Digital Audio with Java™

CRAIG A. LINDLEY

Prentice Hall PTR
Upper Saddle River, NJ 07458
http://www.phptr.com

ISBN 0-13-087676-3

90000

9 780130 876768

Library of Congress Cataloging-in-Publication Date

Lindley, Craig A.
   Digital audio with Java / Craig Lindley
        p.   cm.
   Includes bibliographical references and index.
   ISBN 0-13-087676-3
   1. Sound--recording and reproducing--Digital techniques. 2. Java (Computer program
   language) 3. Real-time data processing. I. Title

   TK7881.4 L5415 1999
   621.389'3'0285--dc21   99-058694

Editorial/Production Supervision: *MetroVoice Publishing Services*
Acquisitions Editor: *Greg Doench*
Editorial Assistant: *Mary Treacy*
Buyer: *Alexis Heydt*
Art Director: *Gail Cocker-Bogusz*
Interior Series Design: *Meg Van Arsdale*
Cover Design: *Anthony Gemmellaro*
Cover Design Direction: *Jerry Votta*
Project Coordinator: *Anne Trowbridge*

© 2000 Prentice Hall PTR
Prentice-Hall, Inc.
Upper Saddle River, NJ 07458

Prentice Hall books are widely used by corporations and government agencies for
training, marketing, and resale. The publisher offers discounts on this book when
ordered in bulk quantities. For more information, contact

   Corporate Sales Department,
   Prentice Hall PTR
   One Lake Street
   Upper Saddle River, NJ 07458
   Phone: 800-382-3419; FAX: 201-236-7141
   E-mail (Internet): corpsales@prenhall.com

Printed in the United States of America

10 9 8 7 6 5 4 3 2 1

ISBN 0-13-087676-3

Prentice-Hall International (UK) Limited, *London*
Prentice-Hall of Australia Pty. Limited, *Sydney*
Prentice-Hall Canada Inc., *Toronto*
Prentice-Hall Hispanoamericana, S.A., *Mexico*
Prentice-Hall of India Private Limited, *New Delhi*
Prentice-Hall of Japan, Inc., *Tokyo*
Pearson Education Asia Pte. Ltd.
Editora Prentice-Hall do Brasil, Ltda., *Rio de Janeiro*

Contents

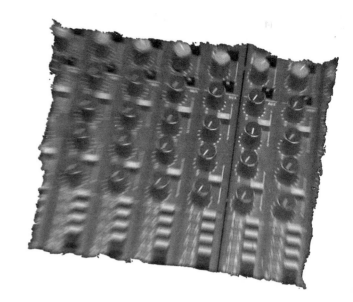

Preface *xix*

    WHO THE BOOK IS WRITTEN FOR *xx*

    WHY JAVA? *xx*

    WHAT YOU NEED TO USE THE SOFTWARE IN THIS BOOK *xxi*

    WHO THE AUTHOR IS *xxii*

Disclaimer *xxiii*

Acknowledgments *xxv*

Processing Effect Front Panels *xxvii*

    INPUT DEVICES—SOURCES *xxvii*

    MONITOR DEVICES *xxix*

    OUTPUT DEVICES—SINKS *xxix*

PROCESSING DEVICES—PROCESSORS   *xxx*

AUDIO APPLICATIONS   *xxxiv*

List of Figures   *xxxvii*

Part 1
Audio Controls and Indicators   *1*

INTRODUCTION   *1*

REQUIRED CONTROLS   *2*

REQUIRED INDICATORS   *2*

1   Audio Control and Indicator Basics   5

INTRODUCTION   *5*

AUDIO COMPONENTS AS JAVA BEANS   *7*

Painting Controls and Indicators   *10*
Control and Indicator Events   *10*
Blinker Component   *12*
DataGen Component   *13*

NOTES   *14*

2   Audio Button Controls   15

INTRODUCTION   *15*

SUPPORT FOR DOUBLE BUFFERING   *17*

PROCESSING LOW-LEVEL MOUSE AND KEYBOARD EVENTS   *18*

PRODUCING HIGHER-LEVEL SEMANTIC EVENTS   *20*

DERIVED BUTTON CLASSES   *21*

RoundButton Class   *21*

SquareButton Class   *23*

ToggleSwitchButton Class   *24*

MISCELLANEOUS INFORMATION   *27*

3 Audio Potentiometers   29

INTRODUCTION   *29*

USER/POTENTIOMETER INTERACTION   *31*

PRESENTATION ISSUES   *32*

POTENTIOMETER CLASS HIERARCHY   *32*

PotBase Class   *33*

Pot Class   *37*

SlidePot Class   *46*

BoostCutSlidePot Class   *47*

IntValuedPot Class   *48*

IntValuedSlidePot Class   *50*

RealValuedPot Class   *50*

RealValuedSlidePot Class   *50*

CONNECTING POTS TO LISTENER DEVICES   *50*

THE PotTypeDemo PROGRAM   *51*

MISCELLANEOUS INFORMATION   *52*

4   LED Indicators   55

INTRODUCTION   *55*

WHAT'S THIS BLINKER THING AND WHY A STATE MACHINE?   *57*

LEDBase BASE CLASS   *59*

RoundLED CLASS   *60*

SquareLED CLASS   *61*

CONNECTING LEDs TO ActionEvent PRODUCERS   *61*

LabeledLED CLASS   *63*

MISCELLANEOUS INFORMATION   *64*

5   Meters—Analog and Digital   65

INTRODUCTION   *65*

METER CLASS   *67*

ANALOG METER CLASS   *69*

LEDMeter CLASS   *73*

RoundLEDMeter CLASS   *74*

METER BALLISTICS   *76*

PROBLEMS WITH LEVEL METERS IN DIGITAL AUDIO SYSTEMS   *77*

MISCELLANEOUS INFORMATION   *78*

6 Display Devices 79

INTRODUCTION *79*

SEVEN-SEGMENT DISPLAY DEVICES *79*

SevenSegmentDisplay Class *79*

LEDDisplayBase Class *81*

IntLEDDisplay Class *83*

ReadoutLabel DISPLAY DEVICE *86*

MISCELLANEOUS INFORMATION *88*

7 Simulated Equipment Front Panels 89

INTRODUCTION *89*

COMPONENT CONNECTIONS *92*

BASE CLASS FUNCTIONALITY *96*

LAYOUT TECHNIQUES *97*

UI CONSISTENCY ISSUES *100*

OTHER SIMULATED EQUIPMENT FRONT PANELS *102*

MISCELLANEOUS INFORMATION *102*

Part 2
Audio Architecture, Processing, and Monitoring   *103*

8   Sound and Audio Basics   *105*

INTRODUCTION   *105*

SOUND   *105*

ANALOG WAVEFORMS AND INPUT/OUTPUT DEVICES   *109*

HEADROOM, CLIPPING, AND DISTORTION   *110*

NON NATURAL SOUND PRODUCTION   *112*

SAMPLED SOUND   *112*

Analog-to-Digital Conversion (A-to-D Conversion)   *113*
Sound Processing Software   *115*
Digital-to-Analog Conversion (D-to-A Conversion)   *116*

MUSICAL RELATIONSHIPS   *117*

9   The Audio Processing Architecture   *119*

INTRODUCTION   *119*

NEGOTIATION   *122*

PASSING SAMPLES BETWEEN DEVICES   *124*

RESET PROPAGATION AND PROCESSING   *125*

AbstractAudio UTILITY METHODS   *125*

THE LinkedListVector CLASS   *126*

THE AudioTest PROGRAM   *127*

    Sample Invocations of the *AudioTest* Program   *129*

BATCH PROCESSING VS. REAL-TIME PROCESSING   *130*

FINAL NOTE   *130*

CONCLUSIONS   *131*

MISCELLANEOUS INFORMATION   *132*

10   Digital Filters   *133*

INTRODUCTION   *133*

FILTER VARIETIES   *134*

    Low-pass Filters   *134*
    High-pass Filters   *135*
    Band-pass Filters   *136*
    Band-stop Filters   *137*

PRACTICAL APPLICATIONS OF FILTERS AND FILTERING   *137*

DIGITAL FILTERS TYPES   *138*

    FIR Filter Advantages   *139*
    FIR Filter Disadvantages   *139*
    IIR Filter Advantages   *139*
    IIR Filter Disadvantages   *139*

IIR DIGITAL FILTER DESIGN TECHNIQUES AND EQUATIONS   *140*

    IIR Band-pass Filters Equations   *141*
    IIR Band-stop Filter Equations   *141*
    IIR High-pass Filter Equations   *141*
    IIR Low-pass Filter Equations   *142*

IIR FILTER DESIGN CLASSES   *143*

IIR FILTER RUNTIME CLASSES   *144*

IIR FILTER USAGE   *145*

MISCELLANEOUS INFORMATION   *147*

11   Audio Sources   149

INTRODUCTION   *149*

OSCILLATOR DEVICES   *149*

Waveform Fidelity   *154*

Use with the AudioTest Program   *157*

Stereo Oscillator   *158*

AUDIO FILE READING DEVICE   *159*

Note and Warning   *160*

FileReaderWithUI Class   *161*

Use with the AudioTest Program   *162*

The AudioFileDecoder Class   *162*

Data Decoders   *163*

AU Files and the AURead Class   *164*

WAV Files and the WaveRead Class   *166*

AUDIO ACQUISITION DEVICE   *168*

WinRecorder Class   *169*

WinRecorderWithUI   *170*

Use with the AudioTest Program   *171*

MISCELLANEOUS INFORMATION   *172*

12 Audio Monitors   175

INTRODUCTION   175

MONITOR DEVICE RECAP   176

THE SAMPLE SCOPE   176

Operation   178

Possible Enhancements   182

Use with the AudioTest Program   183

Operational Note   183

Miscellaneous Information   184

THE SPECTRUM ANALYZER   184

Operation   186

The FFT   188

Use with the AudioTest Program   192

Miscellaneous Information   193

13 Audio Processors   195

INTRODUCTION   195

AMPLITUDE ADJUST PROCESSOR   196

Description   196

Operation   197

Use with the AudioTest Program   198

Miscellaneous Information   198

CACHE PROCESSOR   199

Description   199

Operation   199

Possible Enhancements   *201*

Use with the AudioTest Program   *201*

Miscellaneous Information   *201*

CHORUS/FLANGER PROCESSOR   *202*

Description   *202*

Operation   *203*

The User Interface   *208*

Use with the AudioTest Program   *210*

Miscellaneous Information   *210*

COMPRESSOR/EXPANDER/LIMITER/NOISE GATE PROCESSOR   *211*

Description   *211*

Operation   *215*

The User Interface   *219*

Use with the AudioTest Program   *221*

Miscellaneous Information   *221*

DELAY PROCESSOR   *222*

Description   *222*

Operation   *223*

The User Interface   *226*

Use with the AudioTest Program   *227*

Miscellaneous Information   *228*

DISTORTION PROCESSOR   *228*

Description   *228*

Operation   *228*

The User Interface   *229*

Use with the AudioTest Program   *230*

Miscellaneous Information   *230*

GRAPHIC EQUALIZER PROCESSOR   *231*

Description   *231*

Operation   *232*

Important Note   *236*

The User Interface   *237*

Use with the AudioTest Program   *238*

Miscellaneous Information   *239*

PANNER PROCESSOR   *239*

Description   *239*

Operation   *240*

Use with the AudioTest Program   *244*

Miscellaneous Information   *245*

PARAMETRIC EQUALIZER PROCESSOR   *245*

Description   *245*

Operation   *246*

Important Note   *247*

The User Interface   *247*

Use with the AudioTest Program   *249*

Miscellaneous Information   *250*

PHASER PROCESSOR   *250*

Description   *250*

Operation   *251*

The User Interface   *255*

Use with the AudioTest Program   *257*

Miscellaneous Information   *257*

PITCH SHIFTER PROCESSOR   *258*

Description   *258*

Operation   *259*

The User Interface   *267*

Use with the AudioTest Program   *268*

Miscellaneous Information   *269*

REVERB PROCESSOR   *269*

Description   *269*

Operation   *271*

The User Interface   *274*

Use with the AudioTest Program   *275*

Miscellaneous Information   *276*

NOTE   *276*

14 Audio Sinks   277

INTRODUCTION   *277*

AUDIO FILES   *278*

FileWriterWithUI CLASS   *279*

Use with the AudioTest Program   *282*

WRITING AU FILES   *282*

The AUWrite Class   *282*

AUWriteDevice Class   *286*

WRITING WAVE FILES   *286*

WaveWrite Class   *286*

WaveWriteDevice Class   *288*

SAMPLE PLAYERS   *288*

The PCMPlayer   *289*

USER INTERFACE   *295*

The WinPlayer   *295*

User Interface   *298*

MISCELLANEOUS INFORMATION   *299*

Part 3
Audio Applications   *301*

15   The Phrase Sampler Application   *303*

HOW THE PHRASE SAMPLER IS USED   *304*

HOW THE PHRASE SAMPLER WORKS   *305*

Sampling and Loop Control Device   *306*

The Pitch Shifter Device   *307*

The Sample Doubler Device   *307*

The WinPlayer Device   *308*

UI Controls and Indicators   *308*

POSSIBLE ENHANCEMENTS   *311*

MISCELLANEOUS INFORMATION   *312*

16   The Guitar/Bass Tuner Application   *313*

HOW THE TUNER IS USED   *314*

HOW THE TUNER WORKS   *315*

The Sampler   *315*

The Low-pass Filters   *316*

The FFT Code   *316*

The Note Table   *317*

The Status Indicator LEDs   *318*

The Tuning Meter   *319*

Overall Operation   *319*

Other Design Approaches   *320*

POSSIBLE ENHANCEMENTS   *320*

MISCELLANEOUS INFORMATION   *322*

Appendix A—Building, Documenting, and Running the Code in this Book   323

REQUIREMENTS   *323*

INSTALLATION   *324*

PATH   *324*

CLASSPATH   *324*

BUILDING THE COMPLETE SOURCE TREE   *324*

MAKING JAR FILES   *325*

DOCUMENTING THE CODE   *325*

RUNNING THE AUDIO APPLICATIONS   *325*

RUNNING THE AUDIO PROCESSORS   *325*

SAMPLE INVOCATIONS OF THE AudioTest PROGRAM   *327*

Appendix B—Java Media Framework Version 2.0 (JMF2.0ea)   *329*

INTRODUCTION   *329*

JMF2.0 BACKGROUND   *330*

The Datasource Device   *336*

The Demultiplexer Device   *338*

The Datasink Device   *339*

JMF2.0/AbstractAudio DEVICES   *342*

The JMFMic Device   *342*

The JMFFile Input Device   *346*

The JMFFile Output Device   *350*

The JMFPlayer Device   *354*

SOURCE FILES   *357*

Appendix C—Bibliography   *359*

BOOKS AND ARTICLES   *359*

MISCELLANEOUS PUBLICATIONS   *360*

Appendix D—CDROM Content   *361*

CDROM SOURCE FILES   *361*

CDROM SOUND FILES   *371*

Index   *373*

Preface

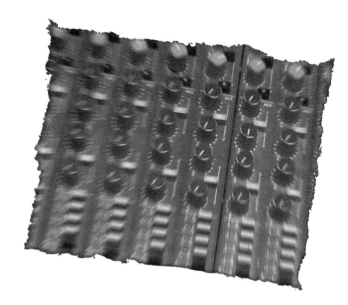

The purpose of this book is to show how to process sound with the Java™ programming language using techniques of digital signal processing (DSP). This is not a traditional DSP book (or Java book for that matter), in that only a limited amount of theory is presented. The approach taken here is much more intuitive, describing how algorithms work instead of necessarily why they work mathematically. Here, hearing is truly believing. You don't need an advanced degree in mathematics or digital signal processing to understand what is going on. You should come away with a toolkit of audio processing tools and effects that can be applied anywhere they are needed. To this end, the book includes code for processing digital audio in various ways (reverb, phaser, delay, equalization, flanger, chorus, etc); for analyzing digital audio (an oscilloscope class and a spectrum analyzer class); a large group of User Interface (UI) controls (potentiometers, LED-like indicators, switches, meters, etc) for building audio processing devices in software, complete with realistic front panels and two full applications (phrase sampler and guitar tuner) for showing practical uses of the code provided.

As anyone interested in audio will know, digital processing of audio is all the rage and is one of the reasons for the falling prices of professional audio equipment. The increase in microprocessor performance over time and falling memory prices has benefitted the recording industry as well as the personal computing industry. Previously, digital audio processing algorithms could only be implemented on dedicated DSP chips because of performance requirements. Now, these same algorithms can be implemented on a personal computer using an interpretive language like Sun's Java. With processing performance doubling roughly every six months, even the lowest-end computer will have or currently does have the power required for manipulation of sound in real time.

In short, this book provides a collection of algorithms for audio processing that I have collected over many years. These algorithms are coded in Java so you can see as well as hear the affect of their application. This book contains *a lot of code* you can use for whatever audio applications you can envision. Audio files are also provided to audibly illustrate the processing algorithms.

WHO THE BOOK IS WRITTEN FOR . . . .

This book is for anyone with a programming background who is interested in the manipulation of sound on a PC and people who are interested in how programs like *Cakewalk* or *Cool Edit* process digital audio. This book is also for anyone who would like a platform for prototyping new audio effects to hear what they sound like. This book is even for someone who would like to make their voice sound like Darth Vader or the Chipmunks on their answering machine (using the pitch shifter effect provided).

Besides the intended use in audio applications, the UI controls and indicators provided in this book can be used for process control and other test applications where values must be displayed to a user and the user has a need to interact with simulated controls on simulated equipment front panels—for example, power system monitors, power plant simulators, mass transit status controls, etc.

WHY JAVA? . . . .

The primary reason for choosing Java is because it is my programming language of choice for application development. Ease of use, object orientation, and portability make it an excellent choice for coding audio algorithms for reuse. Further, since VM (virtual machine) performance is increasing rapidly, Java's performance is approaching that of C++. So by using Java we get portability, the performance we need, and the richness of the Java APIs without the complexity of C++. That's a winning combination as far as I am concerned. I never want to code in C++ again if I can help it.

Almost all of the code in this book is written in Java. I say almost because there is a small amount of code for interfacing to the Windows audio hardware. This was necessary since the initial version of JMF (Java Media Framework) did not provide audio (or video) acquisition when the code for this book was first written. So, I provide a couple of Windows DLLs written in C using JNI (Java native interface) to couple the Windows sound hardware to the Java framework presented in this book. By the time you read this, the need for this system-dependent code will probably have vanished as the next release of JMF/JavaSound promises to provide audio acquisition. See Appendix B for details.

While almost all of the code in this book is written in Java, this book does not pretend or intend to teach Java programming. There are many, many books on the market for that. No one with experience with any high level procedural language should have trouble reading the code provided as it is well-commented and most of the code has javadoc API documentation as well. All of the code is written in a very straight-forward manner with no intentional tricks or obfuscations. I want people to understand what I have provided and use it fully.

One final note is that all programs in this book are written as Java applications. There are no applets provided. Using the framework I provide, it should be an easy task to come up with a Java applet for processing sound but I'll leave it to you to do so. Any Java programming book can be used as a guide for applet development.

WHAT YOU NEED TO USE THE SOFTWARE IN THIS BOOK . . . .

You'll need the software provided on the included CDROM, a Java development environment of your choice (the code is Java 1.1 compliant), a *make* utility of some kind, and a PC with enough horsepower to process audio. Minimum requirements for the PC are a Pentium-class machine with a minimum of 20 megabytes of RAM running at 150MHz or faster. Of course the faster the PC, the higher the sampling rate audio that can be accommodated. Actually, even a slower machine will do, but you'll have to limit your real-time processing to lower sampling rates. My main development machine was a 75MHz Pentium laptop that worked fine except when high sampling rate audio (44100 samples/second) was processed. Also, it will be helpful to have a sound card on your PC that is full duplex. That is, one that can record and play back at the same time. Otherwise, you will not be able to digitize audio and play back audio simultaneously. Fortunately, most modern sound cards support full duplex operation if the required driver is available, so this should not be an issue for most people.

A final note about the software build environment and testing: This code was built and tested on machines running Windows. Ports of the provided code to other platforms will require some work on the user's part that is not within the scope of this book. *Make* files will probably need to be changed when using different *make* programs and even some of the Java code may need to be tweaked depending on the Java development environment and version of Java you use. Please be prepared to face these and similar situations as you attempt to use the code provided.

WHO THE AUTHOR IS . . . .

I have been writing software for a very long time. Recently, I was a founding partner in a startup company that writes multimedia software. I've always been interested in sound and imaging. Actually, the last three books I have written deal with imaging topics.

Before starting my software career, I was involved in the design, production, and deployment of professional recording equipment as a hardware circuit designer. I have now come full circle with this book. It is rather amazing to me to think that what I designed years ago with analog circuitry can now be done totally in the digital domain with software. When I think of all the circuit boards I designed that are now unnecessary, I have to chuckle.

I hope you enjoy reading this book as much as I have enjoyed writing it. There is something very pleasing about having knobs to tweak (even though they are simulated knobs on simulated front panels) and hearing the results of the changes in real time.

If you would like to contact me, e-mail is your best bet. The following e-mail address can be used:

craigl@worldnet.att.net

So long and have fun processing audio. Maybe the next break through audio special effect will be yours.

Craig A. Lindley
Manitou Springs, CO

Disclaimer

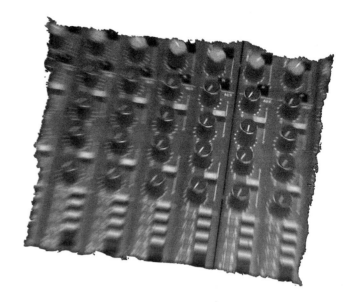

Although I have tried very hard to make sure the code provided in this book and on the accompanying CDROM performs as described and as bug-free as possible, neither myself nor the publisher guarantees the provided code in any way. *The code should be considered proof of concept as opposed to production quality.* The code may or may not fit your needs but that is up to you to decide.

Please realize that as the author of this book I make very little money on each copy of the book that is sold. In fact, I could not go out to lunch at a fast food restaurant for the royalty I made on your purchase. So if you buy this book and use the code provided in it, you must be aware that you do so at your own risk. I cannot be expected to be your personal consultant on your entire new application just because you used some of my code. Also, I cannot help you learn Java or advanced digital signal processing techniques, modify DLLs, or change *make* files for some new Java platform or whatever (you fill in the request). The requests some people make may sound funny to the casual reader, but from my experience as an author, I know a small number of people will attempt to make incredible demands on an author's time and expect them to be fulfilled ASAP. All for the cost of a fast food hamburger. Please understand this is not fair to me because I do feel guilty when I have to turn down people's requests.

Having said all that for my own protection, please realize that all reasonable questions and/or requests will be answered via e-mail as my time allows. I want you to use the code I have written—nothing would make me happier. Also, if you come up with some novel application of the techniques I provide here, I would be interested in knowing about it. If you will be reasonable, I will be reasonable in return. That is all I ask.

Acknowledgments

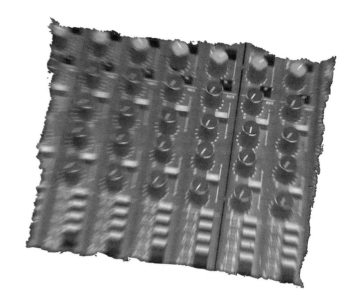

I would first like to dedicate this book to someone who many would consider an unlikely candidate for a dedication. This person's name is Howard Steel and he played a vital role in forming my interest in audio and audio equipment. You might say he was my mentor in this field at the same time he was my boss. As a mentor he taught me how audio circuitry was *supposed* to be designed. As my boss he fired me multiple times because he didn't like someone questioning his judgment as I sometimes did. He also critiqued many of my initial designs right into the ground because he said "they didn't sound good enough." He gave the phrase *back to the drawing board* concrete meaning for me. I want to dedicate this book to him first because, without his influence, I wouldn't know anything at all about the design of professional recording equipment and hence would not have the background to write this book. If you are still out there Howard, I cannot thank you enough.

At the same time I would like to acknowledge a gentlemen named Don Schrotta who allowed me to remain employed each time Howard fired me. They were partners in the small audio company I worked for, you see. Don was also the one who hired me during summers in college to first install high-end stereo gear and later to head up the design and manufacturing arm of Quantum Audio Labs in Torrance, California. Don, I owe you a lot also.

Both Howard's and Don's names are associated with some of the finest rock 'n roll recordings done in the late seventies through the mid eighties. Maybe even to this day, but I don't know because I've lost contact with them. Many of the hits of that era were recorded on equipment that we designed, built, tested, and installed in major recording studios throughout the country.

Another person in the audio business who influenced me is the late John Pritchett. John bought Quantum Audio Labs from Don and Howard and he and I carried on the tradition for many years. It was only my uncontainable interest in microprocessors that yanked me out of the professional audio business. It would be many years until computers and audio equipment would come together and I could satisfy both interests simultaneously.

Next, I have to say that my wife Heather Hubbard has played a large part in my writing this book. Without her support in allowing me to follow my muse, I could not have written this book or any of the previous ones, for that matter. She helps shelter me from the rigors of life. It is Heather who always says okay when I suggest we need yet another pair of speakers somewhere in the house or that I really do need another piece of recording equipment, a new computer, new guitar, or synthesizer. You get the picture, I think. Thanks, wife, for being there for me and allowing me to blow our budget from time to time on cool toys.

Mike Courtney also needs to be acknowledged for volunteering to read the manuscript with an eye towards the technical details. Thanks Mike.

Finally, I must acknowledge my buddy Bob Weisenicker who allowed me access to his rather large collection of DSP books during the research phase of this book. Thanks, Bob, and soon you'll have another book to add to your collection.

Of course you the reader have to be acknowledged as well. If there weren't people out there like you who love audio stuff as much as I do, I wouldn't have had the opportunity to write this book on a subject I dearly love. Thanks in advance for your support in this endeavor. I hope you get as much out of this book as I have in writing it.

Processing Effect
Front Panels

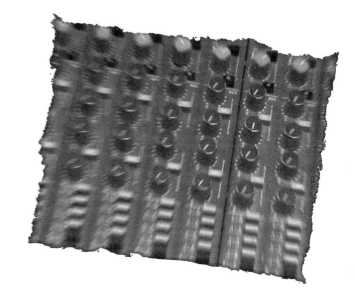

T he following are some of the audio processing effects and devices presented in the book. Each of the processing effects has a simulated front panel and uses simulated audio controls and indicators which can be manipulated in real time. The code for each of these devices is provided on the accompanying CDROM.

INPUT DEVICES—SOURCES . . . .

Input From Line/Mic Input Device

Mono Oscillator Device

Stereo Oscillator Device

Au/Wave File Reader Device

MONITOR DEVICES ....

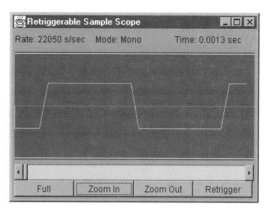

Retriggerable Sample Scope Device

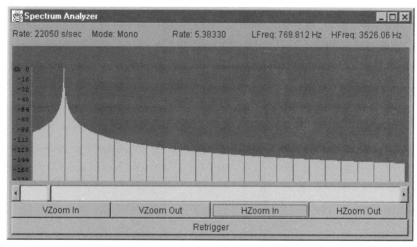

Spectrum Analyzer Device

OUTPUT DEVICES—SINKS ....

Sample Player Using JMF

Sample Player Using Native Windows

Au/Wave File Writer

PROCESSING DEVICES—PROCESSORS . . . .

Amplitude Adjustment Processor

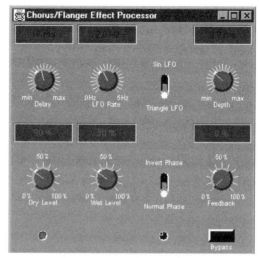

Chorus/Flanger Processor

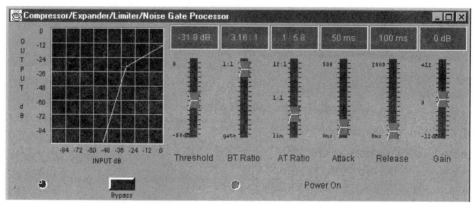

Compressor/Expander/Limiter/Noise Gate Processor

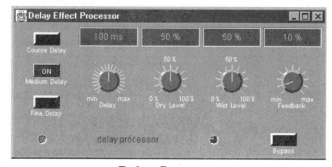

Delay Processor

Distortion Processor

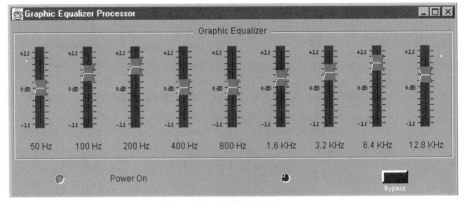

Graphic EQ Processor

Panner Processor

Parametric EQ Processor

Phaser Processor

Pitch Shifter Processor

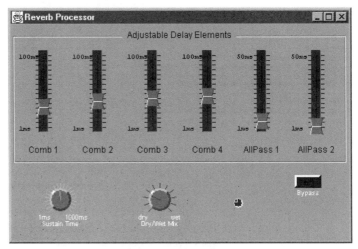

Reverb Processor

AUDIO APPLICATIONS . . . .

Phrase Sampler Application

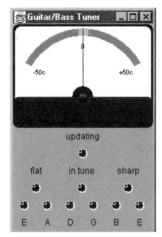

Guitar/Bass Tuner Application

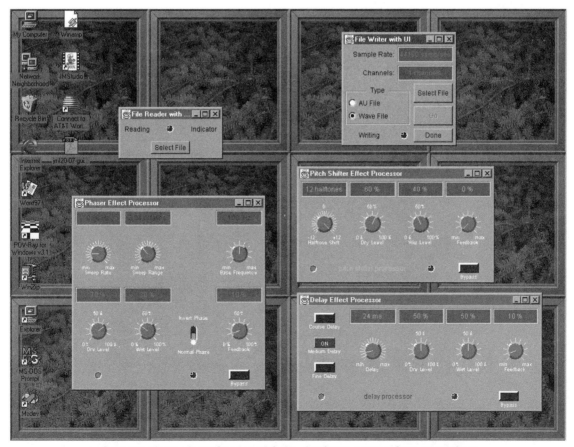

Screen shot showing multiple devices operating together

List of Figures

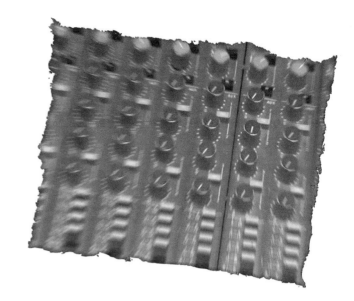

Input From Line/Mic Input Device	xxvii
Mono Oscillator Device	xxviii
Stereo Oscillator Device	xxviii
Au/Wave File Reader Device	xxviii
Retriggerable Sample Scope Device	xxix
Spectrum Analyzer Device	xxix
Sample Player Using JMF	xxix
Sample Player Using Native Windows	xxx
Au/Wave File Writer	xxx
Amplitude Adjustment Processor	xxx
Chorus/Flanger Processor	xxxi
Compressor/Expander/Limiter/Noise Gate Processor	xxxi
Delay Processor	xxxi
Distortion Processor	xxxii
Graphic EQ Processor	xxxii
Panner Processor	xxxii
Parametric EQ Processor	xxxiii
Phaser Processor	xxxiii

	Pitch Shifter Processor	xxxiv
	Reverb Processor	xxxiv
	Phrase Sampler Application	xxxiv
	Guitar/Bass Tuner Application	xxxv
	Screen shot showing multiple devices operating together	xxxv
Figure 2.1	Button Classes and Various Configuration Possibilities	16
Figure 3.1	The Pot Demonstration Program	30
Figure 4.1	LED Demonstration Program	56
Figure 5.1	Meter Demonstration Program	66
Figure 6.1	Seven-Segment Display Layout	80
Figure 6.2	Display Devices Demo Program	86
Figure 7.1	The FileReader Device's Simulated Front Panel User Interface	90
Figure 7.2	The StereoOscillator Device's Simulated Front Panel User Interface	91
Figure 7.3	The SpectrumAnalyzer Device's Simulated Front Panel	91
Figure 7.4	The Compressor/Expander/Limiter/Noise Gate Device's Simulated Front Panel	92
Figure 7.5	Simple UI using a GridLayout layout manager	98
Figure 8.1	Simple Sine Wave	106
Figure 8.2	Complex Waveform	109
Figure 8.3	Sine Wave (no clipping)	111
Figure 8.4	Sine Wave (onset of clipping)	111
Figure 8.5	Sine Wave (severe clipping)	111
Figure 8.6	Digital Signal Path	112
Figure 10.1	Idealized amplitude versus frequency response curve for a low-pass filter	135
Figure 10.2	Idealized amplitude versus frequency response curve for a high-pass filter	136
Figure 10.3	Idealized response curve for a band-pass filter	136
Figure 10.4	Idealized response curve for a band-stop filter	137
Figure 11.1	Mono Oscillator Device User Interface	150
Figure 11.2	Stereo Oscillator Source Device User Interface	150
Figure 11.3	A 1000 Hz Sine Wave	155
Figure 11.4	A 1000 Hz Triangle Wave	155

Figure 11.5	A 1000 Hz Square Wave	155
Figure 11.6	Noise	156
Figure 11.7	Generated Sine Wave Spectrum Analysis	156
Figure 11.8	Simple UI for AU and WAV File Player	160
Figure 11.9	Windows Recorder/Sampler Device User Interface	170
Figure 12.1	The Sample Scope's User Interface	177
Figure 12.2	Time Domain—Sample Amplitude vs. Time	185
Figure 12.3	Frequency Domain—Frequency Component Amplitude vs. Frequency	185
Figure 12.4	The Spectrum Analyzer's User Interface	186
Figure 12.5	Spectrum with Horizontal Zoom and Scrolling Applied	186
Figure 13.1	Simulated Front Panel for Amplitude Adjust Processor	197
Figure 13.2	Chorus/Flanger Block Diagram	202
Figure 13.3	The Chorus/Flanger Processor User Interface	203
Figure 13.4	Compressor/Expander/Limiter/Noise Gate Processor User Interface	211
Figure 13.5	The Delay Processor's User Interface	222
Figure 13.6	Delay Processor Block Diagram	223
Figure 13.7	Delay Effect Buffer	223
Figure 13.8	The Distortion Processor's User Interface	229
Figure 13.9	Idealized Gain for Graphic Equalizer	231
Figure 13.10	Graphic Equalizer Block Diagram	232
Figure 13.11	User Interface for the Graphic Equalizer Processor	237
Figure 13.12	User Interface (Simulated Front Panel) for Panner Processor	240
Figure 13.13	Idealized Gain for the Parametrics Equalizer	246
Figure 13.14	Parametrics Equalizer Block Diagram	246
Figure 13.15	User Interface for the Parametric Equalizer Processor	247
Figure 13.16	Phaser Effect Logical Block Diagram	251
Figure 13.17	The Phaser Effect Processor's User Interface	255
Figure 13.18	Pitch Shifter Block Diagram	260
Figure 13.19	Delay Sequencing and Crossfading Schedule	261
Figure 13.20	The Pitch Shifter Processor User Interface	267

Figure 13.21   Comb Filter Block Diagram   271

Figure 13.22   The Schroeder Reverb Block Diagram   272

Figure 13.23   All-pass Filter Network Block Diagram   272

Figure 13.24   The Reverb Processor's User Interface   274

Figure 14.1   FileWriterWithUI Device User Interface   279

Figure 14.2   PCMPlayer Device User Interface   289

Figure 14.3   WinPlayer Device User Interface   289

Figure 15.1   The Phrase Sampler's User Interface   303

Figure 15.2   The Phrase Sampler Block Diagram   306

Figure 16.1   The Tuner Application's User Interface   313

Figure 16.2   Tuner Logical Block Diagram   315

Figure B.1   JMFPlayer Block Diagram   336

Figure B.2   JMFFile (Output) Block Diagram   337

Figure B.3   JMFMic Block Diagram   341

Figure B.4   JMFFile (Input) Block Diagram   342

Figure B.5   The JMFMic Input Device Based on JMF2.0   342

Figure B.6   The JMFFile Input Device Based on JMF2.0   346

Figure B.7   The JMFFile Output Device Based on JMF2.0   350

Figure B.8   The JMFPlayer Device Based on JMF2.0   354

Part 1

Audio
Controls
and Indicators

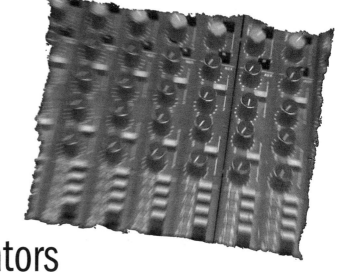

INTRODUCTION ·

When I first thought about writing a book on the processing of sound, I concluded that for this book to be interesting and useful for people, the code presented had to be interactive. Part of this interactivity, of course, is being able to hear the sound as it is processed. It was a given that the user should be able to hear the processed sound in real time or near real time. What I wasn't sure about was another aspect of interactivity. That was, could or should the user be able to manipulate the sound processing parameters in real time and immediately hear the result? Or, should the usage model be that all changes be implemented in code, a recompile and a rerun being necessary to hear the result?

I realized that while the recode/recompile/rerun approach would be the easiest to implement, it would go against the concept of interactivity. It is pretty hard to judge subtle differences in processed sound if one must run a different or modified application to hear them. In the end, it was a relatively easy decision to make even though it meant I had a lot more work to do.

The decision to offer users interactive control of the sound processing parameters meant that user interfaces would have to be implemented for all processing devices. The next question was, should these user interfaces be built using standard AWT controls (again the easy way out) or should the user interfaces try to simulate to some degree actual front panels for equivalent hardware devices?

Again, I decided that, to make the interactivity as compelling as possible, it would be necessary to implement simulated front panels for all processing devices.

Nothing beats the listening experience of being able to tweak a knob and immediately hear a difference in the sound produced. Having made that decision, I started to look around for a set of controls and indicators that I could use for building user interfaces for audio devices. At that point, Sun's Java was still new and few widget sets existed with the capabilities I required. The widget sets I did find were either too limited, too buggy, or just too expensive for my use. So, after much deliberation I decided to explore the idea of building my own sets of controls and indicators for building the simulated front panels. After all, I was interested in the new Java bean technology anyway and it seemed suited for this endeavor. The rest, as they say, is history.

So, what kind of controls and indicators would be required for building these simulated front panels? To determine this, I looked closely at real audio hardware devices, including mixing boards, reverb units, compressors/expanders, special effect units, and other devices and came up with the following lists.

REQUIRED CONTROLS . . . .

1. An assortment of buttons and switches including round and square types with labels and a toggle switch. All types of switches need to operate in either push on/push off or momentary on modes. These buttons must be operated using the mouse.

2. A rotary potentiometer (pot) and a linear slide pot for manipulating parameters in real time using the mouse. These pots need to operate in either linear mode or in pseudo audio taper mode.

REQUIRED INDICATORS . . . .

1. Light emitting diodes or LEDs. These simulated LEDs would need to be available in round and square form factors, be available in various sizes, be available in any color, and have various modes of operation, including on/off solid, blinking at adjustable rates, or single pulse.

2. A seven-segment display capable of displaying the characters 0...9. This display element should be available in any size and with any color and a configurable number of digits.

3. Numerous types of meter indicators, including a simulated analog meter with movable needle, an LED bar graph meter, and a VU-type meter implemented using round LEDs.

Additional requirements placed on the design of these controls and indicators include:

1. The controls must be built using the Java 1.1 event model to provide a uniform and easy-to-use interface to other code.

2. These controls and indicators must be built with a common look and feel so they go together well when used on the simulated front panels.

3. These controls and indicators should provide a three-dimensional presentation to make the simulated front panels appear as real as possible (this is harder to do than you might think).

4. These controls and indicators should be written as Java beans whether they are used that way or not. That way there is maximum flexibility in how they are deployed.

In this section of the book, all of the controls and indicator devices mentioned above will be described and implemented. These devices will be used in Part Two to build simulated front panels for the audio processing devices and also in Part Three for the stand-alone audio applications presented there.

A short discussion is presented at the end of this section detailing how these controls and indicators are used in the construction of simulated front panels.

1 Audio Control and Indicator Basics

INTRODUCTION . . . .

Before we can delve into how all of the various controls and indicators are implemented, we must first provide some background material that will help it all make sense. The choice was made to use the Java 1.1 event model for all controls and indicators presented in this book because it is much cleaner and easier to use

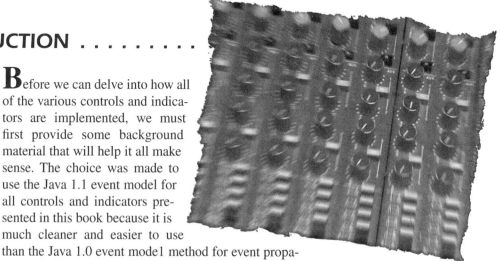

than the Java 1.0 event model method for event propagation. This means this code must be run on a version of Java 1.1 or greater. These devices were first implemented using 1.1.7 and later tested using 1.2 (Java2).

Abstract Window Toolkit (AWT) 1.0 had its problems. To paraphrase Sun's Java documentation,[1] event processing in version 1.0 of the AWT was based upon inheritance. In order for a program to catch and process GUI events, it had to subclass GUI components and override either *action*() or the *handleEvent*()[2] methods. Returning "true" from one of these methods consumes the event so it is not processed further; otherwise the event is propagated sequentially up the GUI hierarchy until either it is consumed or the root of the hierarchy is reached. While this technique worked fine for small applets with simple interfaces, it did not scale well for larger Java programs for the following reasons:

1. The requirement to subclass a component in order to make any real use of its functionality is cumbersome to developers; subclassing should be reserved for circumstances where components are being extended in some functional or visual way.

2. The inheritance model does not lend itself well to maintaining a clean separation between the application model and the GUI because applica-

tion code must be integrated directly into the subclassed components at some level.

3. Since all event types are filtered through the same methods, the logic to process the different event types (and possibly the event targets in #2 above) is complex and error-prone. It is not uncommon for programs to have perplexing bugs that are the result of returning an incorrect result (true or false) from the handleEvent() method. This becomes an even greater problem as new event types are added to the AWT; if the logic of existing handleEvent() methods isn't set up to deal properly with unknown types, programs could potentially break in very unpredictable ways.

4. There is no filtering of events. Events are always delivered to components, regardless of whether the components actually handle them or not. This is a general performance problem, particularly with high-frequency type events, such as mouse moves.

5. For many components, the action() method passes a String parameter which is equivalent to either the label of the component (Button, MenuItem) or the item selected (List, Choice). For programs which use the second approach, this often leads to poor coding and unwieldy string-compare logic that doesn't localize well.

The 1.1 event model, also referred to as the delegation model, was introduced to fix the problems mentioned above and to provide a more robust framework to support more complex Java programs. To this end, the design goals were as follows:

1. Provide a simple and easy-to-learn event model.

2. Support a clean separation between application and GUI code.

3. Facilitate the creation of robust event-handling code which is less error-prone (strong compile-time checking).

4. Provide a design flexible enough to enable varied application models for event flow and propagation.

5. For visual tool builders, enable run-time discovery of the events that a component generates as well as the events it may observe.

6. Support backward binary compatibility with the old model.

In the delegation model, event types are encapsulated in a class hierarchy rooted at java.util.EventObject. An event is propagated from a "source" object to a "listener" object by invoking a method on the listener and passing in the instance of the event subclass which defines the event type generated.

A *listener* is an object that implements a specific EventListener interface extended from the generic java.util.EventListener. An EventListener interface defines one or more methods which are to be invoked by the event source in response to each specific event type handled by the interface.

An *event source* is an object which originates or "fires" events. The source defines the set of events it emits by providing a set of set<EventType>Listener (for single-cast) and/or add<EventType>Listener (for multi-cast) methods which are used to register specific listeners for those events.

In an AWT program, the event source is typically a GUI component and the listener is commonly an "adapter" object which implements the appropriate listener (or set of listeners) for an application to control the flow/handling of events. The listener object could also be another AWT component which implements one or more listener interfaces for the purpose of hooking GUI objects up to each other.

One final note. All controls and indicators presented in this book were written directly on top of the 1.1 version of AWT. An option would have been to write them on top of Sun's UI toolkit, Swing, but that was not done as these devices were being developed at the same time Swing was evolving. This of course could still be done if one had good reason to do so.

AUDIO COMPONENTS AS JAVA BEANS . . . .

When I first began to implement the audio controls and indicators for this book, I thought Java beans were the way to go. I liked the idea of standalone little components that could interact with a visual design environment for building larger applications. The idea of connecting event producers to the event consumers visually (and having the design tool write the simple interface code) seemed compelling. So after analyzing what it meant for a component to be a Java bean, I came up with a short list of requirements including:

1. The component had to use the AWT 1.1 event model.

2. The component had to have a zero argument constructor and a sufficient number of setter methods for configuring the component after it was instantiated.

3. For sizing within the Java bean design environment, the component had to provide a *getPreferredSize* method to tell its environment what size it wanted to be.

4. The component had to use simple, single parameter get and set methods for the various component properties, using a uniform naming convention.

5. The component had to provide special *make* files that compiled the component's code and produced a *jar* file of the code, any icon files, and a manifest describing the jar files content.

In reality, there are more requirements for industrial strength beans than presented in this list but I was not developing a component library for sale as a product, I was developing a library for my own amusement as I had no notion that I would be writing a book on audio any time soon. A real library of audio component beans would possibly need to provide:

1. Multiple icon gif files per component. One for 16×16 pixel icons and one for 32×32 pixel icons depending upon the mode the visual environment wants to operate in.

2. BeanInfo support classes for each component that are used to associate icons with the component for displaying within the design environment and to hide the properties of the component that need not be visible to the component user.

3. Special custom property editors that don't rely on the editors supplied by the Java bean environment for simple data types.

4. Some better design-time vs. run-time differences in behavior. That is, better design-time presentation that would assist in the layout process when used in a graphical Java bean environment.

Be that as it may, I set off down the Java bean path. I coded all controls and indicators to this simple (non-industrial-strength) list of requirements and that is how they are provided to you today. As part of my testing efforts, all controls and indicators have been placed in Sun's bean box and have been connected together and tested. They all interacted with the bean box environment and with each other as expected. They have not, however, been tested with any of the new visual development environments as I don't use these tools yet.

While writing these controls and indicators as Java beans was a good learning experience for me, I found that I was not inclined to use them in a visual development environment for two reasons—first the environments available at the time these components were developed were slow and buggy, and second, any time I found a bug in one of these components, I had to build new jar files for importation into the visual environment. This was time-consuming and, as a result, frustrating.

Instead, I use these components as normal UI component classes within my Java code. In other words, I build my UIs with these components using the traditional approach of using layout managers for component placement. I can then use the setter and getter methods coded into the components to configure the controls or indicators for use after the layout manager has placed and sized them. This is really a testament to the bean architecture that components coded as beans can be used as beans or can be used as standalone Java classes. The standalone Java class approach worked so well I changed the make files to compile these components at the same time all of the other Java code is compiled. If I want to produce jar files containing these components (for use as Java beans), I run make specifying the *beanjarmakefile* makefile.

In keeping with the Java bean tradition, almost every visual aspect of controls and indicators is configurable via simple method calls. Table 1.1 shows the various types of UI controls and indicators provided and the types of attributes that can be manipulated for each. The details of each device's operation and configuration will be described in later chapters. *Note:* The non-visible controls like the *Blinker* and *DataGen* are not shown here even though they too provide simple methods for their configuration. They are not shown because they are not visible in an application that uses them.

Table 1.1   Types of UI Controls and Indicators

Control or Indicator	Configurable Items
Various buttons	Width, height, fonts used for labeling, caption, caption placement (top or bottom), sticky or momentary action mode, initial state, whether component displays a highlight or not, panel color, button color, and text color.
LED display (7-segment variety)	Width, height, number of digits, initial value, fonts used for labeling, caption, caption placement (top or bottom), panel color, LED segment color, LED segment background color, and text color.
Various LEDs	Radius (for round) or width and height for rectangular LEDs, LED color, panel color, mode (solid or blinking), rate (fast or slow blink), and initial state.
Various Meters	Width, height, fonts used for labeling, caption, whether or not the meter has labels and if so where they are to be placed, initial value, the number of sections that make up the meter's display surface, whether meter displays a highlight or not, panel color, needle color, and text color. Additionally, meters have color zones that can be set.
Various Potentiometers	Width, height, fonts used for labeling, caption, whether or not the pot has labels and if so where they are to be placed, initial value, the number of discrete values a pot has, whether pot displays a highlight or not, panel color, knob color, text color, tic mark color, and scale color.

From this table you can see that the controls and indicators provided are highly configurable.

Painting Controls and Indicators

Much of the effort that goes into making fancy controls and indicators goes into the paint method that gets called to render the control or indicator in a graphics context. Not only does the paint method have to perform the mundane tasks of coloring and labeling the device, it must also draw the device with some degree of realism. To enhance realism, the current vogue is to draw controls and indicators with a spectral highlight (bright white spot), as if the lighting was coming from above and to the left of the device. This lighting model is further enhanced by the appropriate use of shadows to simulate depth in places that would be dark due to absence of light. This combination of light and dark is used to give the devices a three-dimensional look.

As straightforward as this sounds, it is not always easy to do. To make controls and indicators life-like requires not only good programming skills but also artistic talent. I refer to this as the "3D challenge" because it is a challenge for those of us with limited or no artistic skills. You may have noticed in the table above that the use of a highlight is configurable for the components provided. You can turn highlighting on and off to see if it provides the affect you desire in your audio applications. How highlighting is done for each specific component will be dealt with in subsequent chapters. Note that some of the components provided don't support highlights at this time even though they may have a method of setting the attribute.

Flickering, which is the result of screen updates that happen too fast for a component to keep up with, reduces realism for components because real components do not flicker. To combat this problem, many of the controls and indicators in this book use double-buffering techniques. That is, the image of the component is drawn onto an offscreen buffer, and when the drawing is complete, it is copied in its entirety into the graphics context. This tends to reduce flickering in that only the portion of a control or indicator that needs to be redrawn is redrawn and the static background will only be updated when needed.

Control and Indicator Events

Table 1.2 summarizes the event types used by the various components described in this section of the book. Also shown are the interfaces these classes of components implement, as required for interoperability within the 1.1 event model and to be usable as Java beans.

Table 1.2   Component Event Types

Generic Component Type	Implements Interface(s)	Collects for Distribution of Events	Fires
blinker		PropertyChangeListeners	PropertyChangeEvent
button(s)		ActionListeners	ActionEvent
datagen	Adjustable	AdjustmentListeners	AdjustmentEvent
leddisplay	AdjustmentListener		
leds	PropertyChangeListener and ActionListener		
meters	AdjustmentListener		
pots	Adjustable	AdjustmentListeners	AdjustmentEvent

PropertyChangeEvent Data Range Values

As shown in the table above, only the *Blinker* component (described shortly) produces (fires) *PropertyChangeEvents*. The only consumer of these events are the *LEDs* described in the next chapter.

ActionEvent Data Range Values

Only *Button* components fire *ActionEvents* and only the *LEDs* consume these events. The only values that *ActionEvents* can have in this book is ON or OFF.

AdjustmentEvent Data Range Values

It is very important to understand that all controls, indicators, and data generators developed in this book that utilize *AdjustmentEvents* were designed to operate over the integer range of values from 0 to 100. Devices that produce *AdjustmentEvents* use 0 as the minimum value and 100 as the maximum or full-scale value. Devices that consume these events interpret the data the same way.

This means that a potentiometer at the minimum value position (rotated fully counter clockwise) generates (or fires) an *AdjustmentEvent* with a value of 0 to all of its listeners. At the maximum value position (fully clockwise), the *AdjustmentEvent* contains a value of 100. On the consumer side, a value of 0 in an *AdjustmentEvent* will not register on a meter, for example. But a value of 100 in an *AdjustmentEvent* will cause the meter to read full scale. Normalization of the range of values of operation makes the interoperability of *AdjustmentEvent* producers and consumers possible.

This range of values was chosen because it was felt that 101 possible values offered enough granularity for our use here and because this range of values maps well into percentage values.

The first two Java bean components, *Blinker* and *DataGen*, are discussed next. These components have no visual aspects but perform important system functions nevertheless. The visual components like *pots* and *LEDs* are discussed in subsequent chapters.

Blinker Component

The *Blinker* is an invisible Java bean component that fires a property change event at a regular, specified interval. A *Blinker* is the data source required for running *LED* indicators. Actually, it drives the state machine that each *LED* runs. A *Blinker* fires a *PropertyChangeEvent* named "blink" that alternatively has the values of Boolean.TRUE and Boolean.FALSE. A *Blinker* can be thought of as a square wave generator with a programmable period. The period can be set in the constructor or by using the *setInterval* method *Blinker* provides. Once started, a *Blinker* runs forever in its own thread. Because a *Blinker* drives *LED* state machines, the shorter the period, the faster the *LED* blinks if in blink mode and the faster the *LED* responds to changes in state in general.

A *Blinker* has methods for adding *PropertyChangeListeners* called *addProperty ChangeListener* and for removing *PropertyChangeListeners* called *removeProperty ChangeListener*. The *Blinker* fires a *PropertyChangeEvent* to each registered listener. Therefore one *Blinker* can support any number of *LEDs* that might be used in an application. The code below illustrates how a *Blinker* is connected to multiple *LEDs*.

```
// Start a blinker for the LEDs with a period of 250 milliseconds
Blinker blink = new Blinker(250);

RoundLED firstLED = RoundLED();
blink.addPropertyChangeListener(firstLED);

RoundLED secondLED = RoundLED();
blink.addPropertyChangeListener(secondLED);
```

Note: The *Blinker* runs the *LED* state machine but does not control the state (off/on) or the mode (solid/blink) of the *LED*. State is controlled through various other means that will be discussed when *LEDs* are described later in this section. Suffice it to say that an *LED* must always be connected to a *Blinker* whether or not the *LED* is programmed to blink.

The blinker is contained in the package *craigl.beans.blinker* and resides in the file *Blinker.java*.

DataGen Component

The data generator class, *DataGen*, was developed for testing other beans, specifically those beans that are *AdjustmentListeners* like the various meters and the seven-segment LED display. It is similar to a *Blinker* in that it fires events periodically and runs forever in its own thread. But instead of firing a *PropertyChangeEvent* like the *Blinker*, it fires an *AdjustmentEvent*. The time between the *AdjustmentEvents* can be set in the *DataGen* constructor or by using the *setInterval* method it provides.

The *DataGen* class has methods for adding *AdjustmentListeners* to its internal list called *addAdjustmentListener* and for removing listeners from its list called *removeAdjustmentListener*. *DataGen* fires an *AdjustmentEvent* to each registered listener on the list. One *DataGen* device can support any number of *AdjustmentEventListeners* that might be used in an application. The code snippet below illustrates how a *DataGen* is connected to an *AnalogMeter* device.

```
// Instantiate a DataGen data source for test with a period of 200
milliseconds
DataGen dg1 = new DataGen(200);

// Instantiate an AnalogMeter to receive the events from DataGen
AnalogMeter leftAnalogMeter = new AnalogMeter();

// Make the meter a listener to the events produced by DataGen
dg1.addAdjustmentListener(leftAnalogMeter);
```

After this code is run and the meter is connected to the *DataGen* source, each *AdjustmentEvent* fired by *DataGen* will result in a new value being displayed on the meter. In the case of the *AnalogMeter* used here, the needle's position will deflect appropriately to the new value.

The data contained in the *AdjustmentEvent* produced by *DataGen* is random. The only constraints placed on the data is that it must be an integer value in the range 0 to 100 as explained previously for all *AdjustmentListener* devices. The code that generates the random data inside of *DataGen* is shown below for reference.

```
.
/**
 * Fire an adjustment event containing random data
 */
void fireAdjustmentEvent() {
    // Generate a random data value between 0 and 100
    value = (int) (Math.random() * 100);

    // Synchronously notify the listeners so that they are
    // guaranteed to be up-to-date with the Adjustable before
    // it is mutated again.
    AdjustmentEvent e = new AdjustmentEvent(this,
        AdjustmentEvent.ADJUSTMENT_VALUE_CHANGED,
        AdjustmentEvent.TRACK, value);

    // Send it out if there is a listener
    if (adjustmentListener != null)
        adjustmentListener.adjustmentValueChanged(e);
}
```

DataGen is contained in the package *craigl.beans.datagen* and resides in the file *DataGen.java.*

The visual components are discussed in the chapters to follow.

NOTES . . . .

[1] Java AWT: Delegation Event Model from jdk1.2\docs\guide\awt\designspec\events.html

[2] In fact, *action*() and *handleEvent*() have been deprecated as of version 1.1 of Java

2　Audio Button Controls

INTRODUCTION · · · · · · · ·

This chapter discusses button controls. Currently, three different classes of button controls are provided. These classes are:

1. Round buttons (represented by the *RoundButton* class), which have a round presentation that sports a lighted cap in the on position. There are no three-dimensional aspects to these buttons.

2. Square buttons (represented by the *SquareButton* class), which have a square presentation that displays the word "ON" when the switch is in the on position. The three-dimensional presentation of this button attempts to give the impression the button is depressed into the surrounding panel when in the on position and sticks out above the panel in the off position.

3. Toggle switch buttons (represented by the *ToggleSwitchButton* class) which mimic a miniature toggle switch in their presentation. This switch has a lever or baton that is embedded into the surrounding panel via an elliptical well and that snaps up and down.

Examples of all three switch classes can be seen in Figure 2.1. The *LED*s shown above these switches indicate the state of the button. If the button is in the on state, the *LED* is on and visa verse. What cannot be seen in this figure is that buttons operate in two different modes. These modes are:

1. Push On/Push Off Mode. This is the normal mode of operation. With buttons operating in this mode, you must click them once to turn them on and

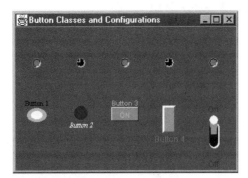

Figure 2.1   Button Classes and Various Configuration Possibilities. Lighted LEDs indicate buttons in the on position.

again to turn them off. They retain their state until the state is changed. This property is referred to as "sticky" in the discussion that follows. If a button is in sticky mode it is a push on/push off type of button.

2. Momentary Mode. When a button is operated in this mode, it is on only while the mouse is selecting it. As soon as the mouse moves or the mouse button is released these buttons return to the off state. When a button's sticky property is false, it is not sticky so it operates in momentary mode.

The mode in which a button operates can be controlled by parameters passed into its constructor or can be controlled by calling methods that control the button's sticky property. Button mode can be changed at runtime if that is a required behavior for the application you are developing.

The button class hierarchy consists of an abstract base class called *Button* which maintains all of the button properties, has the getter and setter methods for those properties, handles the low-level mouse and keyboard events necessary for operating the buttons, and fires an *ActionEvent* every time the state of the button changes. In other words, this base class does all of the work necessary for a button's operation.

Button classes built on top of this base class (*Button*) need provide only two methods; a *paint* method and a *getPreferredSize* method, to be able to take advantage of functionality built into the base class. All three of the button classes provided, *RoundButton*, *SquareButton*, and *ToggleSwitchButton*, are implemented this way.

We delve further into what these two methods do in a moment but first, Table 2.1 is a list of the properties that are supported by the base class that can be used in all derived button classes. It is hopefully obvious what each property does by its name or, in some cases, the short description provided.

Table 2.1 Properties and Methods of Base Button Class

Property	Associated Methods
Width	setWidth(int width), int getWidth()
Height	setHeight(int height), int getHeight()
Font (used for labeling and caption)	setFont(Font f), Font getFont()
	setFontName(String fontName), String getFontName()
	setFontStyle(int fontStyle), int getFontStyle()
	setFontSize(int fontSize), int getFontSize()
Caption	setCaption(String caption), String getCaption()
	setCaptionAtBottom(boolean captionAtBottom), boolean getCaptionAtBottom
Switch mode: sticky = push on/push off	setSticky(boolean sticky), boolean getSticky()
State (on or off)	setState(boolean state), boolean getState()
Highlight (controls 3D presentation)	setHighlight(boolean highlight), boolean getHighlight()
Panel Color	setPanelColor(Color pc), Color getPanelColor()
Button Color	setButtonColor(Color bc), Color getButtonColor()
Text Color	setTextColor(Color tc), Color getTextColor()

As this list shows, there is quite a bit of configurability available for buttons, some of which is apparent in Figure 2.1. When these buttons are used as Java beans in a visual design environment, each of these properties is editable at design time.

SUPPORT FOR DOUBLE BUFFERING . . . .

The *Button* base class has some built-in support for double buffering. As you'll recall from the previous chapter, double buffering is the process by which an image of the component is drawn into an off-screen buffer and, when the drawing is complete, is copied in its entirety into the current graphics context. This tends to reduce flickering in that only the portion of a control or indicator that needs to be redrawn is redrawn and the static background will only be updated when needed.

The support provided by *Button* is in maintaining references to two Java *Images*. One image is called the *onImage* and the other the *offImage*. As you may have guessed, the *onImage*, if used, contains a bitmap of the button in its on state and the *offImage* contains a bitmap of the button in its off state. The *paint* methods in button classes derived from the *Button* base class render the image appropriate to the state of the button every time *paint* is called.

By convention, if double buffering is being used by a component, before attempting to render the image bitmap onto the device context the component would first check to see if the image is null. If the image reference is null, code is called to render the component's bitmap into an off screen buffer as a Java *Image* and return a reference for further use. In this respect, the *onImage* reference is used as a flag to indicate whether an image exists or not. It is important therefore that the *onImage* and *offImage Image* references are set to null as part of initialization to indicate these images have yet to be generated. Failing to do so is an invitation for an exception to be generated the first time the *paint* method is called.

In addition to maintaining the *onImage* and *offImage* references, many of the property setter methods in *Button* set the *onImage* reference to null if the property with which it is associated would alter the visual presentation of the button. Of course, next time through the button's *paint* method, the null *onImage* reference would cause both the *onImage* and *offImage* images to be generated anew. How double buffering is used by the various buttons presented in this chapter is described shortly. Double-buffering techniques such as these are also used for rendering meters, as is discussed in later chapters.

PROCESSING LOW-LEVEL MOUSE AND KEYBOARD EVENTS . . . .

In order to make buttons work, it is necessary to capture low-level mouse and keyboard events that take place over the button and respond to them appropriately. The first step in this process is to indicate that the *Button* base class, derived from *Canvas*, is interested in capturing low-level events. This is done by calling the following code in the constructor of the *Button* class.

```
// Enable low level event processing for mouse and keyboard
enableEvents(AWTEvent.MOUSE_EVENT_MASK | AWTEvent.KEY_EVENT_MASK);
```

Once this is done, methods must be written (one for each event to be processed) to handle the events that will be directed at the button. These methods, which in this case must be called *processMouseEvent* and *processKeyEvent*, are included in the *Button* class for just this purpose. The code below shows how low-level mouse and keyboard events are processed and in turn produces high-level semantic events for consumption by *ActionListeners*. You can also see how the switch mode (sticky property) and the switch's state are directly manipulated as a result of the events received.

```
protected void processMouseEvent(MouseEvent e) {
    // Track mouse presses/releases
    switch(e.getID()) {
        case MouseEvent.MOUSE_PRESSED:
            requestFocus();
            state = !state;
            repaint();
            fireActionEvent();
            break;

        case MouseEvent.MOUSE_RELEASED:
            if (state && !sticky) {
                state = false;
                fireActionEvent();
                repaint();
            }
            break;
    }
    // Let the superclass continue delivery
    super.processMouseEvent(e);
}

// Due to the duration of the key event, using keyboard keys in con-
junction with non sticky
// buttons doesn't always work well.
protected void processKeyEvent(KeyEvent e) {

    // Simulate a mouse click for certain keys
    if (e.getKeyChar() == KeyEvent.VK_ENTER ||
     e.getKeyChar() == KeyEvent.VK_SPACE) {
        if (sticky) {
            state = !state;
            repaint();
        }   else{
            state = true;
            repaint();
            state = false;
            repaint();
        }
        fireActionEvent();
    }
    // Let the superclass continue delivery
    super.processKeyEvent(e);
}
```

PRODUCING HIGHER-LEVEL SEMANTIC EVENTS . . . . .

As briefly mentioned above, buttons fire an *ActionEvent* (by calling the *fireActionEvent* method shown above and below) every time their state changes. The receivers of this event are those entities that have registered interest in the state of a particular button. To support registration, the *Button* base class has a method called *addActionListener* for adding to the interest list and a method called *removeActionListener* for removing those *ActionListeners* no longer interested in the state of a particular button. Again, since registration is handled by the button base class, derived classes get the functionality for free. So, whenever a button fires an *ActionEvent*, that event is delivered to all *ActionListeners* currently registered as interested. *Note:* Registered listeners are delivered the generated *ActionEvent* automatically; however, any Java code can poll a button's state at any time by calling the button's *getState* method directly.

The code below from *Button.java* shows how listeners and events are managed.

```java
// Event processing methods
// Add an ActionListener to the list of listeners interested in this
button's state
public synchronized void addActionListener(ActionListener l) {
actionListener = AWTEventMulticaster.add(actionListener, l);
}


// Remove this ActionListener from the list of interested parties
public synchronized void removeActionListener(ActionListener l) {
actionListener = AWTEventMulticaster.remove(actionListener, l);
}


// Deliver the event to all registered action event listeners
protected void processActionEvent(ActionEvent e) {
    if (actionListener != null)
        actionListener.actionPerformed(e);
}


// Fire off an event to all interested parties. This method is called
whenever the button changes state.
private void fireActionEvent() {
processActionEvent(new ActionEvent(this, ActionEvent.ACTION_PERFORMED,
state ? "ON":"OFF"));
}
```

DERIVED BUTTON CLASSES . . . .

The *Button* base class, being an abstract class, cannot be instantiated on its own. It defines two abstract methods, *paint* and *getPreferredSize*, that derived classes must implement to become concrete classes. The *paint* method is where the button's presentation is developed and rendered onto a graphics context. Since only the derived class knows what presentation is desired, it makes sense that they provide the *paint* method to provide it. Since the *Button* base class is extended from *Canvas*, you can think of this class as providing an empty canvas on which the button will be drawn but leaving the drawing to derived classes. Along a similar vein, only the derived class knows what size the finished button is to be so it must provide the method that all layout managers call, *getPreferredSize*, to ascertain the button's size for layout purposes. The *paint* and the *getPreferredSize* methods for all derived button classes will be described in the following sections.

RoundButton Class

To completely describe the *RoundButton* button class, it is only necessary to describe its *paint* and its *getPreferredSize* methods, as all base button functionality is provided by the *Button* base class. The *paint* method of the *RoundButton* class is the most straightforward of all of the buttons in this book. It consists mostly of finding out the size of the button's *Canvas* area at runtime (and calculating various items from that), filling its piece of the enclosing panel it defines in the panel color, drawing the filled circle that makes up the button, optionally drawing the button's highlight if the button is in the "on" state, and finally drawing the button's caption above or below the button as determined by the *captionAtBottom* flag.

Since this *paint* method is so short, it is shown below as an example of how these paint methods are written. You'll see when you examine this code that double buffering is not utilized for such a simple presentation. This is because there would be as much flashing caused by buffer swapping as there is by doing this simple painting directly onto the graphics context.

```
// Paint method
public synchronized void paint(Graphics g) {

    // Get dimensions of component
    int cwidth = getSize().width;
    int cheight = getSize().height;

    // Paint the panel
    g.setColor(panelColor);
    g.fillRect(0, 0, cwidth, cheight);
```

```
// Set font into the graphics context
g.setFont(font);
FontMetrics fm = g.getFontMetrics();

// Calculate important dimensions
int xCenter = cwidth / 2;
int halfHeight = height / 2;
int yCenter = captionAtBottom ? YPAD + halfHeight :
                          fm.getMaxDescent() + YPAD + halfHeight;
int xLargeOrg = xCenter - (width / 2);
int yLargeOrg = yCenter - (height / 2);

int smallWidth = (width * INNERBUTTONPERCENT) / 100;
int smallHeight = (height * INNERBUTTONPERCENT) / 100;

int xSmallOrg = xCenter - (smallWidth / 2);
int ySmallOrg = yCenter - (smallHeight / 2);

// Draw the button
g.setColor(buttonColor);
g.fillOval(xLargeOrg, yLargeOrg, width, height);

if (state) {
    // Button is on
    g.setColor(Color.white);
    g.fillOval(xSmallOrg, ySmallOrg, smallWidth, smallHeight);
}
// Draw the caption either above or below the button
int captionWidth = fm.stringWidth(caption);
int captionXOffset = (cwidth - captionWidth) / 2;
int captionYOffset = captionAtBottom ? height + YPAD +
fm.getMaxAscent():YPAD;
    g.setColor(textColor);
    g.drawString(caption, captionXOffset, captionYOffset);
}
```

The presentation of a *RoundButton* is codified into the *paint* method above. Now it is easy to write the *getPreferredSize* method also required of the *RoundButton* class. Here, one must decide how big the area of the component must be to accommodate all of its individual pieces. In this case, we have the button area defined by its width and height and we have the caption that is defined by its width and height as well. The width returned in the *getPreferredSize* method call must be the greater of the button's width or the width in pixels of the caption string. A small bit of padding is added to the calculated size for good measure. The height returned in the call must be at least the height of the button plus the maximum height of a character in the caption plus some padding as well. The calculated width and height values are returned via a Dimension object. The code is shown below as an adjunct to the textual description provided.

```
public Dimension getPreferredSize() {

    // Calculate the preferred size based on the label text
    FontMetrics fm = getFontMetrics(font);
    int captionWidth = fm.stringWidth(caption);
    int maxAscent = fm.getMaxAscent();
    int maxDescent = fm.getMaxDescent();
    int maxCharHeight = maxAscent + maxDescent;

    int minWidth = Math.max(width, captionWidth);
    minWidth += 2 * XPAD;

    int minHeight = height + YPAD + maxCharHeight;
    return new Dimension(minWidth, minHeight);
}
```

When a layout manager needs to know the size of a *RoundButton*, it calls the *getPreferredSize* method on the *RoundButton* object. With the width and height information that is returned, the layout manager can adjust the size of the enclosing container appropriately. Once the size issues are resolved, the display area is invalidated which causes the *paint* method of the *RoundButton* object to go to work painting the visual presentation of the round button. As the user interacts with the button via the mouse or by changing its properties, a repaint is scheduled which paints the button using the new properties. So, for example, if the button color is changed via the *setButtonColor* method, the visual presentation will change as soon as the repaint operation completes.

SquareButton Class

The operation of the *paint* and the *getPreferredSize* methods for square buttons is very close to that used for the round buttons described above. In fact the *getPreferredSize* method is identical. The *paint* method, however, is different because of the difference in presentation required between a round and a square button. It is the presentation that makes the buttons different. Double buffering is not used for square buttons either.

A square button provides two attributes that make it more realistic than its round button counterpart. Those are, the square button provides some three dimensional characteristics in that the button looks like it depresses into the surrounding panel in the on position and pops out of the panel in the off position. This option is controlled by the *highlight* property of the button. Secondly, the word "ON" is displayed in the center of the square button when the button is in the on state. This is similar to many mechanical push button switches available today. If you examine the code in the file *SquareButton.java* you will see how these attributes are provided.

ToggleSwitchButton Class

The toggle switch button has the most elaborate presentation of any button presented. That is because it has a more complex geometry than are required for rendering simple round or square buttons. As it exists here today, the *ToggleSwitchButton* is a rather poor representation of a real toggle switch but it proves that a toggle switch can be built over the top of the *Button* base class successfully. Two things set the toggle switch apart from the buttons described previously. They are:

1. The toggle switch button has two captions. One, called the *topCaption* is rendered above the body of the toggle switch and the other, called the *bottomCaption*, is rendered below the switch. The presence of two captions is taken into consideration within the *getPreferredSize* method's code.

2. The toggle switch button is the first to use the double buffering capabilities supported in the base *Button* class. Here a method is provided called *generateSwitchImage* that creates and returns a Java *Image* of the toggle switch button in either the on or the off state depending on the boolean parameter it is passed.

Since this is the first time double buffering has been used it is necessary to show the code which does the image production.

```
private Image generateSwitchImage(boolean isOn) {
    // Calculate important values relative to dimensions
    // of bitmap image.
    int xCenter = minWidth / 2;
    int yCenter = minHeight / 2;

    // Create the toggle switch image
    Image toggleImage = createImage(minWidth, minHeight);

    // Get the graphics contexts
    Graphics gToggleImage = toggleImage.getGraphics();

    // Paint the panel
    gToggleImage.setColor(panelColor);
    gToggleImage.fillRect(0, 0, minWidth, minHeight);
```

```java
// Set font into the graphics context
gToggleImage.setFont(font);
FontMetrics fm = gToggleImage.getFontMetrics();

// Draw the captions. Top then Bottom
gToggleImage.setColor(textColor);
int captionWidth = fm.stringWidth(topCaption);
int captionXOffset = (minWidth - captionWidth) / 2;
int captionYOffset = yCenter - captionOffset;
gToggleImage.drawString(topCaption, captionXOffset, captionYOffset);

captionWidth = fm.stringWidth(bottomCaption);
captionXOffset = (minWidth - captionWidth) / 2;
captionYOffset = yCenter + captionOffset + fm.getHeight();
gToggleImage.drawString(bottomCaption, captionXOffset, captionYOffset);

int hWidth = width / 2;
int hHeight = height / 2;

// Draw the outer switch well
gToggleImage.setColor(Color.white);
int xOrg = xCenter - hWidth;
int yOrg = yCenter - hHeight;
int largeWidth = width + highlightOffset;
int largeHeight = height + highlightOffset;
gToggleImage.fillRoundRect(xOrg, yOrg, largeWidth, largeHeight,
                                            width, width);

// Draw the inner switch well
gToggleImage.setColor(Color.darkGray);
gToggleImage.fillRoundRect(xOrg, yOrg, width, height, width, width);

// Now the switch shaft
gToggleImage.setColor(buttonColor);
int wsShaftWidth = (width * 3) / 4 ;
int hsShaftWidth = wsShaftWidth / 2;
int wlShaftWidth = width;
int hlShaftWidth = wlShaftWidth / 2;
int wShaftLength = (5 * height) / 4;
int hShaftLength = wShaftLength / 2;
```

```
Polygon p = new Polygon();
p.addPoint(xCenter - hsShaftWidth, yCenter);
p.addPoint(xCenter - hlShaftWidth, isOn ? yCenter - hShaftLength :
                                   yCenter + hShaftLength);
p.addPoint(xCenter + hlShaftWidth, isOn ? yCenter - hShaftLength :
                                   yCenter + hShaftLength);
p.addPoint(xCenter + hsShaftWidth, yCenter);
gToggleImage.fillPolygon(p);

// Now the shaft head
gToggleImage.setColor(highlightBrighterColor);
gToggleImage.fillOval(xCenter - hlShaftWidth, isOn ? yCenter -
                      (hShaftLength + hlShaftWidth) : yCenter +
                      (hShaftLength - hlShaftWidth), wlShaftWidth,
                      wlShaftWidth);
    return toggleImage;
}
```

With the *onImage* and *offImage* images created using the function above, the *paint* method is relatively straightforward. You'll notice how the *onImage* reference is used as a flag to determine if new images need to be generated. If the image reference is null, both images are generated/regenerated. Finally, the state of the toggle switch is used to select which of the generated images gets rendered using the *drawImage* method. If the toggle switch should be in the on position because its state is true, the *onImage* image is rendered and visa versa.

```
// Paint method which uses double buffering
public synchronized void paint(Graphics g) {

    int cwidth = getSize().width;
    int cheight = getSize().height;
    int xCenter = cwidth / 2;
    int yCenter = cheight / 2;

    // Calculate position of switch in graphics context
    int toggleOrgX = (cwidth - minWidth) / 2;
    int toggleOrgY = (cheight - minHeight) / 2;

    // See if we have toggle switch images for displaying
    if (onImage == null) {
        onImage = generateSwitchImage(true);
        offImage = generateSwitchImage(false);
    }
```

```
    // State is reversed if not in sticky mode
    boolean newState = state;

    if (!getSticky())
        newState = !state;

    // Render the switch into the device context
    if (newState)
        g.drawImage(onImage, toggleOrgX, toggleOrgY, null);
    else
        g.drawImage(offImage, toggleOrgX, toggleOrgY, null);

}
```

MISCELLANEOUS INFORMATION . . . .

Package:

craigl.beans.buttons

Source Files:

File Name	Description
Button.java	Base class from which all buttons are derived. Provides all basic button functionality, property storage, and getter and setter methods.
ButtonTypeDisplay.java	Test program for showing various button styles and configuration possibilities. This program was used to generate Figure 2.1.
RoundButton.java	Extension of *Button* base class providing a round button presentation.
RoundButtonBeanInfo.java	*BeanInfo* class for associating round button icons with *RoundButton* class.
RoundButtonIcon16.gif	16 × 16 pixel icon associated with this class.
RoundButtonIcon32.gif	32 × 32 pixel icon associated with this class.
SquareButton.java	Extension of *Button* base class providing a square button presentation.
SquareButtonBeanInfo.java	*BeanInfo* class for associating square button icons with *SquareButton* class.

File Name	Description
SquareButtonIcon16.gif	16 × 16 pixel icon associated with this class.
SquareButtonIcon32.gif	32 × 32 pixel icon associated with this class.
ToggleSwitchButton.java	Extension of *Button* base class providing a toggle switch presentation.
ToggleSwitchButtonBeanInfo.java	*BeanInfo* class for associating toggle switch icons with *ToggleSwitchButton* class. Additionally, this class illustrates how the various properties offered by the *ToggleSwitchButton* class can be made visible or invisible.
ToggleSwitchButtonIcon16.gif	16 × 16 pixel icon associated with this class.
ToggleSwitchButtonIcon32.gif	32 × 32 pixel icon associated with this class.

3 Audio Potentiometers

INTRODUCTION . . . .

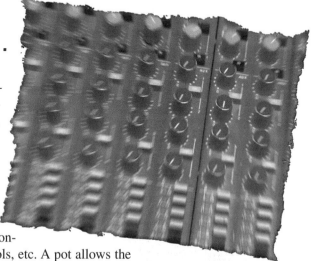

In this chapter, we will be discussing the ubiquitous potentiometer or, for short, the pot. A pot is a variable resistor whose value changes as its knob is manipulated. This is probably the most commonly used component in commercial audio equipment. Pots are used in stereo equipment for volume controls, balance controls, tone controls, etc. A pot allows the user to select a value by rotating (a round potentiometer) or sliding (a slide pot) a knob. A real potentiometer, being an analog device, allows the user almost infinite control over the value of the pot. As we shall see in the discussion to follow, our virtualization of potentiometer isn't quite so flexible, nor does it need to be.

Real potentiometers are manufactured with different *tapers* for use in different applications. A pot's taper describes a graph of value (percent of full scale resistance) vs. travel (the distance a pot is moved as a percentage of its full scale distance). Pots come with linear, logarithmic, and audio tapers among many others. A pan pot (see processor section in Chapter 13) is typically two variable resistance elements (pots) controlled by a single shaft. The taper of the two sections are mirror images of each other so as the pot shaft is rotated in one direction the value of one pot goes up and the value of the other goes down. This is used to fade the panned audio signal up in one channel and down in the other stereo channel in a smooth fashion.

In audio applications both linear and audio taper pots are used. As you might guess, a pot with a linear taper exhibits a linear change in value as the pot is manipulated. By way of example, if a 10K (10000) ohm (the measure of resistance) pot has its shaft at the minimum position, the resistance value is zero ohms. If this pot is at the

50% rotational midpoint, its resistance value is 5K ohms. If the shaft is rotated to the fullest extent possible, its value is 10K ohms.

Audio taper pots have a logarithmic resistance curve. Audio taper pots are used for volume controls in audio equipment because their non-linear response matches the response of the human ear. That is, the pot is made to increase volume logarithmically as required by the human ear to perceive volume increasing in a linear fashion. Thus, the volume control (being an audio taper pot) seems to operate linearly.

In total, five different varieties of pots are described in this chapter. These are:

1. A simple round potentiometer
2. A simple slide pot
3. Audio taper pots
4. Pots with extended integer and real scales
5. Pots with dB scales

You should be able to find a potentiometer here that will work in your audio application. Figure 3.1 shows a few of these pots in operation.

Note: The basic round potentiometer and the basic slide pot present here can be used as Java beans (if packaged into jar files). The other pots described in this chapter cannot. The reason is that some of the specialized pots return floating-point values instead of integer values, as required by the *Adjustable* interface. This prevents their use as beans.

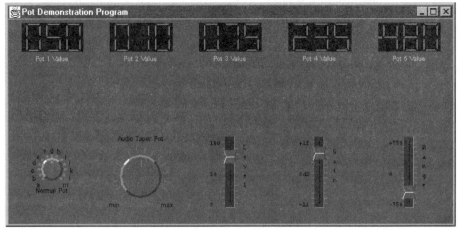

Figure 3.1   The Pot Demonstration Program

USER/POTENTIOMETER INTERACTION . . . .

The pots described in this chapter are designed for use on simulated equipment front panels. Even though these visual devices are made to look three-dimensional, there isn't any real knob to touch or to manipulate. With our virtual pot, the knob is manipulated using the mouse. The mechanics of doing this will be described shortly but now a few points need to be made about the user interaction model.

Round potentiometers respond to mouse events and to keyboard events. If the mouse is clicked within the knob and dragged to the right, the value of the pot will increase by one unit each time a mouse move event is detected. If the mouse is moved to the left, the value will decrease by one unit for each event. If, however, the mouse is clicked outside of the knob but within the pot's containing area, the value of the pot will change by a block increment instead of a unit increment. Clicking the mouse to the left of the center of the pot's area will decrement the pot's value by a block increment but clicking to the right of center (but still outside of the knob) will increment the value by the same block increment.

Round potentiometers also respond to the left and right cursor arrow keys on the keyboard by incrementing their value by two units each time the right arrow is clicked and decrementing by two each time the left arrow is clicked. To use keyboard control, you must first click the mouse on the pot you are interested in manipulating (to give it input focus) and then use the cursor keys.

Slide pots do not react the same as round potentiometers do to mouse and keyboard events. If the mouse is clicked within the knob of a slide pot and dragged up, the value of the pot will increase by one unit each time a mouse move event is detected. If the mouse is moved down, the value will decrease by one unit for each event. If, however, the mouse is clicked outside of the slide pot's knob but within the pot's containing area, the value of the pot will change by a block increment instead of a unit increment. Clicking the mouse above the center of the pot's area will increment the pot's value by a block increment but clicking below center (but still outside of the knob) will decrease the value.

Slide pots respond to the up and down cursor arrow keys on the keyboard by incrementing their value by two units each time the up arrow is clicked and decrementing by two each time the down arrow is clicked.

To define unit and block increments we must introduce the concept of pot sections. Sections are the divisions that a pot's travel is broken up into, be it a round pot or a slide pot. Each pot section is delineated by a graduation mark. Actually, there is always one more graduation mark than there are sections. A pot with two sections would have three graduations: at the minimum value, at the mid value, and at the maximum value. You can think of sections as the detents on the volume control on expensive stereo systems. As you turn these pots, you feel a click at each section.

By definition, the basic pots presented in this chapter produce an integer range of values from 0 to 100. A unit increment increments or decrements a pot's value by one. The block increment amount, however, depends upon how many sections the pot is broken up into. The block increment is equal to 100 divided by the number of sections the pot uses. So for a pot with ten sections (the default) the block increment value is ten. If a pot used 12 sections the block increment value would be eight (the result of dividing 100 by 12 using integer arithmetic). So when a pot is clicked outside of its knob with the mouse, its value will increase or decrease at its specific block increment rate.

Visually, this means the pot will rotate and stop at the next graduation. Clicking outside of the knob will cause the pot to rotate, stopping at each graduation in turn, whereas clicking the mouse inside of a pot's knob and dragging the mouse will give much finer adjustment granularity as the pot's value changes by one each time. Of course, since the pot's value can change by single units this way, the position of the knob doesn't necessarily have to line up with the pot's graduations.

Simple round potentiometers and slide pots have a linear relationship between the amount of knob travel and the value they return. A pot at its minimum position will return a value of zero; a pot at its mid position, the value of 50; and a pot at its maximum position, 100. The other types of pots described here don't necessarily have a linear relationship between travel and returned value. As we shall see, many times a linear ratio is not desired.

PRESENTATION ISSUES . . . .

In order to provide as much flexibility as possible, I made the appearance of round potentiometers and slide pots highly configurable. With the code provided you can make many different-looking pots for use in your applications. Figure 3.1 gives you a few examples of what is possible. In addition to changing the size and the color of the pot, you can change whether tics (short line segments) or dots are used for the scale graduations and for the indicator on the round pot knobs, whether the graduations have labels or not, whether the pot has a caption and, if so, the position of the caption in relation to the pot and other attributes.

POTENTIOMETER CLASS HIERARCHY . . . .

At the base of the potentiometer class hierarchy is the abstract *PotBase* class. It provides the basic functionality and behavior that all pots must have. At the next level in the hierarchy comes the *Pot* and the *SlidePot* classes. *Pot* is a concrete class that provides a round potentiometer and the *SlidePot* class provides a typical slider. Then comes a series of specialized pots that extend *Pot* and *SlidePot*. Those classes that extend *Pot* include: *IntValuedPot* and *RealValuedPot*. Classes that extend *SlidePot* include: *IntValuedSlidePot*, *RealValuedSlidePot*, and *BoostCutSlidePot*. All of these will be described before we are done with this chapter.

PotBase Class

The potentiometer class hierarchy is anchored by an abstract base class called *PotBase*, which maintains all of the common pot properties, has the getter and setter methods for those properties, handles the low-level mouse and keyboard events necessary for operating the pots, and fires an *AdjustmentEvent* every time the value of the pot changes. In other words, this base class does all of the work necessary for a pot's operation. *PotBase* extends the AWT *Canvas* class and implements the *Adjustment* interface.

Being an abstract class, *PotBase* cannot be instantiated on its own. *PotBase* defines two abstract methods

```
public abstract void paint(Graphics g);
public abstract Dimension getPreferredSize();
```

that must be implemented by all derived classes because they have to do with visual presentation of potentiometers, something which *PotBase* does not concern itself with. Potentiometer classes built on top of this base class need only to provide these two methods to be able to take advantage of all of the functionality built into the base class. In summary, the *PotBase* class provides all of the base potentiometer functionality and derived classes provide the presentation. To this end, the *PotBase* class encapsulates all potentiometer properties and methods common to all pots. Table 3.1 itemizes all of these properties and methods.

Table 3.1 Properties and Methods of the PotBase Class

Property	Associated Methods
Font (used for labeling and caption)	setFont(Font), Font getFont() setFontName(String), String getFontName() setFontStyle(int), int getFontStyle() setFontSize(int), int getFontSize()
Caption	setCaption(String), String getCaption()
Highlight (controls 3D presentation)	setHighlight(boolean), boolean getHighlight()
Panel Color	setPanelColor(Color), Color getPanelColor()
Knob Color	setKnobColor(Color), Color getKnobColor()
Text Color	setTextColor(Color), Color getTextColor()

Table 3.1   (continued)

Property	Associated Methods
Tic Color	setTicColor(Color), Color getTicColor()
Grad Color	setGradColor(Color), Color getGradColor()
Labels (for labeling graduations)	setHasLabels(boolean), boolean getHasLabels(), setLabelString(String)
Sections	setNumberOfSections(int), int getNumberOfSections()

These methods can be called on any pot and achieve the specified affect. These methods can be called immediately after pot instantiation or at runtime to change the pot's behavior on the fly. It's hard for me to think up an example of why one would need to change a pot's behavior and/or presentation at runtime, but you might be able to think of a reason. *Note:* All of these properties can also be set in the constructor of the derived pot classes when the pots are instantiated.

The *PotBase* class also implements the *Adjustable* interface. By implementing this interface, all potentiometers are made to produce (fire) *AdjustmentEvents* whenever a pot's value changes. These events are the means to connect pots (*AdjustmentEvent* producers) to *AdjustmentEvent* consumers like meters or seven-segment displays.

Support for Double Buffering

The *PotBase* base class has built-in support for double buffering. As you'll recall from previous chapters, double buffering is the process by which an image of a component (in this case a pot) is drawn into an off-screen buffer, and when the drawing is complete, it is copied in its entirety into the current graphics context. This tends to reduce flickering in that only the portion of a control or indicator that needs to be redrawn is redrawn and the static background is updated only when needed.

The support provided by *PotBase* is in maintaining a reference to a Java *Image* called *potImage*. This *Image* is of the complete pot and associated area and contains all static imagery needed for a pot's presentation. The *paint* method in derived classes renders this image into the device context and then overlays it with any dynamic imagery (the position of the knob for example) required.

In addition to maintaining the *potImage* reference, many of the property setter methods in *PotBase* set the *potImage* reference to null if the property to which it is associated would alter the visual presentation of the pot. Of course, next time through the pot's *paint* method, the null *potImage* reference would cause the off-screen image to be regenerated with its new look before being displayed.

Processing Low-level Mouse and Keyboard Events

In order to make potentiometers work, it is necessary to capture low-level mouse and keyboard events that take place over the pot and respond to them appropriately. The first step in this process is to indicate that the *PotBase* base class, derived from *Canvas*, is interested in capturing low-level events. This is done by calling the following code in the constructor of the *PotBase* class.

```
// Enable low level event processing for mouse and keyboard
enableEvents(AWTEvent.MOUSE_EVENT_MASK | AWTEvent.MOUSE_MOTION_
EVENT_MASK | AWTEvent.KEY_EVENT_MASK);
```

Once this is done, methods must be written in the classes derived from *PotBase* (one for each event to be processed) to handle the events that will be directed at the pot. These methods, called *processMouseEvent*, *processMouseMotionEvent*, and *processKeyEvent*, are implemented in derived classes because round potentiometers and slide pots process these events differently.

Producing Higher-level Semantic Events

Potentiometers fire an *AdjustmentEvent* (by calling the *fireAdjustmentEvent* method shown below) every time their value changes. The receivers of this event are those entities that have registered interest in the state of a particular pot. To support registration, the *PotBase* base class has a method called *addAdjustmentListener* for adding to the interest list and a method called *removeAdjustmentListener* for removing those *AdjustmentListeners* no longer interested in the state of a particular pot. Again, since registration is handled by the pot base class, derived classes get the functionality for free. So, whenever a pot fires an *AdjustmentEvent*, that event is delivered to all *AdjustmentListeners* currently registered as interested. *Note:* Registered listeners are delivered the generated *AdjustmentEvent* automatically; however, any Java code can poll for a pot's value at any time by calling the pot's *getValue* method directly.

The code below from *PotBase.java* shows how listeners and events are managed.

```
// Add an adjustment listener
public synchronized void addAdjustmentListener(AdjustmentListener l) {

    adjustmentListener = AWTEventMulticaster.add(adjustmentListener, l);
}

// Remove adjustment listener
public synchronized void removeAdjustmentListener(AdjustmentListener l){
```

```
        adjustmentListener = AWTEventMulticaster.remove(adjustmentListener, 1);
}

// Indicate to all listeners that the pot's adjustment has changed
public void fireAdjustmentEvent() {

        // Synchronously notify the listeners so that they are
        // guaranteed to be up-to-date with the Adjustable before
        // it is mutated again.
        AdjustmentEvent e = new AdjustmentEvent(this,
                          AdjustmentEvent.ADJUSTMENT_VALUE_CHANGED,
                          AdjustmentEvent.TRACK, value);
        // Send it out if there is a listener registered
        if (adjustmentListener != null)
           adjustmentListener.adjustmentValueChanged(e);
}
```

The *PotBase* class provides one other method of note called *getAttenuation*. This method is the means by which any pot can be made to have an audio taper. This method takes the current linear value of the pot in the range 0…100 and converts it to a logarithmic scale for return from this call. An audio taper pot returns a value of zero at the minimum travel position, a value of .1 at the 50% travel position, and a value of 1.0 at the extreme end of the travel. The code below shows how this is accomplished.

```
// Simulate a pot with an audio taper. Audio taper pots
// have a 10% / 90% value at 50% rotation. Return an
// attenuation factor that takes this into consideration.
// At full scale an attenuation factor of 1.0 is returned.
// At 50 % full scale an attenuation factor of .1 is returned
// At 0% full scale an attenuation factor of 0.0 is returned.
public double getAttenuation() {

    if (value == 0)
        return 0.0;

    else if (value == 100)
        return 1.0;

    else {
        // Calculate log attenuation
        double exp = - (100.0 - (double) value) / (POTRANGE / 2.0);
        return Math.pow(10, exp);
    }
}
```

Pot Class

The *Pot* class implements a very configurable, round potentiometer that responds to mouse and keyboard events. Figure 3.1 shows two different round pots in use. Actually, both are instances of the same round pot class—they are just configured differently. Visual differences are what distinguishes these two pots; operationally, they are the same.

If you examine the two round pots shown, you can see that tics (short line segments) and dots (small diameter circles) can be used to delineate pot sections. These marks are called graduations or graduation marks. You can also see that a tic or a dot can be used on the knob to indicate position. Finally, you can see that textual labels can be used to label the graduations. All of these visual display attributes are controlled by class properties which have getter and setter methods. The *Pot* class provides the properties and methods listed in Table 3.2 for controlling its visual presentation.

Table 3.2   Properties and Methods of Pot Class

Property	Associated Methods
Radius (in pixels)	setRadius(int), int getRadius()
Tic length percentage	setTicLengthPercent(int), int getTicLengthPercent()
Tic start percentage	setTicStartPercent(int), int getTicStartPercent()
Grad gap percentage	setGradGapPercent(int), int getGradGapPercent()
Grad length percentage	setGradLengthPercent(int), int getGradLengthPercent()
Label percentage (placement of labels around the pot)	setLabelPercent(int), int getLabelPercent()
Tics (selects a tic or a dot as a knob position indicator)	setKnobUseTics(boolean), boolean getKnobUseTics()
Graduations (selects tics or dots for use as graduations)	setGradUseTics(boolean), boolean getGradUseTics()
Caption placement	setCaptionAtBottom(boolean), boolean getCaptionAtBottom()

As methods are called to alter a pot's associated property, the pot's *paint* method is called to render a new version of the pot with its changed appearance. Doubling buffering is used by the *paint* method to keep unnecessary rendering to a minimum.

Because the *Pot* class implements round potentiometers, it seemed appropriate that their size would be specified by a radius instead of a length and a width. As expected, increasing the size of the radius increases the size of the round pot.

Tic start and tic length are specified as percentage ratios with respect to a pot's radius, they control the position and the size of the tic or dot used on a knob for indicating position. Increasing tic start moves the position indicator closer to the edge of the knob. Manipulating tic length controls the length of the tic or the size of the dot indicator, depending upon which is used. See *Pot.java* for the default values of these attributes.

Grad (short for graduation) gap and grad length are also percentage ratios that control where the graduation marks surrounding the pot begin in relation to the knob and how large they should be. Increasing the gap moves the graduation marks radially outwards from the pot's center. Increasing the length makes the tic marks longer or the dots larger, depending on which type of graduation mark is being used.

Label percentage controls how far from the pot's center labels are drawn. As this ratio is increased in value, the labeling occurs farther and farther from the center of the pot.

Tics are selected for use as the knob position indicator by calling the function *setKnobUseTic*(true). If false is passed to this method, a dot will be used instead. Along the same vein, if the *setGradUseTics* method is called and passed a true value, tics will be used for graduation markings. If false is passed, dots will be used instead.

Finally, a pot can have a caption that describes its purpose (volume control, treble control, etc). A caption is specified as a string; the position of the caption (either above or below the pot) is controlled by calling the *setCaptionAtBottom* method. Calling this method with a true parameter causes the caption to be placed below the pot, which is the default behavior and is shown in Figure 3.1 on the left. Pot two in this figure shows the caption configured above the pot.

A pot's value can always be gotten by calling its *getValue*() method directly. What has not been mentioned is that a pot's value can also be set using the *setValue*(int) method. Setting a pot's value to the valid range of values from 0…100 will cause the pot's knob position indicator to assume the corresponding position.

As you will notice if you look at the code in *Pot.java*, many of the drawing functions operate in polar coordinates. This seemed appropriate during the design because pots are round and all embellishments made to the pots seem to radiate out from the center of the pot. The method

```
void drawLinePolar(Graphics g, int xCenter, int yCenter, double angle,
int start, int length)
```

draws a line radiating from the specified center point with the specified angle that starts at the radial distance start from the center and extends for length pixels. This method is used to draw tics both on the knob's surface and/or on the panel's surface when tics are used for marking graduations. The method

```
void drawDotPolar(Graphics g, int xCenter, int yCenter, double angle,
int start, int length)
```

draws a circle at the specified angle from the center position specified at a radial distance of start with a diameter of length. This method is used to draw dots both on the knob's surface and/or on the panel surface when dots are used for marking graduations. Finally, the method

```
void drawTextPolar(Graphics g, int xCenter, int yCenter, double angle,
int start, String text)
```

is used for labeling the panel surface surrounding the pot. Text is rendered horizontally at the distance and angle specified from the center point.

Handling Mouse and Keyboard Events

The *Pot* class has its own mouse and keyboard event handling code because pots respond differently to these events than do objects of the *SlidePot* class. As you will recall the base class, *PotBase*, turned on low-level event handling in its constructor. It is up to the derived classes, however, to implement the event handling. How round pots respond to mouse and keyboard events was described in the introduction to this chapter. The following code taken from *Pot.java* illustrates how the *Pot* class handles these events.

```
// Process mouse click events
protected void processMouseEvent(MouseEvent e) {

    // Track mouse presses/releases
    switch(e.getID()) {
        case MouseEvent.MOUSE_PRESSED:
            requestFocus();
            mouseDown = true;

            // Figure out where mouse is
            downPt = e.getPoint();

            // Was mouse clicked within the knob ?
            int deltaX = Math.abs(downPt.x - xCenter);
            int deltaY = Math.abs(downPt.y - yCenter);
            if ((deltaX <= radius) && (deltaY <= radius))
                mouseInKnob = true;
            else
                mouseInKnob = false;
            break;
```

```
        case MouseEvent.MOUSE_RELEASED:
            mouseDown = false;

            // If mouse was clicked outside of knob
            if (!mouseInKnob) {
                // If mouse clicked on left side of knob
                if (downPt.x <= xCenter) {
                    setValue(value - blockIncrement);
                    fireAdjustmentEvent();
                } else{
                    setValue(value + blockIncrement);
                    fireAdjustmentEvent();
                }
            }
            break;
    }
    // Let the superclass continue delivery
    super.processMouseEvent(e);
}

// Process motion events
protected void processMouseMotionEvent(MouseEvent e) {

    // Track mouse drags
    if (e.getID() == MouseEvent.MOUSE_DRAGGED) {
        // Only interested in movement when mouse is down
        if (mouseDown && mouseInKnob) {
            // Figure out where mouse is
            Point pt = e.getPoint();

            // See if movement
            int deltaX = pt.x - downPt.x;
            if (deltaX > 0) {
                // Move by positive unit increment
                setValue(value + unitIncrement);
            } else{
                // Move by negative unit increment
                setValue(value - unitIncrement);
            }
            fireAdjustmentEvent();
```

```
            // Update current position
            downPt.x = pt.x;
            downPt.y = pt.y;
        }
    }
    // Let the superclass continue delivery
    super.processMouseMotionEvent(e);
}

// Process keyboard events
protected void processKeyEvent(KeyEvent e) {

    // Simulate a mouse click for certain keys
    int keyCode = e.getKeyCode();

    if (keyCode == KeyEvent.VK_RIGHT) {
        setValue(value + unitIncrement);
        fireAdjustmentEvent();
    }   else if (keyCode == KeyEvent.VK_LEFT) {
        setValue(value - unitIncrement);
        fireAdjustmentEvent();
    }
    // Let the superclass continue delivery
    super.processKeyEvent(e);
}
```

Pot Class Constructors

Three constructors exist for the *Pot* class. The first, a zero argument constructor is provided because all Java beans must have one. This constructor uses default values for all properties. Its signature is as follows:

```
public Pot()
```

When pots are instantiated using this minimal constructor, they can still be configured using the property setter methods described above. The next constructor has the following signature:

```
public Pot(int radius, String caption, int value)
```

Using this constructor, the size of the pot, its caption, and its initial value can be specified; all other properties are defaulted. The final constructor which exposes all of the *Pots* properties is as follows:

```
public Pot(int radius, String fontName, int fontStyle, int fontSize,
String caption, boolean hasLabels, String labelsString,
boolean captionAtBottom, int value,
boolean knobUseTics, boolean gradUseTics, boolean hasHighlight,
int ticLengthPercent, int ticStartPercent,
int numberOfSections, int gradGapPercent, int gradLengthPercent,
int labelPercent,
Color panelColor, Color knobColor, Color textColor,
Color ticColor, Color gradColor)
```

No default values are provided when this constructor is used. This constructor allows the finest control over the visual aspects of a *Pot*, as all properties must be explicitly specified.

The Paint Method

The *paint* method is one of the two abstract methods defined by *PotBase* that all derived classes must implement. The *paint* code from *Pot.java* is shown below for reference. You can see how the various properties of the pot drive its visual presentation. You can also see how double buffering is used to reduce extraneous rendering and therefore help to reduce display flickering. The operation of the code should be obvious from the comments.

```
// Paint the pot
public void paint(Graphics g) {

    // Get the size of the container
    int width = getSize().width;
    int height = getSize().height;

    // ·Set font into the graphics context
    g.setFont(font);

    // Get the font metrics
    FontMetrics fm = g.getFontMetrics();

    // Get char height
    int charHeight = fm.getAscent();

    // Calculate center of knob
    xCenter = width / 2;
    int adjustedHeight = height - charHeight;
    int halfAdjustedHeight = adjustedHeight / 2;
```

```
if (captionAtBottom)
    yCenter = halfAdjustedHeight;
else
    yCenter = halfAdjustedHeight + charHeight;

// See if we have a knob bitmap image for displaying
if (potImage == null) {

    // No, so create the image area for the knob and surroundings
    potImage = createImage(width, height);

    // Get graphics context for the image
    Graphics gKnob = potImage.getGraphics();

    // Set font into the graphics context
    gKnob.setFont(font);

    // Do some calculations
    int knobWidth = radius * 2;

    // Calc position of knob in graphics context
    int knobOrgX = xCenter - radius;
    int knobOrgY = yCenter - radius;

    // Paint the panel area
    gKnob.setColor(panelColor);
    gKnob.fillRect(0, 0, width, height);

    if (hasHighlight) {
        // The knob is drawn so that it has a highlight towards
        // the upper left and the lower right portion of the knob
        // is darker.
        final int hlw = 3;
        int thlw = hlw * 2;
        final int highlightSpanAngleDegrees = 20;
        int halfSpanAngle = highlightSpanAngleDegrees / 2;

        // Draw the bright highlight color
        gKnob.setColor(highlightBrighterColor);
        gKnob.fillOval(knobOrgX, knobOrgY, knobWidth, knobWidth);

        // Draw the darker arc
        gKnob.setColor(highlightDarkerColor);
        gKnob.fillArc(knobOrgX, knobOrgY, knobWidth, knobWidth, 225, 180);
```

```
    // Draw the white highlight arc
    gKnob.setColor(Color.white);
    gKnob.fillArc(knobOrgX, knobOrgY, knobWidth, knobWidth,
        135 - halfSpanAngle, highlightSpanAngleDegrees);

    // Now fill in the middle of the knob with the
    // knob color
    gKnob.setColor(knobColor);
    gKnob.fillOval(knobOrgX + hlw, hlw + knobOrgY,
        knobWidth - thlw, knobWidth - thlw);
} else {
    // Draw the knob without a highlight
    gKnob.setColor(knobColor);
    gKnob.fillOval(knobOrgX, knobOrgY, knobWidth, knobWidth);
}

// Now draw the graduations and labels, if required
if (numberOfSections != 0) {
    gKnob.setColor(gradColor);
    for (int grad=0; grad < numberOfSections + 1; grad++) {
        double gradValue = ((double) POTRANGE * grad) / NumberOfSections;
        if (gradUseTics) {
            // Draw the tics
            drawLinePolar(gKnob, xCenter, yCenter,
                getAngleFromValue(round(gradValue)),
                getGradStart(), gradLength);
        } else{
            drawDotPolar(gKnob, xCenter, yCenter,
                getAngleFromValue(round(gradValue)),
                getGradStart(), gradLength);
        }
    }
    // Now the labels
    if (hasLabels) {
        gKnob.setColor(textColor);
        for (int grad=0; grad < numberOfSections + 1; grad++) {
            double gradValue = ((double) POTRANGE * grad) /
                            numberOfSections;

            // Get the label
            String label = (String) labels.elementAt(grad);
```

```
                     // Draw the label
                     drawTextPolar(gKnob, xCenter, yCenter,
                         getAngleFromValue(round(gradValue)),
                         labelRadius, label);
                 }
             }
         }
         // Now, draw the centered caption either above or below the pot
         int stringWidth = fm.stringWidth(caption);
         int xPos = (width - stringWidth) / 2;
         int yPos = fm.getAscent() / 2;
         if (captionAtBottom)
             yPos += yCenter + labelRadius;
         else
             yPos += yCenter - labelRadius;
         gKnob.setColor(textColor);
         gKnob.drawString(caption, xPos, yPos);
    }

    // Render the knob and surroundings onto the device context
    g.drawImage(potImage, 0, 0, null);

    // Draw the tic on the knob. Position determined from value
    g.setColor(ticColor);
    if (knobUseTics) {
        // Draw the tic
        drawLinePolar(g, xCenter, yCenter, getAngleFromValue(value),
            ticStart, ticLength);
    } else{
        // Draw the dot
        drawDotPolar(g, xCenter, yCenter, getAngleFromValue(value),
            ticStart, ticLength);
    }
}
```

The getPreferredSize Method

The *getPreferredSize* method is the other abstract method defined in the base class that must be implemented in derived classes. Its purpose is to provide the dimensions of its enclosing area to any and all who might ask. This method is called by layout managers to size the containing area necessary for encapsulating the *Pot* object in a user interface. Here, the dimensions returned include that required for the *Pot* itself and for its caption. Code is as follows:

```
public Dimension getPreferredSize() {

    // Calculate the preferred size based on the caption text
    FontMetrics fm = getFontMetrics(font);
    int charHeight = fm.getMaxAscent() + fm.getMaxDescent();
    int charWidth = fm.charWidth('0');
    minHeight = 2 * (labelRadius + charHeight + PAD);
    minWidth = 2 * (labelRadius + charWidth + PAD);
    int captionWidth = getCaption().length() * charWidth;

    minWidth = Math.max(minWidth, captionWidth);
    return new Dimension(minWidth, minHeight);
}
```

SlidePot Class

The *SlidePot* class implements a slide or slider pot. A slide pot is very similar to a round pot except that all of its knob's travel is in a straight line up and down instead of in a circle. Because its visual presentation differs from that of a round potentiometer, it needs different properties to express those differences. The properties provided by the *SlidePot* class are listed in Table 3.3.

Table 3.3   *Properties and Methods of SlidePot Class*

Property	Associated Methods
Width (in pixels)	setWidth(int), int getWidth()
Length (in pixels)	setLength(int), int getLength()
Knob width percentage	setKnobWidthPercent(int), int getKnobWidthPercent()
Knob length percentage	setKnobLengthPercent(int), int getKnobLengthPercent()
Graduation width percentage	setGradWidthPercent(int), int getGradWidthPercent()
Label positioning percentage	setLabelPercent(int), int getLabelPercent()

The size of a slide pot is specified by a width and a length value both expressed in pixels. By varying these values, you can produce slide pots that are tall and skinny or short and fat. The width dimension is especially important because most other properties that operate on percentages do so in relation to the slide pot's width value.

The size of the slide pot's knob is specified as a ratio to the width of the slide pot. Doing so always keeps the knob the correct relative size regardless of how the slide pot's width changes. The default percentage is 130% which means the knob will always be wider than the slide pot. Since the slide pot's knob is hour-glass-shaped, this ratio defines the size of the widest portion of the knob.

Knob length is specified as a percentage ratio to the length of the slide pot. The default percentage ratio is 23%. The default width and length values of 130% and 23% were chosen because they provide a reasonable-looking knob.

The graduation width percentage controls how far the graduation mark tics extend horizontally from the middle of the slide pot. Larger values make the tics extend further.

Finally, the label positioning percentage determines how far the labels and the caption are from the center of the slide pot. Larger values move the labeling farther from the slide pot's center. Slide pot labeling occurs on the left of the slide pot, whereas its caption shows up on the right-hand side.

Since all other aspects of a slide pot's operation are the same as for a round pot, there is no need to provide any new code for illustration purposes. If you are interested in looking at the code, it can be found in the file *SlidePot.java*. Suffice it to say that the *SlidePot* class provides its own unique *paint* and *getPreferredSize* methods, as required by its inheritance. The slide pot's *paint* method utilizes double buffering as did its round cousin counterpart to avoid flickering as much as possible. Also, the *SlidePot* class has three constructors, as did the *Pot* class.

A *SlidePot* can operate as a Java bean if it is built correctly and packaged in a jar file.

BoostCutSlidePot Class

The *BoostCutSlidePot* was developed exclusively for use in the graphics equalizer processor of section two. It is included in this discussion because I felt all pots should be discussed in one place in this book. This pot is an example of how a specialized pot was created by extending the simple slide pot. To determine the gain in dB, an application must call the *getGain* method of a *BoostCutSlidePot* just as pots with audio taper needed to have their *getAttenuation* method called. The code for this pot is shown below for illustrative purposes.

```
public class BoostCutSlidePot extends SlidePot {

   /**
    * Class constructor
    *
    * @param int length is the length in pixels of the slide pot
    * @param int width is the width in pixels of the slide pot
    * @param String caption is the label to be associated with the pot
    * @param int minDBGain is the min value of gain in dB
```

```
 * @param int maxDBGain is the max value of gain in dB
 * NOTE min and max values are usually the same only different in sign
 */
public BoostCutSlidePot(int length, int width, String caption, int
                        minDBGain, int maxDBGain) {

    super(length, width, caption, 50);

    this.minDBGain = minDBGain;

    potGranularity = ((double) maxDBGain - minDBGain) / POTRANGE;
}

/**
 * Return the value of the gain at the current pot setting
 *
 * @return double gain
 */
public double getGain() {

    // Get the pots current value 0..100
    int potValue = getValue();

    double db = (potValue * potGranularity) + minDBGain;
    double gain = Math.pow(10, db / 20.0);

    if (gain >= 1.0)
        return gain;
    else
        return -gain;
}
// Private class data
private double minDBGain;
private double potGranularity;
}
```

How a *BoostCutSlidePot* is coupled into an application will be shown shortly.

IntValuedPot Class

An *IntValuedPot* is an extension of the basic *Pot* class that allows for returned ranges of other than 0...100. This class was developed because it was found that this functionality was sometimes needed and it made more sense to encapsulate it in its own class than it did to always force the application to provide it. To show how thin a veneer was required to provide this functionality, the code for the class is shown below:

```
// This class extends Pot to provide for integer values other than
0..100 to be returned public class IntValuedPot extends Pot {

    /**
     * Class constructor
     *
     * @param int maxValue is the maximum value the pot should return at
     * max rotation.
     * @param int minValue is the minimum value the pot should return at
     * min rotation.
     */
    public IntValuedPot(int maxValue, int minValue) {
        this.minValue = minValue;
        potGranularity = ((double) maxValue - minValue) / 100.0;
    }

    /**
     * Get the scaled value of the pot at its current position
     *
     * @return int scaled int value
     */
    public int getIntValue() {
        return (int)((super.getValue() * potGranularity) + minValue);
    }

    /**
     * Set the current position of the pot to the scaled value
     *
     * @param int realValue is the scaled int value to set the pot to
     */
    public void setIntValue(int realValue) {

        super.setValue((int)((realValue - minValue) / potGranularity));
    }

    // Private class data
    private double potGranularity;
    private int minValue;

}
```

Note: The minimum and maximum values specified can be positive or negative with respect to each other. For example, it is possible to set the maximum value to +750 and the minimum value to –750. It is also possible to set the maximum value to –750 and the minimum value to +750.

IntValuedSlidePot Class

The code for this class is virtually identical to that shown above except that it extends *SlidePot* instead of the *Pot* class. In other words, this class provides a slide pot with programmable minimum and maximum integer values.

RealValuedPot Class

RealValuedPot are similar to *IntValuedPot* except they return double values within a programmable range.

RealValuedSlidePot Class

RealValuedSlidePot are similar to *IntValuedSlidePot* except they return double values within a programmable range. Slide pots of this type are used in the compressor/expander processor and in the reverb processor of section two.

CONNECTING POTS TO LISTENER DEVICES . . . .

It is a trivial exercise to use any of these pots in an audio application. In the simplest sense, the pot is first instantiated with a variable number of parameters, depending on the constructor used. Next, the pot may or may not be further configured by calling the property setter methods on the pot. Finally, the pot must be connected to whatever device is interested in its operation. A code snippet is shown below:

```
// Create a slide pot with an initial value of zero
SlidePot pot = new SlidePot(85, 13, "Level", 0);

// Connect a display device (an AdjustmentListener) to the output of this pot
pot.addAdjustmentListener(displayDevice);
```

With this code, every time the slide pot is manipulated, it creates an *AdjustmentEvent* which is dispatched to the display device which is an *AdjustmentEvent* listener and therefore knows how to interpret the event and react accordingly.

Things are not so simple when pots other than simple round pots and slide pots are used. In these cases, it is necessary to provide an *AdjustmentListener* that polls the pot's value, possibly manipulates it, and passes it on. Examples of this technique can be found in the *PotTypeDemo* program described below. To make pot number two (second pot from left in Figure 3.1) operate with an audio taper pot, the following code is used:

```
...Create and configure pot2

// Add listener to this pot using an anonymous inner class
pot2.addAdjustmentListener(new AdjustmentListener () {
    public void adjustmentValueChanged(AdjustmentEvent e) {
        amplitudeChanged(pot2, display2);
    }
});

// Called when the amplitude pot is manipulated. Note: amplitude
// pot is modeled with a pseudo audio taper.
public void amplitudeChanged(PotBase p, IntLEDDisplay display) {

    // Get the attenuation factor from this audio taper pot
    double atten = p.getAttenuation();

    // Set the displayed value to 100 times the attenuation
    display.setValue((int)( 100 * atten));
}
```

THE PotTypeDemo PROGRAM . . . .

In this demo program, the output of which is shown in Figure 3.1, five different types of pots are created and coupled to five display devices (the seven-segment display devices will be covered in a subsequent chapter) so you can see how the pots' values change as they are manipulated.

Pot 1 is a round potentiometer that uses dots for the knob and for the graduation markings. It is a standard pot in that it operates over the linear range of values from 0 to 100. At the 50% rotation position shown, the output value is 50 as indicated on the display. This pot is configured so that the caption is below the pot. The pot has 12 sections for a total of 13 graduation marks. The block increment for this pot is eight.

Pot 2 is a larger round potentiometer that uses tics for both the knob and for graduations. This pot is special in that it provides a pseudo audio taper, as has been described. As you can see, at the 50% rotation point the pot's output value is only at the 10% point. This pot is configured to have its caption at the top. Pot 2 is configured for 15 sections.

Pot 3 is a linear slide pot configured with 10 sections. Like all previous potentiometers described here, it has both labels and a caption.

Pot 4 is a special boot/cut pot developed for the graphic equalizer processor of section two. It reads out directly in dB. It provides a double return value but in this demo program, the display is actually showing one hundred times the value returned. At the mid position labeled 0 dB, the value returned from this pot is 1.0. The 0 dB label indicates no gain. At the +12 dB position, the value returned is 3.98 (a voltage gain of 12 dB is a voltage ratio of 3.98:1). At the –12 dB position the value returned from the pot is –0.25.

Pot 5 is a pot based on the *IntValuedSlidePot* class. It is similar to a normal slide pot except the range of values it can return can be configured by the user. In the case here, it is configured to return a minimum value of –750 and a maximum value of +750 instead of the standard 0…100.

All of the pots used in this program are configured to use black for text labeling and to use red for tic marks and graduation marks. Two slightly different colors are used for the pot knobs.

MISCELLANEOUS INFORMATION . . . .

Package:

craigl.beans.pots

Source Files:

File Name	Description
BoostCutSlidePot.java	Special slide pot developed for the graphic equalizer of section two. It reads out in dB gain or loss.
IntValuedPot.java	A traditional round potentiometer that has scaled outputs that allow any integer values to be assigned as min and max values. Not constrained to the range 0…100.
IntValuedSlidePot.java	Same as above except this is a slide pot instead of a round pot.
Pot.java	Traditional round potentiometer class.
PotBase.java	Abstract base class from which all varieties of potentiometers are derived.

File Name	Description
PotBeanInfo.java	*BeanInfo* class for associating round pot icons with the *Pot* class.
PotIcon16.gif	16 × 16 pixel icon associated with this class.
PotIcon32.gif	32 × 32 pixel icon associated with this class.
PotTypeDemo.java	Example program used to produce Figure 3.1. Demonstrates the use of traditional round potentiometers and slide pots.
RealValuedPot.java	A traditional round potentiometer that has scaled outputs that allow any real values to be assigned as min and max values. Not constrained to the range 0...100.
RealValuedSlidePot.java	Same as above except this is a slide pot instead of a round pot.
SlidePot.java	*SlidePot* class code.
SlidePotBeanInfo.java	*BeanInfo* class for associating slide pot icons with *SlidePot* class.
SlidePotIcon16.gif	16 × 16 pixel icon associated with this class.
SlidePotIcon32.gif	32 × 32 pixel icon associated with this class.

probably without much coding required on your part. As we shall also see, LEDs conform to the Java AWT 1.1 event model (as they must to be used as beans).

WHAT'S THIS BLINKER THING AND WHY A STATE MACHINE? . . . .

LEDs, as I have implemented them here, actually run a small state machine to control their operation. A state machine was found necessary for numerous reasons. First, I didn't like LEDs on a simulated device flashing at different rates because this was terribly distracting. The affect was something like being in a line of cars turning left with all the turn signals flashing at different rates. Second, I wanted to keep LED repaints down to a minimum for performance reasons as well as to limit flickering caused by random repainting. Finally, I wanted the duty cycles (the on vs. the off times) of blinking LEDs to be the same. As a corollary to this final item, I wanted the LEDs to operate synchronously as if they were being driven by digital logic. You will see what I mean if you exercise the *LEDTypeDemo.java* application shown in Figure 4.1.

This might seem like a lot of trouble for such a simple indicator but I wanted what I wanted (audiophiles can be terribly fussy!).

To drive the LED state machines (one exists for each LED), I needed a source of regularly timed pulses that would run the state machine through its various states. A *Blinker* as described in Chapter One was just the ticket as it runs in its own thread and fires regularly timed *PropertyChangeEvents* that the LED state machines can listen for. Each time the state machine receives a blink event, the required state of the LED is examined and the on screen LED is repainted as necessary. If the state of the LED has not changed, the blink event is ignored and superfluous repaints are thus avoided. The code below, extracted from *LEDBase.java*, is the code for the LED state machines.

```
/**
 * A small state machine to control the LED. It is meant to
 * limit the number of repaints getting generated so that the
 * LED does not studder as much as it would otherwise.
 */

public void propertyChange(PropertyChangeEvent evt) {
    // Make sure this is a blink property change.
    // Ignore all other types.
    if (!evt.getPropertyName().equals("blink"))
        return;
```

```
// Pulse is set by blinker property value
boolean pulse = ((Boolean) evt.getNewValue()).booleanValue();

// halfPulse toggles at 1/2 the blinker rate
if (pulse)
    halfPulse = !halfPulse;
if (state) {
    // LED needs to be on
    offOnce = false;

    if (mode == MODESOLID) {
        // LED on solid
        if (!onOnce) {
            ledState = true;
            repaint();
            onOnce = true;
        }
    } else if (mode == MODEBLINK)   {
        // LED is blinking
        onOnce = false;
        if (rate) {
            // Rate is fast
            ledState = pulse;
        } else{
            // Rate is slow
            ledState = halfPulse;
        }
        repaint();
    } else{
        // LED needs to pulse
        ledState = true;
        repaint();
        state = false;
    }
} else{
    // LED needs to be off
    onOnce = false;
    if (!offOnce) {
        ledState = false;
        offOnce = true;
        repaint();
    }
}
}
}
```

Two important facts must be noted here about the LED state machines. First, since a source of blink events must be available to advance the state machine through its states, an LED will not even turn on without first being connected to a *Blinker*. Second, the state of an LED, whether it is off or on, is independent of the *Blinker* source. The significance of this statement will become clearer very shortly.

In a typical application utilizing these simulated LEDs, a single *Blinker* would be instantiated and all of the LEDs would be connected to it as *PropertyChange* listeners. If your application required LEDs to blink at more than two rates, multiple *Blinkers* could be used configured to have different blink intervals or periods. The application's code would then connect the LEDs to the appropriate *Blinker* to achieve the desired blink rates.

LEDBase BASE CLASS . . . .

As described, the *LEDBase* class provides all of the base LED functionality and derived classes provide the presentation. To this end, the *LEDBase* class encapsulates all LED properties and methods common to all LEDs. Table 4.1 itemizes all of these properties and methods.

Table 4.1   Properties and Methods of the LEDBase Class

Property	Associated Methods
LED color	setLEDColor(Color), Color getLEDColor()
Panel color	setPanelColor(Color), Color getPanelColor()
LED mode (solid=0/blinking=1/pulse=2)	setLEDMode(int), int getLEDMode()
LED blink rate flag (fast/slow)	setLEDBlinkRate(boolean), boolean getLEDBlinkRate()
LED state (off/on)	setLEDState(boolean), boolean getLEDState()

These methods can be called on any LED and achieve the specified affect. These methods can be called immediately after LED instantiation or at runtime to change LED behavior on the fly. For example, one might want to change the color of an LED from green to red to indicate recording is taking place. Or, to change the LED from being on solid to blinking, as an indication of a state change within the application.

In addition to containing the LED state machine, this base class also implements the *PropertyChangeListener* and the *ActionListener* interfaces. The *PropertyChangeListener* interface is necessary to receive the blink event produced by the *Blinker* which drives the state machine. The *ActionListener* interface is necessary as the means to couple *ActionEvent* producers (like the *Buttons* of Chapter 2) to the LEDs.

LEDBase is an abstract class which cannot be instantiated on its own. *LEDBase* defines two abstract methods

```
public abstract void paint(Graphics g);
public abstract Dimension getPreferredSize();
```

that must be implemented by all derived classes because they have to do with visual presentation of the LED, something which *LEDBase* does not concern itself with.

RoundLED CLASS ·

The *RoundLED* class extends *LEDBase* to provide an LED with a round visual presentation. It implements a *paint* method to render the round LED onto a graphics context and provides a *getPreferredSize* method to return its required size to any Java layout manager that inquires. Also, the *RoundLED* class provides some unique properties of its own and overload some provided by *LEDBase* for rendering purposes. Table 4.2 describes the properties that this class provides:

Table 4.2   *Properties and Methods of the RoundLED Class*

Property	Associated Methods
LED size (in pixels)	setRadius(int), int getRadius()
LED color	setLEDColor(Color).This method overloads the base class method in order to clear the off-screen images used in double buffering the LED's image. This causes the on and off LED images to be recreated with the new color the next time the *paint* method is called.
Panel color	setPanelColor(Color). This method overloads the base class method in order to create a color that is slightly brighter than the specified panel color. This color is used in rendering the round LED.

As simple as a round LED might seem to be (a colored dot in the most trivial case), rendering it with three-dimensional properties takes effort. The difficulty arises because I tried to make the LED look as if it were mounted behind the panel with just the crown of the LED sticking through. This effect was accomplished using nested and filled circles of various sizes and colors. If you examine the code in *RoundLED.java* you will see how this was done. And although double buffering was probably not required, it was used to implement the *RoundLED* class.

SquareLED CLASS . . . .

The *SquareLED* class is even simpler than the *RoundLED* class presented above. It provides the same two methods, *paint* and *getPreferredSize*, but tailors them to a square visual presentation. The properties provided by the *SquareLED* class are shown in Table 4.3.

Table 4.3   Properties and Methods of the SquareLED Class

Property	Associated Methods
LED raised property. See AWT graphics method *fill3Drect*.	setRaised(boolean), boolean getRaised()
LED width (in pixels)	setWidth(int), int getWidth()
LED height (in pixels)	setHeight(int), int getHeight()

The raised property can be either true or false. If true, the square LED looks as if it protrudes out of the panel on which it is placed. If false, it looks as if it extends into the panel. This effect is produced using dark and light highlights that emulate shadows. Because the presentation provided by the *paint* method is so simple, double buffering is not used.

CONNECTING LEDs TO ActionEvent PRODUCERS . . . . . .

The code sample below brings together all the pieces required for using LEDs in an application. First, a *Blinker* is instantiated to provide a data source for the LED state machines. Next, a *SquareButton* is created which will provide the *ActionEvent* source to drive the state of the LEDs. Then a pulsing red *RoundLED* and a slow blinking blue *SquareLED* are created and coupled to the button as *ActiveEventListeners*. With all of this mechanism connected, the LEDs will follow the state of the button. The *RoundLED* will pulse once each time the button changes from the off to the on state and the *SquareLED* will blink slowly while the button is on.

```
// Create the blinker for the LEDs
Blinker blinker = new Blinker(200);

// Create square button
SquareButton ledButton =
    new SquareButton(40, 20,              // Sets the size
        "SanSerif", Font.BOLD, 10,        // Sets the text font
        "Led Button", true,               // Caption and caption at bottom flag
        true, false,                      // Sticky and state
        true,                             // Highlight
        PANELCOLOR,                       // Panel color
        Color.gray,                       // Button color
        Color.green);                     // Text color

// Create the pulsing red LED
RoundLED led1 = new RoundLED();
led1.setRadius(7);
led1.setPanelColor(PANELCOLOR);
led1.setLEDColor(Color.red);
led1.setLEDMode(RoundLED.MODEPULSE);
// Add the LED to a panel
p.add(led1);
// Connect this LED to the blinker for running its state machine
blinker.addPropertyChangeListener(led1);
// Connect the LED to the button to control its state
ledButton.addActionListener(led1);

// Create the slow blinking blue LED
SquareLED led3 = new SquareLED();
led3.setWidth(16);
led3.setHeight(10);
led3.setPanelColor(PANELCOLOR);
led3.setLEDColor(Color.blue);
led3.setLEDMode(RoundLED.MODEBLINK);
led3.setLEDBlinkRate(false);
// Add the LED to the panel
p.add(led3);
// Connect this LED to the blinker for running its state machine
blinker.addPropertyChangeListener(led3);
// Connect the LED to the button to control its state
ledButton.addActionListener(led3);
```

LabeledLED CLASS . . . .

LabeledLED is the final LED device provided in this package. This device is comprised of two components, a *RoundLED* and an AWT *Label*. These two components were packaged together into the *LabeledLED* class because LEDs are usually labeled and it seemed to make sense. You can see how these devices are put to use by examining the *RoundLEDMeter* device of the next chapter or the guitar tuner application of section three.

The *LabeledLED* class is highly configurable to offer as much flexibility as possible. The constructor of this class is shown below to give you an idea of the possibilities.

```
/**
 * Class Constructor for a Labeled LED
 *
 * @param Blinker blinker is the data source for the LED that allows
 * it to change states
 * @param Color panelColor is the color of the panel surrounding
 * the round LED and label.
 * @param Color ledColor is color of the LED
 * @param Color textColor is the color of the labeling text
 * @param Font font is the font used for the labeling text
 * @param int radius is the side of the LED to create
 * @param String label is the labeling string for the LED. This is a
 * static string that cannot be changed at runtime.
 * @param boolean isVertical if true indicates the label and the LED
 * will be aligned vertically. If false the label and the LED will
 * be aligned horizontally.
 * @param boolean topLeftMode if true indicates the LED will be the
 * top or the left component of the pair. If false, the LED will be the bottom
 * or the right component or the pair.
 */
public LabeledLED(Blinker blinker,
        Color panelColor, Color ledColor, Color textColor,
        Font font, int radius , String label,
        boolean isVertical, boolean topLeftMode)
```

The configurability of this class should be obvious from the comments in the constructor but what may not be so obvious is the fact that the LED and the label can be placed on top of one another or placed side by side. Also, the position of the LED in relation to the label can be controlled with the *topLeftMode* boolean. In total there are four possible orientations of the LED and label.

The *LabeledLED* class provides two methods for manipulating the LED. One called *setLEDState*(boolean) to control whether the LED is off or on and *setLEDColor*(Color) for setting the LED's color.

Note: The *LabeledLED* class was not designed to be used as a Java bean but as a standalone software component.

MISCELLANEOUS INFORMATION . . . .

Package:

craigl.beans.leds

Source Files:

File Name	Description
LabeledLED.java	A combination round LED and a label which can have vertical or horizontal orientation. Position of the label with respect to the LED can also be controlled.
LEDBase.java	Base class from which LED subclasses are derived.
LEDTypeDemo.java	Code for the demo program of Figure 4.1.
makefile	Makefile for building this package.
RoundLED.java	Code for round LEDs.
SquareLED.java	Code for square LEDs.

5 Meters–Analog and Digital

INTRODUCTION . . . .

In this chapter, the word meters is used to denote various types of display devices that visually indicate the value of some quantity in relation to a full scale or maximum value. We are all familiar with the ubiquitous progress bar or progress meter that indicates where one is in some time-consuming process like installing software or downloading files from the net. As progress is achieved, the progress bar on the meter moves farther and farther to the right. When the time-consuming operation is completed, the bar reaches it full length. In this example, the progress bar indicates percent completion.

In audio applications, meters have many uses in addition to the simple progress indication described above. Probably the most important use of meters is to indicate audio levels during recording and/or playback. Even the most inexpensive tape deck has some form of meter for setting recording levels appropriately. In many digital audio processing programs, meters are used to help set recording levels, for visually indicating the setting of certain parameters, and for showing progress as various processes are applied to the audio (applying non-real-time effects, for example). As you will soon realize, the meter, in its various forms, is a valuable user interface device for providing status information to users.

Most modern audio equipment uses light emitting diode (LED) meters in its design. These show increasing level by lighting more and more of the LEDs that make up the meter. The LEDs are usually color coded (green to yellow to red) to let the user know the relative level just by the color of the display. The user also knows the recording level is set to high when the red LED segments flash. Older equipment (and some of the ultramodern *retro* equipment) use analog meters with electro-mechanical movements for displaying various values. Meters of this type utilize a needle to indicate the current value. That is, the position of the needle changes as the input stimulus to the meter changes. For the most part, however, the advent of the LED and LED meters has caused the demise of the more expensive analog meter in electronic equipment.

Three types of meters are presented in this chapter. They are:

1. The *AnalogMeter*, which emulates an old fashion analog meter complete with movable needle.

2. The *LEDMeter*, which emulates a bar graph made from small rectangular LED segments.

3. The *RoundLEDMeter*, which uses an array of individual round LEDs to indicate level.

One each of each meter type is shown in Figure 5.1. Which meter type to use in an application is really up to you. Each meter provides the same functionality, so picking one type over another is only a matter of what look you are trying to achieve in your application.

Each meter is extended from the *Meter* base class and they therefore share a lot of the basic meter functionality. Further, each of these meters conforms to Java bean requirements and can therefore be used as such in applications. Other types of meters are possible besides those which are presented here; they can be built on top of the *Meter* base class. Both of the audio applications of section three use meters in their design.

All meters respond linearly to a range of integer values from 0 to 100. A value of zero results in no indication, whereas a value of 100 results in a full-scale indication.

Figure 5.1   Meter Demonstration Program. *Shows instances of an LEDMeter, an AnalogMeter, and a RoundLEDMeter all driven by random*

This is a unitless value in that it doesn't correspond to any physical quantity like dB, voltage, or frequency. Think of the meter value as some percent of full scale from zero to 100 percent. To make the meter read out in some specific units of measurement, conversion software must be written. This will be discussed briefly later in this chapter.

Since all meters are derived from *Meter* and since *Meter* implements the *AdjustmentListener* interface, all meters are adjustment listeners. This means that any meter can be connected to any source of the *Adjustment* events by adding the meter to the event source as an *AdjustmentListener*. Since all UI components that generate *Adjustment* events presented in this book produce values in the range from 0 to 100, they can be directly connected to and can therefore drive a meter directly. The code to connect the output of a potentiometer (see Chapter 3) to an *AnalogMeter* would be similar to the following:

```
// Create an AnalogMeter
AnalogMeter meter = new AnalogMeter();
// Configure the meter as required
...

// Create a round pot
Pot pot1 = new Pot();
// Configure the pot as required
...
// Connect the meter to the pot
pot1.addAdjustmentListener(meter);
```

After this connection is made, every time the potentiometer (pot) value changes (as the user manipulates the pot), the new value will immediately be reflected in the value displayed on the meter. Of course an application could also call the method *setValue*(int) on the meter to set its value directly. No *Adjustment* events or listeners are involved with this more direct method of setting a meter's value.

METER CLASS . . . .

As mentioned, *Meter* is the abstract base class for all meters. *Meter* extends *Panel* for providing an area for presentation and implements *AdjustmentListener*. The majority of the functionality provided by the *Meter* class is in providing properties (with getter and setter methods) that derived classes use for their presentation. The properties and methods provided are shown in Table 5.1

Table 5.1 Properties and Methods of the Meter Class

Property	Associated Methods
Width	setWidth(int), int getWidth()
Height	setHeight(int), int getHeight()
Meter mode—currently unused in this book	setMeterMode(int), int getMeterMode()
Font (used for caption and labeling)	setFont(Font), Font getFont()
	setFontName(String), String getFontName()
	setFontStyle(int), int getFontStyle()
	setFontSize(int), int getFontSize()
Caption	setCaption(String), String getCaption()
Labels	setHasLabels(boolean), boolean getHasLabels
Label position relative to width of meter	setLabelPercent(int), int getLabelPercent()
Labels string used for labeling the meter	setLabelsString(String), String getLabelsString()
Highlight	setHighlight(boolean), boolean getHighlight()
Number of meter sections	setNumberOfSections(int), int getNumberOfSections()
Panel color	setPanelColor(Color), Color getPanelColor()
Needle color	setNeedleColor(Color), Color getNeedleColor()
Text color used for labeling	setTextColor(Color), Color getTextColor()

Classes derived from *Meter* may or may not utilize all of these methods and properties. Derived classes may also need to overload some of these methods for various reasons.

Finally, I should mention the *Meter* class provides various constants and methods for setting and retrieving a meter mode (integer) value. Meter modes would be used to control the functionality implemented in derived meter classes. The following meter mode constants are defined in *Meter.java*. They define all meter modes that I anticipated needing in audio applications.

```
public static final int MODEPEAK = 1;
public static final int MODEPEAKHOLD = 2;
public static final int MODEAVG = 3;
public static final int MODERMS = 4;
public static final int MODEVU = 5;
```

Meter modes aren't used in the code in this book as all meters are peak-reading. These modes have been left in the code for future enhancements.

ANALOG METER CLASS ·····················

This class emulates an analog meter. The distinguishing features of this meter other than its basic appearance are:

1. It uses a movable needle to indicate the current value.
2. It has the ability to set color ranges for the meter scale.
3. It has the ability to label the meter scale with string values.

Because of the complexity of the visual presentation, most of the code used to implement the *AnalogMeter* class is part of the classes *paint* method. Here, double buffering is used to limit the amount of rendering necessary when the meter's value changes to keep flickering to a minimum. The complete meter is rendered in an off screen Java *Image* and is then copied into the device context by the execution of the *paint* method. The off screen image is created anew any time any of the properties that would affect the meter's appearance are changed. After the meter's image is copied to the device context, the needle is drawn over the top. The position and orientation of the needle is determined using the current meter value and some trig. The minimum value position of the needle is to the left while the full scale position is to the right.

The *paint* method is shown below to illustrate the complexity of the rendering required to emulate an analog meter. This code is located in the file *AnalogMeter.java*. The class constants used to control the various aspects of rendering are shown in upper case.

```
/**
 * Paint the Analog Meter onto the graphics context. Double
 * buffering is used to reduce flicker.
 *
 * @param Graphics g is the graphics context on which to draw
 */
public void paint(Graphics g) {
    // Get the size of the container and calculate important
    // values.
    int cwidth  = getSize().width;
    int cheight = getSize().height;
    int xCenter = cwidth / 2;
    int captionHeight  = (cheight * CAPTIONPERCENT) / 100;
    int captionYOffset = cheight - captionHeight;
```

```
int captionXOffset = 0;
int needleLength = captionYOffset - (2 * BORDERWIDTH);

// Is there an image of the analog meter to work with ?
if (meterImage == null) {
    // No, create the image for the meter
    meterImage = createImage(cwidth, cheight);

    // Get graphics context for the image
    Graphics gMeter = meterImage.getGraphics();

    // Fill complete meter
    gMeter.setColor(Color.black);
    gMeter.fillRoundRect(0, 0, cwidth, cheight, CORNERDIAMETER,
                                                CORNERDIAMETER);
    // Fill the panel
    int panelXOffset = BORDERWIDTH;
    int panelYOffset = BORDERWIDTH;
    int panelWidth = cwidth  - (2 * BORDERWIDTH);
    int panelHeight= cheight - (2 * BORDERWIDTH);
    gMeter.setColor(panelColor);
    gMeter.fillRoundRect(panelXOffset, panelYOffset, panelWidth,
                    panelHeight, CORNERDIAMETER, CORNERDIAMETER);
    // Draw color scale
    // First draw the filled arcs
    int xMaxOrg = xCenter - needleLength;
    int yMaxOrg = captionYOffset - needleLength;
    int arcMaxWidth = needleLength * 2;

    for (int colorZone=0; colorZone < colorZones.size(); colorZone++) {
        MeterColorZone mz = (MeterColorZone)
                            colorZones.elementAt(colorZone);

        // Set the colorZone color
        gMeter.setColor(mz.color);

        // Fill the arc
        gMeter.fillArc(xMaxOrg, yMaxOrg, arcMaxWidth, arcMaxWidth,
                        (int) mz.startAngle, (int) mz.spanAngle);
    }
    // Then clean out meter middle
    int bandLength = (needleLength * COLORSCALEPERCENT) / 100;
    int xMinOrg = xCenter - bandLength;
    int yMinOrg = captionYOffset - bandLength;
    int arcMinWidth = bandLength * 2;
```

```
// Fill the arc with the panel color
gMeter.setColor(panelColor);
gMeter.fillArc(xMinOrg, yMinOrg, arcMinWidth, arcMinWidth,
          (int) maxValueAngle - 1, METERRANGEINDEGREES + 2);

// Draw the major meter well
int wellMajDiameter = (WELLMAJDIAMETERPERCENT * cwidth) / 100;
int halfWellMajDiameter = wellMajDiameter / 2;
int wellMaxXOrg = xCenter - halfWellMajDiameter;
int wellMaxYOrg = captionYOffset - halfWellMajDiameter;
gMeter.setColor(Color.black);
gMeter.fillOval(wellMaxXOrg, wellMaxYOrg, wellMajDiameter,
                                            wellMajDiameter);

// Draw the minor meter well
int wellMinDiameter = (WELLMINDIAMETERPERCENT * cwidth) / 100;
int halfWellMinDiameter = wellMinDiameter / 2;
int wellMinXOrg = xCenter - halfWellMinDiameter;
int wellMinYOrg = captionYOffset - halfWellMinDiameter;
gMeter.setColor(Color.gray);
gMeter.fillOval(wellMinXOrg, wellMinYOrg, wellMinDiameter,
                                            wellMinDiameter);

// Fill caption portion
gMeter.setColor(Color.darkGray);
gMeter.fillRoundRect(captionXOffset, captionYOffset, cwidth,
              captionHeight, CORNERDIAMETER, CORNERDIAMETER);

// Draw the caption
gMeter.setFont(font);
FontMetrics fm = gMeter.getFontMetrics();
int labelWidth = fm.stringWidth(caption);
int charHeight = fm.getAscent() / 2;
int xText = xCenter - (labelWidth / 2);
int yText = captionYOffset + (captionHeight / 2) + charHeight;
gMeter.setColor(textColor);
gMeter.drawString(caption, xText, yText);

// Draw the labels
int numberOfLabels = labels.size();
String label, label1;
switch(numberOfLabels) {
    case 0:
        break;
```

```
            case 1:
                label = (String) labels.elementAt(0);
                drawTextPolar(gMeter, xCenter, captionYOffset, 90,
                                            labelDist, label);
                break;
            default:
                double deltaAngle = ((double) METERRANGEINDEGREES) /
                                            (numberOfLabels - 1);
                for (int l=0; l < numberOfLabels; l++) {
                    double angle = minValueAngle - (l * deltaAngle);
                    label = (String) labels.elementAt(l);
                    drawTextPolar(gMeter, xCenter, captionYOffset,
                                            angle, labelDist, label);
                }
        }
    }
    // Render the meter into the device context
    g.drawImage(meterImage, 0, 0, null);

    // Setup to draw the needle
    g.setColor(needleColor);

    double valueAngle = minValueAngle - (value * meterGranularity);
    valueAngle = valueAngle * Math.PI / 180;
    int xOffset = xCenter + (int)(needleLength * Math.cos(valueAngle));
    int yOffset = captionYOffset - (int)(needleLength * Math.sin(valueAngle));

    // Draw the needle
    g.drawLine(xCenter, captionYOffset, xOffset, yOffset);
}
```

The colors used in the meter's scale are set using the *setColorRange* method shown below. Each call to this method creates a new *MeterColorZone* object which encapsulates a starting angle for the new color on the meter scale, the angle of color span, and the new color. These new objects are added to the vector collection of other *MeterColorZone* objects. In the *paint* method above, each element of the *colorZones* vector is extracted and its color is rendered starting at the start angle and continuing for the specified span angle. The *AnalogMeter* in Figure 5.1 has twelve different color zones configured.

```
/**
 * Set a color for a range of values on the meter's scale.
 * Creates a new MeterColorZone object to describe the range. NOTE:
 * there isn't any overlap checking done here so the most recent
 * range set sticks.
```

```
 *
 * @param Color color is the color for the specified range of values
 * @param double minPercentValue is the percentage of full scale value
 * where this color should begin
 * @param double maxPercentValue is the percentage of full scale value
 * where this color should end
 */
public void setColorRange(Color color,
                double minPercentValue,
                double maxPercentValue) {
    double spanAngleRange = maxPercentValue - minPercentValue;
    double spanAngle = spanAngleRange * meterGranularity;
    double startAngle = minValueAngle - (maxPercentValue * meterGranularity);
    colorZones.addElement(new MeterColorZone(startAngle, spanAngle, color));
    meterImage = null;
    repaint();
}
```

The special treatment of labels on an analog meter's face needs to be mentioned here also. If only a single label (string) is specified, it will be drawn centered on the meter's scale. If more than one label string is specified, they will be evenly spaced across the meter's surface. The method *setLabelPercent* controls the radial distance from the origin of the meter's needle to the invisible arc on which the labels are rendered. Label percentage is relative to the height of the meter. The larger the value, the further from the needle's origin the labels are drawn.

LEDMeter CLASS . . . .

The *LEDMeter* class is designed to look like closely spaced rectangular LEDs (with white separators) stacked one on top of another and mounted behind a panel for a three-dimensional effect. *LEDMeters* are always vertical and can have any number of sections (one section per LED). *LEDMeters* also have a vertical caption drawn along the left side of the LED array and labels drawn along the right. These meters, like all others presented in this chapter, respond to the range of values from 0 to 100. When a value of zero is applied to the meter, none of the LED segments are lit and the meter appears dark. As the value applied to the meter increases, the lower segments light and when the meter's value reaches 100, all segments are lit. This meter class is the closest to a progress bar or progress meter of any of the meters presented. It can be used as a progress meter or it can be used to indicate levels of some kind.

The colors of the LEDs in the *LEDMeter* can be set using the *setColorRange* method. For a simple audio level meter, the lower LEDs might be set to green, the next

LEDs might be yellow and the final one or two LEDs might be red. Of course, that is entirely up to you. The *LEDMeter* in Figure 5.1 shows a spectrum of LED colors being used. Similar to what was described for the *AnalogMeter* class, the *setColorRange* method is used to specify a color to be used for a percentage range of values. The simple three-color arrangement might be implemented as follows:

```
// Create an LEDMeter instance
LEDMeter lm = new LEDMeter();

// Now configure the range of colors available
lm.setColorRange(Color.green, 0, 60);
                    // Meter is green from 0% to 60% of full scale
lm.setColorRange(Color.yellow, 61, 80);
                    // Meter is yellow from 61% to 80% of full scale
lm.setColorRange(Color.red, 81, 100);
                    // Meter is red from 81% to 100 % of full scale
```

Then if the level applied to the meter was below 61%, all of the LEDs would be green. As the signal level rose to 80%, it would be yellow and any signal above 81% would be indicated in red. So not only does the number of LEDs lit increase as the signal level does, the color of the LEDs also changes going up the scale. If the number of sections that comprise the *LEDMeter* is equal to the percentage color range specified to calls of *setColorRange* (as is the case in Figure 5.1), each LED can be a different color.

Some of the property methods provided in the *Meter* base class are overloaded by *LEDMeter* in order to handle rendering appropriately. Specifically, the *setHeight*(int) method is overloaded to recalculate the dimensions of the LED segments as the height of the meter is manipulated. The *setNumberOfSections*(int) method is also overloaded so this meter can dynamically change the number of sections (LEDs) at runtime. Finally, the *setPanelColor*(Color) method is overloaded so a lighter and darker shade of the panel color is available for rendering the three-dimensional effect.

RoundLEDMeter CLASS . . . .

The *RoundLEDClass* is not much different from the *LEDMeter* class except that it can be oriented vertically or horizontally and uses round LEDs for its display. Each of these LEDs looks as if it is mounted in a hole behind a panel. All of the three-dimensional aspects of a *RoundLEDMeter* are provided by the *RoundLED* objects that make it up. Similar to the *LEDMeter*, there is one *RoundLED* used per meter section. Similar also to *LEDMeter*, the color of each LED can be set using the *setColorRange* method.

Since the LEDs used in the *RoundLEDMeter* require a *Blinker* data source to run their individual state machines (see Chapter 4), most of the *RoundLEDMeter* class constructors require a *Blinker* to be passed in. This was thought preferable to instantiating a *Blinker* inside each *RoundLEDMeter* class because that way a single *Blinker* can be used per application instead of multiple. The full constructor for the *RoundLEDMeter* class is shown below to give you an idea of how much configurability is provided.

```
/**
 * RoundLEDMeter class constructor with all agruments
 *
 * @param int radius is the radius of the LEDs that will be used in the
 * meter.
 * @param boolean isVertical true if meter is vertical false if meter
 * should be horizontal.
 * @param int meterMode is not currently used
 * @param String fontName is the name of the font for labelling
 * @param String fontStyle is the name of the font style for labelling
 * @param int fontSize is the size of the font for labelling
 * @param String caption is the caption to label the meter with
 * @param boolean topLeftCaption if true causes the caption to be placed
 * at the top of vertical meters and at the left of horizontal meters.
 * False causes the caption to be place at the bottom or the right of
 * the meter.
 * @param boolean hasLabels is true if the meter has labels and it
 * is desired they are displayed.
 * @param String labelsString is the string of comma separated label
 * strings used to label the meter. There should be one entry for each
 * section of the meter.
 * @param boolean labelsOnTopLeft is true if the labels should be on the
 * left of the vertical meter LEDs or on top of a horizontal meter LEDs.
 * If false the labels will be on the right or on the bottom of the LEDs.
 * @param int value is the value the meter should initially display
 * @param int numberOfSections is the number of meter sections. NOTE:
 * this value can only be set in the constructor. It cannot be changed
 * at runtime.
 * @param Color panelColor is the color of the panel surrounding the
 * meter.
 * @param Color textColor is the color used for the labelling text
 * @param Blinker blinker is the blinker used to drive the LED state
 * machine. A blinker is passed in so applications using this meter
 * can have synchronized LEDs.
 */
```

```
public RoundLEDMeter(int radius, boolean isVertical, int meterMode,
        String fontName, int fontStyle, int fontSize,
        String caption, boolean topLeftCaption, boolean hasLabels,
        String labelsString, boolean labelsOnTopLeft,
        int value, int numberOfSections,
        Color panelColor, Color textColor, Blinker blinker)
```

METER BALLISTICS . . . .

Ballistics describes how a meter responds to input stimuli. All of the meters present-ed here are, by their basic nature, linear peak-responding devices in that they display the actual values applied to them on a sample by sample basis. As previously noted, all meters respond linearly to a range of values from 0 to 100, and that this is a unit-less measure that does not represent anything specific like voltage, power, or audio level. Any of these meters can be made to display any quantity desired; it is just a mat-ter of writing a conversion method that accepts input in the desired units and converts those units into the linear range of 0 to 100, which the meters know how to display.

A linear peak response may or may not be the meter response you desire. When trying to emulate an analog meter for example, it might be desirable to emulate the time constant of the electro-mechanical mechanism that drives the needle. Because mechanical devices are involved, real analog meters do not respond to instantaneous peaks. Instead the level they indicate is a mechanical integration of the input signal over time.

In addition, you may want to model a meter that responds in a non-linear way to input signals. For example, you may want to provide a meter with a logarithmic scale to indicate power or you may want your meter to read RMS (root means squared) volt-age levels instead of peak voltage levels.

Many audio applications use a type of meter called a VU meter (short for Volume Units) for indicating audio signal level. What exactly the ballistics are for a VU meter depends on who you talk to. The most consistent definition I have heard is that a VU meter indicates the average signal level over the last 200 to 300 milliseconds. This affect could be achieved by knowing the sampling rate of the samples passing through and saving the last 200 to 300 milliseconds worth (using a FIFO queue that drops older samples) for averaging. The average value would be calculated by summing all of the sample values in the FIFO queue and dividing by the number of samples summed. Once the average was calculated, the value would be compared to whatever a full-scale value might be and the percentage of full scale could be calculated. This quanti-ty could be displayed directly by any of the meters of this chapter.

This VU meter example summarizes the steps necessary to make a meter respond in an application-specific way. Any other desired response would be approached in a similar way.

PROBLEMS WITH LEVEL METERS IN DIGITAL AUDIO SYSTEMS . . . .

As you investigate section two of this book, you will notice a mysterious absence of meters in the processor devices presented. The reason for this is simple. Meters are only really useful for displaying audio levels in an audio application if they reflect what you are hearing instantaneously. Any noticeable delay between what you hear and what the meter indicates is unacceptable and misleading. The problem is therefore the latency between what you hear and what a meter displays and this latency is caused by the buffering used to store and process the audio data. Fewer, smaller buffers decrease latency (thereby making the meters more accurate) but don't allow for doing much audio processing in real time. Larger buffers make more real-time processing possible. So we have typical tradeoffs to make and I chose real-time capability over meter responsiveness and accuracy. Much closer coupling to the underlying sound hardware via Java native methods would allow level meters to be implemented but I didn't want to do that either. I wanted to provide the purest Java code I could that was still usable for audio applications. Of course, multiple processors could be used to perform simultaneous audio processing and metering but that is beyond the scope of what is presented.

In short, I used meters in places in the code where their responsiveness was not an issue. For example, the phrase sampler application of section three uses an *LEDMeter* to show sample acquisition progress and looping points. Additionally, the guitar tuner application also of section three uses an *AnalogMeter* to indicate how close a plucked guitar note is to a reference standard. In both of these cases, meters performed an important function that could not have been satisfied by other visual indicator devices.

MISCELLANEOUS INFORMATION . . . .

Package:

craigl.beans.meters

Source Files:

File Name	Description
AnalogMeter.java	A subclass of *Meter* that provides a mechanical analog meter simulation.
LEDMeter.java	A subclass of *Meter* that provides a bar graph type of display.
makefile	Makefile for building this package.
Meter.java	Base class from which all meters subclasses are derived and which provides properties and methods that derived meter classes use.
MeterDemo.java	Meter demonstration program which was used to produce Figure 5.1. It shows one *LEDMeter*, one *AnalogMeter,* and one *RoundLEDMeter* instance.
RoundLEDMeter.java	A subclass of *Meter* that provides a bar graph type of meter but uses round LEDs for the display elements.

6 Display Devices

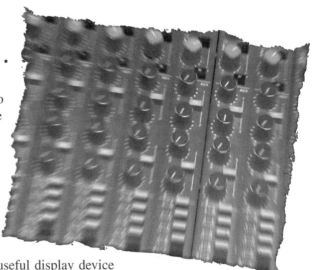

INTRODUCTION · · · · · · · · ·

In this chapter, I will discuss two numeric display devices that are useful in audio applications. The first device simulates the seven-segment LED displays found in many kinds of electronic equipment from digital clocks to frequency counters. The second display device, called the *ReadoutLabel*, while not as exotic as a seven-segment display, is a useful display device for alphanumeric data. Numerous examples of the use of these display devices can be found in other sections of this book.

SEVEN-SEGMENT DISPLAY DEVICES · · · · · · · · · · · · · ·

Three classes cooperate to provide the seven-segment display facility. These are the *SevenSegmentDisplay* class, the *LEDDisplayBase* class, and the *IntLEDDisplay* class. Each will be described below.

SevenSegmentDisplay Class

This class defines the geometry of seven-segment display digits. These digits are used in sets by the higher level display classes to provide multi-digit displays. To define the geometry it is first necessary to number the seven segments that make up a digit display element. The numbering used here is as shown in Figure 6.1.

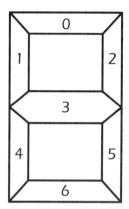

Figure 6.1   Seven-Segment Display Layout.

Once numbered, an array of integers can be produced defining which segments are on and which are off for each possible digit 0...9. The *onSegments* array shown below is indexed by the digits value.

```
private static final int [ ] onSegments = {
/* Bit/Seg Nums 654 3210 */
    /* Character 0 = 111 0111 */ 0x77,
    /* Character 1 = 010 0100 */ 0x24,
    /* Character 2 = 101 1101 */ 0x5d,
    /* Character 3 = 110 1101 */ 0x6d,
    /* Character 4 = 010 1110 */ 0x2e,
    /* Character 5 = 110 1011 */ 0x6b,
    /* Character 6 = 111 1011 */ 0x7b,
    /* Character 7 = 010 0101 */ 0x25,
    /* Character 8 = 111 1111 */ 0x7f,
    /* Character 9 = 010 1111 */ 0x2f
};
```

The next step is to define a polygon that circumscribes each segment of the display digit. If you examine the figure above you will see how each segment is a polygon. Segments 0, 1, 2, 4, 5, and 6 are defined by polygons with four sides while segment three has six sides. The dimensions of these polygons are determined by the required size of the digit. By dynamically calculating these polygons given a required size, seven-segment display digits of any size can be created.

The *SevenSegmentDisplay* class method

```
public static Polygon [] generateSegments(int width, int height)
```

builds an array of *Polygons*, one for each of the seven segments in the digit. The size of the polygon, as mentioned, is determined by the width and height parameters passed into this method.

The final method of interest in this class renders a digit onto a graphics context. The on segments (as determined from the onSegments array shown earlier) in the digit will be rendered with the *ledOnColor*, the off segments will be rendered with the *ledOffColor* (if the constant *DRAWOFFSEGMENTS* is true) and the digit background will be rendered in the *ledBGColor*. The signature of this method is:

```
public static void drawDigit(Graphics g, Polygon [] segments, int
digit, int width, int height,
    Color ledBGColor, Color ledOnColor, Color ledOffColor)
```

Note: If the constant *DRAWOFFSEGMENTS* is set to false, the off segments are not drawn at all.

The code for the *SevenSegmentDisplay* class can be found in the file *SevenSegmentDisplay.java*.

LEDDisplayBase Class

While the *SevenSegmentDisplay* class described above defines and controls the geometry of individual digits, the *LEDDisplayBase* class provides a *Canvas* on which to display the digits and numerous properties for configuring their appearance. This class doesn't provide a *paint* method for rendering the display digits; that will be provided by classes that extend this base class. In fact, the *paint* method is marked abstract in this class so derived classes must implement it.

The properties, and the getter and setter methods, that *LEDDisplayBase* provides to derived classes are shown in Table 6.1.

Table 6.1   Properties and Methods of the LEDDisplayBase Class

Property	Associated Methods
Raised (above or below panel)	setRaised(boolean), boolean getRaised()
Width	setWidth(int), int getWidth()
Height	setHeight(int), int getHeight()
Number of digits in display	setNumberOfDigits(int), int getNumberOfDigits()

Table 6.1   (continued)

Property	Associated Methods
Panel Color	setPanelColor(Color), Color getPanelColor()
LED digit segment color	setLEDColor(Color), Color getLEDColor()
LED digit background color	setLEDBGColor(Color), Color getLEDBGColor()
Text Color	setTextColor(Color), Color getTextColor()
Font (used for caption)	setFont(Font), Font getFont() setFontName(String), String getFontName() setFontStyle(int), int getFontStyle() setFontSize(int), int getFontSize()
Caption	setCaption(String), String getCaption()
Caption position	setCaptionAtBottom(boolean), boolean getCaptionAtBottom()

As these methods are called on derived classes, the corresponding properties are updated, and the appearance of the LED display will change accordingly the next time a repaint occurs.

Besides providing property support, the *LEDDisplayBase* class provides other interesting methods. The first, *renderDigits*, converts the segment *polygons* for the digits 0…9 into individual Java *Image* objects. The size of each digit, and therefore the size of each generated *Image*, is controlled by the width and height properties specified. The code which performs this transformation process is shown below:

```
public void renderDigits() {

    // Generate the polygons for the 7 segment display segments
    Polygon [] segments =
        SevenSegmentDisplay.generateSegments(digitWidth, digitHeight);

    // Generate an image for each digit
    for (int digit=0; digit < 10; digit++) {
        // Create an offscreen image for the digit
        Image digitImage = createImage(digitWidth, digitHeight);

        // Store the digit image into array of digits
        digitImages[digit] = digitImage;

        // Get graphic context for offscreen digit image
        Graphics dg = digitImage.getGraphics();
```

```
        // Render the digit into the offscreen image
        SevenSegmentDisplay.drawDigit(dg, segments, digit, digitWidth,
                   digitHeight, ledBGColor, ledOnColor, ledOffColor);
    }
}
```

LEDDisplayBase also provides a *getPreferredSize* method that returns the dimensions of the LED display (the array of individual digits) and its caption to any who inquire. As has been discussed in previous chapters, the *getPreferredSize* method is primarily called by AWT layout managers in order to size the area which will contain the display device.

```
public Dimension getPreferredSize() {
    // Calculate the preferred size based on the caption text
    FontMetrics fm = getFontMetrics(font);
    int charHeight = fm.getMaxAscent() + fm.getMaxDescent();
    int charWidth = fm.charWidth('0');

    int minHeight = YPAD + height + charHeight;
    int minWidth = (2 * XPAD) + width;
    int captionWidth = getCaption().length() * charWidth;
    minWidth = Math.max(minWidth, captionWidth);
    return new Dimension(minWidth, minHeight);
}
```

IntLEDDisplay Class

IntLEDDisplay, which extends *LEDDisplayBase*, is the first concrete class of LED displays that can be used in applications. These displays can contain any number of individual seven-segment display digits and are used for displaying signed integer values. Another extension of *LEDDisplayBase* is possible for displaying floating-point values (with a movable decimal point) but since that functionality was not required in this book it has not been implemented.

IntLEDDisplay implements the *AdjustmentListener* interface as the means for communicating with devices that generate *Adjustment* events. When an *Adjustment* event is received by an *IntLEDDisplay* object, the integer value is parsed from the event, the value is saved in the object, and a repaint is scheduled. The next paint uses the new value to select the digits for display. If the event contains a negative, a negative sign is painted to the left of the digits. The paint method is shown below:

```
public void paint(Graphics g) {

    int cwidth = getSize().width;
    int cheight = getSize().height;
```

```
// Paint the panel color
g.setColor(panelColor);
g.fillRect(0, 0, cwidth, cheight);

// Set font into the graphics context to get font metrics
g.setFont(font);
FontMetrics fm = g.getFontMetrics();

// Get various text attributes
int charHeight = fm.getHeight();
int charOffset = charHeight / 2;
int textWidth = fm.stringWidth(caption);

// Calculate position of first digit
int xOrg = (cwidth - calcDisplayWidth()) / 2;
int yOrg = captionAtBottom ? YPAD : YPAD + charHeight;

// Fill the background around segments
g.setColor(ledBGColor);
g.fillRect(xOrg, yOrg, width, height);

// Determine if digits have been generated
if (!digitsValid) {

    // Render the digits
    renderDigits();

    // Digit images are now valid for this size 7 segment display
    digitsValid = true;
}

// Draw minus sign if required
if (value < 0) {
    // Draw the minus sign
    int halfHeight = digitHeight / 2;
    int halfSignHeight = MINUSSIGNHEIGHT / 2;
    int x = xOrg;
    int y = yOrg + halfHeight - halfSignHeight;
    int width = separatorWidth - 1;
    int height = MINUSSIGNHEIGHT;

    g.setColor(ledOnColor);
    g.fillRect(x, y, width, height);
}
```

```
    // Display absolute value
    int displayValue = Math.abs(value);

    // Draw the digits. MSD to LSD
    int xDigitPos = xOrg + separatorWidth;
    for (int i = 0; i < numberOfDigits; i++) {
        int div = (int) Math.pow(10.0, (double)(numberOfDigits - i - 1));

        g.drawImage(digitImages[(displayValue / div) % 10], xDigitPos,
                                                    yOrg, this);

        xDigitPos += digitWidth + separatorWidth;
    }

    // Draw the caption
    g.setColor(textColor);
    int textXOffset = (cwidth - textWidth) / 2;
    int textYOffset = captionAtBottom ? YPAD + height + charHeight :
                                        YPAD + charOffset;
    g.drawString(caption, textXOffset, textYOffset);
}
```

The following code segment shows how a three-digit *IntLEDDisplay* is instantiated, configured, and has its value set to negative five.

```
// Create the seven segment display and configure it
IntLEDDisplay display1 = new IntLEDDisplay(130, 150, 3, 0);
display1.setPanelColor(PANELCOLOR);
display1.setLEDColor(LEDCOLOR);
display1.setLEDBGColor(LEDBGCOLOR);
display1.setTextColor(LEDCOLOR);
display1.setCaption("Seven Segment Display");

// Now set its value
display1.setValue(-5);
```

IntLEDDisplays can be used as Java beans (if packaged in jar file form) or as standalone UI software components. In this book, they are used as software components only.

ReadoutLabel DISPLAY DEVICE . . . .

The next display device to be described is called a *ReadoutLabel* device. This device was not designed as a Java bean like the seven-segment devices described previously but is included in this discussion to keep the display devices together in one spot in this book. The *ReadoutLabel* class is an extension of the AWT *Label* class that is used as a display in many of the audio devices in this book. These devices include the chorus, compressor/expander, delay, phaser, and pitch shifter processing devices of section two.

A *ReadoutLabel* is a normal *Label* with an etched border for aesthetic appeal and an optional unit label string. A *ReadoutLabel* display device can be seen on the right in Figure 6.2. Here, the label string is "count." In short, these devices are used for displaying labeled numeric data.

The *ReadoutLabel* class has four constructors. These are:

1. `public ReadoutLabel(Color color, String units, int extraCharCount)`

2. `public ReadoutLabel(Color color, String units)`

3. `public ReadoutLabel(String units)`

4. `public ReadoutLabel()`

The first constructor allows the setting of the *ReadoutLabel*'s color, its unit labeling string and an extra character count. If a non-zero extra character count is specified, it causes the display device to be laid out wider (by a layout manager) when used in an application's UI. This is sometimes necessary to make the *ReadoutLabel* wide enough to display floating-point data with many digits of precision.

The second constructor sets the extra character count to zero while allowing the color and the unit string to be specified.

In the third constructor, the default color of blue is used for the device and only the unit string need be specified. Even this string can be null or empty.

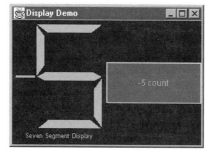

Figure 6.2   Display Devices Demo Program. *Note:* The seven-segment display shown here does not render off segments. See text for details.

The forth and final constructor has no parameters. It creates a *ReadoutLabel* with the default blue color, no label string and no extra character padding.

Two methods exist in the *ReadoutLabel* class for setting the value of the numeric data. The first has a signature of:

```
public void setValue(int value)
```

This method is called when the *ReadoutLabel* device is to be used for displaying integer data. When this method is called, the units string (if used) is appended to the integer data and the result is displayed centered in the *ReadoutLabel* area. The foreground color used to display the data will default to blue if a different color was not specified. The background color will be gray.

The other method

```
public void setValue(double value, int places)
```

is used for displaying floating-point data to a specified number of places. Here, the double value will be converted to a string, truncated to the specified number of places, and then the units string will be appended if available.

To use the *ReadoutLabel* in your programs, simply instantiate the display and then set its value whenever necessary. The code would be similar to the following.

```
ReadoutLabel display1 = new ReadoutLabel(Color.green, "count", 5);
display1.setValue(-5);
```

MISCELLANEOUS INFORMATION . . . .

Package:

craigl.beans.displays

Source Files:

File Name	Description
DisplayDemo.java	Display demonstration program used to generate Figure 6.1. It contains one *IntLEDDisplay* device and one *ReadoutLabel* device. Both of the displays cycle through the values –9 to 9 continuously in this application.
IntLEDDisplay.java	Seven-segment display used for displaying integer values. This display device is a Java bean.
IntLEDDisplayBeanInfo.java	BeanInfo class for associating seven-segment display icons with the *IntLEDDisplay* class.
LEDDisplayBase.java	Base class from which all seven-segment displays are derived.
LEDDisplayIcon16.gif	16 × 16 pixel icon associated with this class.
LEDDisplayIcon32.gif	32 × 32 pixel icon associated with this class.
makefile	Makefile for building this package.
ReadoutLabel.java	Augmented AWT label for displaying numeric data with optional unit label string. *Note:* This code is not structured as a Java bean.
SevenSegmentDisplay.java	Code for constructing seven-segment digits on demand. This code defines which segments are off and on for each digit 0…9 and allows the digits to be rendered as Java *Images*.

7 Simulated Equipment Front Panels

INTRODUCTION . . . .

One of the most fun parts of building software audio processing devices is in building the device's UI component. In this book I refer to the UI component as a simulated front panel because that is in essence what the UI component is—a software simulation of the front panel of a hardware device. A real hardware device like a delay unit, for example, would have potentiometers, LEDs, LED displays, buttons, and switches and possibly a meter or two. The user of the delay unit manipulates the controls on the device to achieve the effect being sought. On our simulated front panels, all of the controls the user manipulates and the displays the user sees are simulated. The only interaction a user can have with the simulated front panels and the controls and indicators they contain are via the mouse and the keyboard. Still, it is very pleasing to be able to manipulate the simulated controls and see simulated indicators being updated and hear the effect on the sound being processed in real time. This draw is what made me write this book in the first place. I started out to find out what it would take to build a simple round potentiometer in software and that quest ended in this book being written. The moral here is be careful what you experiment with because what you choose can cause you a lot of work in the long run.

In the hardware world, the circuitry to perform a processing function is generally designed (and tested) before the packaging is decided upon. The controls and indicators required on the front panel for a new device are dictated by the design. With the number and type of controls and indicators known, the designer then sets about laying out the components on a physical panel. The look, feel, and usability of the new device are established during this highly iterative process. Especially important is the logical grouping of the controls to make the operation of the device as obvious as possible to the user. Once the physical layout is decided upon, the panels to hold the controls and indicators must be machined, painted, and silk-screened with the desired labeling. Finally, the controls and indicators are mounted on the front panel and connected to the circuitry that makes up the complete device. All in all, the design of a new piece of audio equipment is a time-consuming and expensive process. Mistakes and/or redesigns of the look and feel of a piece of gear are very expensive.

The process of designing simulated front panels for audio processing devices is very similar to what a hardware designer goes through when designing front panels for actual devices. First, you must know how the sound processing algorithms you are attempting to implement in your device (equivalent to the circuitry in a hardware device) work and from that you determine the number and type of controls and indicators needed by the user to interact with the equipment. You then go through an iterative design process, deciding how to position and group the controls and indicators to your best advantage. Fortunately, since we are dealing with a simulated front panel, you can try out various designs easily without any cost other than your time. Once you decide on the look of your simulated equipment, you must connect up (via software) the controls and indicators to the underlying algorithms to produce a working device.

With the controls and indicators presented in the previous chapters along with any AWT or Swing UI components you care to throw in, a vast number and variety of simulated equipment front panels can be created. The complexity of the simulated front panels is a measure of the function they need to perform, how much user configuration and interaction is required, and how elaborate you want to be. As always, there is a fine line between too little and too much. I believe the KISS (Keep It Simple, Stupid) principle applies here as it does in many other places.

A relatively complete spectrum of simulated front panels can be seen in the processor devices presented in the next section of this book. From the very simple, like the *FileReader* device shown in Figure 7.1, which contains a single button, one LED and a couple of labels; to the moderately elaborate *StereoOscillator* device in shown in Figure 7.2, which contains AWT radio buttons, grouping boxes, *ReadoutLabel* indicators, round potentiometers, and slide pots; to the spectrum analyzer of Figure 7.3 which looks deceptively simple, but isn't because of the graphical display which is required. In addition to the graphical display, this device uses five AWT *Buttons* and five dynamic labels.

Figure 7.1   The FileReader Device's Simulated Front Panel User Interface

Figure 7.2   The StereoOscillator Device's Simulated Front Panel User Interface

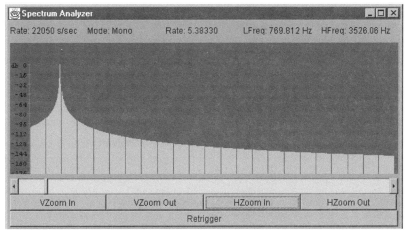

Figure 7.3   The SpectrumAnalyzer Device's Simulated Front Panel

And finally, the Compressor/Expander device shown in Figure 7.4 contains an interactive graphical surface, numerous *ReadoutLabels*, slide pots, a *SquareButton*, and two *RoundLEDs*.

Of course, processor devices with more elaborate simulated front panels than these can be developed if the need is dictated by the application. Further, by using some of the new Java 2D and 3D APIs, it would be possible to make the front panels even more realistic and three-dimensional looking than is shown here.

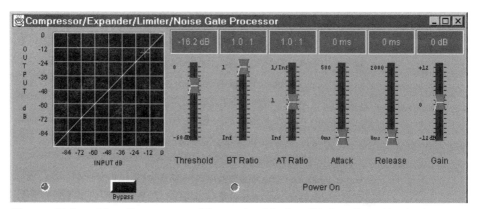

Figure 7.4   The Compressor/Expander/Limiter/Noise Gate Device's
Simulated Front Panel

In the remainder of this chapter, we discuss basic techniques for connecting components and algorithms together; then we discuss techniques used for laying out simulated front panels. Within this discussion, some of the base classes, which may make your layout tasks easier, are covered. Finally, there is a short discussion of look-and-feel consistency issues and how they can be addressed. Once you understand the information presented here, you should be ready to lay out your own simulated equipment front panels.

COMPONENT CONNECTIONS . . . .

There are really two parts to the component connection schema—connecting components together with other components and connecting components to algorithms such that manipulation of the component modifies the operation of the algorithm. Both connections are accomplished using the Java 1.1 event/event listener model. All of the controls presented in previous chapters are sources of Java events. Most indicators presented previously are event listeners. This makes their connection almost trivial.

Table 7.1 summarizes which components produce and which components listen for (consume) events. Any component that listens for a specific type of event can be directly connected to a component that sources the specific event by registering with the event source. Event sources provide methods for doing just that. *addActionListener* registers *ActionListeners* (code which implements the *ActionListener* interface) for interest in *ActionEvents* and *addAdjustmentListener* registers interest in *AdjustmentEvents*.

Table 7.1   Component Event/Listener Summary

Package	Class	Event Source	Event Listener
craigl.beans.blinker	*Blinker*	*PropertyChangeEvent*	
craigl.beans.buttons	*RoundButton*	*ActionEvent*	
	SquareButton	*ActionEvent*	
	ToggleSwitchButton	*ActionEvent*	
craigl.beans.datagen	*DataGen*	*AdjustmentEvent*	
craigl.beans.displays	*IntLEDDisplay*		*AdjustmentListener*
craigl.beans.leds	*RoundLED*		*PropertyChangeListener* and *ActionListener*
	SquareLED		*PropertyChangeListener* and *ActionListener*
	LabeledLED		*PropertyChangeListener* and *ActionListener*
craigl.beans.meters	*AnalogMeter*		*AdjustmentListener*
	LEDMeter		*AdjustmentListener*
	RoundLEDMeter		*AdjustmentListener*
craigl.beans.pots	*Pot*	*AdjustmentEvent*	
	SlidePot	*AdjustmentEvent*	
	Pseudo audio taper pots*	*AdjustmentEvent*	
	BoostCutSlidePot*	*AdjustmentEvent*	
	IntValuedPot*	*AdjustmentEvent*	
	IntValuedSlidePot*	*AdjustmentEvent*	
	RealValuedPot*	*AdjustmentEvent*	
	RealValuedSlidePot*	*AdjustmentEvent*	

*Note: Even though these pots do generate *AdjustmentEvents*, the value contained within the event is the linear integer value from 0 to 100 signifying the current position of the pot. To get the actual value from the pot, direct access methods must be called on the pot instance when the event listener receives the event. These methods are shown in Table 7.2.

Table 7.2   Component Direct Access Method Summary

Package	Class	Getter Method	Setter Method
craigl.beans.buttons	*RoundButton*	boolean getState()	setState(boolean)
	SquareButton	boolean getState()	setState(boolean)
	ToggleSwitchButton	boolean getState()	setState(boolean)
craigl.beans.displays	*IntLEDDisplay*	int getValue()	setValue(int)
craigl.beans.leds	*RoundLED*	boolean getLEDState()	setLEDState(boolean)
	SquareLED	boolean getLEDState()	setLEDState(boolean)
	LabeledLED	N/A	setValue(int)
			setValue(double, int)
craigl.beans.meters	*AnalogMeter*	int getValue()	setValue(int)
	LEDMeter	int getValue()	setValue(int)
	RoundLEDMeter	int getValue()	setValue(int)
craigl.beans.pots	*Pot*	int getValue()	setValue(int)
	SlidePot	int getValue()	setValue(int)
	Pseudo audio taper pots	double getAttenuation()	N/A
	BoostCutSlidePot	double getGain()	N/A
	IntValuedPot	int getIntValue()	setIntValue(int)
	IntValuedSlidePot	int getIntValue()	setIntValue(int)
	RealValuedPot	double getRealValue()	setRealValue(double)
	RealValuedSlidePot	double getRealValue()	setRealValue(double)

Of course, any application can interact with controls and indicators by calling the direct access methods directly and not paying attention to the events that each component generates and/or consumes. The problem with this approach is that the pots, for example, would have to be continually polled to see if their value had changed. Using the Java AWT 1.1 event model, the code is told immediately when the value is changed and what the new value is. This makes an application event-driven and therefore more efficient in the use of CPU resources.

In summary, component-to-component connection is accomplished by adding interested listeners to event sources. Then each time a new event is generated, the listeners will be informed and updated immediately. Numerous examples of this connection mechanism have been presented in previous chapters but some examples need to be shown here as well.

In this first code segment, a *Blinker* and a *RoundLED* are created and connected together. This connection enables the LED to change states when it is later instructed to do so.

```
// Start a blinker for the LEDs with a period of 250 milliseconds
Blinker blink = new Blinker(250);

RoundLED firstLED  = RoundLED();
blink.addPropertyChangeListener(firstLED);
```

In this next code segment, a data generator and *AnalogMeter* are connected together. This will cause the meter to display random data values and is useful for testing new meter devices.

```
// Instantiate a DataGen data source for test with a period of
                                            200 milliseconds
DataGen dg1 = new DataGen(200);

// Instantiate an AnalogMeter to receive the events from DataGen
AnalogMeter leftAnalogMeter = new AnalogMeter();

// Make the meter a listener to the events produced by DataGen
dg1.addAdjustmentListener(leftAnalogMeter);
```

Next, a button is connected to an LED so that whenever the button changes state, the LED follows.

```
// Create the LED to monitor the button
RoundLED led = new RoundLED();

// Add the LED to this panel
p.add(led);

// Connect this LED to the blinker for running its state machine
blinker.addPropertyChangeListener(led);

// Create round button
RoundButton b = new RoundButton();

// Add it to this panel
p.add(b);

// Connect the LED to the button to control its state
b.addActionListener(led);
```

Here, a round potentiometer is connected to a seven-segment type LED display. Then, whenever a user manipulates the pot, the value displayed is automatically updated.

```
// Instantiate a seven segment LED display with 3 digits
IntLEDDisplay display1 = new IntLEDDisplay(90, 40, 3, 0);

// Add the display to the panel
p.add(display1);

// Create a round potentiometer
Pot pot1 = new Pot();

// Add the pot to the panel
p.add(pot1);

// Connect the output of the pot to the seven-segment display
pot1.addAdjustmentListener(display1);
```

The other half of the connection story is connecting control components to algorithms so that manipulation of the control causes changes in the algorithm and hence to the audio being processed. This is hard to illustrate here because neither the audio processing architecture nor any processing algorithms have yet been presented (see the next section). In general, however, it can be said that algorithms are affected by changes in control settings by causing buffer sizes to change, by changing buffer pointer relationships, or by changing various weighting factors applied to samples as they pass through a processor device. Examples of each of these types of coupling will be illustrated in the next section of this book.

BASE CLASS FUNCTIONALITY . . . .

Because many of the processor effects presented in the next section have common UI requirements, it would make sense that they derive their common functionality from the same base class. This class is called *BaseUI* and is contained in the package *craigl.uiutils*. Further, *BaseUI* class extends *CloseableFrame* (also in the same package) which gives all derived classes the closeable window they need to run in. *BaseUI* also provides storage for *AbstractAudio* devices that will be described in the next section. *AbstractAudio* devices know how to connect themselves together for sharing audio samples and provide the framework for processing audio samples.

Many of the user interface classes for the processor devices in the next section are declared as follows:

```
public class SomeProcessorClassUI extends (BaseUI or CloseableFrame)
implements CloseableFrameIF
```

A user interface class would extend *CloseableFrame* and implement *CloseableFrameIF* if it only required a closeable window in which to run but no other derived functionality. Within the constructor of the UI, a call would need to be made to *registerCloseListener*(this) to register the fact that this UI is interested in window-closing events. The UI code would provide a method called *windowClosing*() to satisfy the *CloseableFrameIF*. It is the *windowClosing* method that gets called as the window is closing down. Within the *windowClosing* method, an application can do whatever is necessary to gently shut itself down. In most audio processor cases, this means putting the device in bypass mode so that its affect on samples passing through the device is minimized.

A user interface class would extend *BaseUI* and implement *CloseableFrameIF* if it wanted to run in a closeable window and wanted to take advantage of some of the functionality *BaseUI* provides. The methods listed in Table 7.3 are provided by *BaseUI* to assist with building simulated equipment front panels.

Table 7.3   Methods Provided by the Base UI Class

Method Name	Description
addDefaultComponent (…)	A layout helper function for use with panels using a *GridBagLayout* layout manager.
Pot createPot (…)	Creates and configures a *Pot* with a uniform look.
IntValuedPot createPot (…)	Creates and configures an *IntValuedPot* with a uniform look.
RealValuedPot createPot (…)	Creates and configures a *RealValuedPot* with a uniform look.
configPot (…)	Configure a *Pot* with a uniform look.
createLED (…)	Creates and configures a *RoundLED*.

LAYOUT TECHNIQUES . . . .

Laying out simulated equipment front panels is little different from laying out UIs in other Java applications in that layout managers are used to position the required control and indicator components. Which layout manager to use is driven in a large part by the number and grouping of the components required. Simple UIs like that shown in Figure 7.5 use a *GridLayout* layout manager to place the two *RoundLEDMeter* components onto the panel. A *GridLayout* can be used because of the uniformity of the layout.

Other simulated equipment front panel UIs will require more complicated layout managers to achieve the correct look. The *StereoOscillator* device shown previously makes extensive use of the *GridBagLayout* layout manager to place the controls

Figure 7.5   Simple UI using a *GridLayout* layout manager.

and indicators precisely where they are required. The *addDefaultComponent* method provided by *BaseUI* class helps make this an easier process. The signature for this method is:

```
/**
 * GridBagLayout Helper Function
 * This method is called when adding a component to a UI using a
 * GridBagLayout.
 * @param Panel p is the panel onto which the component is added
 * @param Component c is the component being added
 * @param GridBagLayout gbl is the instance of the layout manager
 * @param GridBagConstraints gbc is the constraint associated with
 * adding this component
 * @param int x is the x position within the panel to add the component
 * @param int y is the y position within the panel to add the component
 * @param int w is the width the added component should take up in the layout
 * @param int h is the height the added component should take up in
 * the layout.
 */
```

```
public static void addDefaultComponent(
          Panel p,
          Component c,
          GridBagLayout gbl, GridBagConstraints gbc,
          int x, int y, int w, int h)
```

To use *addDefaultComponent*, you draw a grid and use that to place the controls and indicators using relative sizes. In the case of the stereo oscillator, the grid on which the UI was designed was 18 sections wide and 10 sections tall. Table 7.4 shows the grid coordinates used for each of the components on the front panel. The coordinates used have their origin at the upper left corner of the grid and the X and Y dimensions increase to the right and down, respectively.

Table 7.4   Grid Layout for Stereo Oscillator UI

Component	X position	Y position	Width	Height
Sample rate component group	0	0	5	5
Left range component group	5	0	5	5
Left Channel label	11	0	3	1
Left ReadoutLabel	11	1	3	1
Left frequency pot	11	2	3	3
Left amplitude pot	15	0	3	5
Oscillator type component group	0	5	5	5
Right range component group	5	5	5	5
Right Channel label	11	5	3	1
Right ReadoutLabel	11	6	3	1
Right frequency pot	11	7	3	3
Right amplitude pot	15	5	3	5

To put the component location information in Table 7.4 to use in creating a UI, code similar to the following is used:

```
// Create the panel the UI is to be built on
Panel mp = new Panel();

// Create the gridbag objects
GridBagLayout gbl = new GridBagLayout();
GridBagConstraints gbc = new GridBagConstraints();
```

```
// Make insets so components don't actually touch
gbc.insets = new Insets(3,3,3,3);

// Set the panel's layout manager to the GridBagLayout instance created above
mp.setLayout(gbl);

// Create the sample rate group control panel
sampleRateGroup = createSampleRateGroup();

// Place it onto the grid
addDefaultComponent(mp, sampleRateGroup, gbl, gbc, 0, 0, 5, 5);
```

Create the other components used in the UI and add them using *addDefaultComponent* with the appropriate location and size coordinates as specified in the table above.

Using this technique, complex user interfaces can be created without having to understand the vagaries of the *GridBagLayout* to any degree.

UI CONSISTENCY ISSUES . . . .

When building numerous audio processing devices that will be used together, it is helpful from a user's perspective to have a common look and feel among them. Users then feel these devices were designed to be used together and have some idea how new devices work from their experience with other devices that have the same look. Of course, I didn't follow this advice in the devices presented in this book because I wanted to give you an idea of what was possible in terms of look and feel. A consistent color scheme, for example, would not have exposed you to the various possibilities from which you could develop your own style.

One way to accomplish this uniformity would be to develop a class or an interface that contains the definition of the properties that should be uniform between devices. Then the individual simulated equipment front panel UIs could access the static definitions or implement the interface and apply the properties accordingly. A class approach similar to the following might be used:

```
public class AudioLookAndFeelConstants {
// Prevent class from being instantiated
private AudioLookAndFeelConstants () {}

// Define colors to be used
public static final Color DEFAULTPANELCOLOR =
    new Color(...);
```

```
public static final Color DEFAULTTEXTCOLOR =
    Color.black;

public static final Color DEFAULTKNOBCOLOR =
    new Color(...);

public static final Color DEFAULTPOTTICCOLOR =
    new Color(...);

public static final Color DEFAULTPOTGRADCOLOR =
    new Color(...);

public static final Color DEFAULTREADOUTLABELCOLOR =
    Color.blue;

public static final Color DEFAULTLEDDIPSLAYCOLOR =
    new Color(...);

// Define the fonts and font specifications to be used
public static final String DEFAULTFONTNAME = "SansSerif";
public static final int DEFAULTFONTSTYLE = Font.PLAIN;
public static final int DEFAULTFONTSIZE = 10;
public static final Font DEFAULTCAPTIONFONT = new Font(DEFAULTFONTNAME ,
                                                       DEFAULTFONTSTYLE ,
                                                       DEFAULTFONTSIZE );

// Define the knob sizes to be used
public static final int DEFAULTLARGEKNOBSIZE = 22;
public static final int DEFAULTMEDIUMKNOBSIZE = 16;
public static final int DEFAULTSMALLKNOBSIZE = 12;

// Misc. items
public static final int DEFAULTLEDRADIUS = 7;
}
```

Then individual applications can import this class definition and use the default values when creating the UI components. A *Pot* instance can be configured from these defaults with code similar to the following:

```
// Instantiate a new Pot for use in the UI
Pot pot1 = new Pot();

// Configure the Pot with the default attributes
pot1.setPanelColor(AudioLookAndFeelConstants.DEFAULTPANELCOLOR);
```

```
pot1.setKnobColor(AudioLookAndFeelConstants.DEFAULTKNOBCOLOR);
pot1.setTicColor(AudioLookAndFeelConstants.DEFAULTPOTTICCOLOR);
pot1.setGradColor(AudioLookAndFeelConstants.DEFAULTPOTGRADCOLOR);
pot1.setTextColor(AudioLookAndFeelConstants.DEFAULTTEXTCOLOR);
pot1.setRadius(AudioLookAndFeelConstants.DEFAULTLEDRADIUS);
```

OTHER SIMULATED EQUIPMENT FRONT PANELS . . . . .

The *frontpanel* package provides four examples of simulated equipment front panels for your study and possible use. Section two of this book offers many more examples of simulated front panels. If you see something that is close to what you need for your application, copy the UI code for the processor device and modify it to fit your needs.

MISCELLANEOUS INFORMATION . . . .

Package:

frontpanels

Source Files:

File Name	Description
CompressorFrontPanel.java	A simulated equipment front panel for an audio compressor device.
DemoFrontPanel.java	A simulated equipment front panel with various controls and indicators.
EQFrontPanel.java	A simulated equipment front panel for a three frequency parametric equalizer.
makefile	Makefile for building this package.
StereoVUMetersFrontPanel.java	A simulated equipment front panel for a stereo VU meter built from two *RoundLEDMeter* objects.

Part 2

Audio Architecture, Processing, and Monitoring

INTRODUCTION

There certainly is a lot to cover in this section of the book. In fact, the information presented here forms the bulk of the book. Once you understand what is here, you will be very far along in your quest for understanding of the basic concepts of audio signal processing and in the implementation of those concepts. Some of the material presented is complex in nature but I have tried to make it approachable for most readers. If you need more information than is provided for any topic, you can consult the bibliography for some additional reading material.

Chapter 8 begins with a discussion of sound and goes on to discuss digital audio basics. The presentation is aimed at people without a substantial background in digital audio and as such can be skipped by readers with adequate background. The approach is as qualitative as possible while still providing useful information.

Chapter 9 continues by describing in detail the audio processing architecture that is used as the basis for all processing done in this book. Understanding this architecture is key to understanding the remainder of the information. In addition, the *AudioTest* program, which is used for linking together various processing elements for experimental purposes, is described.

Chapter 10 covers the concept of IIR digital filters. In this chapter, Java classes are provided for designing and implementing low-pass, high-pass, and band-pass digital filters. These filters show up in some of the audio processing devices detailed in Chapter 13.

All of the audio sources provided in this book are described in Chapter 11. Here you will see how to construct mono and stereo oscillators for sine, triangle, and square waves along with a random noise source. These sources find use for testing other processor devices. Described here as well are devices for reading both AU and WAV audio files and providing the contained samples for subsequent processing. Finally, a device is presented for interfacing to the PC's wave device for acquiring samples for processing from a microphone or line input.

Chapter 12 describes two (virtual) test tools (called audio monitor devices) that can be used to analyze audio samples and test audio processing devices. The first is a sample scope or oscilloscope which is used to visually display the samples passing through it. From the display of the samples one can deduce such attributes as amplitude, wave shape, distortion in some cases, and possibly frequency. The other virtual test instrument provided in this chapter is a spectrum analyzer which is used to measure the frequency content of a group of samples.

In Chapter 13, all of the audio processing devices provided in this book are described. In total, twelve different processing devices are presented. Here the theory and the implementation of that theory are provided.

Finally, Chapter 14 describes all of the audio devices that consume audio samples (sink devices). Devices are included for playback of audio samples using the Java Media Framework (JMF) and for direct interfacing with the PC's wave-out hardware. Also, devices for writing audio samples to AU and WAV sound files are provided.

Note: Appendix B contains other source and sink devices based on an early access version of Java Media Framework (JMF) 2.0. These devices complement and in some cases extend the devices presented in this section of the book.

8 Sound and Audio Basics

INTRODUCTION . . . .

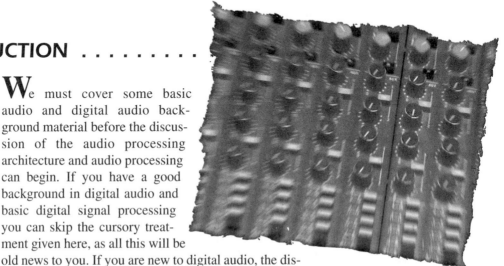

We must cover some basic audio and digital audio background material before the discussion of the audio processing architecture and audio processing can begin. If you have a good background in digital audio and basic digital signal processing you can skip the cursory treatment given here, as all this will be old news to you. If you are new to digital audio, the discussion will cover important topics that you must be made aware of for the remainder of this book to make complete sense. As in other parts of this book, I will try to keep the discussion of theory to a minimum but there is only so much I can shield you from and still provide you with the information you need. Although the discussions to follow are highly simplistic, they do provide all of the background information you will require. The chapter begins with a quick discussion of sound and then moves on to various digital audio topics.

SOUND . . . .

Sound is all around us all of the time. If you listen hard enough, even the quietest moments are filled with sound. The perception of sound is one of the five human senses and we do it quite well. In the simplest sense, sound is vibrations of the air that our eardrums perceive, convert to nerve impulses and send to the brain. It is our brains that interpret the nerve energy and allow us to hear.

Sound is produced by a great many physical processes in nature and can also be produced synthetically. To produce sound, energy is required. Energy is what causes the vibrations of the air that we perceive as sound. There can be no sound where there is no medium (air, water, etc.) to propagate the sound. There is no sound in the void of outer space. Sound moves differently through mediums of different density. The speed of sound, for example, is measured in air at sea level at a reference temperature. A measurement of the speed of sound under water results in a vastly different value.

Natural and/or artificial sounds can be simple or complex. The simplest of sounds tend to be periodic, whereas more complex sounds may have non-periodic tendencies. The simplest of all sounds is the sine wave. A sine wave is a repetitive displacement of air that represents a single frequency. A simple sine wave waveform is shown in Figure 8.1.

Here, the amplitude of the displacement is plotted against time with the middle red line indicating a value of zero. With respect to the zero value, the amplitude of a sine wave has both negative and positive values over time. The total amplitude of the sine wave is the range of values from the negative-most peak to the positive-most peak of the waveform. This is referred to as the peak-to-peak amplitude. The *frequency* of a sine wave expresses how often the sine wave repeats in value. The inverse of the frequency is called the *period*. This is the time between value repeats. The period of a sine wave can be measured from any two points on the waveform, which have the same value and the same slope. The crests of the waveform are typically used but so can the zero crossing of the waveform. The period of a sine wave is sometimes referred to as its wavelength as well but typically only when high frequency electromagnetic spectra are being discussed.

The frequency of a sine wave is typically measured in cycles per second (CPS). The modern unit of frequency measurement is the Hz, which is equivalent to cycles per second. Hz is now used in honor of Heinrich Hertz (1857–1894) for his contribu-

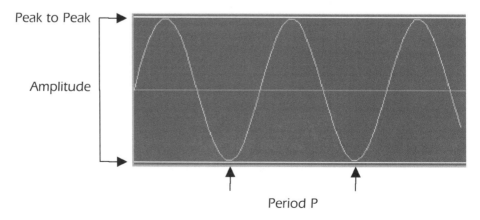

Figure 8.1   A simple sine wave

tion to the understanding of wavelengths and frequency. The definition of frequency relies on the fact that sounds are periodic. Although many of the techniques used for manipulation of sound rely on this fact, very few sounds in nature are truly periodic.

Humans can directly perceive sounds from about 30 Hz up to approximately 20,000 or 20K Hz where K indicates a multiple of 1000 (this is a different K than the K used in the computer industry, which equals 1024, reflecting the computer's binary heritage). Of course, one's ability to perceive sound is influenced by many factors, age and previous exposure being two of the most important. As we grow older, we tend to loose the higher ranges of our hearing. Older adults may not be able to hear frequencies above 12KHz for example unless they are amplified greatly. Exposure to loud sounds for extended lengths of time can also affect our ability to hear. People who listened to extremely loud music in their youth (me being one of them) or who worked near jet airplanes or worked in loud factories before there were safety laws dealing with ear protection have probably suffered some loss of hearing sensitivity. That is, they cannot hear soft sounds without the aid of a hearing device like a hearing aid.

The ear responds to sounds over a very wide range of amplitudes. The ratio of the softest to the loudest sounds we can comprehend represents the ear's dynamic range. If measured in decibels (to be discussed shortly) the dynamic range of the human ear is approximately 180 dB. This is a ratio of amplitude values of about a trillion to one. In other words, the quietest sound we can hear (something like a butterfly's wing flapping) to the loudest (a jet engine up close) represents a vast difference in sound amplitude. Further, the response of the ear is not linear in how we perceive loudness. A sound with twice the amplitude does not necessarily sound twice as loud. In fact the ear has a more logarithmic than linear response.

It turns out that the ear responds to ratios of sound amplitudes instead of arithmetic differences. If a sound's amplitude is increased from 1 to 2, for example, a certain loudness is perceived. To create the equivalent loudness change, again the amplitude must be increased to four times the original (not three times). The notion of logarithmic sound amplitude ratios being necessary to produce linear loudness increases gave rise to the use of the decibel for measurement purposes. A decibel is defined as:

$$1 \text{ decibel} = 20 * \log_{10}(\text{amplitude ratio})$$

when (voltage) amplitude ratios are being compared and

$$1 \text{ decibel} = 10 * \log_{10}(\text{power ratio})$$

when power ratios (in watts) are being compared. This difference is because power varies with the square of the amplitude. The decibel is in reality 1/10 of a *bel*, which was a unit named after Alexander Graham Bell (1847–1922), whose work with the telephone generated the need for such measurements.

If a voltage ratio of 1.00 is chosen as a zero dB reference point, voltage ratios corresponding to various decibel values are as shown in Table 8.1.

Table 8.1   Decibel/Voltage Ratio Correspondense
(Voltage ratio of 1.00 chosen as a zero dB reference point)

Decibels	Voltage Ratio
0	1.0
1	1.122
2	1.259
3	1.412
4	1.584
5	1.778
6	1.995
7	2.238
8	2.512
9	2.818
10	3.162
15	5.623
20	10
40	100
60	1,000
80	10,000
100	100,000
−1	0.891
−2	0.794
−3	0.708
−4	0.631
−5	0.562
−6	0.501
−7	0.447
−8	0.398
−9	0.355
−10	0.316
−20	0.1
−40	0.01
−60	0.001
−80	0.0001

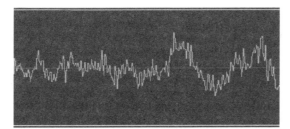

Figure 8.2 Complex Waveform

It is common to hear people speaking of a doubling of amplitude as a 6 dB change in level.

A tuning fork, a flute or pipe organ pipes come closest to producing a pure sine wave sound. Most sounds in nature however are more complex than a sine wave. The waveform shown in Figure 8.2 is an example.

It was Jean-Baptiste Fourier (1768–1830) who first proposed that all sounds could be represented by the summation of a series of simpler sine (and cosine) waves. This gives rise to the concept of a frequency spectrum that describes the set of sine waves that makes up a given sound. A sound has a fundamental frequency which is the frequency of the sine wave with the greatest amplitude of all those that make up the sound. Overtones or harmonics are frequencies that are near multiples of the fundamental frequency. The harmonic content of a sound determines its complexity. The Fourier transform is a mathematical device used to extract the frequency content of a complex sound. FFT or Fast Fourier Transforms are used in various places in this book, including the spectrum analyzer described in this section of the book and the guitar tuner described in section three.

ANALOG WAVEFORMS AND INPUT/OUTPUT DEVICES . . .

As mentioned, sounds exist in nature and it is our ears that allow us to hear them. To electronically process natural sounds, it is first necessary to convert them into electrical impulses that electronic circuitry can act upon. A microphone or other transducer is used to convert a sound's periodic vibrations, which are manifested as changes in sound pressure level, into electrical energy. The minute vibration of a microphone's diaphragm in response to sound creates very small electrical impulses that represent the sound. A good microphone will convert the sound it "hears" to electrical energy with very little coloring of its own. In other words, the electrical signal produced will be a very accurate representation of the sound the microphone was exposed to. The waveform produced by a microphone is considered an analog waveform because it has a unique value for every point in time, unlike a digital waveform, which has only discrete values available at discrete times.

A voltage that varies over time represents the electrical signal from a microphone. Within limits, the louder the sound, the higher the voltage produced by the microphone. Higher frequency sounds cause the voltages to change rapidly whereas lower frequency sounds cause fewer changes to occur.

An audio speaker like that found in a stereo system, in a set of headphones, or in a radio or guitar amplifier performs the opposite function of a microphone. A speaker takes electrical energy representing sound and produces electro-mechanical vibrations of the air that we subsequently hear as sound. This conversion is performed by creating a magnetic field from the electrical energy (within what is called the voice coil) and using it to move a paper or plastic cone in relation to a permanent magnet structure within the speaker. As the level and polarity of the electrical energy changes, the cone is either pushed away from or pulled closer to the speaker's magnet. This movement is converted into sound waves. The more power the electrical signal has, the louder the speaker's sound output will be because the cone will be more violently displaced. Conversion of electrical energy to sound by a speaker is not a 100% efficient process, as both sound and heat in the voice coil are produced. In fact, if too much energy is applied to a speaker, the voice coil can burn out because of excessive heat. Once this happens, the speaker must be replaced or rebuilt with a new voice coil.

A speaker is also considered an analog device because its output is continuously variable over time.

As an aside, even though the operation of a speaker and a microphone are converse in nature, they are more similar than they are different. In fact, it is possible to use some speakers as microphones. For example, if you plug a set of headphones into the microphone input of your stereo system and speak into the headphones you will probably hear your voice in the speakers. In this case, the speakers in the headphones are modulated by your voice and produce a small output voltage that is amplified by your stereo system and sent to the actual speakers for output. Although the same theory applies to microphones as speakers, using a microphone as an output device will, more often than not, damage the microphone and is therefore *not recommended*.

HEADROOM, CLIPPING, AND DISTORTION . . . .

Within audio equipment, there exists a certain maximum level that a signal can obtain without distortion. This level is usually a function of the audio processing circuitry and varies from device to device. Amateur audio gear is designed to operate at a nominal level of –10 dbV whereas professional audio equipment is designed for +4 dbM level. The difference between the average signal applied to a device and the maximum possible level the device can handle is referred to as *headroom*. Generally, the greater the headroom, the better because it allows high-level transient signals to pass through the circuitry without clipping and, therefore, distortion.

Once the signal level exceeds the maximum level, clipping of the signal results. Clipping manifests itself as distortion of the audio signal. Minor clipping can sometimes be tolerated when processing audio; however, severe clipping and the subsequent distortion it causes is probably never desired. Certain guitar-effect devices which are members of the *fuzz tone* family use clipping and its distortion extensively to richen the guitar sound.

A sine wave subjected to varying amounts of clipping can be seen in the three figures that follow.

Figure 8.3 shows a sine wave without any clipping. Figure 8.4 is the same sine wave at the onset of clipping. Finally, the sine wave subjected to severe clipping (Figure 8.5).

The distortion processor described in Chapter 13 can be used to hear the affects of clipping on an audio signal. In fact, the distortion processor in conjunction with the oscillator of Chapter 11 and the sample scope of Chapter 12 was used to produce the figures below.

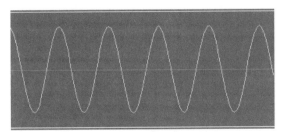

Figure 8.3   Sine Wave (no clipping)

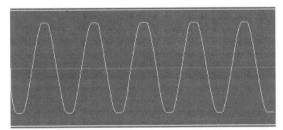

Figure 8.4   Sine Wave (onset of clipping)

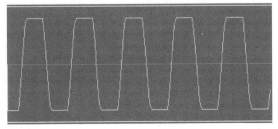

Figure 8.5   Sine Wave (severe clipping)

NON NATURAL SOUND PRODUCTION . . . .

It is possible to produce many realistic sounds using analog electronic circuitry by mimicking physical properties of nature. Pure sine waves can be produced using oscillators that mimic tuning forks, for example, and the sound of bells can be simulated using analog filters with just the right amount of resonance. Change the filter's response and the resonance somewhat and the circuit that was used to produce the sound of bells now sounds like a wooden block being struck. A properly biased germanium diode can simulate the sound of the wind or the surf with the noise it produces. There are even circuits that simulate human speech.

Of course, a whole slew of non-realistic sounds can be produced electronically. The analog synthesizers of the 1970's through the late 1980's used analog circuitry to produce a variety of sounds, some of which were close to natural, and some of which could not be produced naturally. Of course, modern synthesizers are typically digital today—even the ones that model the analog synthesizers of yesteryear.

SAMPLED SOUND . . . .

Today, most sound processing occurs in the digital domain (via digital circuitry and/or microprocessors) instead of in the analog domain (using op-amps, resistors, capacitors, and inductors) as described above. The reasons for this include:

1. Digital circuitry is more stable than the equivalent analog circuitry.
2. Digital signal processing does not introduce the noise into the processed sound as analog signal processing tends to do.
3. There is abundant horsepower in today's PCs and in the embedded microprocessors of sound processing equipment to process sound in software (in real time) instead of building custom hardware to do so.
4. Digital circuitry tends to be cheaper to manufacture and to maintain than the equivalent analog circuitry.

To process sound digitally, most equipment has a signal path similar to that shown in Figure 8.6.

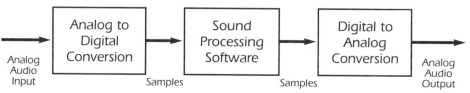

Figure 8.6   *Digital signal path*

The analog-to-digital converter, or A-to-D, is where the continuously variable analog audio signal is converted into discrete digital numbers or samples via the process of quantization. The stream of samples produced by the A-to-D converter represents the input audio information to some degree of accuracy. Numeric algorithms are then applied to the samples (in the sound processing software block) to achieve some desired affect. Finally, the digital samples are converted back to an analog signal via a digital-to-analog converter (called a D-to-A converter). The resultant analog output signal can then be routed to an amplifier and speakers so the processing effect(s) can be heard. As straightforward as this processing sounds, there are many issues with the conversions and with the processing software that affect the resultant sound quality. Under ideal conditions with no sound processing applied, the analog audio output should be exactly equal to the analog audio input. Unfortunately, there is no such thing as ideal conditions in real electronic hardware, so the above statement is never quite true. With some attention to detail however, the output signal can come very close to equaling the input signal. Some of the issues that affect the conversion processes are discussed in the remainder of this chapter.

Analog-to-Digital Conversion (A-to-D Conversion)

An A-to-D converter converts the analog signal in its input to a series of samples that represent the signal in the digital domain. Two forms of quantization are applied in this conversion process—one for bucketizing the amplitude of the signal and another for quantizing the signal in time as samples are taken at regular intervals which have no relationship to the periodicity of the input signal. The bit width of the samples determines how accurately the amplitude of the analog signal can be modeled. Converters exist for many bit widths, up to and including 24 bits. Because amplitude quantization is used, distortion (also called quantization noise) is introduced into the digitized samples. This is because an A-to-D converter attempts to model an input signal with an infinite number of real values with a set of discrete valued integer samples. In the analog realm, amplitude is measured in terms of voltage. In the digital realm, amplitude is a numeric value representing a sample's amplitude.

Once a sample is acquired it must be stored in a known format for processing. Many sampling systems use *Pulse Coded Modulation* (PCM) as the standard for storage. PCM doesn't refer to any specific kind of compression, it only implies the quantization and digitization of an analog signal. The range of values the signal can achieve (called the *quantization range*) is divided into segments and each segment is assigned a unique *code word* (a sequence of bits). The value that the signal achieved at a certain point in time is called a *sample*. To digitize a sample, we look up the segment into which the sample value falls and record the segment's code word. Since the signal is sampled at regular intervals, the progress of the signal through time can be recorded as a sequence of bits.

Whenever the sampled value differs from the actual signal value, distortion/noise occurs. The signal-to-noise ratio is a measurement of how accurately an analog signal can be modeled. For a 16-bit sample size, which is used throughout this book, we can assume an error of not more than one half of one bit and a maximum amplitude of 2^{15} producing a ratio of 2^{16}. Taking $20 * \log_{10}(2^{16})$ yields a signal-to-noise value of 96.3 dB. Quite a respectable value.

Probably the more important contributor to conversion quality is the sample rate. The sample rate, or sampling rate, is the rate at which an analog-to-digital conversion takes place. The result of the conversion is a single sample of digital information. The rate at which samples are taken depends upon the fidelity required. According to Henry Nyquist (1889–1976), the sampling rate determines the maximum frequency information that is preserved in the sampled signal. Nyquist established the fact that in order to recreate an analog waveform accurately from digital samples, it must have been sampled at a rate that was at least twice the frequency of the highest frequency component. This magic number is referred to as the "Nyquist rate" or the "Nyquist criteria" in the literature. Sampling at a lower rate than 2x the highest frequency causes the not-so-subtle effect called *aliasing* to occur. Aliasing is the creation of low-frequency components in the reconstituted waveform that did not exist originally. To prevent aliasing effects from occurring, most modern A-to-Ds are designed to sample at greater than the 2x rate. There is usually a low-pass filter in front of the A-to-D converter (with a very steep rolloff), as well, to enforce the high-frequency limit. The cutoff frequency of the filter may be varied with the sampling rate. In general, the higher the sampling rate (and the better the low-pass filter), the more accurately lower-frequency components of a waveform will be reproduced.

It should also be noted that sampling at exactly 2x the rate of the highest frequency can also cause problems. A good rule of thumb is to sample at something above twice the highest frequency.

However, the higher the sampling rate, the greater the quantity of sample data a system must be prepared to deal with. So it does not make practical sense to sample any faster than is absolutely necessary. Some examples include the telephone system, which samples voice data at 8000 samples per second. This rate was chosen because the highest frequency in a human voice is less than 4KHz or one-half the sample rate. Another example is the 44.1KHz sampling rate used for audio CDs. This rate was chosen because it is slightly faster than double the 20KHz upper limit of human hearing.

Table 8.2 is provided to give you an idea of how much data must be processed for the various sampling rates, number of channels, and the sample word length. As you can see, lots of data must be manipulated when high sample rates are used. This, unfortunately, is the price of fidelity.

Table 8.2   Data Rate as a Function of Sampling Rate and Other Factors

Common Sample Rates in samples/second	Sample Time in seconds	Mono/Stereo Mono=1 channel Stereo=2 channels	Word length in bits	Data Rate in bytes/second
8000	12.5×10^{-5}	Mono	8	8000
			16	16000
			24/32	24000/32000*
		Stereo	8	16000
			16	32000
			24/32	48000/64000*
11025	9.07×10^{-5}	Mono	8	11025
			16	22050
			24/32	33075/44100*
		Stereo	8	22050
			16	44100
			24/32	66150/88200*
22050	4.53×10^{-5}	Mono	8	22050
			16	44100
			24/32	66150/88200*
		Stereo	8	44100
			16	88200
			24/32	132300/176400*
44100	2.27×10^{-5}	Mono	8	44100
			16	88200
			24/32	132300/176400*
		Stereo	8	88200
			16	176400
			24/32	264600/352800*

*Two values are given, the first is the amount of data needing processing and the second is the amount of storage required assuming a 32-bit word is used to store the 24 bits of audio data.

Sound Processing Software

Once PCM samples exist, they can be processed in the digital domain using digital signal processing algorithms and techniques. 16-bit samples are used in this book, which means the valid range of values for a sample is between +32767 and –32768. It is very important when processing samples to prevent numeric overflow or underflow as they create terrible artifacts in the analog signal that is reconstituted from the samples. You will see range checking code in many of the processor devices presented in Chapter 13. Typically the code will look something like this:

```
int sample = buffer[i];       // Get a 16 bit sample from a buffer
                                 somewhere for processing. Hold it in a
                              // 32 bit integer while processing
sample = f(sample)            // Process the sample in some way to
                                 arrive at a new value for this point in time
if (sample > 32767)           // Check for a positive value greater
                                 than the maximum 16 bit value
    sample = 32767            // If greater, set sample's value to the max
                                 value
else if (sample < -32768)     // Check for negative value less than the minimum
                                 16 bit value
    sample = -32768           // If less, set sample's value to the min value
buffer[i] = (short) sample;   // Store the processed sample back into a buffer
                                 for passing along
```

Another important thing for the sound processing software to do is to keep up with the quantity of samples passing through it. If sound is not being processed in real time, this is not an issue. If, however, sound is being processed in real time, the amount of processing must be kept to a minimum; otherwise, breakups (discontinuities) will be heard when the audio is reconstituted. In terms of performance, both the algorithms chosen for the processing of the sound samples and the efficiency of the implementation come into play when running in real time.

Digital-to-Analog Conversion (D-to-A Conversion)

After the digital samples have been manipulated, they must be converted back to an analog signal so we can listen to them. The device which performs the digital-to-analog conversion is a D-to-A converter. The D-to-A converter attempts to create an analog signal by outputting analog voltage values corresponding to the sample values. This process is again hindered by the fact that the samples were quantized to integer values, so the reconstituted analog signal is a stepwise representation of the actual waveform. In general, any finite series of samples can only represent an analog waveform to a finite accuracy. It is important to note that most audio hardware does not produce reconstructed waveforms by traversing data points in a linear fashion. The electrical characteristics of A-to-D converters are such that the conversion of samples to the corresponding voltage levels usually result in a moderately smooth curved waveform.

MUSICAL RELATIONSHIPS . . . .

Musical pitch is closely related to the discussion in this chapter and should therefore be touched upon here briefly. Two important relationships to understand from music are:

1. Two notes that are said to be an octave apart are double in frequency.

2. Since all current western music uses the equal tempered scale which has 12 notes per octave, the notes in the scale are separated in frequency by a ratio that is the twelfth root of two, or approximately 1.0595. Why equal tempered scales are used in today's music is beyond the scope of this discussion but suffice it to say that the use of this scale allows instruments to play music in any key without having to retune for each key.

A440 refers to an A note with a frequency of 440 Hz. This note is often used as a reference in instrument tuning equipment and in electronic music devices.

These musical relationships will be used in the pitch shifter processor in this section of the book and in the guitar tuner of section three.

9 The Audio Processing Architecture

INTRODUCTION · · · · · · · · ·

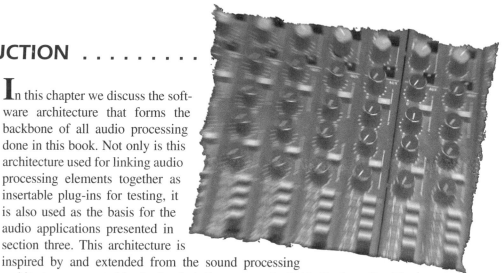

In this chapter we discuss the software architecture that forms the backbone of all audio processing done in this book. Not only is this architecture used for linking audio processing elements together as insertable plug-ins for testing, it is also used as the basis for the audio applications presented in section three. This architecture is inspired by and extended from the sound processing architecture presented in the book *A Programmer's Guide To Sound* by Tim Kientzle, the details of which can be found in the bibliography. This is a great book, by the way, and is one of the few on the market at the time of this writing that deals with sound and music topics in a technical, programmatic way. Similarly to this book, Tim Kientzle's book is written with the programmer/musician in mind.

The sound processing architecture used in this book allows audio processing devices to be linked together in such a way that they can share information and can therefore cooperate in how audio is processed. The term *device* in this context is a software module that operates on digital samples. A series of processing devices connected together make up a signal path or audio processing chain. These can be pictured as a series of blocks in a block diagram where sound enters from the left, is processed in each block and exits from the rightmost block, similar to the following:

Audio Input **Audio Output**

Device 1 → Device 2 ···················· Device N →

Every device has a name and a type associated with it. The name given to a device is informative and should describe the function of the device. Currently there are four types of devices defined. They are:

1. **Source Devices**—A device that provides audio samples for subsequent processing by other devices in the audio processing chain. A device that interfaces to the sound card in your computer and records audio present at the microphone or line input would be a source device. A module that reads sound files like AU and WAV files and provides the samples for processing would also be considered a source device. Finally, an oscillator that synthesizes samples would also be a source device. There can only be one source device in a audio processing chain at a time. A source device will always occupy the leftmost position in the figure above (Device 1).

2. **Processor Devices**—A device that processes, in some manner, the audio samples flowing through it. Typically, the samples exiting a processor device are not the same as the samples entering. How different the output samples are from the input samples depends upon the type of processing the processor device is designed to perform. Many processor devices are presented in this book. Examples include reverbs and phase shifters. Any number of processor devices can exist in a audio processing chain.

3. **Monitor Devices**—A device used to provide a window for analysis into the samples flowing through it but does not alter those samples. Monitor devices are used to implement virtual test equipment in this book. Examples include a sample scope and a spectrum analyzer. Any number of monitor devices can exist in an audio processing chain and they can be placed anywhere they are needed. For example, instances of the sample scope (oscilloscope) could be placed before and after a processor device to aid in the testing process.

4. **Sink Devices**—A device that consumes the samples from the audio processing chain and does something with them. Current sink devices include those that convert samples back into audible form for listening and those that create sound files for storing the result of the audio processing. Currently there can only be a single sink device in an audio processing chain and it must occupy the rightmost position in the chain. In other words, each audio processing chain begins with a source and ends with a sink.

In terms of the diagram above, the first device, Device 1, would be a source device. Devices 2 to N-1 would be either processor devices or monitor devices and the final device, Device N would be a sink device.

This architecture is a *pull architecture,* in that samples are pulled through all devices in the audio processing chain by requests for samples made from the sink device. In practice, the sink device makes a request of samples from the device preceding it which in turn makes requests from the device preceding it and so on, all the way to the source device. As samples are pulled through processor devices, they are subjected to whatever processing the device is designed to perform. When multiple processor devices are present in an audio processing chain they each perform their processing before passing on the altered samples to subsequent devices in the chain. There isn't a limit on the number of processing devices that can be in a signal chain but each device consumes processor cycles and reduces the amount of real-time processing that can be performed.

Since each device has some common requirements placed upon it in order to work within this architecture, it makes sense that all devices would be extended from a common base class. This class is called *AbstractAudio.* The properties of this class will become apparent from the discussion that follows after some of the common device requirements are understood.

One requirement placed upon all varieties of devices is that they must be able to be connected together so they can participate in the processing of samples. Since all devices are implemented as a subclass of *AbstractAudio,* they are essentially of the same type and can therefore be manipulated uniformly. A special collection class called a *LinkedListVector* is used to collect the devices that make up the audio processing chain. Devices are added to the *LinkedListVector* using the *addElement* method, just as normal Java objects are added to a normal *Vector.* This special *Vector* is required because each device must have a reference to the device that immediately precedes it and to the device that immediately follows it. This two-way linking is required because of the process called negotiation, which will be discussed shortly.

The other requirement placed upon devices connected in this manner is that they must all agree on the format of the samples to be manipulated. If each device could only manipulate one format of samples, different devices could not be connected together. To completely specify the format of samples, the following specifications must be agreed upon by all devices in the audio processing chain before processing can begin:

1. sample word size
2. sample rate
3. number of channels

In this book, all processing is performed on samples that are 16-bit signed integers (shorts). Therefore, the range of valid sample values is from −32768 to +32767. Since this constraint is understood inherently by all devices, they don't need to communicate this information between themselves.

State-of-the-art audio processing programs are beginning to use 24- or even 32-bit-wide samples for optimum signal quality instead of the 16 bits used here. In fact, some sound processing applications use floating-point numbers for samples instead of using integers altogether. This is now possible because of the speed at which modern CPUs perform floating-point arithmetic. This decision to use 16-bits here was a compromise between required processor performance and sound quality. I thought since 16 bits were good enough for audio CDs it would be good enough for use here.

The other two sample specification requirements are sample rate and the number of channels the sample stream represents. Since these can change depending on the source of the samples and the playback capability of the sink device, these specifications must be negotiated between all devices that make up the audio processing chain. Negotiation is the process by which all devices agree on all of the sample specifications and modify their behavior accordingly.

In this book, sample rates vary from 11025 samples per second to 44100 samples per second. The number of channels that make up a sample stream is either one for a mono signal or two for a stereo signal. For stereo signals, it is the case that the even-numbered sample is the left channel sample and the odd-numbered sample is the right channel. This fact is important when processing stereo signals. Mixing the left and right channels, either accidentally or intentionally, will result in a compromise in stereo separation.

In most cases, devices in an audio processing chain operate on the number of channels established during the negotiation process. The one exception to this rule is when the panner processor is inserted into the audio processing chain. With the panner processor, it is possible for all devices up to the panner to believe the sample stream is mono yet all devices after the panner believe the sample stream is stereo. You'll see how this is accomplished in section two when the *Panner* processor is described.

NEGOTIATION

For the most part, the process of negotiation is handled automatically by code in the *AbstractAudio* class. The process of negotiation begins whenever any device in the audio processing chain asks for the sample rate or the number of channels that it should expect the sample stream to contain. A device would do this in preparation for allocating buffers, for example, for the processing it is designed to do. Such requests set off a flurry of activity that propagates the full length of the audio processing chain many times. Once all negotiation is performed, the requesting device is returned the sample rate or the number of channels information it requested. At that time, all devices have agreed upon the specification and each has accepted the agreed-upon value. Once the negotiation process has been completed, neither the sample rate nor the number of channels can be changed for the life span of the audio processing chain. In other words, these specifications are frozen.

The process of negotiating the value of the sample rate among all devices in the audio processing chain can be described in the following steps:

1. Any device at any position in the audio processing chain calls the *AbstractAudio* method *getSamplingRate* to ascertain the current sample rate it should plan on using.

2. If the sample rate has already been frozen, the method returns immediately with the agreed-upon sample rate the calling device should use.

3. If negotiation has yet to be performed, a call is made to the *negotiateSamplingRate* method to begin the process. This method makes a call to the *negotiateSamplingRate* method of the next device in the chain closer to the sink device, if there is one. Thus each device calls the next device's *negotiateSamplingRate* method until there are no more devices in the chain and hence the call has arrived at the sink device (as it has no next device to propagate the call to).

4. The sink device then establishes the sample rate it would prefer to use, and the minimum and maximum value it can use, and then calls *minMaxSamplingRate* to propagate this information through all devices between the sink device and the source device. The *minMaxSamplingRate* call also propagates by each device calling the previous device to its immediate left until the source device is found. The source device is identified because it doesn't have a device on its left (a previous device).

5. As each device examines the preferred, min, and max sample rate values it has been passed, it can alter the preferred value to its liking as long as the new preferred value is within the min and max values established by the sink device.

6. After all devices have had a look at the preferred value, the sink then calls another method called *setSamplingRateRecursive* to inform all devices as to the agreed-upon value. This method again propagates from the sink to the source setting all devices to the new value. It also marks the sample rate value as frozen so negotiation will not be performed again.

Even though sample rate negotiation is described by the steps above, negotiation for the number of channels happens in exactly the same way. Here, however, replace *SamplingRate* in all of the noted method calls with *NumberOfChannels*.

With negotiation completed, the individual devices have the information necessary to prepare themselves for the processing of samples. What each device does with this information is device dependent and will be described as each device in this book is presented for discussion.

PASSING SAMPLES BETWEEN DEVICES . . . .

As mentioned, with this pull architecture, samples are pulled between devices in the audio processing chain. This process starts with the sink device asking the device previous to it for a group of samples it requires for playback or for storing into an output file. Here the *AbstractAudio* device comes into play again. First, since each device has a reference to the previous and next devices in the audio processing chain, it can make method calls on those devices. To gather samples from the previous device, the sink devices performs the following call:

```
previous.getSamples(...)
```

This method, *getSamples*, is an abstract method of *AbstractAudio* with the following signature:

```
public int getSamples(short [] buffer, int length);
```

Because *getSamples* is an abstract method, each device must be provided an implementation in order for the device's code to compile. So, each device provides a buffer for the samples and specifies how many samples its would like to the get in the call to *previous.getSamples(buffer, length)*. The previous device fulfills this request by calling the device previous to it, processing the samples it gets in return, and then providing the processed samples to the device who called it. You can see why this is considered a pull architecture with this example.

As long as samples are available, the call to *getSamples* will return a count of the number of samples that have been returned. In most cases, the value returned will equal the length value requested. As the source device begins to run out of samples (from reading a WAV file, for example) at some point the number of samples returned will be less than the length requested. The next call to *getSamples* will most likely return a –1 value which indicates an end of data/end of file (EOF) condition. All devices must be able to cope with the EOF condition without crashing. In most cases, the required behavior is just to return –1 to the device calling it. Sink devices must be written in such a manner as to stop requesting samples when the EOF condition is detected.

The *AbstractAudio* class also supports the concept of device bypassing. That is, the ability to temporarily remove the processing associated with a device from the audio processing chain without physically removing the device. *AbstractAudio* has a class variable called *byPass* that can be set and queried. When set true, the device should be bypassed. If false, the device is not bypassed and should therefore participate in the processing of the samples that flow through it. Although the byPass variable is maintained by the base class, it is up to the *getSamples* method of the derived class to implement the bypass functionality. This is usually as simple as including the following code in the *getSamples* method:

```
if (byPass)
    return previous.getSamples(buffer, length);
```

In essence, if a device is bypassed, the *getSamples* method should simply return the samples read from the previous device. If a device is not bypassed, it should process the samples passing through it before returning them to the next device.

RESET PROPAGATION AND PROCESSING . . . .

Because some devices in an audio processing chain maintain state information, it is necessary to reset these devices between signal processing sessions. An example would be a source device that reads audio samples from a sound file. Once all of the samples from the file have been read and processed in a processing session, this device must be reset so that the file will be read again from the beginning. The cache processor of section two is another example. It must be reset each processing session so that it provides the data from the start of the cache each time.

A reset operation is initiated by any device that calls the *doReset* method of *AbstractAudio*. This causes the reset operation to propagate from this device to the sink device and then from the sink to the source device. As each device receives this reset message, the reset method in each device is called. The default *reset* method provided by *AbstractAudio* does nothing but returns. However, if a device has overridden this default implementation, it can do whatever processing it requires before returning. Reset processing continues back up the audio processing chain to the sink device, where it terminates. Most devices won't need special reset processing but for those that do, it is easy to provide.

AbstractAudio UTILITY METHODS . . . .

Finally, *AbstractAudio* provides a few simple text formatting methods useful for debugging. They are shown in Table 9.1.

Table 9.1   Utility Methods Provided by AbstractAudio Class

Method	Function
public void hexo(int i)	Formats the integer i as a hex string and writes it to standard out.
public void hexo(String s, int i)	Same as above except the string s is prefixed to the formatted integer value.
public static void hexo(long i)	Same as above except used for a long integer value.
public static void hexo(String s, long i)	Labeled and formatted hex long value.
public static void o(String s)	Short cut for System.out.println.

Since all devices are a subclass of *AbstractAudio*, all devices have access to these debugging functions. They help save time by lowering the amount of typing one must do to inspect the values of variables within your code. These may not be necessary if you have access to a good Java debugger.

THE LinkedListVector CLASS . . . .

As hinted at earlier, the *LinkedListVector* class is to *AbstractAudio* devices what the Java *Vector* class is to Java *objects*. This class provides all the methods in the standard *Vector* class tailored specifically for use with *AbstractAudio* objects. This was done because *Vector* could not be extended in older versions of Java. This is no longer true, however, and the ambitious reader could rewrite *LinkedListVector* to take advantage of that fact. As it is, this class provides many methods that could be used in manipulating devices making up an audio processing chain. Currently only a few of the methods provided are actually used in this book. See the code and the javadoc documentation for a complete list of the methods provided.

An audio processing chain is developed by first instantiating a *LinkedListVector* object and then adding devices to it using the *addElement* method. Devices are added in order beginning with the source device, followed by zero or more processor devices, and ending with the sink device. The use of this ordering is important in getting your audio processing chain to work as you would expect.

As an example, consider how a *LinkedListVector* is used to contain the devices which make up an audio processing chain in the guitar tuner application of section three. The audio test program called *AudioTest.java* would be another good example that could be consulted.

```
// Instantiate data structure for linking abstract audio devices
LinkedListVector ll = new LinkedListVector();

// Create a WinRecorder for gathering samples
WinRecorder recorder = new WinRecorder(DEFAULTSAMPLERATE,
                            WinRecorder.DEFAULTCHANNELS,
                            WinRecorder.DEFAULTDEVICEID,
                            null);
if (recorder.initRecorder()) {
    // Open was successful, so continue
    ll.addElement(recorder);

    // Create the tuner device
    Tuner tuner = new Tuner();
    ll.addElement(tuner);

    // Run the tuner code
    tuner.doTuner();
}
```

In this example, *WinRecorder* is the source device and as such is added first to the audio processing chain. Next, the *Tuner* device is instantiated and added to the audio processing chain as a combination processing device and sink device. When the *doTuner* method is called, it causes samples to be pulled from the microphone input of *WinRecorder*, through the *Tuner* and eventually to drive the tuning meter of this application.

THE AudioTest PROGRAM ....

The *AudioTest* program is a simple Java command line application used to string together *AbstractAudio* devices for the express purpose of processing sound. The *AudioTest* program can run in real time or in batch mode, the distinction here being whether the processed sound is available for listening to immediately or if the processed sound samples are written to a file for later listening. Real-time operation places some limitations on the type and number of effects that can be used together simultaneously. Breakup or stuttering of the sound indicates your computer has probably run out of gas. Batch mode has no such limitations because the samples will eventually be written to the output file regardless of how long it takes for the processing to be performed. Batch mode is your best bet when applying lots of effects to audio with a high sampling rate.

The *AudioTest* program performs three functions. First, it instantiates a *Blinker* object (for driving the LED's on the simulated equipment front panels) which will be passed to all processing devices that require one. Next, it instantiates a *LinkedListVector* in preparation for collecting the processing devices to be used during the program run. Finally, the *AudioTest* program parses the command line it is passed, parses all of the devices specified, instantiates them and adds them to the *LinkedListVector* collection. It is important to note that the *AudioTest* program doesn't "terminate" immediately because sink devices don't terminate until their UIs are dismissed. After the audio processing is complete, the collection of processing devices is cleaned up and the program ends.

The *AudioTest* program understands four types of devices: *Source* devices, which provide a source of audio samples to process; *monitor* devices, which allow audio samples to be analyzed but not altered; *processor* devices, which intentionally alter the audio samples algorithmically; and *output* or sink devices, which convert the digital samples to audio files for storage or back to audio for listening to. The *AudioTest* program is told which devices to use by combinations of command line arguments passed to it. One *source* device and one *output* device can be specified for each *AudioTest* program run. Any number of *monitor* devices and *processor* devices can be used in a single run.

The *AudioTest* program is then executed by typing java, the package name/program name, craigl.test.AudioTest, followed by numerous command line arguments. Each command line argument is prefixed with a negative sign. The *AudioTest* command line arguments are as follows:

Source input device: -i (osc | sosc | file | mic sr chs)

Monitor devices: [-m (scope | spectrumanalyzer)+]

Processor device(s):   [-p (aadj cache chorus compexp delay distortion eq pan peq phaser pshift reverb)+]

Output/Sink device: -o (file | player | winplayer)

Items above surrounded with [ ] are optional. Items shown separated by | indicate one of the options can be selected at a time. When items are wrapped in parenthesis as in ( )+ this indicates one or more may be used at a time.

The device mnemonics indicate the following:

osc	mono oscillator source
sosc	stereo oscillator source
file	input from file or output to file
mic sr chs	mic/line input at sample rate sr and chs channels for Windows
scope	sample scope monitor

spectrumanalyzer	spectrum analyzer monitor
aadj	amplitude adjust processor (level control)
cache	sample caching processor
chorus	chorus/flanger effect processor
compexp	compressor/expander/limiter/noise gate processor
delay	digital delay processor
distortion	distortion processor
eq	graphic equalizer processor
pan	panner processor
peq	parametric equalizer processor
phaser	phaser effect processor
pshift	pitch shifter effect processor
reverb	reverberation effect processor
player	sample player based on JMF1.0
winplayer	sample player for Windows

Sample Invocations of the *AudioTest* Program

The following command line will bring up the file reader device for selecting which sound file to convert into audio samples and the winplayer output device for playing the audio samples. Once a file is selected and the play button is clicked, you should hear the audio file being played.

```
java craigl.test.AudioTest -i file -o winplayer
```

The next example (which also only works on Microsoft Windows) will bring up the winrecorder device for sampling a single channel (mono) signal from the mic/line input of your PC at a sample rate of 11025 samples per second and a file writer device for allowing the digital audio to be saved in a WAV or AU sound file.

```
java craigl.test.AudioTest -i mic 11025 1 -o file
```

This next command line will use the mono oscillator as the sample source, will cause the sample scope to come up for monitoring the samples and the pcmplayer device for listening to the samples. NOTE: you won't see the sample scope until the player is commanded to start playing. This will cause the sample scope to trigger and display the samples.

```
java craigl.test.AudioTest -i osc -m scope -o player
```

The final example command line shown below causes the samples to be read from an audio file; brings up and inserts the graphic equalizer processor, the reverb processor, and the pitch shifter into the sample path; and uses the JMF1.0 pcmplayer device for playing the result.

```
java craigl.test.AudioTest -i file -p eq reverb pshift -o player
```

Appendix B has other devices based upon JMF2.0ea that can also be used in an audio signal chain. See Appendix B for details.

BATCH PROCESSING VS. REAL-TIME PROCESSING . . . .

Typically, I use the *AudioTest* program to read audio from a file (-i file), process the sound using one or more processing devices (-p device1 device2 ...), and then use a player (-o winplayer, pcmplayer etc.) to allow me to hear the result in real time. While this provides instant gratification, it takes a while because the processing happens at the speed required by the player for playback. Batch processing, writing the processed output directly to a file, can happen much faster because the samples are processed at the maximum speed of your computer and is not slowed down due to the audio playback rate. Most batch processing using the *AudioTest* program happens in the blink of an eye. You can subsequently double-click on the output file produced by batch processing to hear what you have achieved.

By way of example, if you had a lengthy audio file (say 15 minutes in duration) that you were going to process, it would take 15 minutes to do so in real time. However, if you did the processing in batch mode, it might take one minute from start to finish. Of course the result batch mode file would still take 15 minutes to play back.

Another reason to consider the use of batch processing is if your computer cannot process the sound at a rate sufficient for audio playback. This can happen if you have a slow computer or if you are trying to squeeze too much real-time processing into one run of the *AudioTest* program. By batch processing the output, you will always be guaranteed the processing happens without glitches because the samples will be written to the output file as they are produced even if that rate is less than that required for real-time playback.

FINAL NOTE . . . .

Before ending this discussion, it is important to point out that most devices provided in this book are made up of two basic component parts. The first is the part that is involved with the processing of samples in a sample stream. This part is extended directly or indirectly from *AbstractAudio* and does provide its own *getSamples* method. The second component part is some sort of user interface (UI) for controlling the operation of the device (The UI is usually built, of course, from the visual components provided in section one of this book.) You'll see this pattern repeated throughout this book.

CONLUSIONS . . . .

In this chapter we have discussed:

1. A pull architecture that forms the basis for all audio processing done in this book.
2. The *AbstractAudio* class from which all devices are extended.
3. What negotiation is and how it is used by the processing devices in an audio processing chain to decide on the format of samples that will be processed.
4. How the *AbstractAudio* class encapsulates most of the base functionality required by a sample-processing device except the *getSamples* method that must be implemented by all derived classes.
5. How the *LinkedListVector* class is used to collect devices into an audio processing chain.
6. How the *AudioTest* program is used as the test bed for running the audio processing devices.

MISCELLANEOUS INFORMATION . . . .

Source Files:

File Name	Package	Description
AbstractAudio.java	craigl.utils.	Code defining the base class from which all devices in this book are derived. The code supports naming and typing of devices, provides built-in negotiation facilities, supports the notion of device bypass, provides for reset processing, and has some text formatting methods helpful for debugging.
AudioTest.java	craigl.test	Code for the Java application that is used to run the processing devices presented in this book. This code can be considered a test harness for audio processing devices.
LinkedListVector.java	craigl.utils.	A collection class that has attributes of both a linked list (in that each element knows the elements on both sides) and a Java *Vector*. This class provides a complete *Vector*-like implementation with 15 familiar methods.

10 Digital Filters

. . . .

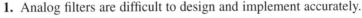

In general terms, audio filters are devices used to manipulate the sonic qualities of audio signals in some predictable way.

In the old days, filtering and equalization of audio signals were performed exclusively using electronic circuits called analog filters. These filters were built with collections of resistors, capacitors, and inductors which are, as a group, generically referred to as passive electronic components. Later, the passive components were augmented with op-amps, making the passive analog filters into active analog filters. Active filters represented a giant leap forward in filter design flexibility and filter operation but still didn't solve all the problems associated with electronic filters. These problems include:

1. Analog filters are difficult to design and implement accurately.
2. Analog filters are subject to component tolerance variations.
3. Analog filters tend to drift over time and with temperature changes.
4. Analog filters cannot easily be made adjustable and still be accurate.
5. It is difficult if not impossible to design analog filters with sharp enough cutoffs for some specialized applications.

Analog filters were used, and still are used, in audio equipment everywhere—from the passive crossovers used in your stereo system's speakers to the tone controls on your receiver and even for equalization on professional recording consoles. It has only been recently that digital filters have begun to make inroads into the mainstream applications usually implemented with active filters. The reasons for this include:

133

1. The price of specialized digital signal processing (DSP) chips, RAM, digital-to-analog converters and analog-to-digital converters have all fallen dramatically over time.
2. The performance of even low-end PCs has risen to the point where signal processing using digital filtering is now possible (hence this book).

And as mentioned, some applications such as brick wall filters (those filters with extremely sharp cutoffs used in front of analog-to-digital converters to prevent aliasing) demand the use of digital filters.

For the purpose of our discussion here, filters are defined as devices that emphasize or de-emphasize certain frequencies to change a signal's timbre. More precisely, filters modify the frequency content and phase of input signals according to some specification. In practice, filters can be used for special effects (like the megaphone sound used in the Beatles song "Yellow Submarine") but in most cases are used for altering the frequency response of recorded instruments to correct some deficiency, real or perceived.

Filter design, analog and/or digital, is a very complex subject that cannot be adequately covered or even summarized in a single chapter of a book. So in keeping with the practical approach taken throughout this book, I'll discuss the filter implementations used in the processor devices of Chapter 13 instead of trying to tackle the whole topic of digital filters. I would like to provide some intuitive insights into digital filters, particularly how the coefficients are calculated in the digital domain so that a desired frequency response is obtained, and to show how to implement IIR digital filters in Java.

For people who need more information about digital filters and filtering than is presented here, there are many books listed in the bibliography that can be consulted.

FILTER VARIETIES . . . .

Four types of filters find application with audio. These four types are described by the shape of their response curve—low-pass, high-pass, band-pass, and band-stop. Each type is described below.

Low-pass Filters

Low-pass filters pass signals below a specified cutoff frequency and reject signals above the cutoff frequency. An idealized amplitude vs. frequency response curve for a low-pass filter is shown in Figure 10.1.

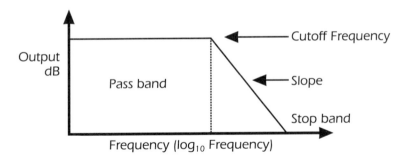

Figure 10.1   *Idealized amplitude versus frequency response curve for a low-pass filter.*

This figure illustrates some very important points about filters. First, the response of a low-pass filter is defined by its cutoff frequency. In actuality, the cutoff frequency is that frequency where the amplitude of the response curve drops by 3 dB. Second, the steepness of the slope (also called rolloff) is determined by the *order* of the filter. A first-order filter has a slope of 6 dB per octave (or 20 dB per decade) above the cutoff frequency. Second-order filters, like those used in Chapter 13, have a slope of 12 dB per octave. Each step increase in order adds an additional 6 dB per octave to the slope, so filters with very high order have a very steep rolloff. Next, the response of a low-pass filter is comprised of two regions: the pass-band region and the stopband region, with a nether region between them which is sometimes referred to as the transition band. Note that although the response of the filter shown above in the pass-band is shown as an absolutely straight line, this doesn't happen in reality. Depending on the filter type (Bessel, Chebyshev, Butterworth, etc.) the amplitude of the response in the pass band can be very flat or full of ripples. Finally, depending on the damping factor of the filter, there may be a peak in the frequency response at the cutoff frequency.

High-pass Filters

High-pass filters pass signals above a specified cutoff frequency and rejects signals below the cutoff frequency. All of the discussion above for low-pass filters applies as well to high-pass filters. The idealized amplitude vs. frequency response curve for a high-pass filter is shown in Figure 10.2.

In electronic engineering terms, low-pass and high-pass filters are just that. In the professional audio world, these filters are generically referred to as *shelving* filters because of the shape of their response curves.

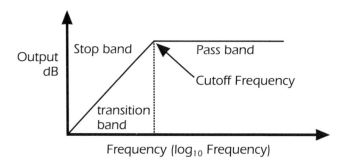

Figure 10.2   Idealized amplitude versus frequency response curve for a high-pass filter.

Band-pass Filters

Band-pass filters boost only those frequencies around its center frequency while attenuating higher and lower frequencies. The idealized response curve is shown in Figure 10.3.

The sharpness of the curve is defined by the quality factor or Q of the filter. Q is defined as

$$Q = Fc / (F_2 - F_1)$$

As Q increases, the range of frequencies acted upon by the filter is reduced. For this reason, band-pass filters can be used to modify the frequency of audio signals in very selective ways, such as enhancing a vocal part by boosting a narrow range of frequencies within a singer's vocal range. In professional audio terms, band-pass filters are often referred to as *peaking* filters due to the shape of the response curve.

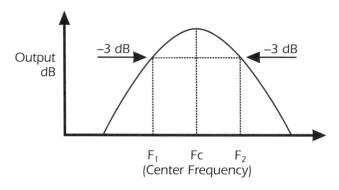

Figure 10.3   Idealized response curve for a band-pass filter.

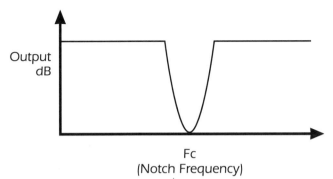

Fc
(Notch Frequency)

Figure 10.4   Idealized response curve for a band-stop filter.

Band-stop Filters

Band-stop or notch filters are the inverse of the band-pass filter. All frequencies around the notch or center frequency are rejected while frequencies above and below the notch frequency pass unimpeded (Figure 10.4). Band-stop filters can be used, for example, to remove a 60Hz hum from an audio recording without affecting frequencies below or above 60 Hz.

PRACTICAL APPLICATIONS OF FILTERS AND FILTERING . . .

As alluded to previously, in audio applications, filters are mainly used for correcting problems introduced by less-than-perfect recording devices and/or recording conditions. But many other uses for filters exist, including:

1. The crossover (a type of filter) within multi-speaker speaker systems is used to route specific ranges of frequencies to speakers designed for their reproduction. Typically, the low-frequency components of the audio signal are sent to the woofer for reproduction, the midrange frequencies to a smaller midrange speaker, and the high frequencies to the tweeter. As you might guess, a low-pass filter is used for screening midrange and high-frequency components from the signal delivered to the woofer. A band-pass type of filter is used to remove the low- and the high-frequency components from the feed to the midrange speaker, and a high-pass filter prevents low and midrange signal components from reaching the tweeter, thus preventing damage.

2. In the control room of many recording studios, a device called a graphic equalizer, consisting of a series of overlapping band-pass filters (typical-

ly centered at ⅓ octave intervals), is used to adjust the frequency response of the room to flat. A room with a flat frequency response is one that does not exhibit any major deviation in response over a wide range of frequencies. It is necessary to have a room with a flat response so that you know what you are hearing is coming from the music and is not artificially influenced by the room. In order to correct the frequency response of a room, the response must first be measured. This is done by placing a pink noise source in the room and miking it with a calibrated microphone known to have a flat response. The signal from the microphone is routed into a spectrum analyzer where a graph of the room's response is produced. This graph will show peaks and valleys in the frequency response of the room. A stereo graphic equalizer is then introduced into the main monitor sound system in the room and anywhere a peak is seen in the room's response, the graphic equalizer is used to attenuate the frequency of the peak. Conversely, anywhere a valley is seen in the response, the graphic equalizer is used to boost the corresponding frequency. By iteratively measuring and compensating, the response of the room can be made virtually flat. Once this is done, a cover is screwed on to cover the equalizer adjustments so they cannot accidentally be changed. Then as long as the geometry of the room is not changed or equipment in the monitoring system is not changed, the response of the room should not change and therefore remain flat.

3. It has already been pointed out that the tone controls on every stereo receiver are implemented with filters. The bass control, for example, boosts or cuts the bass response of the audio passing through the receiver from the flat, unmodified, level. The bass control is implemented using a low-pass filter. The midrange control and the high-frequency control are also filters. What may not be so obvious is that the loudness control found on many receivers is also a type of filter. A loudness control is used to compensate for the non-linear nature of the ear in hearing low- and high-frequency sounds at low volume levels. Compensation is accomplished by boosting the high and low frequencies.

4. Other applications of filters include removing a 60 Hz hum from recorded material and reducing feedback in sound reinforcement applications.

DIGITAL FILTERS TYPES . . . .

Digital filters generally fall into one of two categories, as determined by their response to a unit step impulse. The two varieties are finite impulse response or FIR filters, which respond to the unit impulse with an output of finite duration, and the infinite impulse response or IIR filters, which can have a response that is infinite in duration.

Both types of filters have their advantages and disadvantages so neither filter type is best in all applications. Advantages and disadvantages of each are summarized below.

FIR Filter Advantages

1. FIR filters can be designed to have constant phase characteristics.
2. Non-recursive FIR filters will always be stable.
3. Designs are tolerant of numeric round-off errors in their implementation.

FIR Filter Disadvantages

1. The impulse response, while finite, can be very long in filters where sharp cutoffs are required.
2. Designing an FIR filter with specific requirements is harder than designing the equivalent IIR filter.

IIR Filter Advantages

1. IIR filters are much better at approximating the response of traditional analog filter varieties like Butterworth and Chebyshev filters.
2. IIR filters generally are of lower order than the equivalent FIR filter for filter designs with the same performance requirements. This means they can be implemented in less memory and require fewer CPU cycles to run.

IIR Filter Disadvantages

1. IIR filters are more sensitive to finite-precision arithmetic than their FIR cousins.
2. It is hard if not impossible to design IIR filters with linear phase response.

Because IIR filters are a closer match to traditional analog filters (something I know more about) and because they are easier to design and implement, and because they are computationally less expensive (an important factor when implemented in Java), they have been chosen for our use here. As you shall soon see, IIR filters can be designed and implemented as a neat little package that can be plugged into many audio applications.

Because of the decision made above, only IIR filters will be described from this point on. Consult the bibliography for books on digital filters that can provide in-depth discussions of FIR filters.

IIR DIGITAL FILTER DESIGN TECHNIQUES AND EQUATIONS . . . .

In the digital domain, an IIR filter is implemented as summations of previous inputs (x) and previous outputs (y), multiplied by appropriate scaling factors. Mathematically, this can be represented by the following equation:

Previous inputs   Previous outputs

$$y(n) \cong \sum c[k] * x[n-k] + \sum d[j] * y[n-j]$$

New outputs   Filter Coefficients

Each of the two summations is actually a convolution which is the process of summing samples multiplied by specific weighting factors represented by the filter coefficients. As you might expect, implementing this equation in software is not rocket science; however coming up with the appropriate filter coefficients truly can be. While it is possible to calculate the frequency response of a filter given the digital domain filter coefficients, it is not possible to have a generalized solution for calculating the filter coefficients given a desired frequency response. Various specialized solutions do exist and this is what we will use later in this discussion.

To get around this issue, IIR filters are usually designed in the analog domain (also called the s-domain) using Laplace transforms (s is the Laplace operator) and a transformation called the bilinear transformation is used to convert the s-domain designs into the z-domain (digital domain) for implementation. The form of the formulas for the z-domain filter coefficients thus determined are generalized in terms of the key filter characteristics in the z-domain so that we can design digital filters directly without the necessity of designing the analog equivalent and transforming the design back into the digital domain. Butterworth filters are used as our design model here. The Butterworth filter's response is maximally flat in the pass-band (very little ripple) at the expense of phase linearity and steepness of attenuation slope in the transition band. Butterworth filters seemed to be a good choice for the audio applications presented in this book as flatness of response in the pass-band is very important (we don't want the amplitude of samples jumping around in value now, do we?).

Given the filter type we are trying to emulate in the digital realm (in this case Butterworth filters) and a great deal of very complex mathematics, we can arrive at a set of equations that, when solved at runtime, produce the filter response we desire. Specifically, we need a set of formulas for calculating the filter coefficients alpha, beta, and gamma and a formula, called the difference equation, for solving for the current output value given the filter coefficients and values for the previous inputs and outputs. These formulae are shown below for each of the four filter types.

IIR Band-pass Filters Equations

The filter coefficients for implementing a band-pass filter are shown below. Theta0 is the radians-per-sample at the frequency of interest, which in this case is the center frequency of a band-pass filter. Theta0 is calculated as follows:

$$Theta0(freq) = (2.0 * Math.PI * freq) / sampleRate;$$

The band-pass filter coefficients are:

alpha = (0.5 - beta) / 2
beta = 0.5 * ((1 - tan(theta0/(2*Q))) / (1 + tan(theta0/(2*Q))))
gamma = (0.5 + beta) * cos(theta0)

The band-pass difference equation is:

$$y(n) = 2\{alpha[x(n)-x(n-2)] + gamma * y(n-1) - beta * y(n-2)\}$$

IIR Band-stop Filter Equations

The band-stop filter coefficients are:

alpha = (0.5 + beta) / 2
beta = 0.5 * ((1 - tan(theta0/(2*Q))) / (1 + tan(theta0/(2*Q))))
gamma = (0.5 + beta) * cos(theta0)

The band-stop difference equation is:

$$y(n) = 2\{alpha[x(n) - 2cos(theta) x(n-1) + x(n-2)] + gamma * y(n-1) - beta * y(n-2)\}$$

IIR High-pass Filter Equations

The high-pass filter coefficients are:

alpha = (0.5 + beta + gamma) / 4
beta = 0.5 * ((1 - d/(2*sin(theta0))) / (1 + d/(2*sin(theta0))))
gamma = (0.5 + beta) * cos(theta0)

The high-pass difference equation is:

y(n) = 2{alpha[x(n) - 2x(n-1) + x(n-2)] + gamma * y(n-1) – beta * y(n-2)}

IIR Low-pass Filter Equations

The low-pass filter coefficients are:

alpha = (0.5 + beta - gamma) / 4
beta = 0.5 * ((1 - d/(2*sin(theta0))) / (1 + d/(2*sin(theta0))))
gamma = (0.5 + beta) * cos(theta0)

The low-pass difference equation is:

y(n) = 2{alpha[x(n) + 2x(n-1) + x(n-2)] + gamma * y(n-1) – beta * y(n-2)}

As you can see in each of the difference equations shown above, three values of inputs (x(n), x(n-1), and x(n-2)) and two values of outputs (y(n-1) and y(n-2)) must be available when a difference equation is run. These values represent the current value and two previous values. This fact is key in the implementation of these filters. Remember the previous values are always changing. That is, the value calculated as the current output value now will be a previous value the next time through the difference equation. The same is true for input values. A pseudo-code representation of the algorithm used to execute difference equations is shown below.

```
// Allocate storage for three input and three output values
double input[3];
double output[3];

i = 0;

while input samples are available

    input[i] = get input sample
    j = i - 2
    if (j < 0)
        j = j + 3

    k = i - 1
    if (k < 0)
        k = k + 3
```

```
// Run the difference equation solving for the current output value
output[i] = difference equation using i, j and k

// Output the current value
set output output[i]

// Update array indices
i = i + 1
if (i > 2)
    i = 0
end while
```

In our actual implementation of this code (in the filter runtime classes), we use double values throughout to prevent arithmetic overflow from occurring because, as has been noted, IIR filters are very sensitive to this condition. The extremely large range of double numbers removes many of the constraints placed on DSP code when run in a 16-bit fixed-point environment typical of a DSP chip.

IIR FILTER DESIGN CLASSES . . . .

Three classes are provided for designing the three supported IIR filter types: band-pass, high-pass, and low-pass filters. An IIR band-stop design class is left to the reader for implementation because band-stop filters were not required for the applications in this book. After looking at the three design class examples provided however, a band-stop design class should be trivial to implement if you choose to do so.

These design classes calculate the filter coefficients, alpha, beta, and gamma, for the supported filter types but do not perform any sample filtering. A separate runtime filter class is provided to perform the actual filtering.

These design classes are used in two ways. First, they can be used programmatically (as they are in Chapter 13) to generate the important filter parameters alpha, beta, and gamma from the filter specifications passed into their constructors and, second, they can be used interactively to output filter parameters from filter specifications passed on the command line. To provide this facility, each of the filter design classes is structured as a standalone Java application. If you execute one of these filter design classes from the command line and don't pass any parameters, you will be presented with a usage statement reminding you of what the required parameters are. In all cases, you need to pass the frequency of interest, the sampling rate, and the damping factor or Q required. A typical invocation is as follows:

```
java craigl.filters.IIRHighpassFilterDesign 60 22050 1
```

The output of which would be:

Filter Specifications:

Sample Rate: 22050, Frequency: 60, d/q: 1.0

Alpha: 0.016529823952816793

Beta: -0.4669379360525818

Gamma: 0.033057231863849

Using the design classes programmatically is equally as simple. First, an instance of the class is produced by passing the sample rate, frequency, and damping factor or Q into the constructor of the appropriate design class. Then the method *doFilterDesign* is called to execute the alpha, beta, and gamma equations (shown in the previous section) appropriate for the type of filter being designed. Once this has been done, the instance of the design class can be passed into the runtime filter class that implements the appropriate filter type. Designing digital filters has never been this easy.

IIR FILTER RUNTIME CLASSES . . . .

Just as three filter design classes exist for designing band-pass, low-pass, and high-pass IIR filters, three runtime filter classes exist for executing the difference equations. These classes do the actual sample-by-sample filtering of the input data provided in a buffer. These runtime filter classes differ only in the difference equation they are coded to solve. The code below from *IIRLowpassFilter.java* shows how the low-pass filter difference equation is solved. Other runtime filter classes solve a different difference equation.

```
public void doFilter(short [] inBuffer, double [] outBuffer, int length) {

    for (int index=0; index < length; index++) {
        // Fetch sample
        inArray[iIndex] = (double) inBuffer[index];
        // Do indices maintenance
        jIndex = iIndex - 2;
        if (jIndex < 0) jIndex += HISTORYSIZE;
        kIndex = iIndex - 1;
        if (kIndex < 0) kIndex += HISTORYSIZE;

        // Run the low-pass difference equation
        double out = outArray[iIndex] =
                        2.0 *
```

```
                            (alpha * (inArray[iIndex] + (2 *
                                inArray[kIndex]) + inArray[jIndex]) +
                            gamma * outArray[kIndex] -
                            beta * outArray[jIndex]);

        outBuffer[index] += amplitudeAdj * out;
        iIndex = (iIndex + 1) % HISTORYSIZE;
    }
}
```

IIR FILTER USAGE . . . .

To recap, in the architecture presented here, an IIR filter is made up of two parts: a design class which first calculates and later holds the filter coefficients for the filter and a runtime filter class which performs the filtering based on these coefficients. The runtime filter code must be called as part of the *getSamples* method within the *AbstractAudio* device implementing the filter. *Note:* The filter design class cannot be instantiated until such time as the sample rate is known. In our *AbstractAudio* architecture, this means it cannot be instantiated until sample rate negotiation has been performed and frozen.

A typical *getSamples* method for implementing a low-pass filter is shown below:

```
public int getSamples(short [] buffer, int length) {
    // Ask for a buffer of samples
    int len = previous.getSamples(buffer, length);
    if (len == -1)
        return len;

    // If bypass is enabled or negotiation has yet to be performed,
                                        short circuit filtering
    if (getByPass() || !initializationComplete)
        return len;

    // Realloc buffer as required
    if (dBuffer.length != len)
        dBuffer = new double[len];

    // Apply the low-pass filter
    low-passShelf.doFilter(buffer, dBuffer, len);
```

```
// Convert the double samples back into short samples after
// range constraining them.
for (int i=0; i < len; i++) {
    double dSample = dBuffer[i];
    if (dSample > 32767.0)
        dSample = 32767.0;
    else if (dSample < -32768.0)
        dSample = -32768.0;

    // Convert sample and store
    buffer[i] = (short) dSample;
}
return len;
}
```

In the case where all filter aspects are static, the code for designing the low-pass filter would look similar to the following:

```
// Design the low-pass filter for 5000 Hz cutoff frequency and a
                                        damping factor of 1.0.
lpfd = new IIRLowpassFilterDesign(5000, sampleRate, 1.0);
lpfd.doFilterDesign();

// Implement the filter design
lowpassShelf = new IIRLowpassFilter(lpfd);
```

Once samples begin to be pulled through this *AbstractAudio* device, all frequencies in the digitized audio above 5000 Hz will be removed.

In the actual applications in this book that use filters (the graphic equalizer and the parametric equalizer both of Chapter 13), user inputs (via pots and sliders) are used to control various aspects of filter operation. As a user changes filter parameters (frequency and/or Q), new design classes are instantiated to reflect the changes. In other words, the filters are redesigned on the fly. Say, for example, as the user changes the frequency of the low-pass filter, the method below is called with a new frequency value.

```
public void lowpassShelfFreq(int freq) {

    if (lowpassShelf != null) {
        // Recalculate and install the filter with new freq
        lpfd = new IIRLowpassFilterDesign(freq, sampleRate, DAMPINGFACTOR);
        lpfd.doFilterDesign();
        lowpassShelf.updateFilterCoefficients(lpfd);
    }
}
```

A new filter design is performed to reflect the newly selected frequency and the *updateFilterCoefficients* method is called on the runtime filter to change its parameters and thus its filtering characteristics. The next sample processed in the filters method (*doFilter*) will reflect the changes accordingly.

MISCELLANEOUS INFORMATION . . . .

Package:

craigl.filters

Source Files:

File Name	Description
IIRBandpassFilter.java	This is the runtime filtering code which solves the band-pass difference equation given the appropriate filter coefficient values. This code works on buffers of samples at a time, converting short input samples into double output samples.
IIRBandpassFilterDesign.java	Band-pass filter design class which generates the alpha, beta, and gamma parameters for a band-pass filter for a specific sample rate, center frequency, and Q.
IIRFilterBase.java	Abstract runtime filter base class which manages the filter coefficients for its subclasses. It also implements the three history values for both inputs and outputs.
IIRFilterDesignBase.java	Abstract base class from which all of the design classes are extended. Provides storage for the design parameters (alpha, beta, and gamma) and some helper methods used by all filter types.
IIRHighpassFilter.java	This is the runtime filtering code which solves the high-pass filter difference equation given the appropriate filter coefficient values. This code works on buffers of samples at a time, converting short input samples into double output samples.
IIRHighpassFilterDesign.java	High-pass filter design class which generates the alpha, beta, and gamma parameters for a high-pass filter for a specific sample rate, cutoff frequency, and damping factor.

File Name	Description
IIRLowpassFilter.java	This is the runtime filtering code which solves the low-pass filter difference equation given the appropriate filter coefficient values. This code works on buffers of samples at a time converting short input samples into double output samples.
IIRLowpassFilterDesign.java	Low-pass filter design class which generates the alpha, beta, and gamma parameters for a low-pass filter for a specific sample rate, cutoff frequency, and damping factor.

11 Audio Sources

INTRODUCTION . . . .

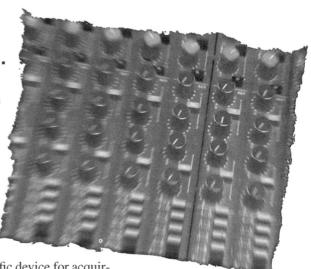

In this chapter, we discuss three class of devices that generate samples for subsequent processing: oscillator devices, which algorithmically generate samples representing sine waves, triangle waves, square waves, and noise; devices for reading AU and WAV audio files and converting their content into samples; and finally, a Microsoft Window's specific device for acquiring samples from the microphone/line input of a PC. Being source devices, only one can be used at a time and they must occupy the first position in any audio processing chain they are a part of. All of the devices described here produce 16-bit (short) samples to be compatible with all of the processing devices presented later. Source devices are specified with the "-i" or input command line switch to the *AudioTest* program of the last chapter.

Note: Additional platform-independent source devices based upon JMF2.0ea are described in Appendix B.

OSCILLATOR DEVICES . . . .

Two varieties of oscillators are described here, a single channel (monaural or mono) oscillator and a two channel, stereo, oscillator. The user interfaces for these devices are shown in Figure 11.1 and Figure 11.2, respectively. From the UI it is possible to set:

1. The sample rate of the generated samples.

2. The type of waveform being generated. Waveform types include a sine wave, triangle wave, square wave, or noise.

3. The frequency of the generated waveform. The stereo oscillator allows the frequency of the right and left channels to be independently adjustable.

4. The amplitude of the generated waveform. The stereo oscillator allows the amplitude of the right and left channels to be independently adjustable.

Figure 11.1 Mono Oscillator Device User Interface

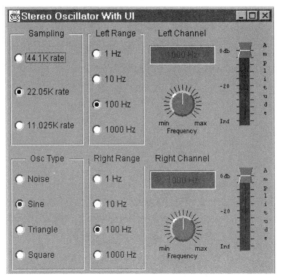

Figure 11.2 Stereo Oscillator Source Device User Interface

These parameters can all be changed in real time except for the sample rate—that can be changed only until the sample rate negotiation with the other devices in the processing chain has been completed. At that point, the sample rate is frozen for all devices in the audio processing chain. The effect of changing any of the runtime-adjustable parameters will be heard after a slight delay caused by sample buffering.

The oscillators use wavetable lookup to produce the selected waveform samples. The wavetable contains one period of the selected (periodic) waveform at the selected sample rate. Said another way, the wavetable contains samples for one second of a one Hz waveform of the selected type. Since the number of samples is directly related to the sample rate, the wavetable cannot be generated until the sample rate negotiations have been completed. If the type of waveform is changed at runtime, the wavetable is reloaded with samples of the new waveform and the production of the new samples begins.

Stepping through the wavetable at a rate controlled by the desired frequency and extracting samples generates a waveform. The samples are placed into a buffer that is passed to subsequent processing elements in the audio processing chain. The code that extracts and stores the samples is shown shortly after the discussion of how the wavetable samples are generated in the first place.

Each of the available waveforms that can occupy the wavetable is generated in a slightly different way. The sine wave, for example, is generated using the *Math.sin* function and a loop that guarantees a complete period of samples (360 degrees or 2π radians of sin values) is produced for the given sample rate. Since the *Math.sin* function returns a value between -1 and 1, each value must be multiplied by 32767 to scale it into the full-scale sample range. In other words, the amplitude of the sin wave samples are such that they occupy the full dynamic range possible using short 16-bit signed samples. In fact, all of the generated waveforms are scaled into this range in a similar fashion.

The first sine wave sample in the wavetable has a value of zero. The value of the samples then rises to 32767 at $\pi/2$ radians. From that point, sample values decrease back to zero at π radians. Sample values then become increasingly negative until $3\pi/2$, when they reach a value of -32767. Samples again become more positive as they move back towards zero at 2π radians.

Since the Java Math library doesn't provide a handy triangle wave function, triangle waves are generated in piecewise linear fashion. Each segment of the triangle wave is constructed separately and concatenated into a complete period of a triangle wave. For the triangle wave the initial sample value is zero and the values increase linearly (along the slope of a line) until reaching maximum value at the quarter waveform point. The slope then turns negative and the sample values decrease until the three quarter waveform point where they reach maximum negative value. The slope then turns positive again and the sample values increase towards zero. The maximum sample values are +/– 32767.

Square waves are constructed by alternating sample values between the values of 32767 and –32768. Samples have the value 32767 for the first half of the wavetable samples and the value –32768 for the second half. There are no transitional values for the square wave.

Noise is the final waveform that can occupy the wavetable. Here the Java *Random* class is used to produce pseudo-random numbers that fall into a Gaussian distribution. Thus white noise is produced. The random numbers are generated in the range 0 to 1 so they are multiplied by 65535 and then have 32768 subtracted from them. This produces a wavetable full of random samples in the proper range.

The code that fills the wavetable is shown below. This code is called when sample rate negotiations are completed and whenever the waveform type is changed by the user at runtime.

```
// Generate a wavetable for the waveform
protected void buildWaveTable() {
    if (type == NOTYPE)
        return;


    // Initialize waveTable index as wave table is changing
    pos = 0;

    // Allocate a table for 1 cycle or period of the waveform
    waveTable = new short[sampleRate];
    switch(type) {
        case NOISE:
            // Create a random number generator for returning gaussian
            // distributed numbers. The result is white noise.
            Random random = new Random();

            for (int sample = 0; sample < sampleRate; sample++)
                waveTable[sample] = (short)((65535.0 *
                                    random.nextGaussian()) - 32768);
            break;

        case SINEWAVE:
            double scale = (2.0 * Math.PI) / sampleRate;

            for (int sample = 0; sample < sampleRate; sample++)
                waveTable[sample] = (short)(32767.0 * Math.sin(sample *
                                                    scale));
            break;
```

```
case TRIANGLEWAVE:
    double sign = 1.0;
    double value = 0.0;

    int oneQuarterWave = sampleRate / 4;
    int threeQuarterWave = (3 * sampleRate) / 4;

    scale = 32767.0 / oneQuarterWave;
    for (int sample = 0; sample < sampleRate; sample++) {
        if ((sample > oneQuarterWave) && (sample <=
                                        threeQuarterWave))
            sign = -1.0;
        else
            sign = 1.0;

        value += sign * scale;
        waveTable[sample] = (short) value;
    }
    break;

case SQUAREWAVE:
    for (int sample = 0; sample < sampleRate; sample++) {
        if (sample < sampleRate / 2)
            waveTable[sample] = 32767;
        else
            waveTable[sample] = -32768;
    }
    break;
    }
}
```

Since the size of the wavetable is the sample rate, you can understand why the wavetable cannot be generated until after the sample rate has been negotiated and frozen.

With an initialized wavetable available, samples of the waveform in the wavetable can be provided to subsequent processing stages or devices in the audio processing chain. Pulling samples from the oscillator is accomplished by the next device in the audio processing chain calling the *getSamples* method in the oscillator. This method fills a buffer with the requested number of samples. The frequency of the samples provided is a function of which samples are picked from the wavetable for return. As mentioned, the wavetable contains a 1 Hz representation of the selected waveform. If all of the samples in the wavetable were returned sequentially, the result would be a frequency of 1 Hz. If every other sample were to be returned, the perceived frequency would be 2 Hz, and so on. If 1000 Hz is desired, the samples returned would be 1000 samples apart in the wavetable. A class variable *pos* keeps track of the index in the wavetable where the next sample should be fetched. *pos* is incremented by the frequency between samples and is kept within the wavetable by a simple range check. The *getSamples* method is shown below:

```
public int getSamples(short [] buffer, int length) {

    int sample = 0;
    int count = length;

    while(count- != 0) {

        buffer[sample++] = (short)(amplitudeAdj * waveTable[pos]);

        pos += frequency;
        if (pos >= sampleRate)
            pos -= sampleRate;
    }
    return length;
}
```

The code above is contained in the file *Oscillator.java*. The code that implements the mono oscillator's UI is contained in the file *OscillatorWithUI.java*.

Waveform Fidelity

One might be interested in how accurate this waveform generation technique is. One way to get a qualitative measure of waveform fidelity is to examine the samples produced using the sample scope of the next chapter. This is a simple thing to set up using the *AudioTest* program described previously. Using the command line below will allow the samples produced by the oscillator to be examined with the sample scope and to be heard as well. The command line says to use the mono oscillator as the sample source, monitor the samples with the sample scope, and play the samples using the winplayer device.

```
java craigl.test.AudioTest -i osc -m scope -o winplayer
```

With this done, as soon as the play button on the *WinPlayer* is clicked, the scope will trigger and the samples can be examined. As will be described in the next chapter, the zoom controls and the scroll bar on the sample scope are used to position the waveform for viewing. The time value displayed in the upper right of the scope is the time interval that the samples currently on the display represent.

A generated 1000 Hz sine wave looks like Figure 11.3.

A 1000 Hz triangle wave looks like Figure 11.4.

A 1000 Hz square wave looks like Figure 11.5.

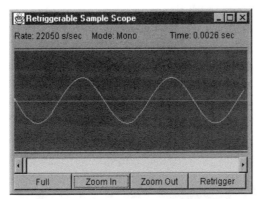

Figure 11.3   A 1000 Hz Sine Wave

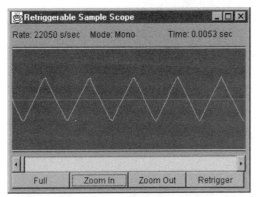

Figure 11.4   A 1000 Hz Triangle Wave

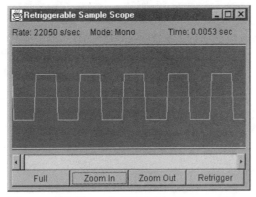

Figure 11.5   A 1000 Hz Square Wave

And finally, noise looks like Figure 11.6.

A more quantitative measurement of waveform fidelity can be had using the spectrum analyzer described in the next chapter. Since a pure sine wave should contain only a single frequency, it is obvious from Figure 11.7 that our generated sine wave is not absolutely pure, as harmonics of the sine wave's fundamental frequency are evident.

What the spectrum analyzer display in Figure 11.7 shows is that there are sonic artifacts in our generated sine wave but that they are at least 32 dB down from the fundamental frequency's level. Since –32 dB represents power, the ratio of the strongest non-fundamental component to the fundamental component is approximately 6.3×10^{-4}. The second harmonic of the 1000 Hz sine wave occurs at 2000 Hz. The component at that frequency is over –128 dB down. All of these spurious components contribute to distortion of the generated sine wave. Fortunately, the generated waveforms are pure enough for our intended use.

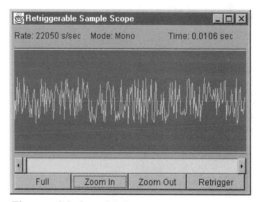

Figure 11.6   Noise

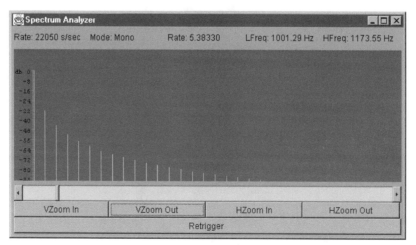

Figure 11.7   Generated Sine Wave Spectrum Analysis

Returning to our discussion of the mono oscillator shown in Figure 11.1, Table 11.1 describes this device's front panel controls and indicators.

Table 11.1   *Oscillator Front Panel Controls and Indicators*

Front Panel Controls and Indicators	Description
Sampling Rate Control Group	These three radio buttons are used to select the sampling rate the oscillator samples should be produced at. Only one sample rate can be used at one time. Once negotiation with the other devices in the audio processing chain has been performed, these controls are disabled to prevent any further change by the user.
Osc Type Control Group	These radio buttons determine the waveform to be used in the production of samples. Noise, sine wave, triangle wave, or square wave can be selected. Only one waveform type can be used at a time. The user can change the selected waveform at any time.
Freq Range Control Group	The selection of frequency range affects the frequencies that can be set with the frequency pot. These buttons allow the single frequency pot to function as a course, medium, and fine frequency control.
Frequency Indicator	The current oscillator frequency is displayed in the *ReadoutLabel* indicator.
Frequency Pot	Using this pot and the frequency range buttons allows the user to dial in the exact frequency of interest.
Amplitude Slide Pot	This control allows the amplitude of the generated samples to be reduced in level from their full-scale values. This slide pot utilizes a pseudo-audio taper as required by audio level controls.

Use with the AudioTest Program

When using the *AudioTest* program, the oscillator is included in the signal path by specifying the command line switch "*–i osc*". To hear the samples produced by the oscillator a command line as follows could be used:

```
java craigl.test.AudioTest -i osc -o winplayer
```

Then when the *Play* button on the *WinPlayer* UI is clicked, you should be able to hear the oscillator at work producing samples. As the samples are being played, the frequency and/or the oscillator waveform can be altered and the effect can be heard in real time.

Stereo Oscillator

The stereo oscillator device is very similar to the mono oscillator device described previously except it allows a different frequency and amplitude of samples to be generated for each channel. You can think of the stereo oscillator as two mono oscillators in a single package with the exception that both the channels must use the same basic wave shape. Even this limitation could be removed with a little more programming effort, if independent waveforms were necessary.

A stereo oscillator finds use mainly in troubleshooting other processing devices. It is very helpful to have a different frequency on each channel when trying to solve crosstalk problems during processing effect development. If the left channel, for example, is set to 1000 Hz and the right channel to 3000 Hz and you can hear both frequencies on both channels in the output, you can be pretty sure you are mixing samples together when you probably shouldn't be.

To implement different frequencies and output amplitudes for both channels, each channel maintains its own wavetable index variable called *posL* and *posR* and its own amplitude multipliers, called *leftAmplitudeAdj* and *rightAmplitudeAdj*, respectively. With individual index values, each channel can sequence through the wavetable at its own rate and adjust the amplitude of the returned samples independently.

The *getSamples* method for the stereo oscillator is as follows:

```
public int getSamples(short [] buffer, int length) {

    int sample = 0;
    int count = length;
    while(count- != 0) {
        if (!toggle) {
            toggle = true;
            buffer[sample++] = (short)(leftAmplitudeAdj * waveTable[posL]);

            posL += frequencyL;
            if (posL >= sampleRate)
                posL -= sampleRate;

        } else{
            toggle = false;
            buffer[sample++] = (short)(rightAmplitudeAdj * waveTable[posR]);
```

```
        posR += frequencyR;
        if (posR >= sampleRate)
            posR -= sampleRate;
    }
  }
  return length;
}
```

Here you can see how the samples placed into the buffer for return are alternately gotten from the left and the right sample sources. As you will recall, stereo samples are interleaved in the architecture used in this book.

The code for the stereo oscillator is contained in the file *StereoOscillator.java*. The code that implements the stereo oscillator's UI is contained in the file *StereoOscillatorWithUI.java*.

It should be noted that both the mono and the stereo oscillator UI classes implement the *NegotiationCompleteIF* interface. This means these classes must implement a method called *signalNegotiationComplete* that is called by the base *Oscillator* class after sample rate negotiation has finished. Calling *signalNegotiationComplete* results in the sample rate radio buttons in the UI being disabled and therefore preventing the user from changing the sample rate again.

AUDIO FILE READING DEVICE . . . .

Computer files are the de facto standard mechanism for exchanging digital audio data in the world today. Regardless of the medium on which the files reside (CDs, DATs, over the Internet, etc.), files contain the bulk of the digital audio data available. A great many different types of audio files currently exist, the two most common being AU files, and WAV files but MP3 and real media files are quickly gaining in popularity.

Audio files consist of a physical format and data. The physical format describes which portions of the information in the file contain control information and which contain audio data. In some cases, the audio data is compressed and in other cases it isn't. The control information extracted from the audio file will indicate whether the data is compressed or not, along with other important information about the contained audio. The minimum amount of information needed to decode the audio data includes:

1. The format of the data in the file. This can mean both the data format (PCM vs. non-PCM) and/or whether the data is compressed or not.

2. The sample rate of the data. This is the rate at which the data contained in the file was sampled and therefore the rate at which it should be played back.

3. The number of channels the data represents. This is usually 1, 2, or 4, meaning mono data, stereo data, or four channel (quad) data.

4. The number of bits contained in each sample of the data. This can range from 8 bits/sample all the way to 32 bits/channel.

To decode a digital audio file for playback, the file must be parsed for control information that is used to extract the audio samples. The parsing techniques, as one might expect, vary from one type of audio file to the next.

The treatment of audio files in this chapter (and in this book for that matter) has been intentionally kept short. A whole book could be written about extracting sample data from the plethora of audio file types in existence today. That would be a book substantially different than this one, however. Here, we will concentrate on AU and WAV files, knowing that any other file type could be processed using the techniques presented. If you wrote the code to parse a new file type, it would be trivial to add that new code to what is presented in this chapter and then be able to utilize the new file type as well as AU and WAV files. For my purposes, AU and WAV files are all that I have needed or desired. The *AudioFileDecoder* class (discussed shortly) was developed to make the audio file parsing framework extendable.

A single source device has been developed that knows how to read most AU and WAV files and to provide the samples for processing. The simple UI for this device is shown in Figure 11.8. The code for this device is contained in the *FileReaderWithUI* class and in the file *FileReaderWithUI.java*. It is this code that would need to be extended if a new audio file format was to be supported. Being a source device, it must occupy the first position in any audio processing chain in which it participates. The use of this device is signaled to the *AudioTest* program with the command line switch "-i file". The *FileReaderWithUI* class's UI will then pop up for selection of the audio file to use for processing.

Note and Warning

Normal use of the *FileReaderWithUI* device is to select and process the file one or more times during a single session with the *AudioTest* program. Once the play button on the sink device in the audio processing chain is clicked, negotiation of the sample rate and the number of channels is frozen. The content of the selected audio file is used to set these values for the whole chain. A problem arises, however, if a new audio file with a

Figure 11.8   Simple UI for AU and WAV file player

different sample rate and/or different number of channels is selected before ending the *AudioTest* program. Less than desirable results will be obtained under these circumstances as the negotiation process is not performed again and the processing devices in the audio processing chain are set to process the samples under erroneous conditions. However, if another file is selected that happens to use the same sample rate and number of channels as the originally selected file, playback will occur normally.

FileReaderWithUI Class

The *FileReaderWithUI* class is unique in that it is not extended from *AbstractAudio* but still must be linked into the chain with other *AbstractAudio* devices to perform its function. This is accomplished by instantiating a placeholder *AbstractAudio* device called *BogusDevice* and providing a method on the *FileReaderWithUI* class (getAA) to return the *BogusDevice* instance. The code from *AudioTest* that shows how this device is linked into the chain is shown here:

```
FileReaderWithUI frwui = new FileReaderWithUI(blinker);
ll.addElement(frwui.getAA());
frwui.showUI(true);
```

The *getAA* method returns the bogus *AbstractAudio* device instance and therefore allows the *FileReaderWithUI* device to be linked into an audio processing chain. Later, when the actual *AbstractAudio* device that will be used to decode the audio file is identified and instantiated, it will replace the *BogusDevice* in the audio processing chain.

FileReaderWithUI provides a simple UI containing a single *Select File* button and a green LED. This class doesn't provide any audio file decoding but it does select the classes that do. When the *Select File* button is clicked in the UI, a standard file selection dialog box is presented to allow an audio file to be selected. Once a file is selected, it is checked to see if this code can handle the file format. This check is performed by calling static methods in the individual file decoding classes. Each supported audio file format would need to provide such a method so the correct file decoder can be determined and instantiated.

Here, the choices are AU files or WAV files. Files that are selected that are not of these formats will cause a message box to pop up with an error message stating that.

If the selected file is of the correct format, a reader class (extended from *AbstractAudio*) for the format will be instantiated and used to replace the *BogusDevice* previously in place. Then, when the *getSamples* method is called by subsequent processing stages, it is directed to a real *AbstractAudio* device which decodes audio samples from the audio file.

While the audio file is being played, the *Select File* button will be disabled and the LED will blink. When the file comes to the end, the *signalReadComplete* method is called by the decoder which stops the LED from blinking and re-enables the *Select File* button.

Table 11.2 descriles the controls and indicators of the *FileReadersWithUI* device, with which the user interacts.

Table 11.2   FileReaderWithUI Front Panel Controls and Indicators

Front Panel Controls and Indicators	Description
Reading Indicator LED	This green LED blinks while the audio data is being readied for reading from the audio file.
Select File Button	Clicking this button brings up the open file dialog box with which the user selects the audio file to process or to listen to.

Use with the AudioTest Program

When using the *AudioTest* program, the *FileReaderWithUI* device is included in the signal path by specifying the command line switch "*–i file*". To play back an audio file without any processing being performed, the following command line can be used:

```
java craigl.test.AudioTest -i file -o winplayer
```

The sequence of events should be that you first select the file to play by clicking the *Select File* button in the *FileReaderWithUI* interface. A file dialog will be presented with which you select the file of your choice. Then when the *Play* button on the *WinPlayer* UI is clicked, you should be able to hear audio file being played. That is, of course, if the audio file is of a format that can be processed.

The AudioFileDecoder Class

The *AudioFileDecoder* class was developed to make adding additional audio file formats to the infrastructure straightforward. This abstract class extends *AbstractAudio* and adds some common functionality required by all audio file decoders. Any new file decoder that you develop should extend from *AudioFileDecoder*. The use of this class forces derived classes to implement a *getSamples* method for returning samples to other processing stages, an *initializeDecoder* method for preparing the decoder needed to extract the samples from the audio file, and a *reset* method that returns the decoder to an initial state so that the audio file data can be reread. The *AURead* and the *WaveRead* classes both extended this common base class. You can examine their code to see how your file decoders should be structured.

Data Decoders

A data decoder is code that converts the byte data read from an audio file into samples appropriate for processing with our system. The purpose of the *initializeDecoder* method is to identify from the format data (metadata) contained in the audio file the type of decoder required to extract (and convert) the samples from the file. Life would be simple if every audio file used the same decoder, but this simply is not the case. Issues such as sample bit width, unsigned vs. signed sample values, byte orientation (little vs. big endian), and compression must be handled by the decoder in such a manner that 16-bit signed integer linear PCM values (shorts) are returned for each sample.

Currently there are five decoders defined that handle most of the AU and WAV audio files that we are interested in. Of course additional decoders could be added as the need arises. The decoders provided with the book are shown in Table 11.3.

Table 11.3   Decoders for AU and WAV Files

Decoder	Function
DecodeG711MuLaw.java	Decodes G711 8-bit mu law data.
DecodePcm16BESigned.java	Decodes 16-bit signed PCM samples that are in big endian format.
DecodePcm16LESigned.java	Decodes 16-bit signed PCM samples that are in little endian format.
DecodePcm8Signed.java	Decodes 8-bit signed PCM samples.
DecodePcm8UnSigned.java	Decodes 8-bit unsigned PCM samples.

The majority of the code within a decoder is involved with bit manipulations of all kinds. If you are interested in learning how these decoders work in detail, see the appropriate Java files.

The *initializeDecoder* method must read enough of the audio file to determine which decoder to instantiate to do the sample conversion. Then the *getSamples* method calls the decoder to retrieve a requested number of samples to return to the next processing stage.

AU Files and the AURead Class

The AU file format has been around for a long time and is the format for audio files used by Sun Microsystems and Next Computers. The format of AU files is simple and easy to decode.

The AU File Format

The format of the AU file consists of a four-byte tag value containing the character string ".snd," followed by six four-byte integer (big endian) informational items, followed by the audio data. The informational data includes:

1. An offset value that tells where the audio data begins in the file.
2. A count of the total bytes of audio data in the file.
3. A value indicating the format of the audio data.
4. The sample rate of the audio data in samples per second.
5. The count of the number of channels present in the audio data.
6. An optional 4-byte storage area for padding. The offset value above will take the presence of this padding into consideration.
7. The sound data.

The *AURead* class provides a static method with the signature

```
public static boolean isAUFile(String fileName)
```

which is used to tell if the file specified by name is an AU audio file. This method is called from *FileReaderWithUI* to make the AU file determination. This method works by checking the tag at the beginning of the file for the ".snd" character sequence. The code from *AURead.java* is shown below:

```
// Determine if file is a AU file
public static boolean isAUFile(String fileName) {

    // Open input stream
    try {

        // Create data stream
        ConvertDataInputStream cdis = new ConvertDataInputStream(fileName);
```

```
    // Read signature from file
    long signature = cdis.readBEInteger(4);

    // Close the file
    cdis.close();

    // See if there is a signature match
    return (signature == WaveRead.chunkName('.','s','n','d'));
  }
  catch(IOException ioe) {
    o(ioe.getMessage());
    return false;
  }
}
```

It is the reading of the informational items in the AU file (by the *initializeDecoder* method) that allows the proper decoder to be identified for use. Specifically, the format value describes the type of audio data in the file and from this value the appropriate decoder is chosen. Table 11.4 shows some of the formats AU files can contain.

Table 11.4   Varieties of AU File Formats

Format Code	Description
1	8-bit mu law G.711*
2	8-bit linear PCM*
3	16-bit linear PCM*
4	24-bit linear PCM
5	32-bit linear PCM
6	Floating-point samples
7	Double-precision floating-point samples
11	8-bit fixed-point samples
12	16-bit fixed-point samples
13	24-bit fixed-point samples
14	32-bit fixed-point samples
18	16-bit linear PCM with emphasis
19	16-bit linear PCM compressed
20	16-bit linear PCM with emphasis and compressed

Table 11.4   (continued)

Format Code	Description
23	ADPCM G.721
24	ADPCM G.722
25	ADPCM G.723.3
26	ADPCM G.723.5
27	8-bit A law G.711

* denotes the formats supported by code in this book

By reading the code in *AURead.java*, you can see how the *getSamples*, *reset*, and *initializeDecoder* methods work together to extract samples from an AU file.

WAV Files and the WaveRead Class

WAV or wave files are the audio files of choice on the Microsoft Windows platform. The WAV file format is an extension to the RIFF file format introduced by Electronic Arts years ago for the Amiga computer. The RIFF file is broken down in chunks of data, each with their own format. Chunks are nested in a RIFF file and each chunk has a size value associated with it. Chunk size specifies the size of all chunks and/or data residing within the chunk. Unlike AU files, WAV files don't have a standard order for the data that makes up the audio file. For this reason, code that decodes WAV files must be more dynamic as it is reading the file and cannot make assumptions about the order in which certain chunks appear.

Chunks are identified by a four-character name. Just as AU files are identified by the four-character sequence, ".snd," a RIFF chunk is named "RIFF," a wave chunk is named "WAVE," a format chunk is named "fmt," and a data chunk is named "data." NOTE: Case and extra spaces in chunk names are significant. Note also that since four-byte integers are read from the audio file, the chunk name data must be read in big endian format. Other informational items read from WAV files are in little endian format.

In the *WaveRead* class, we are only interested in a small variety of chunk types. Any chunks that are found in the file that the code doesn't understand are simply ignored. Specifically, we are interested in verifying that the audio file contains a container chunk called RIFF which is tagged as containing WAVE data, a format or fmt chunk which describes the audio data contained in the file, and a data chunk which contains the encoded audio data. With these chunks in hand, we can extract the audio samples from the WAV file.

The format chunk (named "fmt") contains the informational items that describe the audio data contained in the file. The items consist of two- and four-byte integer values in little endian format. The code from *WaveRead.java* that reads these values from the audio file is shown below. *cdis* is a reference to a *ConvertDataInputStream* object used to randomly access the audio file.

```
// Read the important format parameters
format = (int) cdis.readLEInteger(2);
numberOfChannels = (int) cdis.readLEInteger(2);
sampleRate = (int) cdis.readLEInteger(4);
avgBytesPerSecond = (int) cdis.readLEInteger(4);
blockAlignment = (int) cdis.readLEInteger(2);
bitsPerSample = (int) cdis.readLEInteger(2);

// Skip any other data in this chunk
if (chunkSize > 16)
cdis.skipBytes((int) (chunkSize - 16));
```

All of these items must be read from the format chunk; however, the *avgBytesPerSecond* and the *blockAlignment* entries are not used in this code. Most of the informational items are the same as those used in AU files. The format entry, however, is WAV-file specific. Some of the varieties of WAV file formats in use today are shown in Table 11.5.

Table 11.5   Varieties of WAV File Formats

Format Code	Description
0	Unknown and illegal
1	PCM*
2	Microsoft ADPCM
6	8-bit A law G.711
7	8-bit mu law G.711*

* denotes the formats supported by code in this book

Once the format of the audio data is known, a decoder of the proper variety can be instantiated for use. Then, when a data chunk is found which contains the binary data, the decoder will know how to interpret it.

The *WaveReader* class also has a static method for determining if a file is a wave file or not. This method's signature is:

```
public static boolean isWaveFile(String fileName)
```

This method validates a WAV file by first checking to see if the specified file contains a RIFF chunk and that the RIFF chunk is tagged as containing WAVE data. If both of these checks succeed, a boolean true is returned indicating the file is probably a wave file. If either of these checks fail, false is returned instead.

AUDIO ACQUISITION DEVICE . . . .

No sound processing system would be complete without some method for acquiring digital audio samples from a live audio source via the sound hardware built into virtually every modern computer. This facility is useful for converting live sound into digital audio files for subsequent playback or for allowing live sounds to be the source of samples processed in an audio processing chain. Other uses of an audio acquisition device include the guitar tuner and phrase sampler from section three of this book. Suffice it to say that digitization of live sound is an important aspect of any sound processing system.

Throughout this discussion, the expressions "sample acquisition," "sound acquisition," and "audio acquisition" all mean the same thing and refer to the process of using the sound hardware in a computer to digitize samples of the audio for subsequent storage or processing.

While I was writing the code for this book I tried to figure out how best to provide audio acquisition functionality. I wanted to be as platform-independent as possible as well as Virtual Machine (VM)-independent. Here, however, I ran into problems. I didn't want to be tied directly to Microsoft's VM although that would have been the easiest way to get digital audio input. Unfortunately (fortunately?), I use the Sun VM for all my other development work so using the Microsoft VM was not possible. My next thought was to use JMF1.1 (Java Media Framework), but it was not without its own set of problems and limitations. While JMF1.1 did provide digital audio playback, it didn't have any facility for recording. Later, Javasound was released and it provided some rudimentary sound recording capabilities. Unfortunately, it could not coexist with JMF1.1, so I could have platform-independent sound recording or sound playback, but not both. Finally, since the Microsoft Windows platform is the most ubiquitous, I decided to write platform-specific code for doing recording since that could coexist with JMF for playback. The code presented in this section is one of only two pieces of platform-specific code presented in this book. The other piece is the *winplayer* device that will be described later in this book. I'm sure as Javasound matures, this code can be replaced with a platform-independent version. For now, this is what we've got.

Note: Appendix B shows how platform-independent acquisition and playback are now possible using JMF2.0ea.

To provide Microsoft Windows-specific sound recording capability required the use of Java Native Methods (JNI) and the development of a DLL to interface my Java code with the Win32 sound recording API. *WinRecorder.java* is the Java side of the native method interface and *winrecorderdll.dll* (built from *winrecorder.c*) is the interface DLL providing the native methods. This means that you must have a copy of this DLL for the sound recording mechanism to work and the DLL must reside in the *craig\winrecorder* subdirectory. This also means that this code will only run on a WINTEL PC at the present time.

WinRecorder Class

As mentioned, the *WinRecorder* is the Java side of the native method interface for sample acquisition. This class extends *AbstractAudio* so it can be linked with other devices for processing digital audio samples. Table 11.6 itemizes the important methods provided by this class along with a brief explanation of what they do.

Table 11.6   WinRecorder Class Methods

Method	Function
boolean hasSoundCard()	Returns true if the PC on which it is called has one or more sound cards; false if the PC doesn't have sound hardware.
boolean initRecorder()	Attempts to initialize the sound hardware with the sample rate and number of channels stored in the class. True is returned for success.
boolean closeRecorder()	Called to close down the sound hardware. True is returned if operation is successful.
void minMaxSamplingRate(MyInt min, MyInt max, MyInt preferred)	This method is called during negotiation to convey the sample rate the *WinRecorder* device wants to work at to the rest of the devices in the processing chain.
void minMaxChannels(MyInt min, MyInt max, MyInt preferred)	This method is called during negotiation to convey the number of channels the *WinRecorder* device wants to work at to the rest of the devices in the processing chain.
int getSamples(short [] buffer, int length)	Called by the next device in the processing chain to retrieve samples from the *WinRecorder*. Here the length parameter is ignored and AudioConstants.SAMPLE-BUFFERSIZE samples are always returned instead.

Table 11.6   (continued)

Method	Function
int getSamplesWithOffset(short [] buffer, int offset)	Called by the next device in the processing chain to retrieve samples from the *WinRecorder*. Here the length parameter is ignored and AudioConstants.SAMPLE-BUFFERSIZE samples are always returned instead. The newly acquired samples are stored at *offset* in *buffer*.

The *WinRecorder* class is designed to be used in a stand-alone manner or in conjunction with the *WinRecorderWithUI* class described below.

The native methods are coded in a DLL called *winrecorderdll.dll* that is implemented in the file *winrecorder.c*. If you are interested in how the Win32 portion of this code is written, you can consult that file.

WinRecorderWithUI

The *WinRecorderWithUI* class provides a user interface for operating the sample acquisition device in the context of a processing chain. The UI for this device is shown is Figure 11.9. The function of the controls and indicators provided in the UI are listed in Table 11.7.

Figure 11.9   Windows Recorder/Sampler Device User Interface

Table 11.7   WinRecorderWithUI Front Panel Controls and Indicators

Front Panel Controls and Indicators	Description
Sampling Control Group	These three radio buttons display the rate at which the audio input will be sampled. Choices are 11.025K (11025), 22.05K (22050), or 44.1K (44100) samples per second. The rate is set via command line parameters when using the *AudioTest* program or in the constructor of the class.
Mode Control Group	These two radio buttons control whether mono or stereo samples are acquired from the audio input.
Recording LED	This LED glows red during recording and green when not recording.
Stop Button	This button terminates sample acquisition. The play button on the sink device starts acquisition and this button terminates it. Clicking this button causes an EOF indicator to be placed in the sample stream.

Use with the AudioTest Program

When using the *AudioTest* program, the audio acquisition device is included in the signal path by specifying the command line switch "*–i mic sr chs.*" The *mic* argument identifies the audio acquisition device, the *sr* argument is the sample rate to use, and *chs* should be set to one or two to indicate mono or stereo acquisition. To store the acquired samples as an audio file, this command line would be used:

```
java craigl.test.AudioTest -i mic sr chs -o file
```

Then, when the *Go* button on the sink device is clicked, the samples acquired from the microphone or line input are streamed to the *FileWriterWithUI* device and stored in the audio file of your choice. Clicking the *Stop* button in the *WinRecorderWithUI* user interface terminates sample acquisition.

MISCELLANEOUS INFORMATION . . . .

Source Files and Packages:

File Name	Package	Description
AbstractDecoderIF.java	craigl.utils	Interface specification that all audio file decoders must implement.
AudioFileDecoder.java	craigl.utils	Abstract class on which all audio file decoders are built.
AURead.java	craigl.au	*AbstractAudio* device for decoding various (but not all) AU file formats.
ConvertDataInputStream.java	craigl.utils	Extension of *RandomAccessFile* class which contains methods for reading 4-byte integer values in both little and big endian formats.
DecodeG711MuLaw.java	craigl.utils	Decoder for 8-bit mu law data.
DecodePcm8Signed.java	craigl.utils	PCM decoder for 8-bit signed sample values.
DecodePcm8UnSigned.java	craigl.utils	PCM decoder for 8-bit unsigned sample values.
DecodePcm16BESigned.java	craigl.utils	PCM decoder for 16-bit signed sample values in big endian format.
DecodePcm16LESigned.java	craigl.utils	PCM decoder for 16-bit signed sample values in little endian format.
FileReaderWithUI.java	craigl.filereader	Audio file reader class which provides a simple UI for selecting audio files. This class also selects and instantiates the file decoder appropriate for the selected audio file.
Oscillator.java	craigl.osc	*Oscillator* class which provides basic single channel oscillator operation.
OscillatorWithUI.java	craigl.osc	UI code for the single channel or mono oscillator.
RecorderIF.java	craigl.winrecorder	A simple interface for passing recording status to the *WinRecorderWithUI* device.
StereoOscillator.java	craigl.osc	Extension of *Oscillator* providing dual channel oscillator.

File Name	Package	Description
StereoOscillatorWithUI.java	craigl.osc	UI code for the two channel or stereo oscillator.
WaveRead.java	craigl.wave	*AbstractAudio* device for decoding various (but not all) WAV file formats.
winrecorder.c	N/A	C code for the winrecorderdll DLL that is the native method interface to the Microsoft Windows (waveIn) sound recording subsystem.
WinRecorder.java	craigl.winrecorder	The Java side of the Microsoft Windows specific audio recording native method interface.
WinRecorderUI.java	craigl.winrecorder	The user interface for an *AbstractAudio* device (*WinRecorder*) that acquires samples from hardware and makes them available for subsequent processing.

12 Audio Monitors

INTRODUCTION . . . .

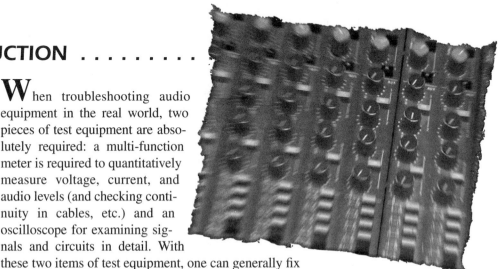

When troubleshooting audio equipment in the real world, two pieces of test equipment are absolutely required: a multi-function meter is required to quantitatively measure voltage, current, and audio levels (and checking continuity in cables, etc.) and an oscilloscope for examining signals and circuits in detail. With these two items of test equipment, one can generally fix most broken audio devices. More subtle problems might require other, more specialized, test equipment, including a spectrum analyzer or distortion analyzer for analysis. Subtle problems are usually much harder to solve than more blatant problems.

In general, test equipment like an oscilloscope can be used in two different ways, for qualitative measurements and for quantitative measurements. Qualitative measurements give a quick indication of signal flow through a device. For example, it might be helpful to know that a signal enters one end of a circuit but doesn't leave it at the other end. An oscilloscope can give you a quick indication of this.

Quantitative measurements are sometimes necessary to determine why a circuit is malfunctioning. Measuring the bias voltage on a transistor in a preamp or the plate voltage of a power amplifier tube are two examples. In these cases, if the voltages are out of range, the devices will malfunction. Both oscilloscopes and multi-function meters are good for these types of quantitative measurements.

In summary, qualitative measurements help isolate the symptoms of a problem, whereas quantitative measurements can help find the cause.

Troubleshooting audio equipment is not usually difficult if one has the correct test equipment and goes about troubleshooting in a logical way. This is equally true if what is being troubleshot is a software audio device under development (like those presented in this book) or a real hardware audio device. The thought processes are the same in both cases. In fact, the logical processes involved in troubleshooting are similar to the logical steps in a binary search algorithm. That is, the system is continuously subdivided into two functional parts; the part that works and the part that doesn't. Once it is known that a portion of the device works, that portion is ignored and the portion of the device that doesn't work is again subdivided into working and non-working parts. This process continues until the device can no longer be subdivided. You then know where the problem lies and hopefully how to fix it. This may mean replacing a blown-out component in a hardware device or rewriting a line of code in a software device.

The gist of this discussion is that to find problems in audio processing devices it is often necessary to have appropriate test equipment available. The monitor devices presented in this chapter, a sample scope (a simple sample oscilloscope) and a spectrum analyzer, are just such tools for troubleshooting the audio processor devices presented in this book. These monitor devices can be used for qualitative as well as some quantitative measurements in the sample domain. Details of their operation and usage are presented.

MONITOR DEVICE RECAP ·

As described in Chapter 9, monitor devices are *AbstractAudio* devices that can be inserted into one or more places in an audio signal chain for purposes of monitoring the samples flowing through them. Unlike processor devices, monitor devices don't modify the samples in any way. They are in essence a portal through which samples can be acquired, analyzed, and subsequently displayed. Monitor devices like the sample scope and the spectrum analyzer take a snapshot of samples in time and display them accordingly. These devices can be retriggered on demand by the user whenever new information is required.

Other monitor devices could also be developed using the techniques presented in this chapter. A meter that could display average, peak, and RMS values of the samples, or a distortion analyzer come to mind. Since troubleshooting software audio processor devices is so similar to troubleshooting hardware devices, any test equipment used in the hardware domain could probably be of use in the sample domain as well.

THE SAMPLE SCOPE ·

In the real world, oscilloscopes are one of the most important tools available for developing and troubleshooting electronic hardware. The reason is simple. The human brain is much better at understanding phenomena it can see than those it cannot. An oscilloscope allows signals to be displayed that happen far too quickly for the unaided human eye to see and thus gives users insight into the domain of subsecond phenomena from which they would ordinarily be excluded. Current oscilloscope technology allows viewing of signals in the picosecond (10^{-12} second) range.

So just as viewing signals in electronic circuitry is important to understanding their behavior, viewing digital samples in our domain also aids in our understanding of what is taking place. It is one thing to be able to hear samples as they are being processed. It is quite another to be able to see them. A visual representation of a stream of digital audio samples can help us understand why something sounds the way it does, right or wrong. And if what we hear is wrong, the visual image of the samples may help us determine what is wrong and possibly how it might be corrected. In fact, the sample scope (short for oscilloscope) presented in this chapter has been used numerous times during the development of code for this book to isolate obscure bugs. Some of these uses will be described later in this chapter. The user interface of the sample scope is shown in Figure 12.1.

The sample scope presented is a monitor device. That is, it does not alter the samples passing through it in any way. The scope simply takes a snapshot in time of the samples passing through it when triggering occurs and displays that snap shot. It can be retriggered by the user at any time to acquire another snapshot for display. It should be noted that this device is crude in its design and offers little in the way of standard oscilloscope functionality. However, it does offer enough functionality to be very useful and is therefore a valuable addition to any audio toolbox even in its current form. Possible enhancements to the basic design are discussed.

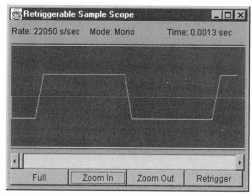

Figure 12.1   The Sample Scope's User Interface

Operation

The operation of the sample scope can best be understood by breaking its functionality into two pieces, sample acquisition and sample display. Each of these is described below.

Sample Acquisition

Because the sample scope is extended from *AbstractAudio*, it can be linked with other *AbstractAudio* derivative devices to form an audio processing chain for the purpose of monitoring digital audio samples. Extending *AbstractAudio* means that the scope must implement a *getSamples()* method for propagating samples and must also have the means for querying the signal path as to the agreed-upon sample rate and number of channels. Sample propagation and audio processing chain querying are both important to the operation of the scope.

The *getSamples()* method from *Scope.java* is shown below. Note how samples pass through this device unaltered and how, when triggered, samples are copied into a separate buffer set aside for viewing. Finally, you can see that a new UI for the scope is created each time the scope is triggered. Retriggering the scope from the UI causes the trigger flag to reset and causes the destruction of the scope's UI. The next time this *getSamples()* method is called, the scope will again trigger, the new data will be copied, and a new *ScopeUI* will be created for display of the new samples.

```java
// Grab samples from previous stage and store for scope
public int getSamples(short [] buffer, int length) {

    if (length == 0)
        return 0;

    // Get samples from the previous stage
    int samples = previous.getSamples(buffer, length);

    // See if scope should trigger
    if (!tf.trigger()) {
        // Indicate scope has triggered
        tf.triggered();

        // Clone the array for the scope
        short [] newBuffer = new short [samples];

        // Copy the data
        System.arraycopy(buffer, 0, newBuffer, 0, length);
```

```
        // Kick off UI for the scope
        sui = new ScopeUI(this, name, newBuffer, tf, sampleRate,
                                                   numberOfChannels);
    }
    // Return samples read
    return samples;
}
```

The scope determines the working parameters of the signal path by overloading two methods provided in *AbstractAudio*. These methods, *minMaxSamplingRate* and *minMaxChannels*, are called during the audio processing chain negotiation process whereby all devices decide on a mutually agreeable format for processing of the audio. This negotiation process is described in detail in Chapter 9. The scope overloads these methods so as to extract the negotiated values for its own use. The code for these simple methods is shown below:

```
// Overload this method to get the current sample rate
public void minMaxSamplingRate(MyInt min, MyInt max, MyInt preferred) {

    super.minMaxSamplingRate(min, max, preferred);
    sampleRate = preferred.getValue();
}

// Overload this method to get the current number of channels
public void minMaxChannels(MyInt min, MyInt max, MyInt preferred) {

    super.minMaxChannels(min, max, preferred);
    numberOfChannels = preferred.getValue();
}
```

The sample rate is important to the scope because it allows the time duration for a group of samples to be displayed to the user. The number of channels is only useful in that it allows the scope's UI to display the mode (stereo or mono) of the samples being viewed.

Sample Display

Most of the programming effort that went into developing the sample scope was in creating the display surface on which the samples are drawn. Like all UIs developed in this book, the processing of button clicks and scroll bar events is handled by anonymous inner classes that follow the Java 1.1 event model. The main UI panel uses a *GridBagLayout* for flexible positioning of components that make up the UI. A separate class, *StatusDisplay*, is used to display the status information at the top of the UI.

This class defines a three-paned panel which displays the current sample rate, whether the signal source is mono or stereo, and an indication of the time interval (in seconds) of the samples being displayed.

Next, the *ScopeSurface* class (an extension of *Canvas*) is developed to provide for the display of samples. All user actions detected by the event code in the *ScopeUI* class are propagated down to the *ScopeSurface* object (via method calls) and modify how the samples are displayed. Specifically, the position of the scroll bar determines which sample will be displayed first on the *ScopeSurface* and the zoom buttons determine how many samples will be displayed per screen. Said another way, the zoom level (controlled by the zoom buttons) sets the magnification used to display the samples.

Most of the mechanism involved in displaying the samples is contained within the *paint* method of *ScopeSurface*. Here, the actual size of the displayable area is calculated and the various horizontal and vertical scaling factors are developed for display of the sampled data. Also, two yellow horizontal lines are drawn to indicate full scale values and a red baseline line is drawn to indicate zero level. Finally, the sample data is drawn at each sample interval by drawing a line from the previous sample's amplitude value to this sample's value. This code that does all of this display formatting can be seen in the file *ScopeUI.java*.

Real World Usage

This scope certainly came in handy while trying to debug the oscillator devices presented in Chapter 11. At one point during their development, I could hear a nasty buzz when listening to the sine wave signal. I knew that this buzz meant there had to be a glitch (discontinuity) somewhere on the waveform but since I had no way of visualizing the waveform I didn't know where the glitch was. This glitch was in fact the motivation for creating the sample scope in the first place. I knew that if I could see where the glitch was and what it looked like, I could find the bug in the code that was creating it. So I side-tracked myself for a while and created the oscilloscope device presented here. Within a few minutes after getting the scope working I isolated the glitch in the oscillator code and immediately fixed it.

The other time this scope was important was during the development of the guitar tuner of section three. My first approach to the tuner was to perform some signal conditioning on the guitar's signal and then count zero crossings of the signal to determine the frequency of the string's pitch. It was only by viewing the processed guitar signal with the scope that I determined this approach was doomed to failure. With the scope, I could see how the rich harmonics of the guitar's signal were defeating my zero-crossing approach. After making this determination, I switched to an FFT-based technique that worked much more reliably.

Sometimes (as in the case of the guitar tuner) it is necessary to examine the digital samples immediately before and after a stage of processing to see what effect the processing had. The scope presented here is useful in that respect because it can be inserted into the signal path at one or more places and the individual instances of the scope can be named so you can always tell which is the signal before the processing and which is the signal after the processing. In the tuner, the code looked something like the following:

```
// Instantiate data structure for linking abstract audio devices
LinkedListVector ll = new LinkedListVector();

// Create a WinRecorder for gathering samples from the guitar
WinRecorder recorder = new WinRecorder(DEFAULTSAMPLERATE,
                        WinRecorder.DEFAULTCHANNELS,
                        WinRecorder.DEFAULTDEVICEID,
                        null);

if (recorder.initRecorder()) {
    // Open was successful, so continue
    ll.addElement(recorder);

    // Create the sample view before processing is done
    Scope s1 = new Scope("Before Processing")
    ll.addElement(s1);

    // Create processor device to filter the guitar's signal
    FilterAndSmoothSignal fss = new FilterAndSmoothSignal ()
    ll.addElement(fss);

    // Create the sample view after processing is done
    Scope s2 = new Scope("After Processing")
    ll.addElement(s2);

    // Create the tuner device
    Tuner tuner = new Tuner();
    ll.addElement(tuner);

    // Run the tuner code
    tuner.doTuner();
}
```

With this code in place, the sample scopes could be retriggered as often as necessary to get a good look at the job the processing code was doing. Since the scope instances are named, it is very easy to tell which is the unprocessed data and which is the post-processed data.

Possible Enhancements

There are numerous enhancements that could be made to the scope's design as presented here. Most obviously, the user interface could be modified to have a gridded surface for display like a real oscilloscope. A welcome addition would also be a controllable (vertical) amplitude scale so that sample amplitude values could be measured accurately. Another neat feature would be scrollable cursors (vertical lines) that measured the time interval between them. These cursors could be positioned over the two peaks in a sine wave signal, for example, and would automatically read out the period and/or frequency of the waveform. Finally, the triggering mechanism could be made more real as well by being able to set triggering levels and to perform automatic retriggering every time the input samples met or exceed the trigger-level values. Finally, the sample scope acquisition code could be altered to allow the display of the left or the right channel of a stereo signal source. Currently, the left and right channels are intermingled on the display when a stereo signal is displayed.

With these additions, a real digital sample scope could be created. However, as has already been described, the scope is already very useful as it is.

Table 12.1   Sample Scope Front Panel Controls and Indicators

Front Panel Controls and Indicators	Description
Rate Display	Shows the current sample rate of the samples being displayed.
Mode Display	Indicates whether the samples represent a stereo or a mono signal.
Time Display	Show the time represented by the samples currently being displayed.
Scope Display Surface	The area in which the samples are displayed. The horizontal yellow lines represent the full scale values (+32767/−32768) for the 16-bit samples. The red center line represents a value of zero.
Scroll Bar	This control allows scrolling within the acquired samples. The position of the scroll bar controls the index of the first sample displayed on the scope's display. The scroll bar works at any zoom level.
Full Button	Compresses the time scale such that all acquired samples are displayed on the scope's display together. This sets the zoom level back to the minimum.
Zoom In Button	Expands the time scale so that fewer samples are displayed on the screen. Each zoom level provides more detail on individual samples or groups of samples. There are a total of 12 zoom levels available. As the zoom level is changed, the full-scale time interval shown on the display is updated.

Table 12.1   (continued)

Front Panel Controls and Indicators	Description
Zoom Out Button	Compresses the time scale so that more samples are displayed on the screen. As the zoom level is changed, the full-scale time interval shown on the display is updated. Clicking the Full Button is like zooming out all of the way.
Retrigger Button	Causes the scope device to acquire a new group of samples for display. This recreates the UI for showing the new samples and resets the zoom level to full out.

Use with the AudioTest Program

When using the *AudioTest* program, the scope is included in the signal path by specifying the command line switch "*–m scope*." To examine the samples produced by the oscillator device, this command line is used:

```
java craigl.test.AudioTest -i osc -m scope -o winplayer
```

Then when the *Play* button on the *WinPlayer* UI is clicked, the scope will trigger and display the samples it acquired.

Operational Note

Currently, the sample scope should only be used with a single channel (mono) signal source as the current design interprets all sample streams as being single channel. Viewing stereo signals with the scope will result in the intermingling of the left and right channel's program material and will be confusing to interpret when displayed.

Miscellaneous Information

Package:

craigl.scope

Source Files:

File Name	Description
Scope.java	Audio device extension of *AbstractAudio* device that controls the scope's triggering, gathers samples to display, and creates the *Scope* UI for displaying the acquired samples. The *Scope* device passes all samples through without alteration. The *Scope* makes a copy of the samples it is processing at the time it is triggered and those are the samples used for display.
ScopeUI.java	The user interface code for the scope. It creates the simulated front panel, instantiates all user interface controls, and displays the samples according to a time scale.
StatusDisplay.java	This class creates a portion of the scope's UI that displays the current sampling rate, whether the signal being viewed is mono or stereo, and the time represented by the samples currently being displayed.
TriggerFlag.java	A convenience class used to encapsulate a boolean value. This flag is used to control the triggering of the scope.

THE SPECTRUM ANALYZER . . . .

A spectrum analyzer is a signal analysis device used to measure and display the frequency content of a signal or, in our case, a sequence of samples. The scope presented earlier in this chapter works in the time domain whereas the spectrum analyzer presented here operates in the frequency domain. This is such an important concept that you must understand it before the spectrum analyzer discussion will make sense. To this end, the time domain can be visualized as a graph of sample amplitudes vs. time. A graph of 11 samples is shown in Figure 12.2.

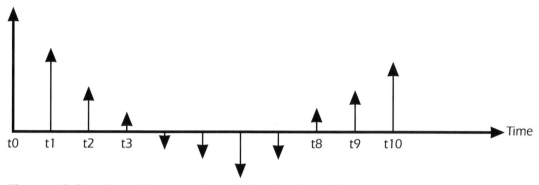

Figure 12.2   Time Domain—Sample Amplitude vs. Time

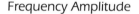

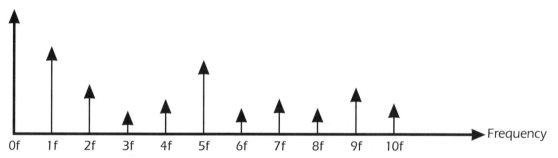

Figure 12.3   Frequency Domain—Frequency Component Amplitude vs. Frequency

Conversely, the frequency domain can be visualized as a graph of frequency component amplitudes versus frequency as shown in Figure 12.3.

Because a spectrum analyzer provides a window into the frequency content of samples passing through it, it makes sense that spectrum analyzers would be used to verify the design of filters and other signal processing transformations that alter frequency content. A spectrum analyzer can be used to quantify the magnitude of such transformation.

Figure 12.4 shows the user interface of the spectrum analyzer presented here. The spectrum shown in this figure is of the 1000 Hz sine wave produced by the digital oscillator of the previous chapter. From this spectrum, you can see that the amplitude of the fundamental frequency is greatest (0 dB) and that the amplitude of the various harmonics drops off quickly. This indicates the purity of the synthesized sine wave signal. Figure 12.5 shows the same spectrum with zoom applied.

The time-domain-to-frequency-domain transformation used in this spectrum analyzer is performed using the fast Fourier transform or FFT, which will be described shortly. First, some operational details for the spectrum analyzer must be discussed.

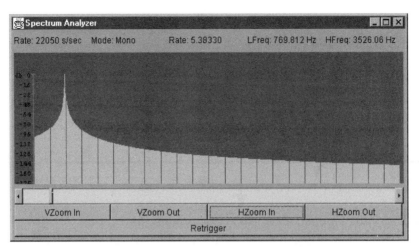

Figure 12.4   The Spectrum Analyzer's User Interface

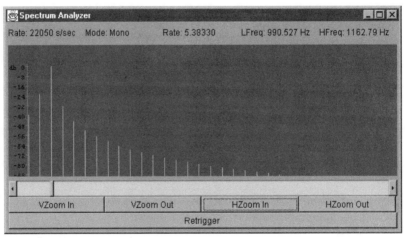

Figure 12.5   Spectrum with Horizontal Zoom and Scrolling Applied

Operation

The operation of the spectrum analyzer can best be understood by discussing how samples are acquired, how they are processed, and then, how they are displayed in the UI.

Sample Acquisition

Because the spectrum analyzer, like the scope presented earlier, is extended from *AbstractAudio*, it can be linked with other *AbstractAudio* derivative devices for the purpose of monitoring digital audio samples. Extending *AbstractAudio* means that the analyzer must implement a *getSamples*() method for propagating samples and must also have the means for querying the signal path as to the agreed upon sample rate and number of channels. Sample propagation and audio processing chain querying are both important to the operation of the analyzer as will become clear in the FFT discussion.

In both of these respects, the spectrum analyzer works exactly the same as the sample scope. Whenever the spectrum analyzer is triggered, a buffer full of samples is extracted from the sample stream for analysis and a new spectrum analyzer UI is created to display the analysis. See the discussion of the sample scope for further details.

Sample Processing

As mentioned, the acquired samples are processed using the FFT. Suffice it to say that the buffer of samples acquired when the spectrum analyzer is triggered is converted from the time domain into the frequency domain by the application of the FFT.

Sample Display

Much of the programming effort that went into developing the spectrum analyzer was spent in creating the display surface on which the frequency components are displayed. Each frequency component is displayed as a vertical line segment whose length determines the relative frequency content. The complete spectrum of the processed audio signal is displayed as an array of these vertical line segments.

Like all UIs developed in this book, the processing of button clicks and scroll bar events is handled by anonymous inner classes that follow the Java 1.1 event model. The main UI panel uses a *GridBagLayout* for flexible positioning of components that make up the UI. A separate class, *StatusDisplay*, is used to display the status information at the top of the spectrum analyzer's UI. This class defines a five-paned panel which displays the current sample rate, whether the signal source is mono or stereo, the rate or ratio by which one frequency component differs from the next, an indication of the lowest frequency component shown on the screen, and an indication of the highest frequency component shown on the screen. These status values are necessary in order to interpret the spectrum information on the main display.

Next, the *ScopeSurface* class (an extension of *Canvas*) is developed to provide for the display of the calculated frequency components. All user actions detected by the event code in the *SpectrumAnalyzerUI* class are propagated down to the *ScopeSurface* object (via method calls) and modify how the frequency component values are displayed. Specifically, the position of the scroll bar determines which portion of the spectrum will be displayed on the *ScopeSurface* and the horizontal zoom buttons determine how many frequency components will be displayed per screen. The vertical zoom level controls determines the granularity of the dB scale used to display the amplitude of the frequency components. This allows the magnitude of any frequency component to be measured fairly accurately.

Most of the mechanism involved in displaying the frequency components is contained within the *paint* method of *ScopeSurface*. Here, the actual size of the displayable area is calculated, and the various horizontal and vertical scaling factors are developed for display of the data, and the dB scale is drawn on the display surface. Finally, the relative frequency component amplitude is drawn at each sample interval by drawing a line from negative infinity to the component's amplitude level. The code that does all of this display formatting can be seen in the file *SpectrumAnalyzerUI.java*.

The FFT

Quite a lot has been written about the Fourier transform and the evolution of the fast Fourier transform or FFT, so I won't repeat that here. If you would like to know some FFT history or see some of the mathematical underpinning, see the books listed in the bibliography for additional references. Also, you could do a search on the Internet and you will find more information about FFT than you care to know. Suffice it to say that the FFT has transformed digital signal processing in that it makes the functionality of the Fourier transform affordable in terms of computational requirements. The FFT and its close algorithmic cousins are used in many engineering disciplines, not just in the processing of sound. Sound, however, is our emphasis here.

As a testament to how useful the FFT algorithm is, note that the FFT code presented is used both in the spectrum analyzer of this chapter and in the guitar tuner application of section three; two rather diverse applications. I should mention that the FFT used here is a Java port of code written by Jef Poskanzer and placed in the public domain. This code is used because it is very concise, relatively fast, and has been used in many applications over the years. In plain English, it does the job. When implemented in Java, this FFT code doesn't have real-time performance but that is not a requirement for the two applications that use it in this book.

It should be noted that FFTs are two-way algorithms. There is therefore a forward and a reverse transformation. The forward transformation, as used here, takes a set of samples in the time domain and manipulates them so as to extract their frequency content. Said another way, the forward transformation takes the amplitude of the samples in the time domain and converts them into the amplitude of the various frequencies they represent in the frequency domain. Access to the frequency content or spectrum of the samples is what is useful in applications. The reverse transformation begins with the frequency component amplitude information and produces a set of time domain samples from that. Reverse FFTs are not used in this book although the Java FFT code provided supports it.

If you take a moment and reflect upon the power that the forward and reverse transforms provide in terms of manipulation of sound, you will see what a powerful tool you have at your disposal. Once a set of samples is converted into the frequency domain, the frequency component coefficients can be manipulated in various ways. Possibilities include:

1. Implementing various filter functions by raising or lowering selected frequency components. Almost any filter you can imagine can be implemented this way.

2. Determining the fundamental frequency of a voice, for example, and augmenting overtones of that frequency to give the voice more impact. Aural exciters do something like this.

3. Alternatively, determining the fundamental frequency of a voice, and trying to add another voice at some interval like a third or a fifth above it (see the discussion of the pitch shifter presented in the next chapter for more information), thereby synthesizing a vocal harmony.

4. Notching out vocal frequencies from a sample stream, thus removing vocals from a song almost completely.

Then, after you have manipulated the frequency component coefficients appropriately, the reverse transformation could be applied to convert back to samples in the time domain. These samples should possess the subtle or not so subtle manipulation you previously applied. As mentioned, however, these types of manipulations will have to be performed in batch mode since the FFT code cannot run in real time. (That is, of course, unless you have a very powerful computer to run your algorithms on. A Cray computer comes to mind.)

Although the mathematics behind the FFT won't be presented here, it is important to understand a few things in order to apply the FFT successfully.

1. The algorithm presented here is a radix 2 algorithm which means that it must work on a group of samples whose number is a power of two. In both applications of the FFT in this book, 4096 sample blocks are used. If only a smaller number of samples are available for analysis, the missing samples should be assigned a value of 0. This will not alter the calculated frequency spectrum of the actual samples.

2. The FFT implementation provided here supports blocks of samples up to 32768 samples in size.

3. Both the input and the output of an FFT are expressed with complex numbers. These complex numbers have both a real and an imaginary component. The arc tangent of the ratio of the imaginary to the real component represents phase shift at each frequency.

4. The FFT implementation used here accepts two arrays for input, one for the real component and the other for the imaginary component of the input samples. For our use here, the imaginary components are always set to zero.

5. The output of the FFT algorithm is also contained in two arrays, one for the real components and one for the imaginary components of the frequency spectra.

6. The consequence of using only real samples for input is that only half of the output calculated frequency components are independent. Therefore, only the first half of the components needs to be examined.

7. The first frequency output component, f0, represents the DC component of the analyzed signal. This value should be zero or nearly zero if the digitized waveform's average signal value was zero. Each sequential frequency component is related to the previous component by the ratio, which is the sample rate divided by the number of points in the FFT. For example, with a sample rate of 22050 samples per second and a 4096 point FFT sample set, the frequency multiplier is 5.383. So the frequency represented by f1 is 5.383 Hz, f2 is 10.766, etc.

8. The output of the FFT algorithm can be interpreted in multiple ways. If it is necessary to determine the power spectrum (Xp), of an FFT result, the power at a frequency, m, is the sum of the squares of both the real (Xreal) and the imaginary (Ximag) components at that frequency.

$$Xp(m) = Xreal(m)^2 + Ximag(m)^2 \quad (1)$$

The power spectrum in decibels is calculated by multiplying 10 times the log base 10 of the above value as follows:

$$Xdb(m) = 10 * \log_{10} (Xp(m)) \quad (2)$$

A normalized power spectrum could be calculated by multiplying 10 times the log base 10 of the power spectrum at frequency m divided by the maximum power spectrum value.

$$Normalized\ Xdb(m) = 10 * \log_{10} (Xp(m)/Xp(m)\ max) \quad (3)$$

The FFT used in the guitar tuning application of section three interprets the FFT result using equation one. The spectrum analyzer presented here interprets the FFT result using equation three.

Table 12.2   Spectrum Analyzer Front Panel Controls and Indicators

Front Panel Controls and Indicators	Description
Sample Rate Display	Shows the current sample rate of the samples acquired and analyzed.
Mode Display	Indicates whether the samples represent a mono or a stereo signal.
Rate Display	The rate or ratio by which one spectral value differs from the next in frequency.
LFreq Display	The frequency corresponding to the leftmost frequency component currently displayed.
HFreq Display	The frequency corresponding to the rightmost frequency component currently displayed.
Scope Display Surface	The area in which the spectral values are displayed. The scale for display is logarithmic and represents the normalized power spectrum of the acquired samples, expressed in decibels. Each spectral value is represented by a vertical line from negative infinity to the normalized spectral power of the signal at this frequency. Since the power values are normalized, the maximum possible value is 0 dB.
Scroll Bar	This control allows scrolling within the spectral values. The position of the scroll bar controls the index of the first spectral value displayed on the spectrum analyzer's display. The scroll bar works at any horizontal zoom level. As the scroll bar's position is changed, the LFreq and HFreq informational displays change to indicate the frequencies of the leftmost and rightmost spectral values currently displayed.
VZoom In Button	Expands the vertical logarithmic scale to allow the amplitude of the spectral values to be measured with more resolution. Each vertical zoom level uses a finer granularity vertical scale. There are a total of 6 zoom levels available. As the vertical zoom level is changed, the on-screen scale changes as well.
VZoom Out Button	Compresses the vertical logarithmic scale to allow the full range of the spectral values to be viewed. The on-screen scale changes as the vertical zoom level changes.
HZoom In Button	Expands the frequency scale so that fewer spectral values are displayed on the screen. Each zoom level provides more detail on individual spectral values or groups of spectral values. There are a total of 9 zoom levels available. As the horizontal zoom level is changed, the HFreq informational display will change as the frequency represented by the rightmost spectral value is reduced.

Table 12.2   (continued)

Front Panel Controls and Indicators	Description
HZoom Out Button	Compresses the frequency scale so that more spectral values are displayed on the screen. As the horizontal zoom level is changed, the HFreq informational display will change as the frequency represented by the rightmost spectral value is increased.
Retrigger Button	Clicking this button causes the spectrum analyzer device to acquire a new group of samples for analysis and display. This recreates the UI showing the new spectral values.

Use with the AudioTest Program

When using the *AudioTest* program, the spectrum analyzer is included in the signal path by specifying the command line switch "*–m spectrumanalyzer.*" To analyze the samples produced by the oscillator device, the command line is

```
java craigl.test.AudioTest -i osc -m spectrumanalyzer -o winplayer
```

Then, when the *Play* button on the *WinPlayer* UI is clicked, the spectrum analyzer will trigger and display the spectrum of the samples it has acquired.

Miscellaneous Information

Package:

craigl.spectrumanalyzer

Source Files:

File Name	Description
FFT.java	A class for performing a fast Fourier transformation. Currently a 4096 point transform is performed to provide accurate frequency content data.
SpectrumAnalyzer.java	Audio device extension of *AbstractAudio* device that controls the spectrum analyzer's triggering, gathers samples for analysis, and creates the spectrum analyzer UI for displaying the acquired samples' spectrum. The spectrum analyzer device passes all samples through without alteration. A copy is made of the samples being passed at the time of triggering and those are the samples used for analysis and display.
SpectrumAnalyzerUI.java	The user interface code for the spectrum analyzer. It creates the simulated front panel, instantiates all user interface controls, and displays the spectrum of the samples in the frequency domain.
StatusDisplay.java	This class creates a portion of the spectrum analyzer's UI that displays the current sampling rate, whether the signal being viewed is mono or stereo, the rate at which one spectral value differs from the next in frequency, the frequency represented by the leftmost sample shown on the display, and the frequency represented by the rightmost sample currently being displayed.

13 Audio Processors

INTRODUCTION . . . .

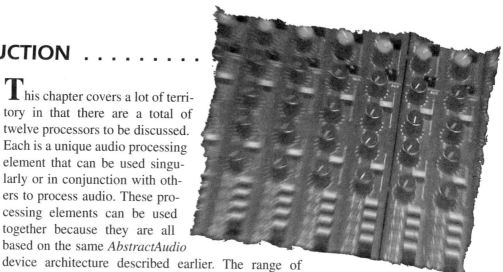

T his chapter covers a lot of territory in that there are a total of twelve processors to be discussed. Each is a unique audio processing element that can be used singularly or in conjunction with others to process audio. These processing elements can be used together because they are all based on the same *AbstractAudio* device architecture described earlier. The range of effects that can be applied to digital audio using these processing elements range from a faint reverb completely across the spectrum to such severe processing that the audio is no longer recognizable. Numerous audio files are provided on the accompanying CDROM to illustrate some of the sonic possibilities available with these processing devices.

In earlier days, recording studios would have had separate hardware devices to perform each processing function. More recently, a single effects unit could perform most if not all of the effects provided here. Now, however, you can apply them all using just your personal computer. That is progress!

The processors to be described in this chapter include:

1. Amplitude adjust processor
2. Cache processor
3. Chorus/flanger processor
4. Compressor/expander/limiter/noise gate processor
5. Delay processor
6. Distortion/clipping processor

7. Graphic equalizer processor

8. Panning processor

9. Parametric equalizer processor

10. Phaser processor

11. Pitch shifter processor

12. Reverb processor

The processors are listed above in alphabetical order and are presented that way in this chapter for organizational reasons. In terms of theoretical and implementation complexity, however, the ordering is different. You may want to study the processors in this alternative order:

1. Amplitude adjust processor

2. Panning processor

3. Distortion/clipping processor

4. Cache processor

5. Delay processor

6. Compressor/expander/limiter/noise gate processor

7. Chorus/flanger processor

8. Phaser processor

9. Parametric equalizer processor

10. Graphic equalizer processor

11. Reverb processor

12. Pitch shifter processor

That way, you are exposed to ever increasing complexity and will hopefully be better prepared for the advanced topics when they arrive. The choice is yours.

AMPLITUDE ADJUST PROCESSOR . . . .

Description

The *Amplitude Adjust* processor is the simplest processor presented in this book and is therefore a good place to start the discussion of processing/processor devices. This *Amplitude Adjust* processor functions as a level or volume control for samples passing through it. It has a slide pot for adjusting the level and a bypass button for removing itself from the signal path. A green bypass LED is provided that blinks when the

Figure 13.1   *Simulated Front Panel for Amplitude Adjust Processor*

bypass mode is in effect. The simulated front panel for this processor can be seen in Figure 13.1.

The only special aspect of this processing element that needs to be pointed out is that the slide pot is provided with a pseudo audio taper, as all good volume controls should be. Audio taper simulation is described in section one of this book. As mentioned there, audio taper pots are used to compensate for the non linearity of the human ear. They make the volume reduction appear linear as the pot's value is changed.

Operation

Like all processing elements presented in this book, the *Amplitude Adjust* processor extends *AbstractAudio* so that it can be linked together with other audio processing elements. This means it must implement a *getSamples* method which it uses to process the samples passing through it. The *getSamples* method that the *Amplitude Adjust* processor implements is shown below. It is the simplest implementation of *getSamples* you'll find in this book.

Basically, samples are pulled through this processing element by subsequent processing stages or, if none, the sink device in the audio chain. These samples are pulled through this device by calls to the *getSamples* method here. As shown, if the bypass mode is in effect, the samples are not altered. When not bypassed, each sample is multiplied in place with the *adjValue* factor. This is the factor that is controlled by the amplitude adjust slide pot. The *adjValue* factor is extracted from the slide pot by calling the method *getAttenuation()* on the pot.

```
public int getSamples(short [] buffer, int length) {

    int len = previous.getSamples(buffer, length);
    if (getByPass())
        return len;
```

```
for (int i=0; i < len; i++)
    buffer[i] = (short)(buffer[i] * adjValue);

return len;
}
```

Table 13.1 lists the front panel controls for the *Amplitude Adjust* processor.

Table 13.1   Amplitude Adjust Processor

Front Panel Controls	Description
Amplitude Adjustment Slidepot	Slide pot with pseudo audio taper that controls the attenuation of the audio samples passing through this processor.
Bypass LED	Green LED that blinks when the amplitude adjust processor is bypassed.
Bypass Button	In the deactivated state, the audio samples passing through this processing stage are subjected to the attenuation controlled by the slide pot. In the activated state, this processing stage is bypassed. Samples out equals samples in.

Use with the AudioTest Program

When using the *AudioTest* program, the Amplitude Adjust processor is included in the signal path by specifying the command line switch "–p aadj."

Miscellaneous Information

Package:

craigl.processors

Source Files:

File Name	Description
AmplitudeAdjustUI.java	User Interface (simulated front panel) for Amplitude Adjust processor.
AmplitudeAdjustWithUI.java	Audio device extension of *AbstractAudio* device that performs the sample manipulation.

CACHE PROCESSOR . . . .

Description

It may be a misnomer to call this device a processor because the *Cache* processor does not alter the samples passing through it in any way. What this device does is fetch processed audio samples from previous stages in the audio signal chain and store them in memory. It caches the processed samples for faster access by subsequent processing stages. Once the cache is filled by pulling samples through it, the processing stages in front of the cache are never accessed again. All requests for samples from subsequent processing stages are satisfied by reading the samples out of the cache.

Introducing the *Cache* processor into a processing signal path can help performance if stages prior to the *Cache* require a lot of real-time processing but always produce the same result. Use of the *Cache* removes the need for repetitive calculations that don't contribute anything to the final result after the first time through. The *Cache* may also be used to buffer sample data read from an audio file, for example.

The *Cache* does not have a user interface associated with it. In other words, its effect can be heard but not seen.

Operation

Like all processing elements presented in this book, the *Cache* processor extends *AbstractAudio* so that it can be linked together with other audio processing elements. This means it must implement a *getSamples* method which it uses to store the samples passing through it. This *getSamples* method is shown below:

```
// Return samples from the cache
public int getSamples(short [] buffer, int length) {

    // Determine if cache already contains samples
    if (cacheSize == 0) {

        // Allocate a move buffer
        moveBuffer = new short [length];

        // Cache uninitialized, determine required cache size
        int len = 0;

        while(len != -1) {
            cacheSize += len;
            len = previous.getSamples(moveBuffer, length);
```

```
        }
        o("Required cache size in samples: " + cacheSize);

        // Allocate buffer for cache
        cacheBuffer = new short [cacheSize];

        // Now fill the cache buffer samples. NOTE: previous
        // stages must have reset for this to work.

        len = previous.getSamples(moveBuffer, length);
        while(len != -1) {
            System.arraycopy(moveBuffer, 0, cacheBuffer,
                                              cacheBufferOffset, len);
            cacheBufferOffset += len;
            len = previous.getSamples(moveBuffer, length);
        }
        // Pt at the beginning of the data in the cache
        cacheBufferOffset = 0;
    }
    // Return samples from the cache
    // Calculate data remaining in the cache
    int dataRemaining = cacheSize - cacheBufferOffset;

    // Return end of file indication if no more data
    if (dataRemaining == 0)
        return -1;

    int samplesRead;

    if (length <= dataRemaining) {
        // Cache has the required amount of data to return
        System.arraycopy(cacheBuffer, cacheBufferOffset, buffer, 0, length);
        cacheBufferOffset += length;
        return length;

    } else    {

        // Cache is short of data
        System.arraycopy(cacheBuffer, cacheBufferOffset, buffer, 0,
                                                    dataRemaining);
        cacheBufferOffset += dataRemaining;
        return dataRemaining;
    }
}
```

Hopefully, the operation of the code above should be obvious from the comments. The following important facts should be noted here, however:

1. The first call made to the *getSamples*() method in the *Cache* processor causes all samples from the previous stage(s) to be read into memory.

2. This code does not place an upper bound on the size of the cache's buffer. The buffer is sized to fit the amount of sample data that the previous stage supplies before it returned an end of file (EOF) indication. This could cause your Java VM to run out of memory. See the possible enhancements section below.

3. Once the cache is full, all subsequent requests for samples are satisfied by reading from the cache's sample buffer. The previous processing stages are never used again.

4. Whenever the *Cache* processor receives the reset message from the signal path, the offset in the cache where the next samples will be read is set back to zero. Subsequent calls to *getSamples*() will return samples from the start of the cached data.

Possible Enhancements

You might want to change this code so that it at least reports insufficient memory if it attempts to allocate too much. As the code is implemented currently, it will happily run your VM into the ground by way of insufficient memory without complaint, although it will tell you first how much memory it will try to allocate before it does so.

Use with the AudioTest Program

When using the *AudioTest* program, the Cache processor is included in the signal path by specifying the command line switch "*–p cache.*" To cache the reading of an audio file, a command line similar to the following can be used:

```
java craigl.test.AudioTest -i file -p cache -o winplayer
```

Miscellaneous Information

Package:

craigl.processors

Source Files:

File Name	Description
Cache.java	The sample caching processor code.

CHORUS/FLANGER PROCESSOR . . . .

Description

Flanging (sometimes spelled planging or even phlanging) and chorus are two distinct audio processing effects produced using delays. Flanging and chorus use variable delays as opposed to the fixed delay used in the delay processor device described later in this chapter. For these effects, the delay is modulated by a low-frequency signal provided by a low-frequency oscillator, or LFO, the result of the modulated delay being the famous syrupy, swishing sound heard on many of the records of the 1960s and 1970s. The difference between flanging and chorus is the amount of delay involved. Flanging uses short delays so no echo affects are perceived. Chorus, on the other hand, uses much longer delays so the echo affects are apparent. Chorus is called chorus because it is used to make a single voice sound like many. Both effects have their uses and it is fortuitous we can create both effects in a single processing device. The block diagram describing how these effects are produced is presented in Figure 13.2. The user interface (UI) for the chorus/flanger processor described in this chapter is shown in Figure 13.3. Using the UI controls provided for this device, a vast number of unique processing effects can be produced that span the spectrum from simple flanging to extreme chorus and everything in between.

Rock and roll folklore says that flanging was discovered by George Martin during a Beatles recording session but I have no idea if this is true or not. What is known

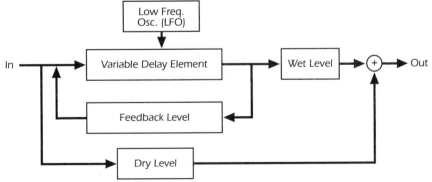

Figure 13.2   Chorus/Flanger Block Diagram

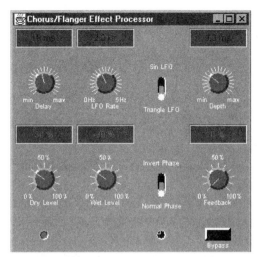

Figure 13.3   The Chorus/Flanger Processor User Interface

is that flanging was first produced by making two identical audio tape copies of some source material and playing them back simultaneously while mixing the outputs together. The swishing sound was produced by riding one's thumb on the *flange* of one of the tape reels, thereby slowing playback of one tape minutely. These small tape speed variations caused a short delay to be introduced into the audio playback and a subsequent variable phase shift which caused the swish.

To hear what this effect sounds like, listen to the files *craig1chorus.wav* and *craig1chorusweird.wav* located in the *sound* directory of the CDROM.

Operation

Modern flanging is produced with the aid of a digital comb filter but the technique is amazingly similar to the tape-based method mentioned above. A comb filter is the type of filter that results when an audio signal is mixed with a delayed copy of itself. This filter is referred to as a comb filter because a plot of its frequency response looks like the teeth of a comb. Each tooth represents a frequency of attenuation. As the amount of delay is varied, the comb filter sweeps up and down the audio spectrum, causing flanging to occur.

In the implementation presented here, the delay is varied or modulated using a low frequency sine or triangle waveform (user selectable) that can range in frequency from zero to five Hz (also user selectable). The depth setting controls how much the delay varies as the LFO oscillates back and forth. Depth can be set anywhere in the range of zero to 30 milliseconds. A depth setting of zero means the delay does not respond to the LFO. At a maximum depth setting, the delay to which the audio samples are subjected ranges from the delay setting set by the user to this delay setting plus 30 milliseconds. When the LFO waveform is at its maximum value, the delay used is that set by the delay pot. When the LFO waveform is at zero level, the total delay is the pot delay plus one half of the depth setting. At minimum value (maximum negative value) of the LFO waveform, the total delay is the pot delay plus the full depth value. So, as the LFO oscillates back and forth over its range of values, the delay element effectively shrinks and expands accordingly.

It should be noted that the LFO waveform is not precomputed and stored as it was in the *Oscillator* devices presented in Chapter 11. Here, the waveform is a computed stepwise representation of a sine or triangle waveform that is built on a sample-by-sample basis. That is, the next value of the waveform is computed as it is needed and not before. Also, the techniques for computing the next value of the sine wave waveform are different from computing the next value of the triangle waveform. This can be seen in the code segment presented shortly.

The operation of the chorus/flanger device is completely sample-synchronous in that a sample is processed, the LFO output is adjusted, and buffer indices are updated after each sample. These processes must occur in lock step or clicks and pops will be evident in the processed audio.

As the delay is varied in duration by the LFO, the point in the delay buffer where the delayed signal is extracted changes dynamically. In fact, the actual extraction point isn't always represented by an integer value but usually lies somewhere between two samples in the delay buffer. In my first implementation of this effect, I simply truncated the extraction point index and fetched the delayed sample from there. This, however, resulted in some sonic artifacts that were objectionable to the ear. Once I realized the cause of the problem, my second implementation utilized linear interpolation. Using this technique I now fetch both samples surrounding the actual extraction point and combine them. The mix ratio is controlled by how close each sample was to the actual computed extraction point. This in essence is providing fractional sampling of the delayed audio samples. The results of this approach are much better.

Leaving aside for the moment the LFO and the variable delay element, how the audio samples are routed from input to output of this processing device should be mentioned. This routing is evident by the numerous arrows used on the block diagram. In order to understand how things work, a few terms must first be defined.

The term *dry level* refers to the percentage of the unprocessed input signal that is coupled into the output. The UI for this device provides a dry level pot for controlling the level. If the dry level pot is set at zero, none of the unprocessed input is fed forward to the output. At a 50% level, input at one half amplitude is mixed into the output. At 100%, the full amplitude of the input is mixed into the output. Of course, in the digital domain in which we are working, amplitude scaling is done via multiplication. Since our potentiometers output a number between 0 and 100, we can scale the input signal by doing the following:

Output Sample = (Input Sample * PotValue) / 100;

The term *wet level* refers to the percentage of processed signal which makes its way to the output to be mixed with the dry signal. A pot is also provided in the UI for varying this parameter. Note that it is quite possible to have 100% dry level and 100% wet level selected at the same time. This just means that the summed output will be larger in amplitude than the input audio signal. By varying the amount of wet and dry level, you can control how in your face the flanging or chorus effect is. The result of some processing effects cannot be heard if some dry level signal is not present in the output along with the wet or processed signal. This is true for most settings of the chorus/flanger effect.

The UI's *Feedback level* pot controls how much of the wet processed signal is coupled back to the input for recirculation. Feedback must be used carefully as oscillation can occur within the device. The feedback phase toggle switch in the UI controls whether the samples are fed back as is or if they have their sign reversed (the inverted position). Inverting the fed-back samples can help reduce feedback if it occurs.

The code from *ChorusWithUI.java* shown below illustrates how single channel (monaural) samples are processed.

```java
// Process mono samples
protected int processMonoSamples(short [] localBuffer,
                                 short [] buffer, int len) {

    // Do the processing
    for (int i=0; i < len; i++) {
        // Fetch the input samples from the local buffer
        int inputSample = (int) localBuffer[i];

        // Calculate sample offsets for fetching two samples
        double sampleOffset1 = sweepValue - halfDepthInSamples;
        double sampleOffset2 = sampleOffset1 - 1;

        // Calculate delta for linear interpolation
        double delta = Math.abs((int) sampleOffset1 - sampleOffset1);
        int actualIndex1 = readIndex + (int) sampleOffset1;
        int actualIndex2 = readIndex++ + (int) sampleOffset2;
        boolean underflow1 = (actualIndex1 < 0);
        boolean underflow2 = (actualIndex2 < 0);

        // Adjust indices for possible under/over flow
        if (underflow1)
            actualIndex1 += delayBufferSize;
        else
            actualIndex1 %= delayBufferSize;
```

```
if (underflow2)
    actualIndex2 += delayBufferSize;
else
    actualIndex2 %= delayBufferSize;

// Fetch two samples and interpolate
int delaySample1 = (int) delayBuffer[actualIndex1];
int delaySample2 = (int) delayBuffer[actualIndex2];
int delaySample = (int) (delaySample2 * delta +
                                delaySample1 * (1.0 - delta));
// Sum wet and dry portions of the output
int outputSample =
    ((inputSample * dryLevel) / 100) +
    ((delaySample * wetLevel) / 100);

// Clamp output to legal range
if (outputSample > 32767)
    outputSample = 32767;
else if (outputSample < -32768)
    outputSample = -32768;
// Store output sample
buffer[i] = (short) outputSample;

// Calculate sample for storage in delay buffer
inputSample +=
    (delaySample * feedbackLevel * (invertPhase ? -1:+1)) / 100;

// Store sample
delayBuffer[writeIndex++] = inputSample;

// Update indices
readIndex %= delayBufferSize;
writeIndex %= delayBufferSize;

// Calculate new sweep value
if (isSinLFO) {
    // LFO is sinusoidal
    sampleNumber %= sampleRate;
    sweepValue = halfDepthInSamples *
        Math.sin(radiansPerSample * sampleNumber++);

} else    {
```

```
            // LFO is triangular
            sweepValue += step;

            // Keep sweep in range
            if ((sweepValue >= halfDepthInSamples) ||
              (sweepValue <= -halfDepthInSamples)) {
                // Change direction of sweep
                step *= -1;
            }
        }
    }
    return len;
}
```

Stereo samples are handled in a similar way by a method called *processStereoSamples* with just about twice the amount of processing being required. Stereo samples are extracted from the interleaved sample stream and processed through separate left and right delays. On output, the separate left and right samples are again combined and interleaved into the output sample stream.

As usual, the *getSamples* method is where the action is. It is the *getSamples* method that is called by subsequent processing stages to pull samples through this device. *getSamples* is shown below for reference. You can see how the number of channels count is used to determine which method to call to perform the sample processing.

```
// Process the samples that pass through this effect
public int getSamples(short [] buffer, int length) {

    // Skip this device if bypassed or initialization is not yet complete
    if (getByPass() || !initializationComplete)
        return previous.getSamples(buffer, length);

    // Read number of samples requested from previous stage
    int len = previous.getSamples(localBuffer, length);
    if (len == -1)
        return -1;

    if (numberOfChannels == 1)
        return processMonoSamples(localBuffer, buffer, len);
    else
        return processStereoSamples(localBuffer, buffer, len);
}
```

The User Interface

The user interface for the chorus/flanger processing device is shown in Figure 13.3. The code that produces the UI is contained in the file *ChorusUI.java* whereas it is the code in *ChorusWithUI* which does the actual sample processing. The *ChorusWithUI* class instantiates *ChorusUI* as it is coming up.

The UI is built with a *GridBagLayout* layout manager using the controls and indicators, presented in section one of this book. Within the UI are numerous pots, buttons, LEDs, *ReadoutLabel* indicators and toggle switches. As with all processing devices, a bypass switch and accompanying LED are provided. Anonymous inner listener classes are used to trap and process events from the pots and switches. Middleware methods are called by the listener classes when the UI controls are manipulated. These methods update the indicators in the UI and then call low-level functions in *ChorusWithUI* to affect processing.

It is within the UI code where all default, minimum, and maximum values for the various pots are established. These values are coded as static final integer values and are shown below.

```
public static final int MAXDELAYINMS = 40;
public static final int MINDELAYINMS = 1;
public static final double MAXRATEINHZ = 5;
public static final double MINRATEINHZ = 0;
public static final double MAXDEPTHINMS = 30;
public static final double MINDEPTHINMS = 0;
public static final int DEFAULTDELAYINMS = 18;
public static final int DEFAULTDEPTHINMS = 10;
public static final int DEFAULTRATEINHZ = 2;
public static final int DEFAULTDEPTHLEVEL= 10;
public static final int DEFAULTDRYLEVEL = 30;
public static final int DEFAULTWETLEVEL = 30;
public static final int DEFAULTFEEDBACKLEVEL = 0;
```

Any of the defaults can be changed with a simple edit of this code and a recompile. The values chosen were ones I thought were appropriate but you may think differently.

Table 13.2 lists the front panel controls and indicators for the chorus/flanger processor.

Table 13.2   *Chorus/Flanger Processor Front Panel Controls and Indicators*

Front Panel Controls and Indicators	Description
Delay Indicator	A *ReadoutLabel* indicator showing the delay in milliseconds (ms) dialed in with the delay pot.
LFO Rate Indicator	A *ReadoutLabel* indicator that indicates the frequency of the low frequency sweep oscillator used in this effect. Readout is in Hz.
A Depth Indicator	A *ReadoutLabel* indicator indicating the depth of modulation in milliseconds.
Delay Pot	This pot sets the static delay used in this effect. The range of values is from 1 to 40 milliseconds. Very short delays result in a flanging effect while longer delays produce chorus.
LFO Rate Pot	This pot controls the frequency of the low frequency oscillator (LFO) used to modulate the delay. Frequencies from 0 Hz to 5 Hz can be selected. The frequency selected is independent of the waveform used for modulation.
LFO Mode Toggle Switch	This toggle switch controls the waveform (shape) used for modulation. In one position a sine wave is used; in the other, a triangle wave is used for the LFO.
Depth Pot	This pot controls the strength with which the LFO modulation is applied to the delay. The range of values is from zero to 30 milliseconds. At full scale, the delay value can be affected by the LFO.
Dry Level Indicator	A *ReadoutLabel* indicator indicating the amount of the dry (unprocessed) signal present in the output.
Wet Level Indicator	A *ReadoutLabel* indicator indicating the amount of the wet (processed) signal present in the output.
Feedback Level Indicator	A *ReadoutLabel* indicator indicating the amount of the output signal fed back to the input.
Dry Level Pot	This pot controls the amount of the dry (unprocessed) signal present in the output.
Wet Level Pot	This pot controls the amount of the wet (processed) signal present in the output.
Phase Invert Toggle Switch	This toggle switch controls the phase of the output signal feedback to the input. Feedback can be in phase (normal) or 180 degrees out of phase (inverted).
Feedback Level Pot	This pot controls the amount of the output signal coupled back to the input.

Table 13.2　　(continued)

Front Panel Controls and Indicators	Description
On LED	A red LED that simulates a power on indicator. It does nothing else and is for looks only.
Bypass LED	A green LED that flashes when this effect is bypassed.
Bypass Button	Clicking this button causes the chorus/flanger effect to be bypassed. In other words, the processor is effectively removed from the signal chain.

Use with the AudioTest Program

When using the *AudioTest* program, the chorus/flanger processor is included in the signal path by specifying the command line switch "*–p chorus.*" To acquire samples from the mic/line input, process the samples using the chorus/flanger effect, and save the results to a file, use the following command line:

```
java craigl.test.AudioTest -i mic 11025 1 -p chorus -o file
```

Miscellaneous Information

Package:

craigl.processors

Source Files:

File Name	Description
ChorusUI.java	The user interface for the chorus/flanging effect.
ChorusWithUI.java	The *AbstractAudio* device that performs the chorus/flanging effect.

COMPRESSOR/EXPANDER/LIMITER/NOISE GATE PROCESSOR ·

Description

Compressors, expanders, limiters, and noise gates are all devices used to control and modify the amplitude dynamics of sound. Each of these devices affects audio passing through them differently. These devices operate on audio amplitude values and are not delay-based effects like most other processing devices presented in this chapter.

To understand how these devices operate and truly why they exist at all, one must understand the concept of *dynamic range* as applied to sound. The dynamic range of sound is the difference between the loudest component of the sound and the softest component. Symphonic music can have a very large dynamic range as a passage of music can change from the quiet chime of a single bell to the fury of the full symphony accompanied by cannons. Blue grass music, in contrast, has a much smaller dynamic range because the differences in amplitude between soft and loud passages is much smaller. Compressors, expanders, limiters, and noise gates all affect dynamic range in very specific ways, as the following discussion will hopefully make clear.

Because compressors, expanders, limiters, and noise gates all function by manipulating audio amplitude levels (and therefore dynamic range), we can conveniently combine their functionality into a single audio processing device. In other words, the device presented in this chapter can function as a compressor, an expander, a limiter, or a noise gate or some combination thereof. This is like getting four processing effects for the price of one. For the purpose of this discussion the term *compressor device* will be used to refer to the *AbstractAudio* device developed in this chapter that performs all four functions.

The UI for the *compressor* device is shown in Figure 13.4. As shown there, the user is presented with a graph of the devices' input/output response and a series of con-

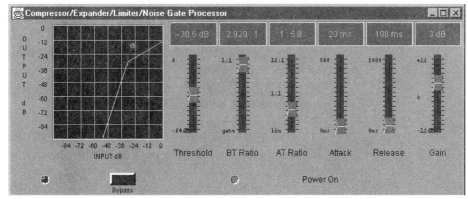

Figure 13.4   *Compressor/Expander/Limiter/Noise Gate Processor User Interface*

trols to change various aspects of that response. Providing a graph helps to illustrate what is going on and the effect each individual control has. The following UI controls are provided:

1. The *Threshold* control controls the sample level at which the amplitude manipulating effect is applied. The range of values is from 0 dB (a full-scale sample value of 32767) to –60 dB (a sample value of approximately 32). A sample value above the threshold prepares the device for operation. As the threshold is lowered, the threshold position on the graph (the red X) moves towards the lower left. How the threshold value is interpreted depends upon the effect being used.

2. The *BT Ratio* controls the response of the device below the threshold (BT = below threshold). As this control is manipulated, the response graph below the threshold point changes from a 225 degree angle indicating output equals input to 270 degrees, which indicates noise gating. This control is used primarily for controlling the noise gate effect.

3. The *AT Ratio* control controls the response of the device above the threshold (AT = above threshold). The slope of the response graph above the threshold determines which processing function is being performed. A slope of 45 degrees indicates output is equal to input and that amplitude dynamics are not being affected. A slope of less than 45 degrees indicates compression. A slope of zero degrees means that limiting (extreme compression) will occur if the audio level exceeds the threshold. A response graph slope of greater than 45 degrees indicates expansion.

4. The *Attack* control determines the time in milliseconds the peak audio level must remain above the threshold before the amplitude processing effect engages. A very small or zero attack time causes the effect to engage very quickly and can result in a *breathing* phenomenon if the gain changes dramatically due to compression or expansion.

5. Release time is controlled by the *Release* control. The release time is the time the amplitude processing effect remains engaged after the audio level drops back below the threshold. If the effect were to release instantaneously, the effect gain would jump up and down instead of only changing during a quiet interval in the processed audio.

6. The *Gain* control is used to make up for signal amplitude lost because of compression or to reduce gain due to expansion.

Before beginning the discussion, two other important topics must be mentioned. First, it must be pointed out that peak audio sample values are used for threshold detection in the device presented here instead of average levels or RMS value levels used in some professional gear. However, most professional gear provides peak threshold detection modes as well. Second, our device provides only a "soft knee" approach to amplitude manipulation, whereas some professional gear provides both hard and soft knee operation. The knee is where the response graph bends and this occurs at the selected threshold value. A hard or soft knee indicates how audio will be processed when its level is close to that of the knee. A hard knee means the audio will be subjected to the amplitude manipulation as defined by the chosen response graph. If the response graph abruptly changes (as in the case of a limiter), the output audio will abruptly change as well. Here abruptness equates to hardness. When a soft knee is used, the abruptness of the knee is mitigated by a curve fitting operation about the threshold point. The smooth curve is then used to determine how the audio levels are adjusted instead of the abrupt change dictated by the response graph. The use of a hard or soft knee is a matter of personal preference and changes depending on the type of audio being processed.

Finally, I should point out that performing these amplitude manipulating effects in the digital domain is much easier than performing them in the analog domain, as gain can be controlled on a sample-by-sample basis using simple multiplication.

Below is a short description of each of the four processing effects and examples of how they might be used.

Compressors

A compressor is a device that is used to reduce the dynamic range of audio passing through it. In essence, a compressor squeezes more audio into a smaller range of amplitude values, thereby making softer passages appear to be louder and loud passages softer.

Of the amplitude manipulating effects described in this chapter, compressors are used the most in the audio industry. In fact, compressors are used at many different stages of the audio recording, production, and distribution process. A compressor might be used when recording an individual track such as a kick drum to keep transients from overloading the recording device. A compressor might again be used during mixing to bring a vocal prominently into the foreground over the top of the mix. A compressor will probably again be used when preparing the completed recording for mastering onto a CD or vinyl to keep track-to-track volume levels approximately constant. And a compressor will be used again when the CD is played over the AM or FM radio air waves as the dynamic range of these transmissions must be very tightly controlled for bandwidth reasons.

A compressor works by automatically reducing audio levels when the audio passes a user-defined threshold. Audio with levels below the threshold are passed through unaffected. Because output levels are reduced by the compression process, most compressors have a gain adjustment control to make up for lost level. As the gain is increased, the softer passages are increased in volume while the louder passes are reduced in volume by compression. This is why compressors cause softer passages to get louder (relatively) and louder passages to get softer.

When using the compressor device presented in this chapter as a compressor, all UI controls might be used except the *BT Ratio* control, which would only be used if a noise gate function in addition to the compressor function was desired.

Expanders

Whereas a compressor attempts to reduce the dynamic range of the audio passing through it, the expander expands it. Expanders are not used as frequently as compressors, but their effect can be dramatic if used correctly. Consider a recorded violin part that is fine in terms of the melodic aspects but lacks the dynamics required to really bring it out in the mix. Under these conditions, an expander can be used to increase the dynamics and make the violin really stand out.

An expander works by boosting the level of the audio when the audio passes a user-defined threshold. Audio below the threshold is passed through unaffected.

Limiters

A limiter is a device that guarantees audio output will never exceed a preset limit. A limiter does not manipulate the audio passing through it until the level of the audio exceeds a user-defined threshold. At that point, the audio is *limited* to the maximum output level, regardless of how large the input signal becomes. When the audio input level falls below the threshold, the limiting action is turned off.

Noise Gate

A noise gate is a device used to remove extraneous background noise from an audio segment. A noise gate works by monitoring the audio input level and, if the level falls below an adjustable threshold, the noise gate forces the output to zero. This device is called a gate because audio flows freely (and unmodified) if the gate is open and doesn't flow at all if the gate is closed.

Consider a recording of an electric guitar through a very noisy guitar amplifier. As long as the guitar player is playing, the noise of the amplifier is masked by the music. When the guitar player stops playing in a soft portion of the tune, for example, the noise of the amplifier becomes prominent. A noise gate set to the appropriate threshold will allow the guitar music to pass through unimpeded but will prevent the noise of the amplifier from passing to the output during the quiet intervals.

Operation

As with virtually all processing devices presented in this book, this device is comprised of two main components, one that does the manipulation and processing of samples and one that provides the user interface for the device. The sample manipulation code is contained in the file *CompExpWithUI.java* and the user interface code in the file *CompExpUI.java*. When user interaction occurs in the UI component, methods in the sample manipulation component are called to affect processing. The sample manipulation code is discussed in this section and the UI code is discussed briefly in the next. Upon inspection of the code, it will quickly become obvious that the real work in performing the compressor/expander/limiter/noise gate functionality is done in the *getSamples* method of *CompExpWithUI.java*. All of the other code surrounding this method is for support only.

```java
public int getSamples(short [] buffer, int length) {
    // Get samples from previous stage
    int len = previous.getSamples(buffer, length);

    // If bypass is enabled, short circuit processing
    if (getByPass() || !initializationComplete)
        return len;

    // We have samples to process
    for (int i=0; i < len; i++) {

        // Get a sample
        double sample = (double) buffer[i];

        if (Math.abs(sample) >= thresholdValue) {
            // Sample value exceeds threshold

            releaseCount++;
            releaseCount %= (calcReleaseCount + 1);

            if (attackExpired) {
                // Attack satisfied, process sample
                if (!limiting)
                    sample *= atRatio;
                else
                    sample = (sample < 0) ?
                        -thresholdValue : thresholdValue;
```

```
        }   else    {
            attackCount-;
            if (attackCount <= 0) {
                attackExpired = true;
                releaseCount = calcReleaseCount;
            }
        }
    }   else    {
        // Sample value did not exceed threshold
        if (attackExpired) {
            if (!limiting)
                sample *= atRatio;

            releaseCount-;
            if (releaseCount <= 0) {
                attackExpired = false;
                attackCount = calcAttackCount;
            }
        }   else    {
            attackCount++;
            attackCount %= (calcAttackCount + 1);
        }
        // Now process below threshold noise gating
        sample *= btRatio;
    }
    // Apply gain
    sample *= gain;

    // Range check results
    if (sample > 32767.0)
        sample = 32767.0;
    else if (sample < -32768.0)
        sample = -32768.0;

    // Store sample back into buffer
    buffer[i] = (short) sample;
}
// Return count of sample processed
return len;
}
```

This relatively short code segment is performing a remarkable amount of processing on the samples flowing though it. Remember, that this one piece of code performs compression, expansion, limiting, and noise gating all with user-adjustable attack and release timing. Because of the timing requirements needed by this effect, the code has a state machine feel to it. Every sample processed represents a quantum of time, so the count of the processed samples is the reference used for timing. Attack and release timings are handled by counting the number of samples represented by their respective time interval. For example, if we are processing audio samples which occur at the rate of 22050 samples per second, each sample represents a time interval of 0.0453 milliseconds. If an attack time is set at 300 milliseconds, then 6623 samples will pass during the attack time interval. *Note:* If a stereo signal is being processed, twice that many samples will need to pass for the same time interval.

Within the code, separate attack and release counters are maintained. These counters are initialized to the value *calcAttackCount* and *calcReleaseCount*, respectively, as these numbers represent the count of samples that represent the current attack and release times. As the user manipulates the attack and release controls in the UI, new values are calculated for the *calcAttackCount* and *calcReleaseCount* values.

In this implementation, the compression/expansion effect is applied across both channels if a stereo signal is being processed. That is, a very loud transient in one channel will affect the gain applied to both channels. This may or may not be the behavior you expect or like so you are free to modify this behavior to fit your needs.

As each individual sample is being processed, the sample is first tested to see if it exceeds the user-selected threshold value. Peak detection acts across both left and right channels if a stereo source is being used. The processing that the sample undergoes is determined by whether or not it exceeds the threshold value. If the sample's value is greater than or equal to the threshold, a test is made to see if the attack time expires (attackCount <= 0). If not, the sample is passed through untouched but the attack time counter is decremented and a test is made to see if the attack time has expired. If it has, the value of the sample will be manipulated. If limiting is not being applied, the sample is simply multiplied by the above-threshold ratio (*atRatio*) value, which is set indirectly by the user. This multiplication can result in compression if *atRatio* is less than 1.0 and expansion if the value is greater than 1.0. How *atRatio* is calculated will be discussed shortly. If limiting is being applied, the value of the sample is set to that of the threshold. In other words, the sample's value is clipped to the threshold's value regardless of the value of the input signal.

If the sample's value is less than the threshold, another branch of the code is taken through *getSamples*. Here a check is made to determine if the timeout occurs here and if so the sample is subjected to the same type of processing (sans limiting) it would have experienced had its value exceeded the threshold. Samples will continue to receive like treatment until the release timeout occurs. At that time, the attack counter is reset and the amplitude processing effects are turned off until the attack again times out.

Additionally, if the value of a sample falls below the threshold, it is subjected to the below-threshold ratio, or *btRatio*. This again is a multiplier effect applied to the value of the sample. At its nominal value, *btRatio* is set to 1.0 so no gain reduction occurs. However, as the user manipulates the BT Ratio control in the UI, the value of *btRatio* falls, reducing the value of the sample accordingly. When the BT Ratio control is set to noise gating, the sample value becomes zero below the threshold, thereby turning off output completely below the threshold.

To understand how gain manipulation is performed, one must understand something of the compression and expansion processes. Compression ratios are typically expressed as a decibel ratio* like 1:2. Where the numerator represents how much the output will change in dB as a result of the dB change in the input level (shown in the denominator). Compression ratios from 1:1 (no compression) to 1:12 are typical of today's devices. Compression ratios of greater than 1:12 are considered limiting. The gain reduction that occurs as a result of compression is then the difference between the input and output gain values. Table 13.3 shows various values of compression and the actual numeric ratio they represent. In the case of compression and expansion, the variable *atRatio* in the code is given the value of Ratio from the table for a given output/input gain setting.

Table 13.3   Compression Ratio

Output Change in dB	Input Change in dB	Delta (in dB)	Ratio
1	1	0	1.0
1	2	−1	0.8913
1	3	−2	0.7643
1	4	−3	0.7079
1	5	−4	0.6310
1	6	−5	0.5623
1	7	−6	0.5012
1	8	−7	0.4467
1	9	−8	0.3981
1	10	−9	0.3548
1	11	−10	0.3162
1	12	−11	0.2818

As shown in Table 13.3, if a sample's value exceeds the threshold and compression is set at 1:12, the resultant sample value will be 0.2818 that of the original value.

Expansion happens in a converse way. For expansion, we need to figure out how much a sample's value will increase due to a 1 dB increase in input signal. The amount of increase depends on the selected ratio and is illustrated in Table 13.4.

---

* Many times the ratios are given in reverse, such as 2:1, meaning how much the input changed vs. how much the output changed. Regardless of which form the ratios are expressed in, they indicate the same thing. I use the output:input convention throughout this discussion.

Table 13.4 Expansion Ratios

Output Change in dB	Input Change in dB	Delta	Value
1	1	0	1.0
2	1	+1	1.1220
3	1	+2	1.2589
4	1	+3	1.4125
5	1	+4	1.5849
6	1	+5	1.7783
7	1	+6	1.9953
8	1	+7	2.2387
9	1	+8	2.5119
10	1	+9	2.8184
11	1	+10	3.1623
12	1	+11	3.5481

As you can see with large expansion ratios like 12:1, the value of a sample increases quickly as the ratio of the sample is multiplied by is 3.5481.

The User Interface

The user interface for this device is the most complex presented in this book. In fact, it was more difficult to write the UI code than it was to write the sample manipulation code that does the actual work. The UI is built with a *GridBagLayout* using controls and indicators presented in section one of this book. Within the UI are numerous slide pots, buttons, LEDs, *ReadoutLabel* indicators, and a special *LabeledGraphSurface* display component that is used to draw the device's input/output response graph.

As with all processing devices presented in this book, a bypass switch and accompanying LED are provided. Anonymous inner listener classes are used to trap and process events from the pots and buttons. Middle-ware methods in *CompExpUI* are called by the listener classes when the UI controls are manipulated. These methods update the *ReadoutLabel* indicators in the UI, then update the graph presented by the *LabeledGraphSurface* component, and then call low-level functions in *CompExpWithUI* to affect the sample processing.

The *LabeledGraphSurface* component combines a *GraphSurface* component which is the UI graph itself with custom classes for labeling both the horizontal and vertical axes of the graph. Updating the graph is accomplished by calling methods on *GraphSurface*. This component understands the concepts of threshold, above-threshold ratio, and below-threshold ratio and how they need to be represented on the graph. In all, three points are calculated and drawn on the graph with a red cross (+). Then yellow lines are drawn connecting the points on the graph.

The front panel controls and indicators are listed in Table 13.5.

Table 13.5 Compressor/Expander/Limits/Noise Gate Processor

Front Panel Controls and Indicators	Description
Graph Surface	This is the area on which the compressor's input/output response graph is drawn. It provides a pictorial representation of how samples passing through the device will be processed.
Threshold Indicator	This *ReadoutLabel* indicator shows the current setting in dB of the threshold slide pot.
BT Ratio Indicator	This *ReadoutLabel* indicator shows the below threshold ratio selected by the *BT Ratio* slide pot.
AT Ratio Indicator	This *ReadoutLabel* indicator shows the above threshold ratio selected by the *AT Ratio* slide pot.
Attack Indicator	This *ReadoutLabel* indicator shows the current setting of the *Attack* slide pot.
Release Indicator	This *ReadoutLabel* indicator shows the current setting of the *Release* slide pot.
Gain Indicator	This *ReadoutLabel* indicator indicates the gain being applied within the effect.
Threshold Slide Pot	This slide pot controls the threshold at which the device begins processing audio. It ranges in value from 0 dB to –60 dB, where the reference is the maximum 16-bit signed value 32,767.
BT Ratio Slide Pot	This below threshold slide pot controls the processing of audio samples that fall below the current threshold value. In its extreme position, noise gating is enabled.
AT Ratio Slide Pot	This above threshold slide pot controls the processing of audio samples that exceed the current threshold value. In its extreme position, limiting is enabled. Values above mid-point indicate expansion whereas values below mid-point indicate compression.
Attack Slide Pot	This slide pot controls the attack time in milliseconds. Attack time is the length of time audio samples must exceed the threshold before processing begins. For noise gating, the attack time is the time audio samples must fall below the threshold before noise gating occurs.

Table 13.5 (continued)

Front Panel Controls and Indicators	Description
Release Slide Pot	This slide pot controls how long the processing effect still occurs after the sample values have returned to the below-threshold values. Release time is measured in milliseconds.
Gain Slide Pot	This slide pot controls how much gain is applied to each sample. At mid-point, no gain is applied. Above mid-point gain is applied to each sample, whereas below mid-point, a loss is applied.
Bypass LED	A green LED that blinks when this processor device is bypassed.
Bypass Button	A *Button* control which, when clicked, puts this device in bypass mode.
Power On LED	A red LED that is always on to simulate power. It does nothing else.

Use with the AudioTest program

The compressor/expander/limiter/noise gate effect is included in the signal path by specifying "–*p compexp*" on the command line to the *AudioTest* program.

Miscellaneous Information

Source Files:

File Name	Package	Description
CompExpUI.java	craigl.processors	The user interface for the compressor/expander effect device.
CompExpWithUI.java	craigl.processors	The *AbstractAudio* device that performs the compressor/expander effect.
GraphSurface.java	craigl.compexp	A class providing the black surface with green grid lines on which the input/output response graph is drawn.
LabeledGraphSurface.java	craigl.compexp	The graph surface and surrounding horizontal and vertical labels.

DELAY PROCESSOR . . . .

Description

The delay effect processor described in this section is the simplest of the delay-based effects presented. Using this effect, delays from 1 millisecond to 2 seconds in duration can be introduced into the signal chain. The UI provided for the delay processor is shown in Figure 13.5. As shown there, numerous controls are provided to allow the delay effect to be tailored to the user's requirements. This delay processor presented works equally well with mono or stereo sources.

The use of delay is common in the recording industry and delay is also a commonly used effect by electric guitarists. When used in small doses, delay tends to fatten up a sound and can help strengthen a vocal part or make a guitar part really stand out. Delays of short duration (< 50 milliseconds) are not perceived as echoes but give the source material an added presence. Delays between 50 milliseconds and 100 milliseconds give a nice doubling effect still without apparent echo. Delays above 200 milliseconds produce a noticeable echo which can be used to advantage in various situations. A two-second delay gives one the urge to yodel as it sounds like the sound is bouncing around in a huge canyon.

It should be noted that delay is not the same as reverb and in fact reverb is a much harder effect to produce correctly. A reverb processor will be presented later in this chapter and the delay vs. reverb question will be taken up there.

To hear what this effect sounds like, listen to the files *craig2delay10ms.wav*, *craig2delay50ms.wav*, *craig2delay100ms.wav,* and *craig2delay1000ms.wav* located in the *\sound* directory of the CDROM.

Figure 13.5   The Delay Processor's User Interface

Operation

The complete block diagram of the delay is shown in Figure 13.6. From this diagram you can see the various signal paths that samples can traverse. The delay effect is implemented as a simple circular buffer the length of which is controlled by the amount of delay requested by the user. The code used for calculating the buffer size given the required delay, the sample rate, and the number of channels is shown below:

```
// Allocate delay buffer
int delayOffset = (delayInMs * sampleRate * numberOfChannels) / 1000;
delayBufferSize = AudioConstants.SAMPLEBUFFERSIZE + delayOffset;

// Allocate new delay buffer
delayBuffer = new short[delayBufferSize];

// Initialize indices
// Index where dry sample is written
writeIndex = 0;

// Index where wet sample is read
readIndex = AudioConstants.SAMPLEBUFFERSIZE;
```

The circular buffer can be visualized as shown in Figure 13.7.

The difference in the position between the read index and the write index is the number of sample times that make up the selected delay. Once a delay is selected, the buffer size is calculated and the buffer is allocated. Once that is done, the read and

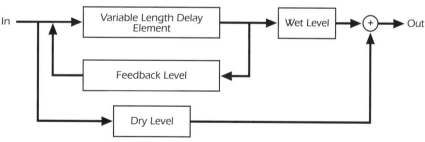

Figure 13.6   Delay Processor Block Diagram

Figure 13.7   Delay Effect Buffer

write indices are positioned. Buffer size doesn't change again until the user changes the delay.

Because this is a circular buffer, the read and write indices must always be kept synchronized with each other and must also be kept within the confines of the buffer. This is easily accomplished using the *mod* operation as shown here:

```
readIndex %= delayBufferSize and writeIndex %= delayBufferSize
```

Using this technique, the indices are guaranteed to wrap around from the end of the buffer back to its beginning without further effort. I should mention that the left and right samples of a stereo signal always occupy adjacent slots in the delay buffer.

At each sample time, new samples entering the circular buffer are written at the *writeIndex* and the index is advanced. Delayed samples are extracted at the *readIndex* and it, too, is advanced. These indices chase each other around the buffer until no more samples are available for processing.

As has been discussed, the term *dry level* refers to the percentage of the unprocessed audio input signal that is coupled into the output. The block diagram shows this signal path clearly. The UI for this device provides a dry level pot for controlling this level. If the dry level pot is set at zero, none of the unprocessed input is fed forward to the output. At a 50% level, input at one-half amplitude is mixed into the output. At 100%, the full amplitude of the input is mixed into the output.

Wet level refers to the percentage of delayed signal which makes its way to the output to be mixed with the dry signal. A pot is also provided in the UI for varying this parameter. By varying the amount of wet and dry level you can control how prominent the delay effect is. Note that you won't hear the effects of the delay if some dry level signal is not present in the output along with the wet delayed signal.

The feedback control in the UI controls how much of the delayed signal is coupled back to the input for recirculation through the delay buffer. Note, that large amounts of feedback will cause the delay processor to function as a comb filter. A comb filter is created when an audio signal is mixed with a delayed copy of itself. Comb filters have been mentioned previously. You'll hear the comb filter effect as the feedback control is increased in value. The sound will change from a typical delay effect with little or no feedback to a metallic or robotic sound as feedback is increased. This effect, which is really a side effect of operation, may also come in handy in some situations.

Since all of the action within the delay processor effect happens in its *getSamples* method, this method is shown below. It is the *getSamples* method that is called by subsequent processing stages to pull samples through this device.

```java
// Process the samples that pass through this effect
public int getSamples(short [] buffer, int length) {

    if (getByPass() || !initializationComplete)
        return previous.getSamples(buffer, length);

    // Read number of samples requested from previous stage
    int len = previous.getSamples(localBuffer, length);

    // Do the processing
    for (int i=0; i < len; i++) {
        int inputSample = (int) localBuffer[i];
        int delaySample = (int) delayBuffer[readIndex++];
        int outputSample =   ((inputSample * dryLevel) / 100) +
                             ((delaySample * wetLevel) / 100);

        // Clamp output to legal range
        if (outputSample > 32767)
            outputSample = 32767;
        else if (outputSample < -32768)
            outputSample = -32768;

        // Store in output sample
        buffer[i] = (short) outputSample;

        // Calculate feedback
        inputSample += (delaySample * feedbackLevel) / 100;

        // Clamp output to legal range
        if (inputSample > 32767)
            inputSample = 32767;
        else if (inputSample < -32768)
            inputSample = -32768;

        delayBuffer[writeIndex++] = (short) inputSample;

        // Update indices
         readIndex %= delayBufferSize;
         writeIndex %= delayBufferSize;
    }
    return len;
}
```

The User Interface

The user interface for the delay processor device is shown in Figure 13.5. The code that produces the UI is contained in the file *DelayUI.java* whereas it is the code in *DelayWithUI.java* which does the actual sample processing described above. The *DelayWithUI* class instantiates *DelayUI* as it is coming up.

The UI is built with a *GridBagLayout* using the controls and indicators presented in section one of this book. Within the UI are numerous pots, buttons, LEDs, and *ReadoutLabel* indicators. As with all processing devices, a bypass button and accompanying LED are provided. Anonymous inner listener classes are used to trap and process events from the pots and buttons. Middle-ware methods are called by the listener classes when the UI controls are manipulated. These methods update the indicators in the UI and then call low-level functions in *DelayWithUI* to affect processing.

Special effort was required to support the concept of varying resolutions of the Delay pot as required for this application. The UI provides course, medium, and fine delay buttons that allow the single Delay pot to function at all three levels. If you play with the UI for a minute, you'll get the idea. If you are interested in how this was done, consult the code in *DelayUI.java*.

Table 13.6   Delay Processor Front Panel Controls and Indicators

Front Panel Controls and Indicators	Description
Course Delay Button	This button is part of the three-button set used to control the granularity of the delay set using the Delay pot. When clicked, each tic of the Delay pot corresponds to 100 milliseconds of delay. Total delay can be very exactly set (to the millisecond) using a combination of the three delay granularities provided.
Medium Delay Button	This button is also part of the three-button set used to control the granularity of the delay set using the Delay pot. When clicked, each tic of the Delay pot corresponds to 10 milliseconds of delay.
Fine Delay Button	This button is also part of the three-button set used to control the granularity of the delay set using the Delay pot. When clicked, each tic of the Delay pot corresponds to 1 millisecond of delay.
Delay Indicator	A *ReadoutLabel* indicator showing the delay in milliseconds (ms) dialed in with the Delay pot.
Delay Pot	This pot sets the static delay used in this effect. The range of values is from 1 to 2000 milliseconds. Short delays tend to fatten up the sound. Long delays result in echo.

Table 13.6   (continued)

Front Panel Controls and Indicators	Description
Dry Level Indicator	A *ReadoutLabel* indicator indicating the amount of the dry (unprocessed) signal present in the output.
Dry Level Pot	This pot controls the amount of the dry (unprocessed) signal present in the output.
Wet Level Indicator	A *ReadoutLabel* indicator indicating the amount of the wet (delayed) signal present in the output.
Wet Level Pot	This pot controls the amount of the wet (delayed) signal present in the output.
Feedback Indicator	A *ReadoutLabel* indicator indicating the amount of the delayed output signal fed back to the input.
Feedback Pot	This pot controls the amount of the delayed output signal coupled back to the input. Large amounts of feedback result in a very metallic sound as the delay becomes a comb filter.
On LED	A red LED that simulates a power on indicator. It does nothing else.
Bypass LED	A green LED that flashes when this effect is bypassed.
Bypass Button	Clicking this button causes the delay effect to be bypassed. In other words, the processor's effect is removed from the signal chain.

Use with the AudioTest Program

When using the *AudioTest* program, the delay processor is included in the signal path by specifying the command line switch "*–p delay.*" To process an audio file using the delay effect and be able to listen to the results, the following command line might be used:

```
java craigl.test.AudioTest -i file -p delay -o winplayer
```

Miscellaneous Information

Package:

> craigl.processors

Source Files:

File Name	Description
DelayUI.java	The user interface for the delay effect as shown in Figure 13.5.
DelayWithUI.java	The *AbstractAudio* device that performs the delay.

DISTORTION PROCESSOR . . . .

Description

The distortion effect processor described here uses clipping to distort an audio signal. This is a very crude device whose only purpose is to illustrate how clipping is done. I doubt whether this device in its present form will find any useful application, but who knows?

This device clips samples to produce distortion just like the first generation of guitar fuzz tone pedals clipped the guitar's signal to produce distortion. The problem with this approach is the harshness of the result. Newer generations of distortion boxes for guitars have a much richer sound, reminiscent of the type of distortion tube amplifiers produce when driven at high volume levels. Unfortunately, the modeling of distorting tubes with DSP is beyond the scope of this processing device—and this book, for that matter.

To hear what this effect sounds like, listen to the file *craig1distortion.wav* located in the *\sound* directory of the CDROM.

Operation

As you might have guessed, clipping samples in the digital domain is very easy. One only has to compare the value of the sample to the threshold value and replace the sample's value with the threshold if the threshold was exceeded. The code in the *getSamples* method of the distortion processor shown below illustrates how this is done. Things couldn't get much simpler.

```
public int getSamples(short [] buffer, int length) {

    int len = previous.getSamples(buffer, length);
    if (getByPass())
        return len;

    for (int i=0; i < len; i++) {
        int sample = buffer[i];
        if (sample > threshold)
            sample = threshold;
        else if (sample < -threshold)
            sample = -threshold;

        buffer[i] = (short)(sample * gain);
    }
    return len;
}
```

You'll note that the sample amplitude lost as a result of clipping can be compensated for by increasing the gain. Here the gain adjustment is performed with a simple multiplication.

The User Interface

The user interface for the distortion processor is shown in Figure 13.8. The code that produces the UI is contained in the file *DistortionUI.java* whereas it is the code in *DistortionWithUI* which does the actual sample processing described above. As is typical, the *DistortionWithUI* class instantiates *DistortionUI* as it is coming up. Since there is nothing special about the UI for this device, no discussion will be given.

Figure 13.8   *The Distortion Processor's User Interface*

Table 13.7 lists the front panel controls and indicators for the distortion processor.

Table 13.7   Distortion Processor Front Panel Controls and Indicators

Front Panel Controls and Indicators	Description
Distortion Pot	This pot controls the threshold at which clipping occurs. At the "more" end of the distortion scale, the threshold is set at 3276 and samples with values equal to or greater than this will be set to this value. At the "less" end of the scale the threshold is at 32767. As this pot is rotated through its range of values, the threshold where clipping occurs changes accordingly.
Gain Slide Pot	Since clipping samples tends to reduce their level, this gain control is provided to make up for the lost level.
Bypass LED	A green LED that flashes when this effect is bypassed.
Bypass Button	Clicking this button causes the distortion effect to be bypassed. In other words, the processor's effect is removed from the signal chain.

Use with the AudioTest Program

When using the *AudioTest* program, the delay processor is included in the signal path by specifying the command line switch "–*p distortion*."

Miscellaneous Information

Package:

craigl.processors

Source Files:

File Name	Description
DistortionUI.java	The user interface for the distortion effect as shown in Figure 13.8.
DistortionWithUI.java	The *AbstractAudio* device that generates the distortion using clipping.

GRAPHIC EQUALIZER PROCESSOR · · · · · · · · · · · · · · ·

Description

Graphic equalizers are a somewhat common piece of equipment in personal stereo systems and a very common component in professional recording studios. Even some car audio systems are equipped with a graphic equalizer to adjust the frequency content of the sound according to the driver's preferences. Typically, a graphic equalizer consists of a series of slide pots each controlling a band-pass filter centered at a specific frequency. Inexpensive graphic equalizers have a limited number of wide frequency ranges whereas professional graphic equalizers place the center frequencies every 1/3 octave and have much narrower frequency bands.

Typically the slide pots are placed side by side and the center position of each pot represents the flat (unmodified) position. As the position of the slide pot is moved above center, the frequencies affected by the pot are accentuated. When the pot's position is below center, the corresponding frequencies are attenuated. In professional audio terms, the frequencies are boosted or cut. With this side-by-side arrangement of frequency pots, the position of the pots' sliders provide a visual graph of the selected frequency response.

The amount of boost or cut each frequency pot provides is a function of an equalizer's design. Here, 12 dB of boost or cut is provided. That is, the frequencies in each band can be adjusted by +/– 12 dB. The center frequencies in this design are placed at 50 Hz, 100 Hz, 200 Hz, 400 Hz, 800 Hz, 1.6 kHz, 3.2 kHz, 6.4 kHz, and 12.8 kHz. A 1/3 octave equalizer could easily be built by extending this design.

A plot of the idealized gain for the equalizer with all slide pots set to full boost would be similar to the one shown in Figure 13.9. *Note:* The response would only look like this if the X axis is plotted on a log scale.

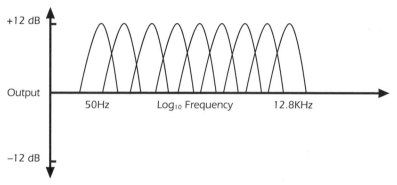

Figure 13.9   Idealized Gain for Graphic Equalizer. All slide pots are set to full boost.

The Q or the sharpness of the individual bandpass filters was chosen to be 1.4 so that the troughs between peaks at the full boost position are minimized (necessary to limit extreme ripple in the amplitude response).

To hear what this effect sounds like, listen to the files *craig1eq1.wav*, *craig1eq2.wav*, and *craig1eq3.wav* located in the *sound* directory of the CDROM.

Operation

This graphic equalizer is implemented using nine IIR band-pass filters of the variety described in Chapter 10. See the graphic equalizer block diagram shown in Figure 13.10. Each filter is designed for a different center frequency and each is also designed with a constant Q of 1.4 for the reasons mentioned. Because each filter introduces gain into the signal path, special treatment of the input samples is necessary to keep the gain of this device similar to that when the device is bypassed.

The overall gain calculation is complicated by the fact that we also have to worry about aliasing caused by low sampling rates. Specifically, the filters that manipulate the two highest frequency bands are selectively enabled or disabled, depending on the sample rate of the audio being processed. The sample rate must be above twice the highest frequency 12.8 kHz (25.6 kHz) for all slide pots to function correctly. If the sample rate is below this value, the highest frequency filter and then the second highest frequency filter will be dynamically disabled.

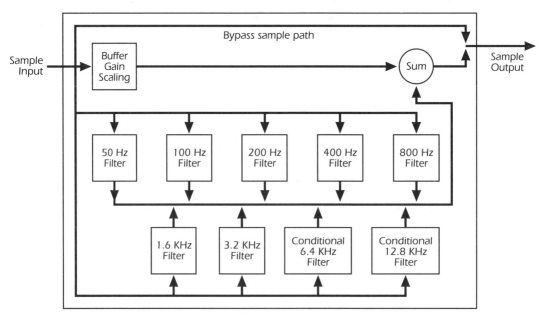

Figure 13.10   Graphic Equalizer Block Diagram

This complicates the gain calculations because the number of filters changes depending on the sample rate and of course the sample rate won't be known until after negotiation has been performed. The code which does the filter design (after the sample rate is known) and the gain determination is shown below:

```java
private void doInitialization() {

    // Total the number of filter gain elements in chain
    gainElements = 1;

    // Design the filters now that the sampling rate is known.
    // Design the filter
    fd50Hz = new IIRBandpassFilterDesign(50, sampleRate, Q);
    fd50Hz.doFilterDesign();

    // Implement the filter design
    f50Hz = new IIRBandpassFilter(fd50Hz);
    gainElements++;

    // Design the filter
    fd100Hz = new IIRBandpassFilterDesign(100, sampleRate, Q);
    fd100Hz.doFilterDesign();

    // Implement the filter design
    f100Hz = new IIRBandpassFilter(fd100Hz);
    gainElements++;

    // Design the filter
    fd200Hz = new IIRBandpassFilterDesign(200, sampleRate, Q);
    fd200Hz.doFilterDesign();

    // Implement the filter design
    f200Hz = new IIRBandpassFilter(fd200Hz);
    gainElements++;

    // Design the filter
    fd400Hz = new IIRBandpassFilterDesign(400, sampleRate, Q);
    fd400Hz.doFilterDesign();

    // Implement the filter design
    f400Hz = new IIRBandpassFilter(fd400Hz);
    gainElements++;
```

```
// Design the filter
fd800Hz = new IIRBandpassFilterDesign(800, sampleRate, Q);
fd800Hz.doFilterDesign();

// Implement the filter design
f800Hz = new IIRBandpassFilter(fd800Hz);
gainElements++;

// Design the filter
fd1600Hz = new IIRBandpassFilterDesign(1600, sampleRate, Q);
fd1600Hz.doFilterDesign();

// Implement the filter design
f1600Hz = new IIRBandpassFilter(fd1600Hz);
gainElements++;

// Design the filter
fd3200Hz = new IIRBandpassFilterDesign(3200, sampleRate, Q);
fd3200Hz.doFilterDesign();

// Implement the filter design
f3200Hz = new IIRBandpassFilter(fd3200Hz);
gainElements++;

// Conditionally design and implement the higher freq filters
if (sampleRate > 12800) {
    // Design the filter
    fd6400Hz = new IIRBandpassFilterDesign(6400, sampleRate, Q);
    fd6400Hz.doFilterDesign();

    // Implement the filter design
    f6400Hz = new IIRBandpassFilter(fd6400Hz);
    gainElements++;
}

if (sampleRate > 25600) {
    // Design the filter
    fd12800Hz = new IIRBandpassFilterDesign(12800, sampleRate, Q);
    fd12800Hz.doFilterDesign();

    // Implement the filter design
    f12800Hz = new IIRBandpassFilter(fd12800Hz);
    gainElements++;
}
gainFactor = 1.0/ gainElements;
```

```
    // All filters designed, indicate initialization is complete
    initializationComplete = true;
}
```

As you can see, the number of gain elements is counted and the count is what is used for gain scaling later.

As shown in the block diagram of Figure 13.10, each filter operates on the samples provided by the previous *AbstractAudio* device in the signal chain. The filters are effectively applied to the input data in parallel even though they are executed sequentially. Samples are processed a buffer at a time. The block marked Buffer Gain Scaling on the diagram converts a buffer of the input (short) samples into a buffer of double samples while applying gain reduction proportional to the number of gain elements (filters). The output of each filter is summed with the converted samples to form the final output.

The *getSamples* method for the graphic equalizer which does all of this is shown below.

```
public int getSamples(short [] buffer, int length) {

    // Ask for a buffer of samples
    int len = previous.getSamples(buffer, length);
    if (len == -1)
        return len;

    // If bypass is enabled, short circuit filtering
    if (getByPass() || !initializationComplete)
        return len;

    // Realloc buffer as required
    if (dBuffer.length != len)
        dBuffer = new double[len];

    // Move short samples into summation buffer for processing
    // Prescale the data according to number of filter elements
    for (int i=0; i < len; i++)
        dBuffer[i] = (double) buffer[i] * gainFactor;

    // Apply the filters sequentially
    f50Hz.doFilter(buffer, dBuffer, len);
    f100Hz.doFilter(buffer, dBuffer, len);
    f200Hz.doFilter(buffer, dBuffer, len);
    f400Hz.doFilter(buffer, dBuffer, len);
    f800Hz.doFilter(buffer, dBuffer, len);
```

```
f1600Hz.doFilter(buffer, dBuffer, len);
f3200Hz.doFilter(buffer, dBuffer, len);
if (sampleRate > 12800)
    f6400Hz.doFilter(buffer, dBuffer, len);

if (sampleRate > 25600)
    f12800Hz.doFilter(buffer, dBuffer, len);

// Convert the double samples back into short samples after
// range constraining them.
for (int i=0; i < len; i++) {
    double dSample = dBuffer[i];
    if (dSample > 32767.0)
        dSample = 32767.0;
    else if (dSample < -32768.0)
        dSample = -32768.0;

    // Convert sample and store
    buffer[i] = (short) dSample;
}
return len;
}
```

Double samples are processed by the filters to avoid numeric inaccuracies that would compromise the performance of the IIR band-pass filters.

What is not apparent from the code seen thus far is how the user's boost/cut selections are applied to the audio samples passing through the graphic equalizer. As you may recall from the discussion in Chapter 3, the *BoostCutSlidePot* produces a value that represents a gain value in dB. These pots are configured here to have a range of +/– 12dB. This means the gain at the maximum (+12 dB) position would be returned as a factor of +3.98; at the mid (0 dB) position, the gain would be returned as +1.0; and the factor returned at the minimum (–12 dB) position of the slider would be –0.25. These gain values are set directly into the filters with a call to the filter's *setAmplitudeAdj* method. The additive or subtractive filtered sample values are added directly into the double samples passed in the buffer from previous stages and the filter's effect is thus achieved.

Important Note

The graphic equalizer presented should be used only with mono audio sources. When used with a stereo source, the equalizer combines the frequency content of both channels inappropriately. A stereo version of this equalizer would have a set of filters for each channel and the interleaved stereo data would need to be demultiplexed and routed to the appropriate filter bank.

The User Interface

The user interface for the graphic equalizer is shown in Figure 13.11. As shown there, the equalizer consists of a group of nine slide pots, each centered at a different frequency. There is also a bypass button with corresponding LED and a simulated power-on LED. The UI was designed to simulate what a rack-mounted graphic equalizer really looks like. The slide pots are placed side by side so that the position of the sliders gives a visual indication of the frequency response currently dialed in.

The user interface is managed using a *GridBagLayout*, which allows maximum flexibility in component placement. Each of the slide pots is of the *BoostCutSlidePot* variety. These specialized slide pots were described in Chapter 3. Anonymous inner listener classes are used to trap and process events from the slide pots and button. Middle-ware methods in *GraphicEQUI* are called by the listener classes when the UI controls are manipulated. These methods, in turn, call methods in *GraphicEQWithUI* to update the gain adjustment for the individual filter sections and/or to take the equalizer into and out of bypass mode.

Table 13.8   Graphics Equalizer Front Panel Controls and Indicators

Front Panel Controls and Indicators	Description
50 Hz Slide Pot	Control that determines the amount of boost or cut that occurs around 50 Hz.
100 Hz Slide Pot	Control that determines the amount of boost or cut that occurs around 100 Hz.
200 Hz Slide Pot	Control that determines the amount of boost or cut that occurs around 200 Hz.

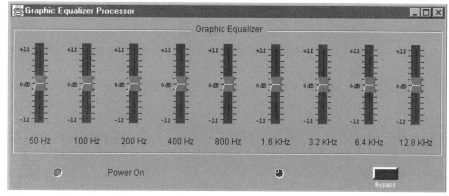

Figure 13.11   User Interface for the Graphic Equalizer Processor. All slide pots shown in the flat position.

Table 13.8   (continued)

Front Panel Controls and Indicators	Description
400 Hz Slide Pot	Control that determines the amount of boost or cut that occurs around 400 Hz.
800 Hz Slide Pot	Control that determines the amount of boost or cut that occurs around 800 Hz.
1.6 kHz Slide Pot	Control that determines the amount of boost or cut that occurs around 1.6 kHz.
3.2 kHz Slide Pot	Control that determines the amount of boost or cut that occurs around 3.2 kHz.
6.4 kHz Slide Pot	Control that determines the amount of boost or cut that occurs around 6.4 kHz.
12.8 kHz Slide Pot	Control that determines the amount of boost or cut that occurs around 12.8 kHz.
Power On LED	A red LED that simulates a power indicator. Its does nothing else.
Bypass LED	Green LED that blinks when the graphic equalizer is bypassed.
Bypass Button	In the unbypassed state, the audio samples passing through the graphic equalizer are subjected to the filter response curve set up by the user. In the bypassed state, this processing stage is bypassed. Samples out equals samples in.

Use with the AudioTest Program

When using the *AudioTest* program, the graphic equalizer processor is included in the signal path by specifying the command line switch "*–p eq*." To capture sound from the mic/line input of your PC at a sample rate of 11025 samples per second and to use the graphic equalizer to manipulate it, the following command line would be used:

```
java craigl.test.AudioTest -i mic 11025 1 -p eq -o winplayer
```

Miscellaneous Information

Package:

craigl.processors

Source Files:

File Name	Description
GraphicEQUI.java	User interface code (simulated front panel) for the graphic equalizer processor as shown in Figure 13.11.
GraphicEQWithUI.java	*AbstractAudio* device which performs the graphic equalizer function.

PANNER PROCESSOR . . . .

Description

Panning is the process of positioning an audio signal in the sound panorama. When dealing with two channel stereo audio, an audio signal can be positioned totally in the left channel, equally in the left and right channels (in the center), totally in the right channel, or anywhere in between. Panning is accomplished by rotating a pan pot to the desired position (see Figure 13.12).

How panning operates depends on whether the sample source for the panner processor is mono or stereo. The output of the panner processor is always stereo. If the signal source is mono, the position of the pan pot determines how much of the mono signal is routed into the left and/or right channels. If the signal is panned hard to either the left or the right, 100% of the mono signal is routed to the appropriate output channel and the opposite channel level drops to zero. If the pan pot is placed in the center, one half of the mono signal goes to the left output channel and one half goes to the right output channel.

If the signal source for the panner is stereo, panning works differently. In fact there are two different modes of operation possible: pre-mix and non pre-mix. In pre-mix mode, the left and right stereo channels are added together, thus creating a mono signal, before panning is applied. The composite mono signal is then panned as described above for mono signal sources. In non pre-mix mode, a panner acts like a balance control on a stereo receiver. In this mode stereo separation is maintained in that the left input channel is routed to the left output channel and right input channel

Figure 13.12   User Interface (Simulated Front Panel) for Panner Processor

is routed to the right output channel. The position of the pan pot controls the attenuation applied to each channel. In the extreme left position, 100% of the left input channel is routed to the left output but 0% of the right input goes to the right output. In the center position, 50% of the left signal goes to the left output and 50% of the right input goes to the right output. In the extreme right position, 0% of the left signal is propagated to the left output but 100% of the right input is propagated.

To hear what this effect sounds like, listen to the file *craig1panner.wav* located in the *sound* directory of the CDROM.

Operation

The panner processor is the only processor in this book that manipulates the channel negotiation process. In the normal channel negotiation process, the sample source and the sample sink agree on the number of channels to process and all processing stages in between are bound to this agreement. When a panner processor is one of those intermediate stages, the number of channels before and after the panner can be different. The audio processing chain before the panner can be mono or stereo but it is always stereo after the panner. This manipulation is performed by overloading the *minMaxChannels* and the *setChannelsRecursive* methods provided by the *AbstractAudio* base class. As can be seen in the code fragment that follows, when the *minMaxChannels* method is called during the negotiation process, the call is propagated all of the way to the source to get its min, max, and preferred channel requirements. As the call to *minMaxChannels* in each stage returns, the min, max, and preferred parameters are available to the stage. The *minMaxChannels* method for the panner saves the preferred channel count from the previous stages and then sets the min, max, and preferred values to stereo for all subsequent stages. Thus, the audio processing chain can be mono up to the panner but is always stereo afterwards.

```
// Override this method to capture the preferred number
// of channels from the stages preceding the panner but
// return a stereo preference from this panner stage. This is
// done because the output of the panner is always stereo.
public void minMaxChannels(MyInt min, MyInt max, MyInt preferred) {

    // Propagate call towards the source
    if (previous != null)
        previous.minMaxChannels(min,max,preferred);
    // Save the preferred value from previous stages
    preferredChannels = preferred.getValue();
    // Set flag to indicate source mode
    monoSource = (preferredChannels == 1);

    // Set up for stereo as the output of the panner is
    // always stereo.
    min.setValue(2);
    max.setValue(2);
    preferred.setValue(2);
}
```

The stereo channel assignment propagates from the panner to the sink which then calls *setChannelsRecursive* in each stage to set the agreed-upon number of channels into the stage. When this method is called for the panner, the number of channels for the stages preceding the panner are set appropriately and the number of channels for the stages after the panner are set to stereo.

```
// Override this method so that all stages before the panner
// use their negotiated preference (stereo or mono). All
// stages afterwards are stereo.
public void setChannelsRecursive(int ch) {

    ch = preferredChannels;
    super.setChannelsRecursive(ch);
    // Update panner UI with source mode
    pui.setSourceChannels(ch);
}
```

The real work in panning an audio source takes place in the *getSamples* method of the panning processor, the code for which is shown below. Its operation should be obvious from the comments in the code. The important thing to understand about this code is how a single buffer is used for acquiring and manipulating the samples. All processing is done on this single buffer for efficiency.

```
// Apply the panner effect to the samples passing through this
// stage.
public int getSamples(short [] buffer, int length) {

    // If the previous stage constitutes a mono (single channel)
    // source, then halve the number of samples requested. This
    // allows the use of a single buffer for processing.

    int halfLength = length / 2;

    // Request samples from previous stage
    int len = previous.getSamples(buffer, monoSource ? halfLength : length);

    // Was EOF indication returned?
    if (len == -1)
        return -1;

    // If bypass in effect and we have a stereo source, don't do
    // anything as samples are already in the buffer. If we have
    // a mono source, copy mono samples to both the left and right
    // channels.
    if (getByPass()) {
        if (monoSource) {
            // We have a mono source to process. Work from back to front
            // of buffer to prevent over writing unprocessed data.
            int sourceIndex = halfLength - 1;
            int destIndex = length - 2;

            for (int i=0; i < halfLength; i++) {
                short s = buffer[sourceIndex-]; // Read mono sample
                buffer[destIndex] = s;          // Write left channel
                buffer[destIndex+1] = s;        // Write right channel
                destIndex -= 2;
            }
        }
        return length;
    }
    // Bypass not in effect, do some panning
```

```
    // What is done depends upon source and mode
    if (monoSource) {
        // We have a mono source to process. Work from back to front
        // of buffer to prevent over writing unprocessed data.
        int sourceIndex = halfLength - 1;
        int destIndex = length - 2;
        for (int i=0; i < halfLength; i++) {
            short s = buffer[sourceIndex-];
            buffer[destIndex] = (short) (s * leftPanFactor);
            buffer[destIndex+1] = (short) (s * rightPanFactor);
            destIndex -= 2;
        }

    } else {

        // We have a stereo source to process. Check the mode.
        if (mixMode) {
            // Mix left and right before panning
            for (int i=0; i < length; i+=2) {
                double s = (buffer[i] + buffer[i+1]) / 2.0;
                buffer[i] = (short) (s * leftPanFactor);
                buffer[i+1] = (short) (s * rightPanFactor);
            }

        } else {
            // Leave stereo separation intact
            for (int i=0; i < length; i+=2) {
                buffer[i] = (short) (buffer[i] * leftPanFactor);
                buffer[i+1] = (short) (buffer[i+1] * rightPanFactor);
            }
        }
    }
    return length;
}
```

Table 13.9 lists the front panel controls and indicators for the panner processor.

Table 13.9   *Panner Processor*

Front Panel Controls and Indicators	Description
Mono LED	Yellow LED that is lit when the processing stages previous to the panner processor are supplying mono samples.
Stereo LED	Green LED that is lit when the processing stages previous to the panner processor are supplying stereo samples.
Pan Pot	Controls where in the sound panorama the audio source appears. Signal can be panned hard left, center, or hard right or anywhere in between.
Stereo Pre-mix Button	If activated (pre-mix mode) and a stereo sample source is being processed, the left and the right samples are mixed together to create a mono signal before being panned. In pre-mix mode, stereo separation of the source is lost. If deactivated and a stereo sample source is being processed, the pan pot determines the attenuation of the left and right channel samples. That is, panning hard left will allow the left channel samples to pass unattenuated but the right channel samples will be fully attenuated. In non pre-mix mode, stereo separation is maintained. If a mono source is being processed, this button has no effect in either position.
Bypass LED	Green LED that blinks when the panner processor is bypassed.
Bypass Button	In the deactivated state, the audio samples passing through this processing stage are panned according to the position of the pan pot. In the activated state, this processing stage is bypassed. Samples out equals samples in.

Use with the AudioTest Program

When using the *AudioTest* program, the panner processor is included in the signal path by specifying the command line switch "*–p pan.*" To read an audio file, process it with some delay, and then use the panner processor, the following command line would be used:

```
java craigl.test.AudioTest -i file -p delay pan -o winplayer
```

Miscellaneous Information

Package:

craigl.processors

Source Files:

File Name	Description
PannerUI.java	User Interface (simulated front panel) for panner processor as shown in Figure 13.12.
PannerWithUI.java	Audio device extension of *AbstractAudio* device.

PARAMETRIC EQUALIZER PROCESSOR . . . .

Description

A parametric equalizer is a set of specialized tone controls which have adjustable frequency and often adjustable sharpness or Q. This type of equalizer is an important audio tool in that it allows very specific audio frequencies to be manipulated without affecting surrounding frequencies to any significant degree. Parametric equalizers are different from the graphic equalizer presented earlier in that the boost and cut frequencies of the graphic equalizer are fixed.

Parametric equalizers come in many configurations. In general there are three- and four-frequency band varieties, with some varieties having a sharpness control for each band. The parametric equalizer presented here is a three-band variety that has a sharpness control for the mid-range frequency group only. Of course, since you have access to the source code for this device, you can extend it in any way you see fit. Adding a fourth band or adding sharpness controls to each band is a trivial extension of the design presented.

In this design, three filters make up the parametric equalizer: a low-pass filter with an adjustable cutoff frequency; a band-pass filter with adjustable center frequency and adjustable sharpness; and a high-pass filter, again with an adjustable cutoff. As a user makes changes to the front panel controls of the parametric equalizer, changes to the filter's parameters are routed to the appropriate filter. A new filter is instantly realized with the new parameters and immediately takes effect.

A plot of the idealized gain for the parametric equalizer with all slide pots set to full boost (+12 dB) would be similar to the one shown in Figure 13.13.

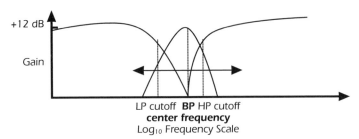

Figure 13.13   *Idealized Gain for the Parametrics Equalizer. All pots set to full boost.*

The dotted lines represented the cutoff and the center frequencies that can be manipulated by the user. The double-headed arrow indicates that each of the three frequencies can be independently varied over a limited range. Note that, the response pictured would only look like this if the frequency (X-axis value) is plotted on a log scale.

Operation

The filters used in this parametric equalizer were described in detail in Chapter 10. The high-pass, band-pass, and low-pass filters are all of the IIR type and are fully digital in nature. A block diagram of the parametric equalizer can be found in Figure 13.14.

Except for the types of filters employed, this parametric equalizer is of very similar design to the graphic equalizer presented previously. The gain management technique used in the graphic equalizer is used in this design as well. Also, the concept of parallel sample data filtering with subsequent summing of the results is employed both here and in the design of the graphic equalizer. If you are interested in a more detailed

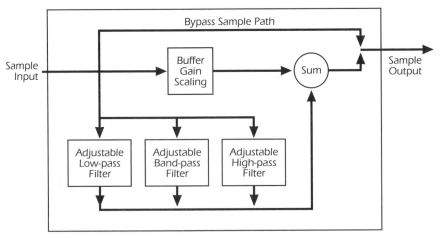

Figure 13.14   Parametrics Equalizer Block Diagram

discussion of how the filtering works, consult the discussion provided in the graphic equalizer section or look at the code in *ParametricEQWithUI.java*.

Important Note

The parametric equalizer presented should only be used with mono audio sources. When used with a stereo source, the equalizer combines the frequency content of both channels inappropriately. A stereo version of this equalizer would have a set of filters for each channel and the interleaved stereo data would need to be demultiplexed and routed to the appropriate filter bank.

Note also that the operation of the high-frequency and mid-frequency controls is limited to those frequencies that fall below the Nyquist limit. In other words, these controls are automatically disabled for those frequencies that are higher than twice the sampling rate of the audio passing through this device.

The User Interface

The user interface for the parametric equalizer is shown in Figure 13.15. The simulated front panel was designed to emulate a channel strip (or module) of a recording con-

Figure 13.15 *User Interface for the Parametric Equalizer Processor. Each group of controls is color coded for group association.*

sole where parametric equalizers are typically found. This UI design is but one possible layout for this device. You might want to change the layout to better suit your needs. This can easily be accomplished without even changing the code that performs the parametric filtering function.

The equalizer's UI consists of three groups of controls plus the requisite bypass button and LED. There is one group of controls for the high frequencies, one for the mid frequencies, and one for the low frequencies. Two controls, a pot and a slide pot, comprise the high- and low-frequency group. The mid-frequency group has an additional sharpness (Q) pot. Each control group is color coded as a visual indication of which controls make up which group. The high frequency controls are red, the mid frequency controls are green, and the low frequency controls are dark blue.

The user interface is managed using a *GridBagLayout*, which allows maximum flexibility in component placement. Each of the frequency pots are *IntValuedPots*, each of the boost/cut slide pots are of the *BoostCutSlidePot* variety, and the sharpness (Q) pot is a *RealValuedPot*. Each of these varieties of pots is described in detail in Chapter 3.

Anonymous inner listener classes are used to trap and process events from the pots, the slide pots, and the bypass button. Middle-ware methods in *ParametricEQUI* are called by the listener classes when the UI controls are manipulated. These methods, in turn, call methods in *ParametricEQWithUI* to update the frequency, gain, and Q adjustment values for the individual filter sections and/or to take the equalizer into and out of bypass mode.

Table 13.10 shows the front panel controls and indicators for the parametric equalizer processor.

Table 13.10   Parametric Equalizer Processor Front Panel Controls and Indicators

Front Panel Controls and Indicators	Description
High Frequencies Frequency Adjustment Pot	Control that sets the cutoff frequency of the high-pass shelving filter. The range of frequency values is adjustable from 5 kHz to 16 kHz, assuming the sampling rate is above 32 kHz. This control is disabled for frequency selections above one half the sampling rate.
High Frequencies Gain Slide Pot	Control that determines the amount of boost or cut that occurs at and above the frequency set by the high-frequencies frequency adjustment pot. Range of values is +/– 12 dB.
Mid-Range Frequencies Frequency Adjustment Pot	Control that sets the center frequency of the band-pass peaking filter. The range of frequency values is adjustable from 1.5 kHz to 6 kHz. This control is disabled for frequency selections above one half the sampling rate.

Table 13.10 (continued)

Front Panel Controls and Indicators	Description
Mid-Range Frequencies Gain Slide Pot	Control that determines the amount of boost or cut that occurs at and around the center frequency set by the mid-range frequencies frequency adjustment pot. Range of values is +/– 12 dB.
Mid-Range Frequencies Sharpness (Q) Adjustment Pot	Control that determines the sharpness of the mid-range frequencies bandpass filter. The selectable range is from 1 to 16 with 16 being the narrowest or sharpest peak, which is the most selective in terms of frequency.
Low Frequencies Frequency Adjustment Pot	Control that sets the cutoff frequency of the low-pass shelving filter. The range of frequency values is adjustable from 40 Hz to 1.5 kHz.
Low Frequencies Gain Slide Pot	Control that determines the amount of boost or cut that occurs at and above the frequency set by the low-frequencies frequency adjustment pot. Range of values is +/– 12 dB.
Bypass LED	Green LED that blinks when the parametric equalizer is bypassed.
Bypass Button	In the unbypassed state, the audio samples passing through the parametric equalizer are subjected to the filter response set up by the user. In the bypassed state, this processing stage is bypassed. Samples out equals samples in.

Use with the AudioTest Program

When using the *AudioTest* program, the parametric equalizer processor is included in the signal path by specifying the command line switch "*–p peq.*"

Miscellaneous Information

Package:

craigl.processors

Source Files:

File Name	Description
ParametricEQUI.java	User interface code (simulated front panel) for the parametric equalizer processor. See Figure 13.15.
ParametricEQWithUI.java	*AbstractAudio* device which performs the parametric equalizer function.

PHASER PROCESSOR . . . .

Description

Phasers or phase shifters (or sometimes even phasors) were very important sound processing devices for guitarists and vocalists in the 1970s. These classic devices produced a dream-like, ethereal sound that permeated the music of the psychedelic era. In the opinion of many, these devices were seriously overused. I still have an old phaser foot pedal (stomp box in today's vernacular) that I use with my acoustic guitar from time to time. When used with restraint, these devices can add a presence to the guitar or to a vocal that is hard to beat.

Phasers can sound a lot like flangers as the affect they have on the audio passing through them is similar. Both devices cause notches in the audio frequency spectrum as they are swept up and down. Flangers typically use a linear sweep of these notches whereas phasers use a logarithmic one. Even though these effects sometimes sound the same, the techniques used to produce them are very different. The flanger device presented earlier in this chapter used delay elements to produce a comb filter. The phaser presented here uses a series of all-pass filters to do its work.

In about 1976 I built a phaser for electric guitar that consisted of numerous opamps, four FETs (field effect transistors), and four resistor/capacitor networks. An adjustable frequency sweep drove the FETs. The FETs behaved like variable resistors and were used to change the phase of the resistor/capacitor networks. The output of each phase shifter stage was wired to the input of the next. When I finally got it all to work, I was really proud of myself. If I recall correctly, it didn't work for very long however, due to my marginal assembly techniques.

Now jump ahead 23 years. I still enjoy the phaser effect, so I had to implement one for inclusion in this book. This time, however, phasing is done entirely in the digital domain in software. Boy, how things have changed. Now, instead of the two crude controls I had in my hardware implementation (sweep frequency and depth) this design gives the user a great many controls for fine tuning the phasing effect. The capabilities of the phase shifter device presented here far exceeds anything available in the 1970s or 1980s.

By the way, the device presented here uses four all-pass filter stages to emulate the four filter stages used in the hardware device I built years ago. If I still had the hardware version, and if it still worked, it would have been interesting to compare their sounds. Oh, well…

To hear what this effect sounds like, listen to the files *craig2phaser1.wav*, *craig2phaser2.wav,* and *craig2phaser3.wav* located in the *\sound* directory of the CDROM.

Operation

The block diagram of the phase shifter processor device is shown in Figure 13.16. Please consult this diagram during the discussion that follows.

This phase shifter device is built from four cascaded, first order, all-pass filters. An all-pass filter is different from the other filters described in this book in that it passes all frequencies uniformly (doesn't filter them) but instead modifies the phase of the signals passing through it. Depending on the parameters of the all-pass filter, the phase can be modified from 0 to 180 degrees. The phase is 90 degrees at the frequency that would be the cutoff frequency of a normal filter.

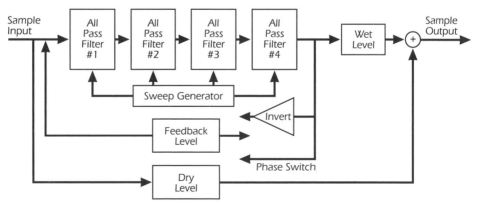

Figure 13.16   *Phaser Effect Logical Block Diagram*

The digital all-pass filters used here were first designed in the analog domain using Laplace transforms and then converted into the digital domain by the application of the bilinear transformation. In doing so you arrive at the following difference equation which can be solved in the digital domain:

$$y(n) = a * [x(n) + y(n\text{-}1)] - x(n\text{-}1)$$

where the only coefficient, a, is calculated as:

$$a = (1 - wp) / (1 + wp)$$

where wp is the radians per sample value. wp is calculated with the simple formula:

$$wp = (2 * PI * baseFrequency) / sampleRate$$

Of course y(n) in the difference equation represents the current output value and y(n-1) is the previously calculated output value. Similarly x(n) is the current input value and x(n-1) is the previous input value. In this design, wp is swept logarithmically over the range of octaves selected by the user with the sweep range control. This sweep of wp causes the phase of the audio passing through this device to be altered accordingly.

Given wp and the current input value, in, the four cascaded all-pass filters are implemented as follows:

```
// Calculate A in difference equation
double A = (1.0 - wp) / (1.0 + wp);

// Do the first allpass filter
thisOut1 = A * (in + thisOut1) - prevIn1;
prevIn1 = in;

// Do the second allpass filter
thisOut2 = A * (thisOut1 + thisOut2) - prevIn2;
prevIn2 = thisOut1;

// Do the third allpass filter
thisOut3 = A * (thisOut2 + thisOut3) - prevIn3;
prevIn3 = thisOut2;

// Do the forth allpass filter
thisOut4 = A * (thisOut3 + thisOut4) - prevIn4;
prevIn4 = thisOut3;
```

Notice how each stage of filtering works with its previous inputs and previous outputs to do its thing and how the current values of inputs and outputs become the previous inputs and outputs on the next pass. Looking at all-pass filters like this shows how really simple they are.

Leaving aside all-pass filters, the routing of audio samples within this processing device should be mentioned. This routing is evident by the numerous arrows used on the block diagram. As is typical of many of the processor devices presented in this book, this device is equipped with a dry, a wet, and a feedback control. The dry level control controls the percentage of the unprocessed input signal that is coupled into the output. The wet level control controls the percentage of processed (phased) signal which makes its way to the output to be mixed with the dry signal. And finally, the feedback control controls how much of the wet processed signal is coupled back to the input for reintroduction into the sample path. Feedback must be used carefully as oscillation can occur within the device. The feedback phase toggle switch in the UI controls whether the samples fed back are in or out of phase. Inverting phase in the digital domain is as simple as multiplying by −1. Inverting the fed back samples can help reduce feedback if it occurs and actually adds another dimension to the phase shifter's capabilities.

The code from *PhaserWithUI.java* shown below illustrates how monaural samples are processed.

```java
protected int processMonoSamples(short [] buffer, int len) {

    // Do the processing
    for (int i=0; i < len; i++) {

        // Calculate A in difference equation
        double A = (1.0 - wp) / (1.0 + wp);

        int inSample = (int) buffer[i];
        double in = inSample + (((invertPhase ? -1:1) * feedbackLevel *
                                                thisOut4) / 100.0);

        // Do the first allpass filter
        thisOut1 = A * (in + thisOut1) - prevIn1;
        prevIn1 = in;

        // Do the second allpass filter
        thisOut2 = A * (thisOut1 + thisOut2) - prevIn2;
        prevIn2 = thisOut1;

        // Do the third allpass filter
        thisOut3 = A * (thisOut2 + thisOut3) - prevIn3;
        prevIn3 = thisOut2;
```

```
        // Do the forth allpass filter
        thisOut4 = A * (thisOut3 + thisOut4) - prevIn4;
        prevIn4 = thisOut3;

        double outSample =    ((thisOut4 * wetLevel) / 100.0) +
                              ((inSample * dryLevel) / 100.0);

        // Clip output to legal levels
        if(outSample > 32767.0)
            outSample = 32767;
        else if(outSample < -32768.0)
            outSample = -32768;

        buffer[i] = (short) outSample;

        // Update sweep
        wp *= currentStep;      // Apply step value

        if(wp > maxWp)          // Exceed max Wp ?
            currentStep = 1.0 / step;
        else if(wp < minWp)     // Exceed min Wp ?
            currentStep = step;
    }
    return len;
}
```

Stereo samples are handled in a similar way with just about twice the amount of processing being required. Stereo samples are processed by a method called *processStereoSamples*. Stereo samples are extracted from the interleaved sample stream and processed through separate left and right paths. On output, the separate left and right samples are again combined and interleaved into the output sample stream.

As usual the *getSamples* method is where the action is. Remember, it is the *getSamples* method that is called by subsequent processing stages to pull samples through this device. *getSamples* is shown below for reference. You can see how the number of channels count is used to determine which method to call to perform the sample processing.

```
// Process the samples that pass thru this effect
public int getSamples(short [] buffer, int length) {
    int len = previous.getSamples(buffer, length);

    if (getByPass() || !initializationComplete)
        return len;
```

```
// Not in bypass mode, process the samples
if (numberOfChannels == 1)
    return processMonoSamples(buffer, len);
else
    return processStereoSamples(buffer, len);
}
```

The operation of the phase shifter device is completely sample synchronous in that a sample is read from the input and presented to the first all-pass filter element, each filter element in turn calculates its new output sample value based upon its new input, the output from the final filter is range checked and stored, and finally the value of wp is updated. The process repeats for each sample processed by the device.

Since mono and stereo signals are processed differently and since wp cannot be calculated until the sample rate is established, the phaser device must interpose on the negotiation process to gather the number of channels and the sample rate set by the *AbstractAudio* devices in the signal chain. Armed with this information, the effect can process the samples passing through it correctly.

The User Interface

The user interface for the phase shifter processing device is shown in Figure 13.17. The code that produces the UI is contained in the file *PhaserUI.java* whereas the code in *PhaserWithUI.java* does the actual sample processing. *PhaserWithUI* instantiates *PhaserUI* during its initialization.

Figure 13.17   *The Phaser Effect Processor's User Interface*

The UI is built with a *GridBagLayout* using the controls and indicators presented in section one of this book. Within the UI are numerous pots, buttons, LEDs, *ReadoutLabel* indicators, and toggle switches. As with all processing devices, a bypass switch and accompanying LED are provided. Anonymous inner listener classes are used to trap and process events from the pots and switches. Middle-ware methods are called by the listener classes when the UI controls are manipulated. These methods update the indicators in the UI and then call low-level functions in *PhaserWithUI* to affect processing.

All default, minimum, and maximum values for the various pots are established within the *PhaserUI* code. These values are coded as static final integer values. Any of the defaults can be changed with a simple edit of this code and a recompile. The values chosen were ones I thought were appropriate but you may think differently.

Table 13.11 lists the front panel controls and indicators for the phaser processor.

Table 13.11   *Phaser Processor Front Panel Controls and Indicators*

Front Panel Controls and Indicators	Description
Sweep Rate Indicator	A *ReadoutLabel* indicator showing the frequency of the phaser sweep in Hz.
Sweep Rate Pot	This pot controls the sweep rate of the phasing effect. The range of sweep rates is from 0.2 Hz to 5 Hz.
Sweep Range Indicator	A *ReadoutLabel* indicator indicating the currently selected sweep range in octaves.
Sweep Range Pot	This pot controls the range in octaves over which the sweep occurs. The sweep range can be varied from 1 to 7 octaves.
Base Frequency Indicator	A *ReadoutLabel* indicator indicating the currently selected base frequency.
Base Frequency Pot	This pot controls the base frequency used for the phasing calculations. Base frequency can range from 50 Hz to 150 Hz.
Dry Level Indicator	A *ReadoutLabel* indicator indicating the amount of the dry (unprocessed) signal present in the output.
Dry Level Pot	This pot controls the amount of the dry (unprocessed) signal present in the output.
Wet Level Indicator	A *ReadoutLabel* indicator indicating the amount of the wet (processed) signal present in the output.
Wet Level Pot	This pot controls the amount of the wet (processed) signal present in the output.

Table 13.11   (continued)

Front Panel Controls and Indicators	Description
Phase Invert Toggle Switch	This toggle switch controls the phase of the output signal feedback to the input. Feedback can be in phase (normal) or 180 degrees out of phase (inverted).
Feedback Level Indicator	A *ReadoutLabel* indicator indicating the amount of the output signal to be fed back to the input.
Feedback Level Pot	This pot controls the amount of the output signal coupled back to the input.
On LED	A red LED that simulates a power on indicator. It does nothing else.
Bypass LED	A green LED that flashes when this effect is bypassed.
Bypass Button	Clicking this button causes the phase shifter effect to be bypassed. In other words, the processor's effect is removed from the signal chain.

Use with the AudioTest Program

When using the *AudioTest* program, the phaser processor is included in the signal path by specifying the command line switch "*–p phaser.*" To insert the phaser effect between the file source and winplayer sink devices, the following command line would be used:

```
java craigl.test.AudioTest -i file -p phaser -o winplayer
```

Miscellaneous Information

Package:

craigl.processors

Source Files:

File Name	Description
PhaserUI.java	The user interface for the phaser shifter effect as shown in Figure 13.7.
PhaserWithUI.java	The *AbstractAudio* device that performs the phase shifting effect.

PITCH SHIFTER PROCESSOR . . . .

Description

The pitch shifter device presented here can manipulate the frequency of the audio signal flowing through it in such a way that the tempo of the audio content remains the same. This, as you will soon realize, is no easy task for a number of reasons, whereas it is easy to lower pitch by an octave, for example, by doubling the number of samples while keeping the sample rate the same or conversely, raise the pitch by throwing away every other sample. Both of these techniques suffer from two problems. First, when the pitch is lowered, the tempo slows down by half and, if the pitch is raised, the tempo is doubled. The second problem is that the pitch adjustment can only happen in integer increments unless special treatment is given to the processed samples.

In contrast, with the device presented here, pitch can be manipulated in half tone increments. What is meant by a half tone is described in the next section. Suffice it to say that pitch can be raised in small increments up to an octave above its original pitch and it can be lowered by the same amount. This gives the pitch shifter device a total range of two octaves.

Using this device and a microphone in conjunction with one of the sample acquisition devices presented earlier, you can make your voice sound like you just inhaled helium at one extreme or sound like James Earl Jones at the other.

Pitch shifting and similar effects are used a lot in the recording industry though you may not recognize this fact overtly. That is because they are often used to correct minor recording problems so you don't hear the problems any longer. Often it is more expedient to process and fix a small error in an otherwise great recorded track than it would be to re-record the full track. Sophisticated pitch-shifting devices can be used to correct minor errors in pitch in a vocal recording, for example by raising or lowering single notes or groups of notes that were sung out of pitch. When mixing audio tracks from different sources, pitch shifting is sometimes used to correct for minor tuning differences of the recorded instruments, allowing them to be mixed together successfully. According to George Martin, the legendary producer of the Beatles, pitch shifting was used to marry two different versions of the song "Strawberry Fields Forever" together into the version we know today. Harmonizers that create harmonies from vocal or instrumental inputs use pitch shifters as well in their operation.

With the device presented here it is possible to demonstrate synthesized harmonies by setting up a mix of the dry, unprocessed signal (say 70%) with a pitch shifted wet signal (at 30%) that has been shifted up in frequency a musical third or a fifth. The result is that you hear the unprocessed signal clearly but you also hear the pitch shifted signal as well. Hearing both signals at once results in harmony that is absolutely locked together. If your voice or instrument goes higher, up goes the harmony the exact same amount. Of course this doesn't sound real life-like because a real harmony singer varies the relationship between their voice and the voice of the main singer over time. The pitch shifter presented here is not that smart, but could form the basis of a device that was.

Note: A lot of processing is happening inside this processor device and the results are not what could be called high fidelity although they are adequate for many applications. In fact, this pitch shifter algorithm is used in the phrase sampler application of section three, where it performs admirably.

The pitch shifter presented here is capable of handling both monaural and stereo sample streams. The code dynamically adjusts itself to the number of channels the sample stream's source provides.

To hear what this effect sounds like, listen to the files *craig1pshift12d.wav*, *craig1pshift12u.wav*, *craig1pshift3u.wav*, *craig1pshift5u.wav*, *craig1pshiftharmony.wav,* and *craig1pshiftwierd.wav* located in the *\sound* directory of the CDROM.

Operation

Before starting a discussion of how this device works, I must give credit where credit is due. The algorithm underlying this device was adapted from an article by Dennis Cronin called, "Examining Audio DSP Algorithms." I found this article on the *Dr. Dobb's Journal* on CD-ROM. This is a very well written article that talks about various digital processing effects and is definitely worth finding and reading.

As alluded to earlier, pitch shifting is a complicated effect to achieve. In fact, the code that performs this function is probably the most complicated processing code in this book. The complexity is partially due to the extent to which the design goes to limit audible artifacts that result from the application of the basic pitch-shifting algorithm. These artifact reduction techniques will be described after the basic pitch-shifting process is described.

Pitch shifting is performed here by the practical application of the Doppler effect. The Doppler effect, for those who don't know this name, is the effect that is heard when you are stationary and a train, for example, is speeding toward you. As it approaches, the pitch of its sound increases in frequency. The closer the train gets, the higher its pitch. As the train passes you, the opposite affect occurs. As it speeds away, the pitch drops lower and lower until it fades away completely. How, you might ask, do we harness the power of a train in software. I was hoping you would ask.

Pitch shifting is done in software by cleverly manipulating delay. The block diagram of the pitch shifter device is shown in Figure 13.18. Specifically, the rate at which delay changes over time controls how much pitch shift is generated. Assume we want to raise the pitch of an audio signal. We start with a 100 millisecond delay in the signal path and ramp the delay towards zero. That is, the length of delay is decreased at each sample time by an amount proportional to the frequency rise desired. Can you picture this in terms of the train? Conversely, to lower pitch, we start with a near zero

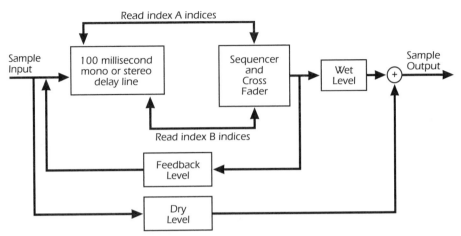

Figure 13.18   Pitch Shifter Block Diagram

delay and ramp it towards 100 milliseconds (resulting in a longer and longer delay) at a controlled rate.

The problem with this approach is what happens when we run out of delay. Say the delay goes from 100 milliseconds to zero. We must restart the delay back at 100 milliseconds to continue with the effect but to do so directly would result in a discontinuity that is definitely audible. This problem is solved in this implementation by having two delay lines that are offset from each other by the amount of delay. When one delay line approaches zero the other delay is restarted at 100 milliseconds. In essence, the delays are ping-ponged back and forth.

This solves the main problem with the discontinuity but introduces another. That is, as one delay line approaches zero delay, its contribution to the output must be faded out and the contribution of the alternate delay line must be faded in. The fade out must be completed by the time of the discontinuity or it will be heard. This process of fading between delay lines is referred to as cross fading. In this design, the cross fade time is set at 12 milliseconds. It is very important to make the cross fade as smooth as possible so fading coefficients based upon sines and cosines are used. These coefficients provide smooth and complimentary fading between the delay channels. The cross fade times are also staggered in time. Figure 13.19 shows graphs of the delay times and gains of the two delay channels A and B.

The final problem to be solved has to do with fractional sample values. Since the value of the delay (actually the delay index) does not always represent an integer sample value, the code must be able to deal with fractional ones. To do this, the process of linear interpolation is employed. That is, the two integer sample values that surround the non-integer index are both fetched and a new sample value is calculated from them. The value of this new sample depends upon how close the index is to each sam-

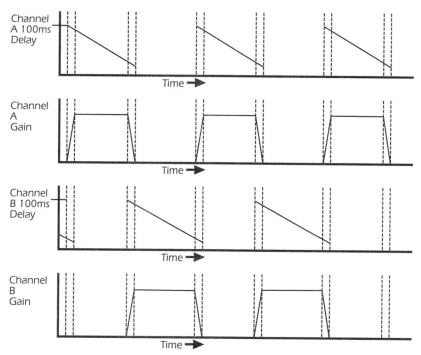

Figure 13.19 Delay Sequencing and Crossfading Schedule. The time between the dotted lines is considered a transition zone.

ple. An example will help illustrate this. The code below is extracted from the pitch shifter. Here the values of the two samples are *dsAHigh* and *dsALow* and the value of the real valued index is *sweep*.

delaySampleA = (dsAHigh * sweep) + (dsALow * (1.0 - sweep));

The new, calculated, sample value is contained in *delaySampleA* and is the weighted sum of the actual integer samples. The weighting applied to each is the proximity of the sample to the real valued index.

At the 10,000 foot altitude level, the description of how the pitch shifter works can be summarized as follows. At each sample time:

1. A sample is written into the delay buffer.
2. Four samples from specific locations are read out of the delay buffer and combined using linear interpolation in preparation for output.
3. The wet and dry signals are combined and a sample is outputted.
4. Delay times are then modulated and the cross fades are applied.

5. Delay indices are updated and wrapped as necessary to keep them within the legal buffer limits.

6. The process repeats until there are no more samples to process.

This is a highly choreographed and synchronized series of tasks that must be perfect or audible artifacts will be apparent.

The code that actually performs the pitch-shifting function is the ultimate reference. It is shown here so you can see how the pitch shifter algorithm is implemented. Hopefully, its operation will be apparent from the contained comments.

```
// Process the samples that pass thru this effect
public int getSamples(short [] buffer, int length) {

    // Don't perform processing until initialization is
    // complete and bypass is not active.
    if (getByPass() || !initializationComplete)
        return previous.getSamples(buffer, length);

    // Read number of samples requested from previous stage
    int len = previous.getSamples(localBuffer, length);
    double delaySampleA, delaySampleB;

    // Do the processing over the new buffer of samples
    for (int i=0; i < len; i++) {

        // Get a sample to process
        long inputSample = localBuffer[i];

        // Grab four samples at a time. This is required for
        // interpolation and blending.
        long dsALow = delayBuffer[readIndexALow];
        long dsAHigh = delayBuffer[readIndexAHigh];
        long dsBLow = delayBuffer[readIndexBLow];
        long dsBHigh = delayBuffer[readIndexBHigh];

        // Do the linear interpolation
        if (sweepUp) {
            delaySampleA = (dsAHigh * sweep) + (dsALow * (1.0 - sweep));
            delaySampleB = (dsBHigh * sweep) + (dsBLow * (1.0 - sweep));
        } else {
            delaySampleA = (dsAHigh * (1.0 - sweep) + (dsALow * sweep));
            delaySampleB = (dsBHigh * (1.0 - sweep) + (dsBLow * sweep));
        }
```

```
// Combine delay channels A and B with appropriate blending
double outputSample = (delaySampleA * blendA) + (delaySampleB *
                                                        blendB);

// Store sample in delay buffer
delayBuffer[writeIndex] = (long)
    (inputSample + ((outputSample * feedbackLevel) / 100));

// Update write index
writeIndex = (writeIndex + 1) % delayBufferSize;

// Prepare sample for output by combining wet and dry
// values
outputSample =
    ((inputSample * dryLevel) / 100) +
    ((outputSample * wetLevel) / 100);

// Clamp output to legal range
if (outputSample > 32767)
    outputSample = 32767;
if (outputSample < -32768)
    outputSample = -32768;

// Store output sample in outgoing buffer
buffer[i] = (short) outputSample;
// Update cross fade blending values each sample interval
if (crossFadeCount != 0) {
    crossFadeCount-;

    // Get new blending values for both channels
    blendA = fadeA[crossFadeCount];
    blendB = fadeB[crossFadeCount];
}

// Update sweep value for each pass if processing
// mono signal and every other pass if processing
// stereo.
if ((numberOfChannels == 1) || ((i + 1) % 2 == 0))
    sweep += step;

if (sweepUp) {
    // Upward frequency change
```

```
// Advance indices to reduce delay
readIndexALow = readIndexAHigh;
readIndexAHigh = (readIndexAHigh + 1) % delayBufferSize;
readIndexBLow = readIndexBHigh;
readIndexBHigh = (readIndexBHigh + 1) % delayBufferSize;

// Check for overflow
if (sweep < 1.0) {
    // No overflow, continue with next sample
    continue;
}

// Octave exceeded bump ptrs again
sweep = 0.0;
readIndexALow = readIndexAHigh;
readIndexAHigh = (readIndexAHigh + 1) % delayBufferSize;
readIndexBLow = readIndexBHigh;
readIndexBHigh = (readIndexBHigh + 1) % delayBufferSize;

// See if it is time to switch to other delay channel
if (activeCount- == 0) {
    // Reset fade in/out count
    crossFadeCount = numberOfCrossFadeSamples;
    activeCount = activeSampleCount;
    if (channelA) {
        channelA = false;
        readIndexBHigh =
            (writeIndex + AudioConstants.SAMPLEBUFFERSIZE) %
            delayBufferSize;
        // Swap blend coefficient arrays
        fadeA = fadeOut;
        fadeB = fadeIn;
    } else   {
        channelA = true;
        readIndexAHigh =
            (writeIndex + AudioConstants.SAMPLEBUFFERSIZE) %
            delayBufferSize;
        // Swap blend coefficient arrays
        fadeA = fadeIn;
        fadeB = fadeOut;
    }
}
```

```
    }   else    {
        // Downward frequency change

        // Check for overflow
        if (sweep < 1.0) {
            // No overflow, advance indices
            readIndexALow = readIndexAHigh;
            readIndexAHigh = (readIndexAHigh + 1) % delayBufferSize;
            readIndexBLow = readIndexBHigh;
            readIndexBHigh = (readIndexBHigh + 1) % delayBufferSize;

            // Continue with processing the next sample
            continue;
        }
        // Octave exceeded don't bump indices so the delay
        // is increased
        sweep = 0.0;

        // See if it is time to switch to other delay channel
        if (activeCount- == 0) {
            // Reset fade in/out count
            crossFadeCount = numberOfCrossFadeSamples;
            activeCount = activeSampleCount;
            if (channelA) {
                channelA = false;
                readIndexBHigh = (writeIndex + AudioConstants.
                                                SAMPLEBUFFERSIZE)
                                % delayBufferSize;
                // Swap blend coefficient arrays
                fadeA = fadeOut;
                fadeB = fadeIn;
            }   else    {
                channelA = true;
                readIndexAHigh = (writeIndex + AudioConstants.
                                                SAMPLEBUFFERSIZE)
                                % delayBufferSize;
                // Swap blend coefficient arrays
                fadeA = fadeIn;
                fadeB = fadeOut;
            }
        }
    }
    }
}
return len;
}
```

The pitch shifter varies pitch in halftone increments. A halftone is the smallest distance between notes in the musical scales used in western music. Since an octave represents a doubling of pitch and since there are 12 notes in an octave, the frequency difference between two notes, a halftone apart, is defined as the 12th root of 2. In Java terms,

```java
// Constant by which one tone differs from the next when the
// interval is a halftone.
private static final double twelvethRootOfTwo = Math.pow(2, 1.0 / 12.0);
```

The amount by which the delay is varied is controlled by the number of half tones selected by the user. The method shown below takes the user input frequency shift value and calculates the *step* rate from it.

```java
// Called when the user changes the pitch shift value
public void setPitchShift(int pitchShift) {

    // Values are in half steps (semitones) in the
    // range -12..0..+12 corresponding to -/+ 1 octave for
    // a range of 2 octaves.

    // Determine which direction the sweep is going
    sweepUp = (pitchShift >= 0);

    setIndices();

    double newStep = 1.0;

    // If pitch shift is 0 short circuit calculations
    if (pitchShift == 0)
        step = 0;

    else{
        // Step is rate at which samples read out
        for (int i=0; i < Math.abs(pitchShift); i++) {
            if (pitchShift > 0)
                newStep *= twelvethRootOfTwo;
            else
                newStep /= twelvethRootOfTwo;
        }
        step = Math.abs(newStep - 1.0);
    }
}
```

```
// Reset the following values whenever pitch shift value changes
sweep = 0.0;
crossFadeCount = 0;
activeSampleCount = numberOfDelaySamples -
    (int)(numberOfCrossFadeSamples * (newStep - 1.0) - 2);
}
```

The User Interface

The user interface for the pitch shifter processing device is shown in Figure 13.20. The code that produces the UI is contained in the file *PitchShifterUI.java*, whereas it is the code in *PitchShifterWithUI.java* (shown above) that does the actual sample processing. *PitchShifterWithUI* instantiates *PitchShifterUI* as it is coming up. It is interesting that the UI for this device is one of the simplest presented in this book, whereas the code behind the UI is definitely the most complex.

The UI is built with a *GridBagLayout* using the controls and indicators presented in section one of this book. Within the UI are numerous pots and *ReadoutLabel* indicators. As with all processing devices, a bypass switch and accompanying LED are provided. Anonymous inner listener classes are used to trap and process events from the pots and button. Middle-ware methods are called by the listener classes when the UI controls are manipulated. These methods update the indicators in the UI and then call low level functions in *PitchShifterWithUI* to affect processing.

Table 13.12 lists the front panel controls and indicators for the pitch shifter processor.

Figure 13.20   The Pitch Shifter Processor User Interface

Table 13.12   *Pitch Shifter Processor Front Panel Controls and Indicators*

Front Panel Controls and Indicators	Description
Halftone Shift Indicator	A *ReadoutLabel* indicator showing how much pitch shift is in effect.
Halftone Shift Pot	This pot controls the amount of pitch shift applied to the audio signal. It is graduated in halftones over the range –12 to +12 halftones. A negative halftone shift indicates pitch frequency reduction whereas a positive halftone shift indicates increased pitch frequencies. A shift of 0 means the pitch stays the same. A halftone represents a frequency ratio that is the twelfth root of two.
Dry Level Indicator	A *ReadoutLabel* indicator indicating the percentage of the dry (unprocessed) signal present in the output.
Dry Level Pot	This pot controls the amount of the dry (unprocessed) signal present in the output.
Wet Level Indicator	A *ReadoutLabel* indicator indicating the percentage of the wet (processed) signal present in the output.
Wet Level Pot	This pot controls the amount of the wet (processed) signal present in the output.
Feedback Level Indicator	A *ReadoutLabel* indicator indicating the percentage of the output signal fed back to the input.
Feedback Level Pot	This pot controls the amount of the output signal coupled back to the input.
On LED	A red LED that simulates a power on indicator. It does nothing else.
Bypass LED	A green LED that flashes when this effect is bypassed.
Bypass Button	Clicking this button causes the pitch shifter effect to be bypassed. In other words, the effect is removed from the signal chain.

Use with the AudioTest Program

When using the *AudioTest* program, the pitch shifter processor is included in the signal path by specifying the command line switch "*–p pshift.*" To pitch shift the samples read from an audio file, the following command line would be used:

```
java craigl.test.AudioTest -i file -p pshift -o winplayer
```

Miscellaneous Information

Package:

craigl.processors

Source Files:

File Name	Description
PitchShifterUI.java	The user interface for the pitch shifter effect as shown in Figure 13.20.
PitchShifterWithUI.java	The *AbstractAudio* device that performs the pitch shifting effect.

REVERB PROCESSOR . . . .

Description

Reverb is probably the most frequently used audio effect in existence today. Reverb is used to add life and sparkle to just about any musical source. This is especially important in electronic music, where the synthesized sounds tend to sound flat and lifeless. Adding reverb to electronic generated sounds make them sound much more organic and natural. Adding reverb to an acoustic guitar during recording brings out the fullness of the guitar's sound so that it can compete with other instruments in a mix. Vocal parts typically have a small amount of reverb added for the same reason, to fill out the weak parts and make the vocalist sound as powerful as possible.

Reverbs have been built using many different technologies in the past although digital reverbs similar to what is presented here are quickly replacing most of them. Various historical approaches have included:

1. Speaker at one end of a long hose and a microphone at the other. The length of the hose and the material from which the hose was made affected the reverb effect achieved.

2. Using springs that are rotated by a transducer at one end and a pickup at the other end. The rotational spin placed onto the spring would propagate the length of the spring and stimulate the pickup at the other end. The propagating audio signal would also bounce back and forth on the spring. This is the way most guitar amp reverbs are made to this day. Most

mechanical spring reverb units use dual springs wound in opposite directions to minimize the pickup of spurious vibrations. The same drive signal would drive both springs (in opposite directions) and the pickup outputs would be summed on the other end. Any common vibration would be subtracted away (common mode rejection).

3. Large metal plates with various transducers and pickups placed at various positions on the plate. Plate reverbs, as these devices are called, are large devices. The smallest I've seen was probably three feet by four feet in size. A good plate reverb might be twice that big and would be hung from the ceiling in a back room of a recording studio. Not only were plate reverbs large, they were equally expensive. Plate reverbs were considered state of the art through the late 1980s.

4. Actual rooms with adjustable partitions that have speakers at one end and microphones placed at various positions at the other end. As you might guess, it was an expensive proposition to have a reverb/echo room set aside specifically for this purpose, but it did produce the most natural reverb available. The reverb times were, by necessity, short because they were dependent on the room size. Really long reverb times were not possible because most recording studios didn't have access to a cathedral or canyon close by.

You can see the appeal of a software-only approach to reverb. It doesn't take up large amounts of space, doesn't require any electromechanical devices, can have switchable algorithms for producing reverb, and is almost infinitely adjustable to fit the most specific of situations.

The reverb device presented here is for demonstration purposes only for a couple of reasons. First, the user interface is not designed for non-technical people to interact with. The UI reflects the physical model used to simulate the reverb, not the more intuitive space (or volume) modeling approach used in most commercial reverb devices. Of course, with the application of more software, the space modeling model could be grafted onto the design presented here.

The second reason is that the algorithm used is somewhat dated. There has been a lot of research into algorithms for producing realistic reverb in the last ten years but these advances are not incorporated into the presented design. Still, the reverb algorithm presented works and can be a valuable addition to your bag of audio processing effects tools.

To hear what this effect sounds like, listen to the files *craig2reverb1.wav*, *craig2reverb2.wav,* and *craig2reverb3.wav* located in the *\sound* directory of the CDROM.

Operation

If you think about what happens when you yell (or yodel) into a big canyon you can begin to understand how reverb processors might work. Most people yell hello into a canyon and are answered by hello, hello, hello…. In other words, what you hear, after a short delay, is your voice repeated back to you at periodic intervals but at reduced levels. Again after a short period of time, echoes of the echo with different periodicity begin to be heard as your voice and its echoes fade off into the background noise. If one were to write an equation (in the digital domain) for this effect, the equation would be in the form of an infinite geometric series that trails off to zero (because of the reduced level of each echo) at infinity. Then, except for the initial delay before the first echo is heard, the series can be reduced to a simple equation that resembles a comb filter network with loop gain (actually loss) and feedback. The comb filter would be similar to that shown in Figure 13.21. Of course, in a big canyon or even in a concert hall, there would be many obstacles the sound would impinge itself upon in the round trip from the source to the reflective surfaces and back to your ears. In a concert hall, reverberation is very complex because of the number of surfaces the sound bounces off and because of the shorter paths the sound travels before bouncing. Added to this, in a concert hall, your ears would perceive some direct, non-reflected sound, as well as the reflected sound, further adding to the complexity of the phenomenon.

As you might guess, due to the complexity of reverberation, it can be very difficult to model accurately enough to sound natural. According to Ken Steiglitz in his book *A Digital Signal Processing Primer*, "The best reverb filters have evolved through trial and error, guided by physical measurements of concert halls and by inspired intuition." In other words, designing a good reverb processing effect is still more art than science.

Most digital reverbs are derived from work done by M.R. Schroeder and J.A. Moorer over the last 20 years. Information about Schroeder's work can be found in the book *Computer Music—Synthesis, Composition and Performance* by Charles Dodge and Thomas Jerse. Information on Moorer's work can be found in the article, "About this Reverberation Business," which appeared in the *Computer Music Journal*, vol. 3, no. 2, 1979.

The reverb processor presented here is called a Schroeder reverb because it was Schroeder who suggested the organization of parallel comb filters and series-connect-

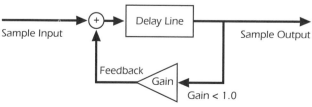

Figure 13.21   Comb Filter Block Diagram

ed all-pass filters which make it up. The block diagram of the Schroeder reverb is shown in Figure 13.22. As shown there, four parallel comb filters operate on the input samples simultaneously and their outputs are summed together, reduced in gain, and then passed through two all-pass filters to modulate the phase. The block diagram of the all-pass filter network is shown in Figure 13.23. The code for the Schroeder reverb is contained in the file *SchroederReverb.java*. The code for the comb filter can be found in *CombFilter.java* and the code for the all-pass network in the file *AllpassNetwork.java*. There is way too much code to list here, so if you are interested in the details, consult the files on the CDROM.

The Dodge book mentioned above suggested the following values for the comb filter and all-pass filter delays to simulate the characteristics of a medium-sized concert hall. These are the default values coded into the *SchroederReverb* class and therefore the values that are used to initialize the slide pots in the UI.

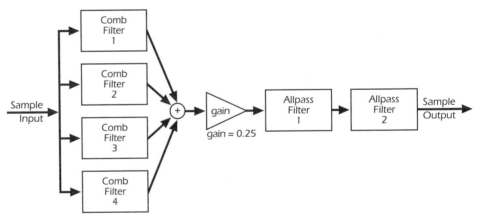

Figure 13.22   The Schroeder Reverb Block Diagram

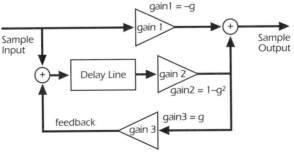

Figure 13.23   All-pass Filter Network Block Diagram

```
public static final double COMB1DELAYMSDEF = 29.7;
public static final double COMB2DELAYMSDEF = 37.1;
public static final double COMB3DELAYMSDEF = 41.1;
public static final double COMB4DELAYMSDEF = 43.7;
public static final double ALLPASS1DELAYMSDEF = 5.0;
public static final double ALLPASS2DELAYMSDEF = 1.7;
```

Of course, you can change the defaults to whatever makes sense to you. The sustain values for the all-pass filter networks are also defined here. These values are fixed in the design and aren't user adjustable.

```
public static final double ALLPASS1SUSTAINMSDEF = 96.8;
public static final double ALLPASS2SUSTAINMSDEF = 32.9;
```

Sustain is the time it takes after the input signal is exhausted until the output completely dies away (is at least 60 dB down). In all other processors presented in this book, the duration of the output samples were the same as the duration of the input samples. This is not true here. In this reverb, after all input samples are exhausted, output samples will continue to be produced by the audio re-circulating through the comb and all-pass filter delay lines. After the user-specified sustain time has been exhausted, the output samples cease to be produced.

The gains utilized in each comb and all-pass filter are calculated from the length of the individual delay for each filter and the sustain interval. For the comb filters, the gain calculation is:

```
public void calcGain() {
    // Calculate gain for this filter such that a recirculating
    // sample will reduce in level 60db in the specified
    // sustain time.
    gain = Math.pow(0.001, delayInMs / sustainTimeInMs);
}
```

Gain in this context is actually a loss because it will always be less than one. If the gain were ever greater than one, the reverb would be unstable and prone to severe oscillations. You can get an intuitive feel for what the gain does by thinking about our canyon echo example. We need to choose a value for the gain such that the samples recirculating through the delay line will be reduced by –60 dB (1 / 1000th) of their initial value in the time allotted for the sustain. In other words, the samples will effectively die out by the time the sustain period ends. Just what happens when you hear the final hello in the canyon.

The gain calculation is done the same way in the all-pass filter network but it is applied in three different places. These places are shown as gain 1, gain 2, and gain 3 in the block diagram. The method that calculates gain in an all-pass network is shown below:

```
private void calcGain() {

    // Calculate gain for this filter such that a recirculating
    // sample will reduce in level 60db in the specified
    // sustain time.
    double gain = Math.pow(0.001, delayInMs / sustainTimeInMs);

    // Now update the network gain
    gain1 = -gain;
    gain2 = 1.0 - (gain * gain);
    gain3 = gain;
}
```

Note: The reverb device presented here works equally well with both monaural and stereo sample sources.

The User Interface

The user interface for the reverb processing device is shown in Figure 13.24. The code that produces the UI is contained in the file *ReverbUI.java*, whereas it is the code in *ReverbWithUI* (described above) which does the actual sample processing. *ReverbWithUI* instantiates *ReverbUI* as it is coming up.

The UI is built with a *GridBagLayout* using the controls and indicators presented in section one of this book. Within the UI are numerous slide pots, pots, a button, and an LED indicator. As with all processing devices, a bypass switch and accompanying LED are provided. Anonymous inner listener classes are used to trap and pro-

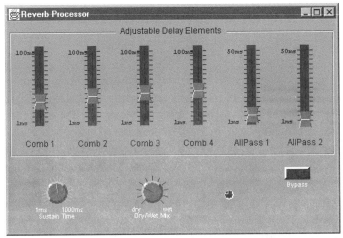

Figure 13.24   *The Reverb Processor's User Interface*

cess events from the slide pots, the normal pots, and the button. Middle-ware methods are called by the listener classes when the UI controls are manipulated. These methods update the indicators in the UI and then call low level-functions in *ReverbWithUI* to affect processing.

Table13.13 describes the front panel conrols and indicator used in the Reverb processor.

Table 13.13   Reverb Front Panel Controls and Indicators

Front Panel Controls and Indicators	Description
Comb 1 Slide Pot	Controls the delay used in the first comb filter. Delays can range from 1 millisecond to 100 milliseconds.
Comb 2 Slide Pot	Controls the delay used in the second comb filter. Delays can range from 1 millisecond to 100 milliseconds.
Comb 3 Slide Pot	Controls the delay used in the third comb filter. Delays can range from 1 millisecond to 100 milliseconds.
Comb 4 Slide Pot	Controls the delay used in the forth comb filter. Delays can range from 1 millisecond to 100 milliseconds.
AllPass 1 Pot	Controls the delay used in the first all-pass filter. Delays can range from 1 millisecond to 50 milliseconds.
AllPass 2 Pot	Controls the delay used in the second all-pass filter. Delays can range from 1 millisecond to 50 milliseconds.
Sustain Time Pot	Controls the length of sustain after the audio input has gone away. Sustain can range from 1 millisecond to 1000 milliseconds.
Dry/Wet Mix Pot	Controls the proportion of the dry unprocessed audio mixed in with the wet reverberated audio.
Bypass LED	A green LED that flashes when this effect is bypassed.
Bypass Button	Clicking this button causes the reverb effect to be bypassed. In other words, the effect is removed from the signal chain.

Use with the AudioTest Program

When using the *AudioTest* program, the reverb processor is included in the signal path by specifying the command line switch "*–p reverb.*"

Miscellaneous Information

Source Files:

File Name	Package	Description
AllpassNetwork.java	craigl.reverb	All-pass network implementation as used in reverb.
CombFilter.java	craigl.reverb	Comb filter used in the reverb.
ReverbUI.java	craigl.processors	The user interface for the reverb effect. See Figure 13.24.
ReverbWithUI.java	craigl.processors	The *AbstractAudio* device that performs the reverberation effect.
SchroederReverb.java	craigl.reverb	Reverb module consisting of four comb filter sections and two all-pass network sections.

14 Audio Sinks

INTRODUCTION . . . .

In this architecture, devices that consume samples are termed *sink devices*. Sink devices must be the final device in any audio processing signal chain. Without a sink device, samples cannot be pulled through the various processing stages that are a part of the chain. When instructed to do so, sink devices begin pulling samples from a previous processing device until an End of File or EOF (length return from *getSamples* method call == –1) indication is found in the sample stream. At that point, sink devices stop pulling samples until instructed to do so again either by a user, if a UI is present, or if commanded programmatically via a method call.

Sink devices may or may not have user interfaces associated with them. All of the sink devices presented in this chapter for use with the *AudioTest* program do have UIs, but having a UI is not a prerequisite for a sink device. User interfaces for sink devices follow a special design paradigm as required for use with the *AudioTest* program. That is, the *showUI* methods of sink device UIs don't return to the calling program until the user has finished processing audio and has intentionally dismissed the UI. Think of the UI has a modal dialog box which does not end until the user dismisses it. Code similar to the following is found in all sink devices with UIs to emulate the modal dialog box effect.

```
// This code keeps the UI up until the recording is completed and
// done is set.
public void showUI(boolean isVisible) {
```

```
// Set visibility
setVisible(isVisible);

// Start a thread to stop return
Thread t = new Thread() {
    public void run() {
        while(!done) {
            // Sleep
            try {
                sleep(250);
            } catch (InterruptedException ie) {}
        }
    }
};
t.start();
try {
    t.join();
} catch (InterruptedException ie) {}
}
```

If sink devices with UIs did not use this paradigm, the *AudioTest* program with which they are designed for use would terminate before audio processing began. Nothing would prevent the main program's thread from terminating immediately after all of the processing devices were instantiated. Having the *showUI* method block prevents the main thread from terminating and allows the user to interact with the devices in the audio processing chain. When the user has finished, the *done* variable is set, which allows the *showUI* thread to terminate and the main thread to follow suit.

In this chapter, sink devices for writing audio files and for playing (listening to) audio samples will be presented. The discussion will begin with a device for writing AU or wave audio files.

AUDIO FILES . . . .

Processing sound and hearing the results in real time is very important. Just as important however is being able to save the results of your processing so that others can appreciate what you have done. Audio could be saved as raw binary data in a file but it makes more sense to save the audio data in a *standard format* that not only your application can understand but that many other applications can understand and use as well. There are many audio file formats in existence today but two of the most ubiquitous are the AU format and more recently the wave file format. Each of these formats are general enough to allow the storage of many types of audio data. For our uses here, however, we are only interested in the storage of 16-bit linear PCM samples. The code that you find in this chapter is skewed towards that end.

Later in this chapter, code is presented for creating both AU and wave files directly from audio samples. Before that however, a higher-level sink device called *FileWriterWithUI* is presented which knows how to create both AU and wave files on demand.

FileWriterWithUI CLASS . . . .

The *FileWriterWithUI* class was created for use with the *AudioTest* program. By including this device in the audio processing path, it is possible to create audio files that contain the results of your processing efforts. The user interface of this device is shown in Figure 14.1. The functionality provided by the *FileWriterWithUI* class can be broken down into the following categories:

1. Building the UI that the user will see and interact with.
2. Processing all UI events that occur as the user clicks buttons in the UI.
3. Negotiating with the other devices in the audio processing chain to determine the sample rate and the number of channels the samples correspond to. This information is necessary because created audio files have these values coded into their headers.
4. Instantiation of the correct low-level device, either *AUWrite* or *WaveWrite* objects, for actually creating the audio file.

The majority of the *FileWriterWithUI* code is taken up in building the UI and making it functional. The majority of the effort directly involved in the production of an audio file can be seen in the *goButtonClicked* method from the file *FileWriterWithUI.java* and shown below:

Figure 14.1   FileWriterWithUI Device User Interface. Device writes AU or Wave files.

```
public synchronized void goButtonClicked() {

    // Change component states
    writingLED.setLEDState(true);
    goButton.setEnabled(false);

    // Get parameters for audio file
    if (!negotiateParameters())
        return;

    // Set display values
    rl1.setValue(sampleRate);
    rl2.setValue(numberOfChannels);

    // Spawn a separate thread to do the file writing otherwise the UI
    // will be starved and the buttons sometimes won't work.
    Thread t = new Thread() {
        public void run() {
            // Successfully nogotiated parameters
            FileWriterIF fwif = null;
            if (fileType == AUTYPE) {
                // Instantiate AUWrite and write the file
                fwif = new AUWrite(fileName, sampleRate, numberOfChannels);
            }   else   {
                // Instantiate WaveWrite and write the file
                fwif = new WaveWrite(fileName, sampleRate, numberOfChannels);
            }
            // Write the file
            fwif.writeFile(aa);

            // Writing done change component states
            writingLED.setLEDState(false);
            fileSelectButton.setEnabled(true);
            goButton.setEnabled(false);
        }
    };
    t.start();
}
```

This code is called when the *Go* button in the user interface is clicked. Its operation begins by changing the state of the front panel LED which begins to blink and the *Go* button itself which is disabled for the present. Next, negotiation is performed to gather the sample rate and channels information from the previous devices in the audio processing chain. After negotiation has been completed, the two front panel indicators for sample rate and channels are updated for the user.

Next, a new thread is created as an anonymous inner class that instantiates either an *AUWrite* or a *WaveWrite* device depending upon which type of file the user had selected when the *Go* button was clicked. The *writeFile* method call performs the actual audio file creation. The *AbstractAudio* device, *aa*, is passed to this method so samples can be acquired from the device preceding this one in the processing chain. On return, the LED state is changed to stop it from blinking, the *File Select* button is again enabled and the *Go* button is disabled in preparation for another file being written. When all of this code has been executed, the thread *t* falls off of the end and quietly terminates. At this point, the audio file just created is available for use.

The User Interface controls and indicators present on the *FileWriterWithUI* front panel are detailed in Table 14.1.

Table 14.1   FileWriterWithUI Front Panel Controls and Indicators

Front Panel Controls and Indicators	Description
Sample Rate Indicator	Indicates the sample rate negotiated with the audio processing chain. The negotiated rate will be written into the header of the audio files created.
Channels Indicator	Indicates the number of channels negotiated with the audio processing chain. The negotiated number of channels will be written into the header of the audio files created as well.
File Type Control Group	Controls the type, AU or wave, of audio files to be produced.
Select File Button	Brings up a File Save As dialog box to allow the user to enter a filename and select a path for the audio file to be created in. The user should specify the correct file extension for the file to be saved that matches the file format. AU files should have an".au" file extension and wave files should have an extension of ".wav". This convention is not enforced programmatically, although it could be.
Go Button	Clicking the go button after performing file selection and file type selection causes the audio file creation process to begin. Samples will be pulled from the audio processing chain until the EOF indication is detected. At that time, file writing will terminate and the audio file will be available for subsequent use. If go is clicked again, the same process will occur again. The filename or path could be changed, however, so that other copies of the audio file can be created.

Table 14.1 (continued)

Front Panel Controls and Indicators	Description
Done Button	After the audio file creation has been performed, clicking this button will terminate both the operation of the *FileWriterWithUI* device but also the complete *AudioTest* program.
Writing LED	This red LED will blink while the audio file is being created and written to. This is analogous to a *recording* LED on other audio equipment.

Use with the AudioTest Program

When using the *AudioTest* program, the *FileWriterWithUI* device is specified for inclusion in the audio processing path by specifying the command line switch "–o file." The UI for this device will then pop up and the user will be able to interact with the device through the front panel controls described above.

WRITING AU FILES . . . .

AU files have a very simple format. AU files are the audio files of choice for Sun Microsystems machines and Next computers.

The AUWrite Class

The lowest level class for writing AU files is *AUWrite.java*. This class understands the required format of AU files and creates an audio file adhering to that format. In the simplest sense, the AU file consists of only two parts; a header and the audio data. More information about AU files can be found in Chapter 11.

The header consists of the ".snd" character string sequence followed by six 32-bit big endian integers that describe the content of the data in the file. The audio data is written to the AU file following the header and consists of 1 or more bytes of data per sample. Since our software uses only 16-bit sample values, two bytes of data are written to the output file for each input sample.

The *AUWrite* class implements the *FileWriteIF*, which means it must implement a method with the following prototype:

```
public boolean writeFile(AbstractAudio aa)
```

This method is where the bulk of the code for writing AU files lives. The code is shown below for reference:

```
// Write the incoming samples into a 16 bit AU file
// Writing terminates when samples are exhausted
public boolean writeFile(AbstractAudio aa) {

    // Open output stream
    try {
        out = new RandomAccessFile(fileName, "rw");

        // Specified file is now open for writing
        // Create AU file header with zero data length
        byte [] header = build16BitAuHeader(sampleRate, numberOfChannels, 0);

        // Write the header to the file
        out.write(header);

        // Now write all the file data
        int totalBytes =0;

        // Read first buffer of samples
        int length = aa.previous.getSamples(sampleBuffer,
                                AudioConstants.SAMPLEBUFFERSIZE);

        while (length > 0) {
            int index=0;
            for (int i=0; i < length; i++) {
                short sample = sampleBuffer[i];
                sampleBufferBytes[index++] = (byte) (sample >> 8);
                sampleBufferBytes[index++] = (byte) (sample & 255);
            }
            // Write bytes to output file
            out.write(sampleBufferBytes, 0, length * 2);

            // Update total byte count
            totalBytes += length * 2;

            // Read the next buffer full
            length = aa.previous.getSamples(sampleBuffer,
                                AudioConstants.SAMPLEBUFFERSIZE);
        }
        // Go back to the start of the file and rewrite header
        out.seek(0);
```

```
        // New header has correct audio byte count
        header = build16BitAuHeader(sampleRate, numberOfChannels, totalBytes);

        // Write the header to the file again
        out.write(header);

        // All done
        out.close();
        return true;
    }
    catch(IOException ioe) {
        System.out.println(ioe.getMessage());
        return false;
    }
}
```

The important things to understand here are:

1. The header is written to the file twice, the first time as a placeholder so that the audio data subsequently written to the file resides in the correct location after the header, and the second time when the header content is finalized—specifically, when the total number of bytes of audio data has been determined.

2. Rewriting the header is possible because the *RandomAccessFile* class is used for writing the file and it supports seeking to an arbitrary location within the file. Here of course, we only seek back to the beginning of the audio file (offset 0) to rewrite the header. The size of the header written in both cases is exactly the same, it only differs in content and then not to any significant degree.

3. The 16-bit samples to be written to the audio file are gathered by pulling them from the previous stage of processing. The *getSamples* method of the previous device of the device passed is called to acquire the samples. The call looks like this:

```
aa.previous.getSamples(sampleBuffer, AudioConstants.SAMPLEBUFFERSIZE);
```

Writing the AU file header requires that the integer values written to the file be in big endian format. A method called *writeIntMsb* in the *AUWrite* class provides this functionality. With that out of the way, the AU file header can be generated as an array of bytes (to be written to the audio file later) using the code below:

```
// Synthesize an AU file header for writing to the file
public static byte [] build16BitAuHeader(int sampleRate,
                int channels,
                int length) {
    // Header is 28 bytes long
    byte [] header = new byte[28];

    // Write magic string
    header[0] = (byte) '.';
    header[1] = (byte) 's';
    header[2] = (byte) 'n';
    header[3] = (byte) 'd';

    // Write offset to sound data of 28 bytes
    writeIntMsb(header, 4, 28, 4);

    // Write number of bytes of sound data.
    writeIntMsb(header, 8, length, 4);

    // Write sound format 16 bit linear PCM
    writeIntMsb(header, 12, 3, 4);

    // Write sample rate
    writeIntMsb(header, 16, sampleRate, 4);

    // Write number of channels
    writeIntMsb(header, 20, channels, 4);

    // Write four bytes of padding
    writeIntMsb(header, 24, 0, 4);

    // Return the header as a byte array
    return header;
}
```

You'll note that the sound format used in building the header is hardcoded to 16-bit linear PCM. All AU files written using the *AUWrite* code will therefore be of this format.

The *writeFile* method calls the *build16BitAuHeader* method (twice) to build the header and then calls *out.write(header)* to write it to the output audio file.

AUWriteDevice Class

This class, although currently unused in the book, may come in handy in your audio processing experiments. *AUWriteDevice*, by extending *AbstractAudio*, can be linked directly into an audio processing chain for writing AU files when a UI is not needed or required. The file/path name of the audio file to write is passed into the class constructor and it should have the correct file extension. The *writeFile* method is then called to cause the audio file to be written.

The *writeFile* method, when called, causes negotiation to occur in the audio processing chain. This is necessary before writing the audio file because the number of channels and the sampling rate must be known in advance. Once negotiation is completed, an instance of *AUWrite* file is created to write the AU file.

There are no provisions for using a *AUWriteDevice* with the *AudioTest* program at this time.

WRITING WAVE FILES . . . .

The processing of writing wave files is similar to the process for writing AU files and because of this, the code provided is structured in the same way. Wave files, however, have a slightly more complex file format that must be produced by the wave file writer. As previously, there is the lowest level class called *WaveWrite* and an *AbstractAudio* device extension called *WaveWriteDevice* built on top of it. These classes are given a cursory description below.

WaveWrite Class

The only difference in *WaveWrite* and the *AUWrite* code is in the code which produces the header for the audio file. Wave files, as explained in Chapter 11, are contained in RiFF files and consists of a set of hierarchically organized chunks of data. Each chunk is named and sized for easy parsing. The code in *build16BitWaveHeader* for producing the wave file header, shown below, is as simple as it can get and still produce a valid wave file. You'll notice in the code that some of the content is written using big endian integers (writeIntMsb) and some is written using little endian integer values (writeIntLsb). This is partly because of the RIFF file history on big endian machines (the Commodore Amiga, for example) and partly because of the more recent Intel (little endian) utilization.

```
// Synthesize an Wave file header for writing to the file
public static byte [] build16BitWaveHeader(int sampleRate,
                int channels,
                int fileLength,
                int dataLength) {
   // Header is 44 bytes long
   byte [] header = new byte[WAVEHDRSIZE];

   // Write RIFF tag
   long tag = WaveRead.chunkName('R', 'I', 'F', 'F');
   AUWrite.writeIntMsb(header, 0, (int) tag, 4);

   // Write RIFF chunk size
   writeIntLsb(header, 4, fileLength, 4);

   // Write WAVE tag
   tag = WaveRead.chunkName('W', 'A', 'V', 'E');
   AUWrite.writeIntMsb(header, 8, (int) tag, 4);

   // Write fmt_ tag
   tag = WaveRead.chunkName('f', 'm', 't', ' ');
   AUWrite.writeIntMsb(header, 12, (int) tag, 4);

   // Write fmt_ chunk size
   int d = 16;
   writeIntLsb(header, 16, d, 4);

   // Write format type. Type 1 is PCM.
   d = 1;
   writeIntLsb(header, 20, d, 2);

   // Write number of channels
   writeIntLsb(header, 22, channels, 2);

   // Write sample rate
   writeIntLsb(header, 24, sampleRate, 4);
   int bitsPerSample = 16;
   int bytesPerSample = 2;

   // Write avg bytes per second
   int avgBytesPerSecond = channels * bytesPerSample * sampleRate;
   writeIntLsb(header, 28, avgBytesPerSecond, 4);
```

```
    // Write block alignment
    writeIntLsb(header, 32, bytesPerSample * channels, 2);

    // Write bitsPerSample
    writeIntLsb(header, 34, bitsPerSample, 2);

    // Write data tag
    tag = WaveRead.chunkName('d', 'a', 't', 'a');
    AUWrite.writeIntMsb(header, 36, (int) tag, 4);

    // Write data chunk size
    writeIntLsb(header, 40, dataLength, 4);

    // Return the header as a byte array
    return header;
}
```

You'll notice that the code above uses hardcoded values for fmt_ chunk size, format type, *bitsPerSample*, and *bytesPerSample*. These produce a wave file that matched my needs but may not match yours. Making this more generic would be easy if there were a compelling reason to do so.

WaveWriteDevice Class

The *WaveWriteDevice* is virtually identical to the *AUWriteDevice* presented earlier with the only exception being that an instance of *WaveWrite* (instead of *AUWrite*) is created to do the audio file writing. All of the description supplied previously for *AUWriteDevice* applies equally well to the *WaveWriteDevice*.

SAMPLE PLAYERS . . . .

The next class of sink devices to be discussed are sample players. These devices can be considered an interface between the audio processing chain and the underlying sound hardware on the computer on which they are running. These devices consume samples from the audio chain and make them available to the hardware for playing. Hearing the end result is the most gratifying part of the audio processing experience, especially if it can be heard in real time (for example, as if a phaser were attached to the instrument currently playing).

Two sample player devices are presented in this chapter. The first device is built upon JMF (Java Media Framework) and is therefore a platform-independent sample playing solution. The second device is a Win32-specific solution built with JNI (Java

Native Method Interface). Both devices provide the same basic API to application programs and both have a UI component built around them to allow for user interaction in the context of the *AudioTest* program. The UIs for these devices can be seen in Figures 14.2 and 14.3, respectively.

These sample players pull samples through the various processing stages until such time as no more samples are available. The indication (termed EOF for End Of File) is detected when the *getSamples* call from the stage preceding the sample player returns a –1 for the number of samples read. At that instant, sample playback halts and the audio processing chain is issued a reset command in preparation for replaying.

As you may recall from the discussion in Chapter 9, a reset command is propagated from the issuing device to the sink device in the processing chain and from there back through all devices until the source device is encountered. All stages that have implemented a *reset* method, by overriding the one in the *AbstractAudio* base class, have their method called to perform whatever processing they require to prepare themselves for restarting playback. Most devices don't implement a *reset* method. The *Cache* device of Chapter 13 is an exception, as are the audio file reader devices *AURead* and *WaveRead*. The *Cache* device resets itself so that the next request for samples is pulled from the start of the cached data instead of from the current position in the cache. The file read devices perform a reset by closing the audio file and nulling out the sample decoder so that the file will be reread from the beginning when playback resumes.

The PCMPlayer

The JMF player is based upon the 1.1 version of the JMF. JMF is Sun and Intel's attempt at a platform-independent API for multimedia application development in Java. In the words of Sun Microsystems, "The Java Media Framework (JMF) is an

Figure 14.2   *PCMPlayer Device User Interface. Plays samples using JMF.*

Figure 14.3   *WinPlayer Device User Interface. Plays samples using Windows Win32 platform-dependent code.*

application programming interface (API) for incorporating media data types into Java applications and applets. It is specifically designed to take advantage of Java platform features. The 1.0 version of the JMF API supports the synchronization, control, processing, and presentation of compressed streaming and stored time-based media, including video and audio." The 2.0 version of the API will support capture of audio and video in addition to its existing features and will eliminate many of the problems found in 1.1. See Appendix B for information on JMF2.0.

JMF is worthy of a complete book of its own (and much has been written elsewhere), so a complete discussion is not provided here. Just enough of the JMF's operation will be described so you can understand how the player works.

To use JMF1.1 you must have installed the JMF1.1 code and you must have the *JMF1.1\lib\JMF.jar* file in your classpath and have *JMF1.1\lib* in your shared library path.

When I first began writing the code for this book, I needed a method for playing back processed audio samples so that I could hear the effect of the processing I was studying. My only recourse at the time was to write native methods to interface the sound processing code written in Java to the underlying sound hardware of my PC. I started down this path but before I was finished, JMF became available. I felt that a platform-independent playback solution was the correct approach, so I abandoned my native method approach and began studying JMF.

As my knowledge of JMF increased, I became aware that JMF1.1 did not allow any direct access to the samples it read from audio files that were subsequently made available for playback. JMF only knew how to play audio files in a select number of well-known formats. It did not provide a means of playing raw PCM samples. I was disappointed, to say the least. Initially it seemed as if JMF wasn't going to work for me after all.

In thinking about this problem I decided to try and fool JMF into accepting a stream of audio data that looked like a streamed AU file. I reasoned that if JMF couldn't play raw PCM samples it probably could play the samples if they were preceded by an AU header of proper construction. So that was the tack I took and it worked except for one small problem.

The problem with this approach was latency. Since JMF thought it was playing an AU file, it attempted to read the majority and in some cases all of the sampled data into its internal buffers before playback would begin. Something like two megabytes of samples would be read in prior to playback beginning and this would result in a rather long pause every time playback was requested. So, while my clever little hack got around one problem, it couldn't help with the other latency problem. Therefore my native method interface approach was still the best bet at that point. I still decided to present the JMF code here to show you how it was done. The native code approach will be shown in the next section. If you examine the code for both solutions you will see that they are more similar than they are different.

JMF2.0 has the concept of a *processor* built in that can have direct access to the PCM samples before playback. Using a processor, it is possible to feed the playback engine piecemeal, thereby reducing the latency problem substantially. When JMF2.0 finally arrives, my AU file hack will no longer be necessary and JMF2.0 will become my playback mechanism of choice.

JMF can be thought of as a state machine that traverses through various states in preparation for audio/video playback. There are six possible states in all. There are a lot of rules about what can and cannot be done in each state that are explained in depth in the Sun documentation.

At the lowest level is the code in *PCMSourceStream.java* which:

1. Extends *PullSourceStream*, which implies that samples will be pulled from it for playback by code which calls its read method.
2. Builds an AU file header, given the sample rate and the number of channels negotiated with the other devices in the audio processing chain. The AU header is initialized to indicate the pseudo AU file is comprised of 16-bit linear PCM data, the very kind produced by the audio processing chain.
3. Provides first the bytes of AU header data and, when those are exhausted, provides data pulled from the audio processing chain as necessary to satisfy requests made to the *read* method. In other words, the JMF playback engine calls the *read* method of this class, which in turn pulls samples through the audio processing chain by calling the *getSamples* method of the previous device in the chain.

The code that builds the AU header is provided by the *build16BitAuHeader* method of the *AUWrite* class which was shown earlier. Since the *read* method is where all of the action is, it is reproduced below for reference.

```
public int read(byte[] buffer, int offset, int nToRead) {

    if (endOfMedia)
        return -1;

    if (nToRead == 0)
        return 0;

    int numberOfBytesProvided = 0;

    // Supply the synthesized header as the initial data
    if (headerBytesLeft != 0) {
        if (headerBytesLeft >= nToRead) {
```

```
            // Header can supply all data requested
            headerBytesLeft -= nToRead;
            System.arraycopy(header, headerByteOffset, buffer, offset,
                                                        nToRead);
            headerByteOffset += nToRead;
            return nToRead;
        } else {
            // Header cannot supply all required data
            System.arraycopy(header, headerByteOffset, buffer, offset,
headerBytesLeft);
            offset += headerBytesLeft;
            nToRead -= headerBytesLeft;
            numberOfBytesProvided = headerBytesLeft;
            headerBytesLeft = 0;
        }
    }
    // Loop until all of the data requested has been provided or
    // until the end of the media has been reached.
    while(numberOfBytesProvided < nToRead) {
        // If samples exhaused, pull in some more from previous
        // processing stages.
        if (samplesAvailable == 0) {
            sampleOffset = 0;

            samplesAvailable =
                aa.previous.getSamples(sampleBuffer,
                                    AudioConstants.SAMPLEBUFFERSIZE);

            endOfMedia = ((samplesAvailable == 0) || (samplesAvailable
== -1));
        }
        if (endOfMedia)
            return numberOfBytesProvided;

        // Convert the 16 bit signed PCM samples into two bytes
        short sample = sampleBuffer[sampleOffset++];
        buffer[offset++] = (byte) (sample >> 8);
        buffer[offset++] = (byte) (sample & 255);
        numberOfBytesProvided += 2;
        samplesAvailable -= 1;
    }
    return numberOfBytesProvided;
}
```

At the next higher level, the *PCMDataSource* class extends *PullDataSource* and connects up the *PCMSourceStream* as the source of data for this data source. Stepping up the ladder again, the class *_PCMPlayer* is what associates *PCMDataSource* with a JMF media *controller*. A controller is the basis for JMF operation and is what runs the state machine mentioned above. *_PCMPlayer* extends *ControllerAdapter* so as to intercept all controller events that it must monitor for proper operation of the controller. *_PCMPlayer* overrides the empty methods of *ControllerAdapter* for all events it is interested in. *ControllerAdapter* provides the following event hooks, only some of which are used by *_PCMPlayer*:

```
public void cachingControl(CachingControlEvent e) {}
public void controllerClosed(ControllerClosedEvent e) {}
public void controllerError(ControllerErrorEvent e) {}
public void connectionError(ConnectionErrorEvent e) {}
public void internalError(InternalErrorEvent e) {}
public void resourceUnavailable(ResourceUnavailableEvent e) {}
public void durationUpdate(DurationUpdateEvent e) {}
public void mediaTimeSet(MediaTimeSetEvent e) {}
public void rateChange(RateChangeEvent e) {}
public void stopTimeChange(StopTimeChangeEvent e) {}
public void transition(TransitionEvent e) {}
public void prefetchComplete(PrefetchCompleteEvent e) {}
public void realizeComplete(RealizeCompleteEvent e) {}
public void start(StartEvent e) {}
public void stop(StopEvent e) {}
public void dataStarved(DataStarvedEvent e) {}
public void deallocate(DeallocateEvent e) {}
public void endOfMedia(EndOfMediaEvent e) {}
public void restarting(RestartingEvent e) {}
public void stopAtTime(StopAtTimeEvent e) {}
public void stopByRequest(StopByRequestEvent e) {}
```

If you look at the code in *_PCMPlayer* you can see that a lot of events just cause a debug message to be generated as an aid in understanding what the controller is doing. Other event hooks call JMF methods to move the controller between states.

The *createPlayer* static method is what is called to instantiate a *PCMDataSource* as the sample source and to make a Player out of it. This code is shown next:

```
public static Player createPlayer(AbstractAudio aa, int channels, int
                                                          sampleRate) {

    // Create a PCM data source from the parameters
    PCMDataSource pcmds = new PCMDataSource(aa, channels, sampleRate);
```

```
    // Create an instance of a player for this data source
    try {
        return Manager.createPlayer(pcmds);
    }
    catch(NoPlayerException e) {
        o("Error:" + e.getMessage());
        return null;
    }
    catch(IOException e) {
        o("Error:" + e.getMessage());
        return null;
    }
}
```

The *PCMPlayer* class is an *AbstractAudio* device that knows how to deal both with the audio processing chain as the source of sample data and a *_PCMPlayer* object as the engine for playing the samples. *PCMPlayer* provides methods for starting and stopping playback. These methods are called *play* and *stop,* respectively. When *play* is called, negotiation is performed with the other devices in the audio processing chain if it hasn't been done before and then a new *_PCMPlayer* object is created by the code below:

```
// Create a player each time through
Player player = _PCMPlayer.createPlayer(this, channels, sampleRate);
if (player == null)
    return false;

// Wrap the player
pcmPlayer = new _PCMPlayer(player);
```

After the *_PCMPlayer* is created, it is started by a call to the *startPlayer* method. At this point, the JMF mechanism cranks up and the controller starts to transition states in preparation for playback. After some spin-up time and prefetch interval, samples start being pulled from the audio processing chain. This process continues until no more samples are available and sample playback terminates. The *startPlayer* method sleeps until playback is complete or playback is terminated.

The *stop* method of *PCMPlayer* calls the *stopPlayer* method of *_PCMPlayer* which in turn calls close on the *Player* to terminate playback and then performs a *notify* so *startPlayer* will return from its sleep. If playback is later restarted, a new *_PCMPlayer* is created as described above and the complete process repeats.

In order to provide a user-friendly method of sample playback to be used in the context of the *AudioTest* program, *PCMPlayerWithUI* was created. This class wraps a *PCMPlayer* device with the simple UI shown in Figure 14.2. *PCMPlayerWithUI* converts button clicks into the appropriate *PCMPlayer* method calls. If you are interested in how this works, consult the code on the CDROM.

USER INTERFACE . . . .

The controls and indicators on the *PCMPlayerWithUI* device front panel are detailed in Table 14.2.

Table 14.2   PCMPlayerWithUI Front Panel Controls and Indicators

Front Panel Controls and Indicators	Description
Playing Indicator LED	This red LED blinks while samples are being played.
Play Button	Starts the playback of audio samples pulled through the audio processing chain. Playback continues until the EOF indication is detected in the sample stream or the playback is stopped by the user.
Stop Button	Stops the playback of sample at the users' request. The play button can be used to restart playback after playback has been stopped.
Done Button	Stops playback and closes down the UI, causing the execution of the *AudioTest* program to end.

Use with the AudioTest program

When using the *AudioTest* program, the *PCMPlayerWithUI* device is specified for inclusion in the audio processing path by specifying the command line switch "*–o player.*" The UI for this device will then pop up and the user will be able to interact with it.

The WinPlayer

WinPlayer was developed because the *PCMPlayer* solution (described above) built with JMF had much too much latency to be practical. While latency was reduced substantially, this WinPlayer solution suffers from platform dependence and will only run on Win32 machines. The *WinPlayer* works via a choreographed dance between code running in the Java VM and code running in the Win32 environment. Code running in the Java environment is responsible for providing samples to the Win32 code. The Win32 code is busy asynchronously playing samples and it signals the Java code when it is running low on samples and requires more. This is a highly synchronized process that cannot get out of sync without causing corrupted playback to occur. Even under the best of conditions if the audio processing chain cannot provide samples faster than the Win32 wave subsystem is playing them, breakup of the played back audio will occur. Of course playback of stereo (two channels) sources is harder to do for performance reasons than playback of monaural audio and faster sample rates are worse than slower ones.

As you probably have guessed, Java native method interface (JNI) is used to connect the Java code to the Win32 wave code. The native methods are implemented in a Windows DLL called *winplayerdll.dll* which is loaded by the Java code when a *WinPlayer* object is instantiated. The code which implements these native methods (and makes up the DLL) is contained in the file *winplayer.c*. This C code provides five methods which are shown and described in 14.3.

Table 14.3   *WinPlayer Methods*

Native Method	Description
nativeSelectDevice	Initializes a *WAVEFORMATEX* structure with playback parameters and calls *waveOutOpen* to prepare for playback. The four buffers are then prepared for use by calling the Win32 function *waveOutPrepareHeader*. Returns true if the initialization was successful and false if problems occurred.
nativePlay	Calls back into *WinPlayer* Java code to gather samples for playback. Enters a loop waiting for the EOF indication to occur in the sample stream. Calls *WaitForSingleObject* method to wait for a buffer to free up and then calls into Java again for more samples to fill the empty buffer.
nativeReset	Calls *waveOutReset* to terminate playback and mark all buffers as available.
nativeClose	Calls the Win32 function *waveOutClose* to close the wave device and free the underlying resources.
nativeStoreSamples	This native method is called by the Java code whenever enough samples have been pulled through the audio processing chain to fill a Win32 buffer. The samples are copied into a Win32 buffer and the method *waveOutWrite* is called to inform the wave subsystem that a new buffer is ready for playback. The buffers are used in a round-robin manner.

We will skip the gory details of how the Win32 wave subsystem works but if you are interested in finding out, the C code in the DLL is well commented and hopefully easy to understand. You'll see if you examine the code that four buffers of 7500 samples (16-bit samples) each are used for playback. The size of the buffers used by the C code must match the size of the buffers used in the Java code or else problems will occur. The buffer size used in the Java code is defined in *AudioConstants.SAMPLE-BUFFERSIZE* and is currently set to 7500 samples.

Another item of information that needs to be conveyed is how the include file, *craigl_winplayer_WinPlayer.h*, required by the C code gets built. For those who have built Java native methods before, the answer is obvious. For those that haven't, the header file is built using the *javah* utility program with the following command line:

```
javah -jni craigl.winplayer.WinPlayer
```

Invocation of javah will cause the header file to be built. The header file contains the prototypes that the native methods must be coded to.

Final note: Building the DLL requires a Win32 development environment which is not included with the code from this book. The good news is the DLL comes pre-built on the accompanying CDROM so you won't need to rebuild the DLL unless you need to add functionality to it or fix a bug.

The Java side of the native method interface is implemented by the *WinPlayer* class contained in the file *WinPlayer.java*. It is here that the native method signatures are defined and where the Java methods for controlling sample playback are implemented. One important function of *WinPlayer* is to load the native method interface DLL, thus making the native methods available. The code which does the loading is shown below:

```
// Load the WinPlayer interface DLL
static {
    // Load the interface DLL
    System.loadLibrary("craigl/winplayer/winplayerdll");
}
```

WinPlayer is a sink device that is extended from *AbstractAudio*. As such, it can be linked into an audio processing chain to pull samples from the chain and store them in native code buffers for playback. *WinPlayer* negotiates with the other devices in the processing chain and determines if the audio playback hardware can support the negotiated sample rate and number of channels. If it is determined the hardware can support the negotiated parameters, playback can occur.

Playback begins when the *play* method of *WinPlayer* is called. This method calls *nativePlay* (a native method in the DLL) to start Win32 wave playback. Initially, the native code doesn't have any samples for playback so it immediately calls back into Java, the *requestSamples* method of *WinPlayer*, to gather some. *requestSamples* pulls samples from the previous device in the audio chain and calls the native method *nativeStoreSamples* to copy the samples from Java into the native sample buffers for playback. Every time a native buffer frees up, *requestSamples* is called again and the process repeats until playback runs out of samples or until the *stop* method is called to terminate playback.

To use the functionality provided by *WinPlayer* within the context of the *AudioTest* program, the *WinPlayerWithUI* device was developed. This class provides the user interface shown in Figure 14.3, which allows a user to control sample playback interactively. The majority of the code within this class is used in building the UI and in controlling the states of the various buttons and indicators. *WinPlayerWithUI* instantiates a *WinPlayer* object and couples the UI button events to method calls in *WinPlayer*. The details of the code's operation can be ascertained by looking at the source.

User Interface

The controls and indicators on the *WinPlayerWithUI* device front panel are detailed in Table 14.4.

Table 14.4   WinPlayerWithUI Front Panel Controls and Indicators

Front Panel Controls and Indicators	Description
Playing Indicator LED	This red LED blinks while samples are being played.
Play Button	Starts the playback of audio samples pulled through the audio processing chain. Playback continues until the EOF indication is detected in the sample stream or the playback is stopped by the user.
Stop Button	Stops the playback of sample at the users' request. The play button can be used to restart playback after playback has been stopped.
Done Button	Stops playback and closes down the UI, causing the execution of the *AudioTest* program to end.

Use with the AudioTest program

When using the *AudioTest* program, the *WinPlayerWithUI* device is specified for inclusion in the audio processing path by specifying the command line switch "–o winplayer." The UI for this device will then pop up, allowing the user to interact with it.

MISCELLANEOUS INFORMATION . . . .

Source Files:

File Name	Package	Description
_PCMPlayer.java	craigl.pcmplayer	A JMF controller for playing PCM samples. Traps all controller events and reacts accordingly.
AUWrite.java	craigl.au	Lowest level AU file writer class that understands the format of AU files and can to produce them.
AUWriteDevice.java	craigl.au	Audio device extension of *AbstractAudio* device that writes AU files from the samples streamed into it.
ControllerAdapter.java	craigl.pcmplayer	Adapter class which provides hooks for derived classes to trap controller events.
FileWriterIF.java	craigl.utils	Interface that all audio file writers must implement. Forms a consistent interface to all audio file writing code.
FileWriterWithUI.java	craigl.filewriter	*AbstractAudio* sink device for writing audio samples to either AU or wave files. It provides the user interface shown in Figure 14.1 when used in conjunction with the *AudioTest* program.
PCMDataSource.java	craigl.pcmplayer	A PCMPlayer data source that utilizes *PCMSourceStream* for samples.
PCMPlayer.java	craigl.pcmplayer	An *AbstractAudio* sink device for playing samples, built on JMF.
PCMPlayerWithUI.java	craigl.pcmplayer	Code which builds a UI around a *PCMPlayer* which allows a user to control sample playback. Produces the UI shown in Figure 14.2.
PCMSourceStream.java	craigl.pcmplayer	Lowest level PCMPlayer class that fools JMF into thinking that it is playing an AU file when in reality it is playing a stream of 16-bit PCM samples prefaced with an AU file header.
WaveWrite.java	craigl.wave	Lowest level wave file writer class that understands the format of wave files and how to produce them.
WaveWriteDevice.java	craigl.wave	Audio device extension of *AbstractAudio* device that writes wave files from the samples streamed into it.
WinPlayer.c	N/A	Platform-specific native method code for interfacing to the Microsoft Windows Win32 wave subsystem. This code becomes the winplayerdll.dll.

File Name	Package	Description
WinPlayer.java	craigl.winplayer	A class that provides the Java side of the native method interface to the Win32 wave subsystem. This class implements *AbstractAudio* so it can be linked into an audio processing chain with other *AbstractAudio* devices.
WinPlayerWithUI.java	craigl.winplayer	Code which builds a UI around a *WinPlayer* that allows a user to control sample playback. Produces the UI shown in Figure 14.3.

Part 3

Audio
Applications

INTRODUCTION . . . .

In this portion of the book, two complete audio applications are presented. These applications use much of the technology described in this book. These are but two of the many possible applications that can be built by combining the functionality described in sections one and two of the book. Because I am a guitar player, the two applications presented are especially useful for guitarists. The first application, a phrase sampler, allows up to 30 seconds of audio to be captured in memory and to be played back with controlled looping. More importantly, the tempo can be cut in half during playback with the pitch remaining the same. This slows down the sampled audio such that fast instrumental riffs are easier to hear and therefore learn by ear.

The second audio application is a guitar tuner modeled after hardware devices currently on the market. This device can be used to tune six-string guitars and four- and five-string bass guitars to near perfect pitch. This device automatically detects the string being tuned and has a meter that displays the difference between the string's pitch and the reference pitch. Simulated LED's show the note being tuned and whether the string is sharp, flat, or in tune.

With these two devices, your PC can become a very useful tool for a guitarist/musician.

As mentioned, these are only two applications built using the provided code. Many more are possible, including:

1. A device that samples from the microphone/line input, has extensive tone controls like the graphic equalizer presented earlier, and writes the output

to a file. This application would allow substantial changes in the tonal character of what is being recorded as it is being recorded.

2. A program that transforms wave to AU files and vise versa.

3. A program that converts songs from an audio CD to a wave or AU file.

4. A full-featured spectrum analyzer that could be used to tune personal recording studio rooms for flatness (neutral frequency response).

5. Any of the source processing devices presented could be recoded in C++ as a direct X audio plug-in and then be used with programs like Cakewalk or other digital audio applications.

6. With some effort, a sampler with sequencer could be developed that grabs samples from various sources and combines them into interesting sequences.

7. A vocal harmonizer could be designed based on the pitch shifter of section two that automatically sings in harmony with a singer.

8. A processing effect like an aural exciter could be developed that selectively modifies harmonics of incoming audio to change them in useful and interesting ways.

This list could go on and on. If you have an idea for an audio application, chances are the code in this book can be used to implement your idea.

15 The Phrase Sampler Application

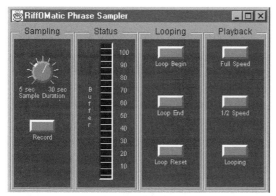

The first full application presented is a specialized phrase sampler. This device allows from 5 to 30 seconds of audio to be sampled and then played back with controlled looping. Most importantly though, playback can be at the normal rate or it can be slowed to half the normal rate while the pitch is kept unchanged. This magic is done by careful use of the pitch shifter processor (presented in section two) along with some additional supporting code. The user interface of the phrase sampler can be seen in Figure 15.1.

The purpose of such a device is to slow down instrumental riffs (a riff for all you non-musicians is a short sequence of notes, usually played at high speed) so that they can more easily be learned. This device is therefore a tool for musicians who learn

Figure 15.1　　The Phrase Sampler's User Interface

songs by ear. Although this application was written with the guitar in mind, it is equally useful for other instruments as well.

It must be noted that this pitch shifting magic does not come without a severe cost in sound quality. While listening to the reduced-speed playback you will hear an incredible array of background noises generated by the digital signal processing being performed. In some cases the background noises can almost obscure the notes you are listening for. This is the price one must pay for having half-speed playback. I can say that this phrase sampler is no worse than the commercial unit I own. Enough said.

The phrase sampler program was chosen for implementation because it is an interesting application of many of the technologies that have been presented previously, because it is useful and valuable in and of itself, and, most importantly, I wanted to see if I could do it. I think I was reasonably successful but you'll have to be the judge of that.

The phrase sampler draws upon the following topics that have been described previously in this book:

1. Using UI devices including potentiometers, multi-color LEDs, LED bar graph meters, and various types of buttons. All of these control and indicator devices are in the form of Java beans. Each has been described in section one of this book.
2. The use of the *WinRecorder* device to sample the microphone/line input connected to a guitar or bass.
3. The use of the pitch shifter described in section two of this book as an integral part of the phrase sampler.
4. The chaining of *AbstractAudio* devices for acquiring and processing digital audio samples.

Since these topics have been given substantial treatment elsewhere, they will only be discussed here in brief.

HOW THE PHRASE SAMPLER IS USED . . . .

To use the phrase sampler, follow the steps listed below:

1. Connect a cable from your audio source (cassette deck, CD player, record player after the preamp) to the line level input of your PC.
2. Adjust the recording level using the volume control/mixer available on your PC. The level should be adjusted to be as high as possible without distorting.

3. Execute the phrase sampler application by typing

```
java apps.phrasesampler.RiffOMatic
```

at the command line. This assumes your classpath is set up correctly.

4. Rotate the *Sample Duration* pot to the desired sampling time. You should set it for just a little longer than the riff/phrase you are trying to capture.

5. Start your audio source at the point you want to capture audio from and then click the *Record* button. The software will acquire audio for the selected sampling time and then will terminate acquisition. During this period, the *Status Indicator* bar graph will be updated with acquisition progress.

6. Next, click the *Full Speed* playback button and you should hear the phrase you just sampled. You may have to acquire a few times to get the musical phrase you are interested in captured correctly.

7. Now you should narrow down the captured audio to just the musical phrase you are interested in learning. You do this by clicking the *Full Speed* playback button and then clicking the *Loop Begin* button just at the start of the phrase and the *Loop End* button just at its end. The *Status Indicator* will be updated to show where in the acquired audio data your loop resides.

8. Clicking the *Full Speed* playback button now will only play back the selected portion of the initially acquired audio. If you find the begin and/or end loop positions to be incorrect, click the *Loop Reset* button and repeat step seven above.

9. Once you have your loop set up correctly, click the *Looping* button. Now when the playback button is clicked, your loop will be repeated over and over until you turn off the *Looping* button.

10. Now, the ½ *Speed* playback button can be clicked to play back the looped audio at half the rate. This is where the magic becomes apparent.

HOW THE PHRASE SAMPLER WORKS . . . .

Halving the tempo while keeping pitch the same is accomplished by using a pitch shift processing element to double the frequency of the incoming audio and then cutting the playback rate in half by doubling the number of samples. The net result is what we want. To understand how the phrase sampler accomplishes this, consider the block diagram shown in Figure 15.2. This entire application consists of four *AbstractAudio* devices linked together in the usual fashion. These devices are:

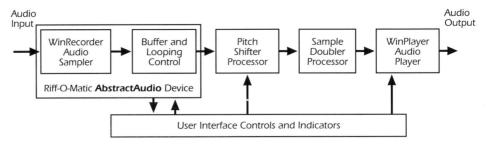

Figure 15.2   The Phrase Sampler Block Diagram

1. The combination of the *WinRecorder* and the buffering and loop control form the first *AbstractAudio* device in the audio processing chain. Collectively, these components make up what shall be referred to as the *Sampling and Loop Control* device for the sake of discussion.

2. The second *AbstractAudio* device is the *Pitch Shifter* processor of section two.

3. The third device, called the *Sampler Doubler*, is used to double and massage the audio samples.

4. The final device in the chain is a *WinPlayer* for playing the processed samples.

Each of these devices is described below.

Sampling and Loop Control Device

Audio data is sampled using a *WinRecorder* device configured for acquisition of a mono signal at a sampling rate of 11025 samples per second. After this device is initialized, samples are returned from it by calling its method *getSamplesWithOffset(short [] buffer, int offset)*. This method acquires *AudioConstants.SAMPLEBUFFERSIZE* samples and stores them into a buffer at the specified offset. This method allows a buffer of arbitrary size be filled with sampled audio data. In this case, the size of the sample buffer is determined by the length of sampling time dialed in by the user via the *Sample Duration* pot.

The *Loop Begin* and *Loop End* buttons in the UI set the starting and ending playback positions in the sample buffer. When samples are requested from this device, the *getSamples* method shown below is called to return the appropriate samples. Note that samples from the sample buffer are copied into the buffer passed in to this method and that the number of samples copied is specified by the length parameter also passed in. The *arraycopy* method in the *System* class is used for this purpose.

```java
// Get samples from the sampled and stored data
public int getSamples(short [] buffer, int length) {

    int count = stopPlayIndex - currentPlayIndex + 1;
    if (count == 0)
    return -1;

    if (count >= length) {
        System.arraycopy(sampleBuffer, currentPlayIndex,
                buffer, 0, length);
        currentPlayIndex += length;
        return length;

    }   else   {
        System.arraycopy(sampleBuffer, currentPlayIndex,
                buffer, 0, count);
        currentPlayIndex += count;
        return count;

    }
}
```

The Pitch Shifter Device

The pitch shifter device is identical to the one described in section two of this book. Here, however, the *Pitch Shifter* is configured as follows:

1. To shift the pitch upward 12 halftones (or semitones), thereby doubling the pitch of the incoming audio samples.
2. The dry level signal is set to zero so that none of the original audio at the original pitch feeds through.
3. The wet level signal is set to 100% as we are only interested in the processed signal.
4. The feedback level is set to zero because no feedback is desired.

As a side note, interesting audible affects may be produced if any of these configuration items are changed. Please experiment!

The Sample Doubler Device

The Sample doubler device is implemented as an inner class of *RiffOMatic* and it too extends *AbstractAudio*. Its sole purpose is to double the number of samples it produces from the number that it consumes. In operation, it passes the first sample through without modification but synthesizes the additional output sample by averaging the first and second input sample. Next time through, the second input sample is passed on and the second and third samples are used in the output sample synthesis. All of this process takes place in the *Sample Doubler's getSamples* method, which it must implement. See the file *RiffOMatic.java* for the details.

The WinPlayer Device

The *WinPlayer* device is as described in section two of this book. There is nothing new of note here. Just remember that it is the *WinPlayer's* inexhaustible hunger for samples for playback that pulls the audio samples from the sample buffer through the various processing stages to eventually end up as the audio you hear.

UI Controls and Indicators

Although the UI is not an *AbstractAudio* device, it does interact with the various devices which make up the phrase sampler. Consider what happens when each of the controls is manipulated.

The Sample Duration Potentiometer

When the *Sample Duration* pot is manipulated, the required size of a new sample buffer is calculated and the new buffer is allocated for the next audio acquisition cycle. The size of this new buffer is rounded up to a multiple of *AudioConstants.SAMPLEBUFFERSIZE* because the *WinRecorder* device always returns buffers of this size. Additionally, the granularity of the LED status indicator is recalculated so that it reflects the acquisition status correctly. That is, the indicator's scale reaches 100% as the sample acquisition time is finished. Finally, the loop begin and end points are set to the beginning and end of the new sample buffer, effectively canceling any previously set loop points.

The Record Button

When the *Record* button is clicked, the *WinPlayer* device is initialized for acquisition and the required number of sample buffers are filled with digitized data from the audio input. As each buffer is being filled, the *Status Indicator* is updated to reflect the portion of the buffer that has been filled. When all of the required samples have been acquired, the *WinPlayer* is closed, thereby terminating its sampling operation.

Loop Begin Button

When the *Loop Begin* button is clicked during playback, the index of the audio sample playing at that moment is saved as *startPlayIndex*. This is the position that will be used for the start of playback next time round. (Due to the latency of audio playback, the recorded start position will vary somewhat from where you think you set it). Finally, a marker will turn red in the *Status Indicator* showing approximately where in the acquired audio the start index was set.

Loop End Button

When the *Loop End* button is clicked, the index of the audio sample playing at that moment is saved as the stop play index. This delineates the end of playback for the acquired audio. Another red marker shows up on the *Status Indicator* indicating the position of the end of audio playback. Latency will again affect the actual loop ending point.

Loop Reset Button

When the *Loop Reset* button is clicked, *startPlayIndex* is set to the beginning of the sample buffer and *stopPlayIndex* is set to its end. The markers on the *Status Indicator* are also cleared to indicate that the full buffer is again available for playback.

Full Speed Playback Button

When the *Full Speed Playback* button is clicked, the *Pitch Shifter* device is set into the bypass mode as is the *Sample Doubler* device. This effectively removes these devices from the audio processing chain and defeats their processing. Then, after some buffer maintenance is performed, the *WinPlayer* device is commanded to begin pulling samples through the audio processing chain. The samples that are returned to *WinPlayer* are from the start to the stop indices in the sample buffer. After these samples are exhausted, a check is made to see if looping is in effect. If so, the indices are reinitialized and the playback process starts over. If looping is not turned on, the playback process ends when the samples are depleted.

½ Speed Playback Button

When the *½ Speed Playback* button is clicked, the *Pitch Shifter* device is set to shift the pitch up a full octave and bypass is reset for both the *Pitch Shifter* and the *Sample Doubler* devices. This puts these devices back into the signal path and makes their processing count. As described above, the *WinPlayer* is again commanded to pull the processed samples through the processing stages and to make them audible. Thus, the reduction in tempo is now heard.

Looping Button

Contrary to all other buttons in this user interface, the *Looping* button is of the push on/push off variety instead of the momentary variety. When this button is on, the *loopingMode* variable in the code is set true, which causes playback to loop between the begin and end looping points in the sample buffer. Looping continues until the looping mode is terminated by clicking this button back to the off state.

Table 15.1 lists the phrase sample application front panel controls and indicators.

Table 15.1   Phrase Sample Application

Front Panel Controls and Indicators	Description
Sample Duration Pot	Allows the user to control the duration of audio sampling. Durations of approximately 5 seconds to approximately 30 seconds are possible.
Record Button	Causes audio samples to be acquired in sufficient quantity to fill the user-defined sample buffer size.
Status Indicator Bar Graph (LED Meter)	This indicator shows the progress of sample acquisition. It goes from 0 to 100% as the sample buffer is filled. Also, as looping is set by the user, loop start and loop end markers will be shown on this indicator, as well.
Loop Begin Button	Clicking this button during playback establishes a new beginning position for audio playback the next time through. This also sets the start of a loop when looping mode is in effect.
Loop End Button	Clicking this button during playback establishes a new ending position for audio playback the next time through. This also sets the end of a loop when looping mode is in effect.
Loop Reset Button	Clicking this button clears the beginning and ending loop information, allowing the full sample buffer to be played back once more.
Full Speed Playback Button	Clicking this button begins playback of the samples in the sample buffer. If no looping points have been set, the full buffer is played back. If looping points have been set, the playback occurs between the beginning and ending loop points.

Table 15.1   (continued)

Front Panel Controls and Indicators	Description
½ Speed Playback Button	Clicking this button begins playback of the samples in the sample buffer at one half the normal rate but at the normal pitch. If no looping points have been set, the full buffer is played back in this mode. If looping points have been set, the playback occurs between the beginning and ending loop points.
Looping Button	This button is of the push on/push off variety. When on, this causes playback to loop continually. That is, as soon as the buffer of samples is exhausted, the playback process starts over from the beginning. Looping occurs from the beginning to the end of the sample buffer unless loop points have been set. In this case, playback loops from the loop begin position up to and including the loop end position.

POSSIBLE ENHANCEMENTS . . . .

An additional playback mode could be added that would allow playback of the audio at something like ⅔ the normal rate. Then three playback speeds would be available: full speed, ⅔ speed, and ½ speed. This new playback rate would allow you to play along at less than full speed as your skill in playing the new riff increases. This new playback rate would require some fractional sampling techniques which would make for an interesting problem which I will leave to you to solve.

Finally, if the JMF2.0 devices of Appendix B were retrofit into this design, this phrase sampler device would probably be more reliable than it currently seems to be and platform independent as well.

MISCELLANEOUS INFORMATION . . . .

Package:

apps.phrasesampler

Source Files:

File Name	Description
RiffOMatic.java	This code performs all of the processing on the audio samples including acquisition, buffer management, looping control, pitch shifting, sample doubling, and sample playback. It also instantiates the user interface code in RiffOMaticUI.java.
RiffOMaticUI.java	This is the user interface code for the phrase sampler. This code instantiates all front panel controls and indicators and handles all of the events generated by user interaction.

16 The Guitar/Bass Tuner Application

The second full application presented here is a guitar/bass guitar tuner. This device allows a user to visually tune an instrument by watching indicators on their PC instead of having to rely on their ears. This device is very useful for people with "tin ears" who need all the help they can get to get and keep their guitars in tune. This device looks like and performs like many of the inexpensive guitar tuners currently on the market. Figure 16.1 shows what the tuner's user interface looks like. The advantage of this tuner over commercial ones is, of course, that you get it included with this book.

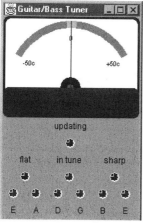

Figure 16.1   The Tuner Application's User Interface

A tuner program was chosen for implementation here because it is an interesting application of many of the technologies that have been presented previously and because it is useful and valuable in and of itself. This guitar tuner is a direct application of theory to practice. Previous topics drawn upon within this application include:

1. Using UI devices including multi-color LEDs and an analog meter on a simulated front panel. Both of these indicator devices are in the form of Java beans.

2. The use of the *WinRecorder* device to sample the microphone/line input connected to a guitar or bass.

3. The use of low-pass IIR filters for removing unwanted high-frequency components from the audio samples.

4. The use of fast Fourier transforms (FFTs) like those used in the spectrum analyzer to analyze the pitch of plucked guitar strings.

5. The chaining of *AbstractAudio* sample provider devices with *AbstractAudio* sample consumer devices.

Since these topics have been given substantial treatment elsewhere, they will only be discussed here in brief. In addition, some new information is provided and used in the *Tuner* application. This includes:

1. Calculation of note pitch or frequency from standard MIDI note numbers.

2. The use of cents to denote differences in pitch.

3. Various other musical relationships: octaves and frequency, cents for measuring frequency differences, whole tones and halftones, etc.

HOW THE TUNER IS USED . . . .

To use the tuner, follow the steps listed below:

1. Connect a microphone to your PC and hold it close to your guitar or connect the guitar directly to the microphone or line input of your PC, if your instrument has a built in preamp (preamplifier).

2. Adjust the recording level using the volume control/mixer available on your PC. The level should be adjusted to be as high as possible without distorting.

3. Execute the tuner application by typing

```
java apps.guitartuner.Tuner
```

at the command line. This assumes your classpath is set up correctly.

4. Pluck a single string on the guitar, making sure that the other strings are muted. Adjust the string's pitch while watching the LED indicators and the meter on the tuner. The string will be in tune when the correct string LED lights and the meter's needle is in the straight up position. The update LED will blink each time a corroborated frequency measurement is taken.

5. Continue tuning until all strings are in tune.

HOW THE TUNER WORKS . . . .

Figure 16.2 shows a block diagram of the tuner from a data flow perspective. In actuality, this application consists of two *AbstractAudio* devices connected so as to share samples. The devices are the *WinRecorder* device for acquiring audio samples from the connected instrument and the *Tuner* device, which consumes and processes the samples produced by the *WinRecorder*. Each block of the block diagram will be described below.

The Sampler

Basically, a *WinRecorder* device is configured to sample a mono signal at 11025 samples per second (or, said another way, with a sampling frequency of 11025 Hz). Once the *WinRecorder* is instantiated, it is placed first on the *LinkedListVector* of devices as it will be the device providing the samples for the tuner software. The *Tuner* device is placed on the list after *WinRecorder*. Every call to

```
previous.getSamples(buffer, length)
```

in the tuner application fetches a buffer of samples from the microphone/line input. As noted in section two, the length parameter is ignored when fetching from

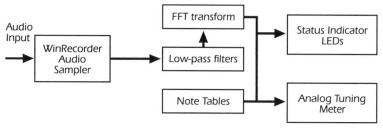

Figure 16.2 *Tuner logical block diagram*

WinRecorder. The *getSamples* call always returns exactly *AudioConstants.SAMPLE-BUFFERSIZE* samples from the recorder. Currently, this value is set at 7500 samples. At a sampling rate of 11025 samples per second, 7500 samples represents 0.68 seconds of sample time.

The Low-pass Filters

Because the PC is such a noisy environment for audio, the sampled audio is first run through two second order low-pass IIR filters to clean it up before passing it on to the FFT transformation. The two filters result in a rather sharp cutoff of 24 dB/octave, with the filter's knee or –3 dB point positioned slightly above the pitch of the little E string on the guitar. The use of the filters guarantees that only guitar range frequencies are involved in the spectrum analysis that follows. These are the same filters which were used in the graphics equalizer processor in section two. The design of these filters was discussed in Chapter 10.

The FFT Code

After the audio samples have been filtered to restrict them to the frequencies of interest, they are processed with a fast Fourier transform to determine their spectral content. The FFT code is the same that was used in the spectrum analyzer discussed in Chapter 12. This code is a Java port of the original C code written by Jef Poskanzer and placed in the public domain. The Java class, FFT, is small and fast and works well in this application. As an additional benefit, this FFT code can perform inverse FFTs, but this facility was not needed here.

The FFT code is configured to perform a 4096 sample forward transformation. This number was chosen as a compromise between accuracy and performance. With a sampling rate of 11025 samples per second, each frequency band or bucket of the transformed data represents 11025 / 4096, or approximately 2.69 Hz. That is, each bucket is 2.69 Hz greater than the previous bucket's frequency. Bucket zero is of course the DC component of the sampled audio and is ignored in this application. Our error in detecting the correct pitch of a guitar string can vary no more than this. It should be noted (and should be obvious) that error is a more serious problem for lower frequencies (lower strings) than for higher ones.

The FFT transformation is applied only to the real component of the sampled audio. If you look at the code in the file *ComputeFrequencyWithFFT.java*, you will see that the array of imaginary data is set to all zeros before being passed to the FFT. Because all of the imaginary data is zero, the FFT results contain two identical copies of the output data. For this reason, it is only necessary to examine the first half of the transformed data during spectral analysis.

For the tuner application, we are only interested in what string's pitch the audio samples represent. Since the fundamental frequency of a guitar note will contain the most energy, we use the FFT code to look for the frequency with the most energy or power present in a buffer of samples. This is done by walking through the first half of the FFT data and finding the frequency corresponding to maximum power. Power is calculated by summing the real and the imaginary components, each squared. After all of the FFT data is examined, the frequency corresponding to the bucket with the most power is returned. This should represent the current pitch of the open guitar string.

The Note Table

In order to determine how close a given guitar's open string is to the ideal, we must have a table of frequencies to compare the pitch against. Just such a table is generated in the tuner code by computing the frequencies from MIDI note numbers. Table 16.1 shows the pitch of the open strings on six-string guitars, and four- and five-string basses. This table also shows the MIDI note associated with each open string. The function

Pitch = (A440 / 32) * Math.pow(2.0, ((MIDINoteNumber - 9.0) / 12.0))

shows how MIDI note numbers are converted to frequencies. The note table is built by iterating over each of the six guitar strings, extracting the corresponding MIDI note number, and using the function shown to calculate the frequency.

Table 16.1 Guitar/Bass Note Values and Approximate Frequencies

Instrument String	MIDI Note Number	Note Frequency
5 string bass guitar		
B string	23	30.8677063285 Hz
E string	28	41.2034446141 Hz
A string	33	55.0000000000 Hz
D string	38	73.4161919794 Hz
G string	43	97.9988589954 Hz
4 string bass guitar		
E string	28	41.2034446141 Hz
A string	33	55.0000000000 Hz
D string	38	73.4161919794 Hz
G string	43	97.9988589954 Hz

Table 16.1   (continued)

Instrument String	MIDI Note Number	Note Frequency
6 string guitar		
E string (big E string)	40	82.4068892282 Hz
A string	45	110.0000000000 Hz
D string	50	146.8323839587 Hz
G string	55	195.9977179909 Hz
B string	59	246.9416506281 Hz
E string (little E string)	64	329.6275569129 Hz

With the initialized note table and the pitch information returned from the FFT code, two things are now possible. First, it is possible to determine which note in the note table is closest to the pitch of the guitar string the user is trying to tune and second, it is possible to calculate how close the guitar string's pitch is to that note in the note table.

In musical applications, differences in pitch are measured in cents. A cent is one one hundredth of the difference between two notes that are separated by a semitone (also referred to as a halftone). An octave which is a two-to-one frequency ratio is made up of 1200 cents. Cent difference between two pitches is calculated with the following formula:

Cents difference = (-CENTSPEROCTIVE * Math.log(ReferenceFreq/freq) / Math.log(2.0));

For our tuner application, the reference frequency is the pitch from the note table which is being compared to the pitch detected from the guitar string via the FFT code.

Please realize that if a guitar string is extremely out of tune, the wrong LED in the user interface may light. The LEDs indicate the note closest to the strings pitch but not necessarily the correct pitch for the string. If you are tuning the G string, for example, it won't be tunable and the G LED will not light until the string's pitch is within +/– 50 cents of the reference frequency for the G string.

The Status Indicator LEDs

The status LEDs on the tuner's front panel incorporate the LED beans developed in section one of this book. An additional class, *LabeledLED*, is layered on top of the *RoundLED* class to provide for the labeling of the individual LEDs as can be seen on the front panel. A labeled LED is created in *TunerUI* for the updating indicator, the note flat indicator, the in tune indicator, the note sharp indicator, and one LED each for the six guitar strings. Each of these LEDs is updated whenever new string frequency data becomes available.

Each LED has its own behavior. The updating LED blinks whenever new string frequency data is available. The flat indicator comes on when the string's frequency is more than –3 cents below the reference. The in tune LED comes on when the string's frequency is within +/– 3 cents of the reference frequency. The sharp indicator comes on when the string's frequency is greater than 3 cents above the reference. The string LED indicators come on when the guitar's string frequency matches one of the note indicators.

The Tuning Meter

The analog meter bean developed in section one is used to visually indicate how close a guitar's string is to the corresponding reference frequency. The meter is setup with a range of –50 to +50 cents with 0 cents being straight up. If the string's frequency is within this range of a valid guitar string's pitch, the meter will register the difference. If the string is outside of this range, the meter doesn't register at all.

Overall Operation

The tuner, once connected to the sampler, runs code in an infinite loop. This loop is contained within the *doTuner* method of *Tuner.java*. Within this infinite loop, another loop is executed two times each pass through the outer loop. Within this loop a request is made of the sampler for a buffer full of samples. When the samples become available, the low-pass filters are run against the samples to clean them up and limit the range of frequencies contained in the samples. Finally, the FFT code is used to determine the fundamental frequency (the string's pitch) contained within the sampled data.

The results of the two inner loops are compared to make sure that the detected frequencies are very close to each other. This is how the application filters out extraneous readings. If the two frequencies are close together, they are averaged and then used to update the front panel indicators. If the frequencies differ, the calculated frequency data is thrown away and the outer loop is begun again.

With new string pitch data available, the updating LED on the front panel is pulsed as an indication of this fact. A method called *findClosestNoteIndex* is used to find the index of the note in the note table that is closest to the note being sampled from the guitar. This method will return –1 if the sampled frequency is out of range. If the sampled pitch is found to be within range, the method *calculateFrequencyDifference* is called to see how close in cents the sampled pitch is from the reference pitch for the identified note. It is this difference value that drives most of the LEDs on the front panel. The note index value, being the exception, is driven from the index of the identified note.

With the difference value available, the appropriate flat, in tune, or sharp LED indicator is lit. Which one is lit is determined by the magnitude of the difference value. If the difference is with the range –50 to +50 cents, the value is indicated on the meter as well.

After the UI indicators are updated, the main loop is begun again and the complete process continues until the tuner application is terminated.

Other Design Approaches

During the design of the tuner, I suspected running FFTs in real time to perform the frequency analysis would be prohibitively expensive in terms of processor time so I looked for a different approach to take. Initially I attempted to perform large amounts of signal conditioning and then counting zero transitions of the conditioned input samples to detect the frequency. While this approach did work, it did not always work reliably. Different instruments with different harmonic characteristics would cause the tuner to fail or to produce spurious results. Because I wanted a tuner that was accurate and stable, I opted for the FFT approach documented here instead. I found that my 300Mz machine was more than fast enough and that the results were much more stable. The stability of this tuner rivals that of the commercial tuner I use on a daily basis.

POSSIBLE ENHANCEMENTS · · · · · · · · · · · · · · · · · · ·

The code for this application could easily be extended to become a general purpose chromatic tuner instead of a guitar-specific tuner. A chromatic tuner has an LED for each of the twelve notes of the chromatic scale. Typical chromatic tuners have LEDs for C, C♯/D♭, D, D♯/E♭, E, F, F♯/G♭, G, G♯/A♭, A, A♯/B♭ and B. Also, a chromatic tuner could be used over a much wider range of frequencies then the guitar tuner presented. Since a 4096 point FFT and a 11025 Hz sample rate is used in the code, the practical range of frequencies that can be detected is from about 10 Hz to about 5500 Hz, in 2.69 Hz increments. This is a frequency range that encompasses many musical instruments.

Table 16.2 lists the Guitar/Bass Tuner application front panel controls and indicators.

Table 16.2   Guitar/Bass Tuner Application

Front Panel Controls and Indicators	Description
Tuning Meter Indicator	The analog meter used to indicate how close the string being tuned is to the string's reference frequency. The meter reads in cents or 1/100 of a halftone. The string should be tuned until the meter's needle is in the green portion of its range which is +/− 3 cents. The overall range of the meter is +/− 50 cents.
Updating LED Indicator	This red LED blinks whenever the UI is updated. It indicates that new string frequency data is available for display. If this indicator never blinks, the audio level should be adjusted.
Flat LED Indicator	This red LED is lit whenever the string being tuned is flat in relation to the string's desired pitch. Flat means lower in frequency than desired. If this LED is lit, the in tune and the sharp LEDs are extinguished.
In Tune LED Indicator	This green LED is lit whenever the string being tuned is within +/− 3 cents of the desired pitch—in other words, close enough to be considered in tune. If this LED is lit, the flat and the sharp LEDs are extinguished.
Sharp LED Indicator	This red LED is lit whenever the string being tuned is sharp in relation to the string's desired pitch. Sharp means higher in frequency than desired. If this LED is lit, the flat and the in tune LEDs are extinguished.
Note LED Indicators	These cyan LED's are lit when the software decides which string is being tuned. Only one is lit at a time and only if the string is within the range attributed to the LED.

MISCELLANEOUS INFORMATION . . . .

Package:

apps.guitartuner

Source Files:

File Name	Description
ComputeFrequencyWithFFT.java	This code prepares the FFT code and the sampled audio data for analysis. It also determines which pitch is dominant in the sampled audio.
FFT.java	An implementation of a fast Fourier transformation. This is the code that converts the time domain audio into the frequency domain as required for analysis.
LabeledLED.java	A simple class that associates an LED bean with a text label.
Tuner.java	This is the Tuner application code. It sets up the WinRecorder *AbstractAudio* device for sampling the input, it determines from the FFT data what string is being tuned and how close it is to the reference pitch's and updates the tuner's UI accordingly. This code runs in an infinite loop: sampling, analyzing, and UI updating until it is terminated.
TunerUI.java	This is the code for the tuner's user interface. It instantiates all of the front panel indicators such that the audio processing code in Tuner.java can manipulate them.

Appendix A–
Building, Documenting,
and Running the Code
in this Book

The following instructions are provided to help you utilize the code in this book. I assume you know how to install the Java SDK on your computer. If not, consult the installation documents provided by Sun Microsystems, Inc. I also assume you know how to compile and run Java applications. If you don't, consult any good Java book for details.

Because of the sophistication of the modern PC/workstation, there are lots of ways your computer's environment may be slightly different from the environment I used to develop the code in this book. Because of this, you may need to use a little ingenuity to get the code building and running on your machine.

REQUIREMENTS . . . .

To build and run the code on the CDROM, you must have access to the following:

1. A Java compiler/development environment capable of compiling version 1.2 of the Java language (Java2). I use the SJ compiler from Symantec version 2.20.32n.

2. A *Make* utility program. I use the one that comes with the Cygnus tools.

3. If you are going to use the *PCMPlayer* (player) as the sound output device you will need the Java Media Framework files available directly from Sun. *PCMPlayer* is based upon JMF version 1.1.

4. If you are going to use the devices from Appendix B that rely on JMF2.0, you must have JMF2.0 installed on your machine.

5. Of course, to use the code in this book after you build it you will need a computer with working sound hardware.

INSTALLATION . . . .

1. Make sure your Java development environment is installed and working correctly by compiling and running other Java applications, maybe some of the examples provided by Sun.

2. Make sure your make utility program is installed and working correctly.

3. Install the Sun JMF software. Run the test applications that come with the version of JMF you are using to verify a correct installation.

4. Copy the complete contents of the CDROM to a directory on your hard drive. For the sake of example, call the directory *audiostuff*.

PATH . . . .

Your path must be extended to include the path to the new *audiostuff* directory on your hard drive.

CLASSPATH . . . .

Your classpath must be extended to include the path to the new *audiostuff* directory on your hard drive.

BUILDING THE COMPLETE SOURCE TREE . . . .

Once the book's code is installed on your system, you should be able to change directory to the *audiostuff* directory on your hard drive and type *make*. If everything is set up correctly, make will traverse the complete source tree, building all of the source files. If errors occur, you probably have a path or a classpath problem that you will need to resolve. *Make* must run to completion, *without errors*, before you can use the software provided. Since there is a make file at every level in the source tree, you can change directory to any level, type make, and build the source tree from that point forward. You may need to modify the make file provided if you are using a *make* utility that is different from one I wrote the make files for. Alternatively, the BAT file *batch-make* can be used to build the source code instead of using *Make.*

MAKING JAR FILES . . . .

If you wish to make the jar files for the Java bean components presented in section one of the book, change directory to the *audiostuff* directory on your hard drive, create a *jars* subdirectory (if it doesn't already exist) and type *make –f beanjarmakefile.* The Java bean components are then built and packaged into jar files and stored in the *jars* directory. Again, the make file may need alteration, depending upon the *make* utility used.

DOCUMENTING THE CODE . . . .

Once the code builds successfully, the *javadoc* utility program can be run against the source tree to produce substantial documentation. To do this, change to the *audiostuff* directory and run the DOS batch file *javadocs.bat.* This will create an HTML subdirectory containing all of the automatically generated documentation. Clicking on *index.html* in this subdirectory will bring up the documentation in your browser.

RUNNING THE AUDIO APPLICATIONS . . . .

The instructions for running the phrase sampler and the guitar tuner applications of section three are found in Chapters 15 and 16, respectively.

RUNNING THE AUDIO PROCESSORS . . . .

The audio processor devices described in section two of the book are run using a shell window (MS-DOS window on a WinTel box). The *AudioTest* program understands four types of devices: *Source* devices, which provide a source of audio samples to process; *monitor* devices, which allow the audio samples to be analyzed but do not alter them; *processor* devices, which intentionally alter the audio samples algorithmically; and *output* (sink) devices, which convert the digital samples to audio files for storage or back to audio for playback. The *AudioTest* program is told which devices to use by combinations of command line arguments passed to it. One *source* device and one *out-*

put device can be specified for each *AudioTest* program run. Any number of *monitor* devices and *processor* devices can be used in a single run.

The *AudioTest* program is then executed by typing *java*, the package/program name, *craigl.test.AudioTest*, followed by numerous command line arguments. Each command line argument is prefixed with a negative sign. The *AudioTest* command line arguments are as follows:

Source input device:	`-i (osc | sosc | file | jmffile | mic sr chs | jmfmic sr chs)`
Monitor devices:	`[-m (scope | spectrumanalyzer)]`
Processor device(s):	`[-p (aadj cache chorus compexp delay distortion eq peq pan phaser pshift reverb)+]`
Output device:	`-o (file | jmffile | player | jmfplayer | winplayer)`

The device mnemonics indicate the following:

osc	mono oscillator source
sosc	stereo oscillator source
file	input from file or output to file
jmffile	input from file or output to file using JMF2.0
mic sr chs	mic/line input at sample rate sr and chs channels for Windows
jmfmic sr chs	mic/line input at sample rate sr and chs channels using JMF2.0
scope	sample scope monitor
spectrumanalyzer	spectrum analyzer monitor
aadj	amplitude adjust processor (level control)
cache	sample cacheing processor
chorus	chorus/flanger effect processor
compexp	compressor/expander/limiter/noise gate processor
delay	digital delay processor
distortion	distortion processor
eq	graphic equalizer processor
peq	parametric equalizer processor
pan	panner processor
phaser	phaser effect processor
pshift	pitch shifter effect processor
reverb	reverb effect processor
player	sample player based on JMF

| **jmfplayer** | sample player based on JMF2.0 |
| **winplayer** | sample player for Windows |

SAMPLE INVOCATIONS OF THE AudioTest PROGRAM ...

On Windows platforms, the following command line brings up the file reader device for selecting which sound file to convert into audio samples and the *winplayer* output device for playing the audio samples. Once a file is selected and the play button is clicked, you should hear the audio file being played.

```
java craigl.test.AudioTest -i file -o winplayer
```

The next example (which also works only on Microsoft Windows) brings up the *winrecorder* device for sampling a single channel (mono) signal from the mic/line input of your PC at a sample rate of 11025 samples per second and a file writer device for allowing the digital audio to be saved in a wave or AU sound file.

```
java craigl.test.AudioTest -i mic 11025 1 -o file
```

This next command line uses the mono oscillator as the sample source and causes the sample scope to come up for monitoring the samples and the *pcmplayer* device for listening to the samples. *Note:* You won't see the sample scope until the player is commanded to start playing. This causes the sample scope to trigger and display the samples.

```
java craigl.test.AudioTest -i osc -m scope -o player
```

The final example command line shown below causes the samples to be read from an audio file; brings up and inserts the graphic equalizer processor, the reverb processor, and the pitch shifter into the sample path; and uses the *pcmplayer* device for playing the result.

```
java craigl.test.AudioTest -i file -p eq reverb pshift -o player
```

Appendix B–
Java Media Framework
Version 2.0
(JMF2.0ea)

INTRODUCTION . . . .

Immediately before this book went to the publisher for printing, Sun released an early access version of the Java Media Framework, or JMF2.0ea. I thought it important to prototype some devices using this technology for the following reasons:

1. JMF2.0 provides audio and video capture, something that the 1.0 version of JMF didn't offer.

2. JMF2.0 promises platform-independent capture, processing, and presentation of audio and video media, something I wish I had had when this book project started.

3. JMF2.0 also offers a plug-in technology that will allow audio and video processing devices to plug into and manipulate media data as it flows from its source to its destination.

4. I wanted to make sure that the *AbstractAudio*-based audio processing code presented throughout this book could be used in the JMF2.0 environment.

Of course, we are only concerned with the audio aspects of JMF2.0 in this book. I'm sure the video aspects of JMF will get plenty of press elsewhere.

To prove to myself the viability of JMF2.0, I created four new devices that illustrate various aspects of JMF2.0's operation. These include a platform-independent device for acquiring samples from an audio input (called *jmfmic*) and coupling them into an *AbstractAudio* signal chain for processing; a platform-independent device for reading various audio files (types include wave, au, gsm, aiff, and mp3) and providing their samples for processing (called *jmffile*); a platform-independent device for writing audio samples output from the *AbstractAudio* signal chain to audio files (also called *jmffile*); and finally, a platform-independent device for playing *AbstractAudio* samples (called *jmfplayer*).

With these four devices, I proved that JMF2.0 is indeed a viable technology but that in some cases the code was not quite ready for prime time. Some parts of the API are missing, whereas other parts are broken while still some other parts are only partially implemented. What this means is that the devices presented in this appendix are only of prototype quality and will require some tweaking when the final version of JMF2.0 is released. Speaking of which, the production version of JMF2.0 is scheduled for release sometime in the late fall of 1999.

What I did not attempt to illustrate with these prototype devices was the ability to use some of the audio processing devices of section two as JMF2.0 plug-ins. This will be left as an exercise for the interested reader. This probably wouldn't be very hard to do, but is probably not trivial, either. Things usually turn out harder than one thinks when working with new, unproven technology.

JMF2.0 BACKGROUND ....

JMF2.0 is a big topic, too big in fact to be presented here in any detail. The first step in learning how JMF2.0 works is to get the *Java Media Framework API Guide* provided by Sun Microsystems, Inc., in the JMF2.0ea package. This 245-page manual (version 0.7) presents a cursory overview of how JMF works but leaves a great many of the necessary details to one's imagination. This means that one must read the jmf-interest group's mailing list for clues and do a lot of experiments to see how things really work. I must admit there were more than a few experiments necessary before I understood enough about JMF2.0 to build the devices presented in this chapter. I'm still not sure I have my arms completely around JMF2.0, but its architecture and operation become clearer by the day.

JMF2.0 is a completely open platform, allowing companies and individuals to extend its base functionality in any way they see fit. Further, if some part of JMF2.0 does not fit your needs, you can develop your own replacement components that do (within the confines of your application). At a high level, JMF2.0 consists of the following component parts. The descriptions of these components comes from the Sun documentation:

1. *Datasources*—Datasources manage the transfer of media content. A datasource encapsulates both the location of media and the protocol and software used to deliver the media.

2. *Datasinks*—A datasink is used to read media data from a datasource and render the media to some destination generally other than a presentation device. A particular datasink might write data to a file or write data across the network.

3. *Processors*—A processor is a specialized type of player that provides control over what processing is performed on the input media stream.

4. *Players*—A player processes an input stream of media data and renders it at a precise time. A datasource is used to deliver the input media stream to the player. The rendering destination depends on the type of media being presented.

5. *Plug-Ins*—Plug-ins are software components placed between datasources and datasinks for manipulating the audio/video data. Five types of plug-ins are currently supported by JMF2.0.

   a) *Multiplexers/Demultiplexers*—Demultiplexers break the audio and video information contained in a media stream into separate tracks that can be processed separately. Multiplexers are used to combine separate audio and video tracks into a single media stream for output.

   b) *Codecs*—A codec performs media data compression and decompression. When audio is encoded, it is converted to a compressed format suitable for storage or transmission; when it is decoded, it is converted to a non-compressed (raw) format, suitable for presentation.

   c) *Effect Filters*—An effect filter modifies the audio data in some way, often to create special effects such as echo. Effect filters are typically applied to raw data.

   d) *Renderers*—A renderer is an abstraction of a presentation device. For audio, the presentation device is typically the computer's hardware audio card that outputs sound to the speakers.

6. *Managers*—JMF uses four manager classes for organizing classes and devices local to a machine.

   a) *Manager* handles the construction of players, processors, datasources, and datasinks. This level of indirection allows new implementations to be integrated seamlessly with JMF. From the client perspective, these objects are always created the same way, whether the requested object is constructed from a default implementation or a custom one.

   b) *PackageManager* maintains a registry of packages that contain JMF classes, such as custom players, processors, datasources, and datasinks.

   c) *CaptureDeviceManager* maintains a registry of available capture devices.

   d) *PlugInManager* maintains a registry of available JMF plug-in processing components, such as multiplexers, demultiplexers, codecs, effects, and renderers.

> **7.** *JMF Registry*—JMF maintains a persistent registry containing information about the system and the software configuration of the local machine. Included in the registry is information about the standard datasources, datasinks, processors, and plug-ins provided by Sun, along with information about any custom versions of the same that you or someone other than Sun has developed.

In order to integrate JMF2.0 into the *AbstractAudio* device architecture presented in this book, it was necessary to develop a custom datasource device, a custom demultiplexer device, and a custom datasink device. Before these devices can be used, however, certain entries must be made in the JMF registry so that the devices can be found at run time by JMF and used for audio sample processing. First, the package prefix of the custom devices' code package must be registered. All of the devices presented are part of the "craigl.jmf20" package, so this prefix is what is registered. The code that does this registration is shown below:

```
/**
 * Register the specified package prefix with the package manager
 *
 * @param String prefix is the package prefix string to register
 *
 * @return boolean true if registration was successful
 */
public static boolean registerPackagePrefix(String prefix, boolean ver-
bose) {
    // Get the vector of registered packages
    Vector packagePrefixes = PackageManager.getContentPrefixList();

    // Has prefix already been registered ?
    if (packagePrefixes.contains(prefix)) {
        if (verbose)
            System.out.println("Package prefix: " + prefix + " already
                                                           registered");
        return false;
    }

    // Register new package prefix by appending the new prefix
    // to end of the package prefix list
    packagePrefixes.addElement(prefix);
    PackageManager.setContentPrefixList(packagePrefixes);

    // Save the changes to the package prefix list
    PackageManager.commitContentPrefixList();
```

```
     if (verbose)
         System.out.println("Package prefix: " + prefix + " registered");
     return true;
}
```

To use this code, the package prefix is passed as the first parameter and a verbose boolean flag is passed as a second parameter. If verbose is true, you see, via message written to standard out, the status of the registration process. Once you know the process works, you can set verbose to false to prevent these messages from being produced.

In order for a custom datasource to be usable in the JMF2.0 environment, it must be associated with a specific protocol. Our datasource is associated with a protocol we made up called "intfc." Intfc stands for interface, as the datasource is the interface between the JMF2.0 environment and the *AbstractAudio* environment. In JMF2.0, the packages used for protocol processing must also be registered. Actually, the package prefixes are what is registered. In our case here, the same package prefix that was registered above is registered here again. This is because the code for our custom datasource lives in the same portion of the source code tree as do the other custom devices, specifically under the "craigl.jmf20" branch.

The code to register the protocol package prefix is shown below. It has the same parameters as described above.

```
/**
 * Register the specified protocol prefix with the package manager
 *
 * @param String prefix is the protocol prefix string to register
 *
 * @return boolean true if registration was successful
 */
public static boolean registerProtocolPrefix(String prefix, boolean ver-
bose) {
    // Get the vector of registered packages
    Vector packagePrefixes = PackageManager.getProtocolPrefixList();

    // Has prefix already been registered ?
    if (packagePrefixes.contains(prefix)) {
        if (verbose)
            System.out.println("Protocol package prefix: " + prefix + "
already registered");
        return false;
    }
```

```
    // Register new package prefix by appending the new prefix
    // to end of the package prefix list
    packagePrefixes.addElement(prefix);

    PackageManager.setProtocolPrefixList(packagePrefixes);

    // Save the changes to the package prefix list
    PackageManager.commitProtocolPrefixList();

    if (verbose)
        System.out.println("Protocol package prefix: " + prefix +
                                                " registered");

    return true;
}
```

Finally, JMF2.0 requires any custom plug-ins to be registered before use and our custom demultiplexer is a plug-in device. Here, besides the package name of the plug-in, the registration process requires information about supported input and output formats and about the type or variety of the plug-in device. As you will recall from previous discussion, there are in fact five different plug-in types including:

> DEMULTIPLEXER = 1
>
> CODEC = 2
>
> EFFECT = 3
>
> RENDERER = 4
>
> MULTIPLEXER = 5

Using this information in the registry, JMF2.0 can decide on a plug-in-by-plug-in basis where or not a device is suitable for incorporation into the sample processing path. Generalized code for checking in a plug-in is shown below:

```
/**
 * Register a plug-in with the plug-in manager
 *
 * @param String className is the package.class name of the plug in to register
 * @param Format [] inputFormats is the input formats supported by
 * the plug in
 * @param Format [] outputFormats is the output formats supported by
 * the plug in
 * @param int type is the type of the plug in see PlugInManager javadocs
 * @boolean verbose if true causes status messages to be output
 *
```

```
* @return boolean true if registration was successful
*/
public static boolean registerPlugIn(String className,
                Format [] inputFormats,
                Format [] outputFormats,
                int type, boolean verbose) {
    // Attempt registration
    boolean result = PlugInManager.addPlugIn(className, inputFormats,
                                                outputFormats, type);
    if (!result) {
        if (verbose)
            System.out.println("Problem registering plug in: " +
                                                    className);
        return false;
    }
    // Plug in registered successfully, commit the registry
    try {
        PlugInManager.commit();
        if (verbose)
            System.out.println("Plug in registration successful");
        return true;
    }
    catch(IOException e) {
        if (verbose)
            System.out.println("Problem registering plug in: " +
                                                    className);
        return false;
    }
}
```

Our demultiplexer is specifically designed to process audio samples of the "audio_raw" variety (since that is the variety our data source produces). The code below calls the code above to register our demultiplexer for processing just these types of samples. Here, the *className* passed in is "craigl.jmf20.media.parser.audio.RawParser", which is the java class for our custom demultiplexer.

```
/**
 * Register a demultiplexer plug in
 *
 * @param String className is the package name of the demultiplexer
 * @boolean verbose if true causes status messages to be output
 *
 * @return boolean true if registration was successful
 */
```

```
public static boolean registerDemultiplexer(String className,
                                            boolean verbose) {
    Format [] inputFormats = new Format[1];
    inputFormats[0] = new ContentDescriptor("audio_raw");
    return registerPlugIn(className, inputFormats, null,
                          PlugInManager.DEMULTIPLEXER, verbose);
}
```

That's all there is to registration. Now, with the subject of registration behind us, we can discuss the various custom devices that were developed to couple JMF2.0 into the *AbstractAudio* architecture.

The Datasource Device

A custom datasource is required for coupling the *AbstactAudio* device signal chain into the JMF2.0 environment. This custom datasource is the source of samples in the JMF2.0 environment; the actual source of the samples, however, is the *AbstractAudio* device signal chain. Using this approach, a series of *AbstractAudio* devices can be chained together to perform some processing task and the result can be piped (figuratively) into JMF2.0 for playback or for writing to an audio output file. How we use this custom data source in the context of the *AbstractAudio* device environment can be seen in Figures B.1 and B.2. These figures are the block diagrams of the *JMFPlayer* and *JMFFile* (output) devices, respectively.

It should be mentioned that our custom datasource knows only how to stream samples. It knows nothing at all about the sample rate of the data it is streaming or about the number of audio channels the sample data represents. Our datasource man-

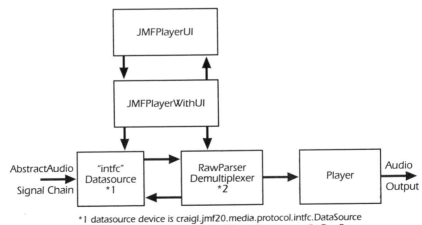

*1 datasource device is craigl.jmf20.media.protocol.intfc.DataSource
*2 demultiplexer device is craigl.jmf20.media.parser.audio.RawParser

Figure B.1   JMFPlayer Block Diagram

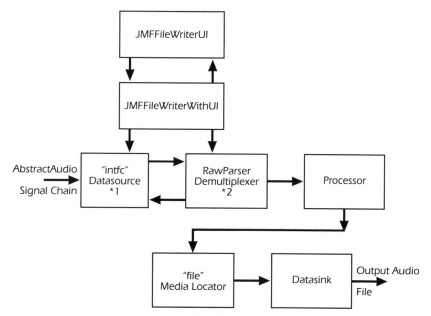

*1 datasource device is craigl.jmf20.media.protocol.intfc.DataSource
*2 demultiplexer device is craigl.jmf20.media.parser.audio.RawParser

Figure B.2   JMFFile (Output) Block Diagram

ages a single *PullSourceStream* stream called *JMFSourceStream*. The read method in *JMFSourceStream* is what pulls samples from the previous *AbstractAudio* device in the signal chain and returns them in a byte array for use by our custom demultiplexer.

Our custom data source extends *PullDataSource* and therefore must provide numerous abstract methods from the *DataSource* base class. If the code is examined, you will see that most of the methods we supply don't do anything in our implementation. In other words, they are not needed to perform the functions we are asking of our datasource.

A custom datasource is specified for use in an application by initializing a media locator for a specific protocol and using the *Manager* class to instantiate a datasource for that protocol. The *createDataSource* method is used to instantiate the datasource. Since our datasource is designed to handle the "intfc" or interface protocol (interface between *AbstractAudio* devices and JMF2.0), it can be instantiated using the code shown below:

```
// Create a media locator for our datasource using the intfc protocol
MediaLocator sourceMediaLocator = new MediaLocator("intfc:");
```

```
// Create a data source from the media locator
PullDataSource dataSource = (PullDataSource)
                    Manager.createDataSource(sourceMediaLocator);
```

To allow the *Manager* to find our custom data source, the package prefix must be registered in the JMF registry, the datasource's code must be in the proper package and the class must be called *DataSource*. In our case, the *DataSource* class is in the package *craigl.jmf20.media.protocol.intfc*. Note the protocol name is part of the package name. Our package prefix as explained earlier is *craigl.jmf20*. Correct package naming is very important in the operation of JMF2.0. If a JMF2.0 element (datasource, datasink, demultiplexer, etc.) is named incorrectly, the corresponding manager will not be able to find and use it.

Finally, I must point out that our custom data source supports "audio_raw" content. This restriction is enforced by the *getContentType* datasource method returning this string. Just as we invented a protocol above ("intfc") to allow our datasource to be found and instantiated, here we invented a content type so that our custom demultiplexer would always be associated with our custom datasource.

It was mentioned previously that our custom datasource has no knowledge of the sample rate or the number of channels the samples passing through it represent. It might have been more correct to have said that the datasource makes no use of the information even though it has access to it. In actuality, the application calls three methods on the datasource to convey information to it. The application calls *setAA* to set a reference to the *AbstractAudio* device from which the samples should be pulled. The application calls *setSampleRate* to set the sample rate of the samples passing through the data source. And finally, the application calls *setChannels* to set the number of channels the samples represent. This information is used by the custom demultiplexer that is described next.

The Demultiplexer Device

A demultiplexer is typically used to break the audio and video portions of a multimedia data stream into separate *tracks* for processing. This allows the audio and video information to undergo different types of processing appropriate to its type. In breaking the stream into the individual tracks, information about the format of the data (audio or video) is bound to the track. Subsequent processing stages can therefore identify the specific format of the audio or video track data and process the samples accordingly and correctly.

For our application, video is unimportant, as we will only be streaming audio sample data into JMF2.0. A custom demultiplexer is needed here, however, to bind information about the sample rate and the number of channels the samples represent onto the track which will be output by the demultiplexer. As a result, subsequent JMF processing stages will know the specifics of our sample data.

Because our demultiplexer advertises its support for the "audio_raw" input content, it will always be bound to our custom datasource described above. This binding happens automatically whenever our data source is instantiated without any actions required on the part of our applications.

The code for the custom demultiplexer is contained in the package/class *craigl.jmf20.media.parser.audio.RawParser.java*. You should consult that file if you are interested in the specifics of how this demultiplexer works and/or is implemented. Remember that since a demultiplexer is a type of JMF plug-in, it must be registered with the plug-in manager before it can be used. Plug-in registration was described previously.

Figures B.1 and B.2 illustrate how our custom demultiplexer fits into the overall application picture.

To recap, our custom datasource is what streams samples from the *AbstractAudio* device signal chain into JMF but it is our custom demultiplexer that gives the samples enough context to be processed by JMF.

The Datasink Device

Whereas a datasource is a source of data in the JMF environment, a datasink is the consumer of data in the same environment. Above we showed how a custom datasource and demultiplexer were used to accept samples produced by the *AbstractAudio* device signal chain for use within JMF. Here, we will use a datasink to route samples produced by JMF into the *AbstractAudio* device signal chain for further processing. In other words, the datasink will provide an operation complementary to that performed by a data source.

Like datasources, datasinks are designed for use with a specific protocol. Here, we again use the "intfc" protocol as our datasink and also an interface between JMF and *AbstractAudio* devices, only in the other direction. Also like datasources, package and class naming is very important for correct integration with JMF. Datasinks must be implemented in a class called *Handler* and must have a package name that denotes the protocol with which they are associated. Our custom datasink is therefore called *Handler* and is part of the package *craigl.jmf20.media.datasink.intfc*.

Our data sink is instantiated using the *Manager* class as was our datasource. Given a datasource, which in this case is a JMF processor, instantiating our datasink is simple. The technique is shown below.

```
// Create a MediaLocator for our datasink
MediaLocator destMediaLocator = new MediaLocator("intfc:");

// Create a datasink from the media locator
DataSink datasink = Manager.createDataSink(processor.getDataOutput(),
                                            destMediaLocator);
```

Once started, a datasink will consume all samples produced by the associated datasource.

Our custom datasink is implemented as an *AbstractAudio* device so that it can be linked into the chain of other *AbstractAudio* devices and inter-operate correctly. This means our datasink must be involved with sample rate and channel negotiation processes and in fact must set these parameters for the entire processing chain. The information for setting these parameters is extracted from the *TrackControl* associated with the audio track of the data source.

Being an *AbstractAudio* device means our datasink must implement a *getSamples* method that subsequent devices in the *AbstractAudio* signal chain call to pull samples from. When samples are read from the datasink, buffers of byte samples are pulled from the data source and converted to 16-bit short samples as required by our architecture. The code in our datasink that does this is shown below.

```java
// Called by next processing stage to retrieve samples
public int getSamples(short [] buffer, int length) {

    int samplesRead = 0;
    int i = 0;
    if (!playbackStartSignalled) {
        cbif.signalPlaybackBegun();
        playbackStartSignalled = true;
    }

    if (EOMMode)
        return -1;
    // While there are still samples needing to be provided
    while(samplesRead < length) {
        // Are there any bytes left in last read?
        if (bytesRemaining <= 0) {
            try {
                // Read another buffer full of data
                pbs.read(bufferObj);

                // Reset index and get new buffer
                dataIndex = 0;
                data = (byte []) bufferObj.getData();
            }
            catch(IOException e) {
                System.out.println("IOException");
                System.exit(1);
            }
```

```
        // Read the number of bytes read in the buffer
        bytesRemaining = bufferObj.getLength();
    }
    // See if we've reached end of media
    if (bufferObj.isEOM() && (bytesRemaining == 0))
        return -1;

    // We've got bytes to return as samples
    buffer[i++] = (short)((((int) data[dataIndex++]) & 255) +
        (((int) data[dataIndex++]) << 8));
    bytesRemaining -= 2;
    samplesRead++;


}

    return length;
}
```

The block diagrams of the JMF devices which use this custom datasink are shown in Figures B.3 and B.4. These are the diagrams for our *JMFMic* and *JMFFile* (input) devices, respectively.

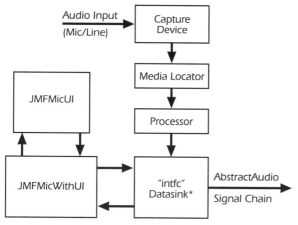

*datasink device is craigl.jmf20.media.datasink.intfc.Handler

Figure B.3   JMFMic Block Diagram

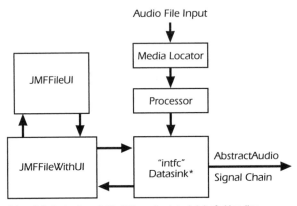

*datasink device is craigl.jmf20.media.datasink.intfc.Handler

Figure B.4   JMFFile (Input) Block Diagram

JMF2.0/AbstractAudio DEVICES . . . .

Each of the four prototype devices based upon JMF2.0 is discussed below.

The JMFMic Device

This device is used to capture audio from the mic/line input of the sound hardware on your computer and make the samples available for use in the *AbstractAudio* device signal chain. The UI for the *JMFMic* device is shown in Figure B.5. The block diagram of this device is shown in Figure B.3. As with most processing devices in this book, the code consists of two parts—a UI part, implemented in the file *JMFMicUI.java*, and an interface part, implemented in *JMFMicWithUI.java*.

Figure B.5   The JMFMic Input Device Based on JMF2.0

Use with the AudioTest Program

When using the *AudioTest* program, the *JMFMic* device is included in the signal path by specifying the command line switch "*–i jmfmic sr chs.*" The *jmfmic* argument identifies this device, the sr argument is the sample rate to use, and chs should be set to one or two to indicate mono or stereo acquisition. As an example, to acquire samples from the microphone input and store them as an audio file, the command line below could be used:

```
java craigl.test.AudioTest -i jmfmic sr chs -o file
```

Using the JMFMic Device

The *Sampling* and *Mode* radio buttons in the UI are used to filter the capture devices (registered with JMF) displayed in the device list. As these are changed, the devices listed will change accordingly. Once a device is found that meets your requirements, it should be highlighted in the list and the *Select Device* button clicked. Once a device is selected it can no longer be changed without restarting the *AudioTest* program. The selected capture device will then be used to acquire samples from the microphone input until sample acquisition is terminated.

The code from *JMFMicWithUI.java* that performs the interesting work within the *JMFMic* device is shown here for reference.

```
// Given the capture devices media locator, create devices for
// acquiring samples and passing them to the AbstractAudio signal
// chain.
public boolean jmfPrepare(MediaLocator sourceMediaLocator) {
    try {
        // Create a data source from media locator
        dataSource = Manager.createDataSource(sourceMediaLocator);

        if (DEBUG)
            System.out.println("DataSource: " + dataSource);
        // Create a processor from the data source
        processor = Manager.createProcessor(dataSource);

        if (DEBUG)
            System.out.println("Processor: " + processor);
        if (processor == null) {
            System.out.println("createProcessor method returned null");
            return false;
        }
```

```java
// Advance processor to configure state to get its track controls
processor.configure();

// Wait until it gets there
waitForState(processor, Processor.Configured);

// Get the track controls from the processor
TrackControl [] controls = processor.getTrackControls();

// Attempt to find any audio track control
TrackControl tc = null;
for (int t=0; t < controls.length; t++) {
    TrackControl tc1 = controls[t];
    // Get format of track
    Format f = tc1.getFormat();

    // Skip if not an audio format track
    if (f instanceof AudioFormat) {
        tc = tc1;
        break;
    }
}
if (tc == null) {
    System.out.println("Couldn't find an audio track in media");
    return false;
}
// We found an audio track to use
AudioFormat af = (AudioFormat) tc.getFormat();

// Extract parameters of audio source needed for configuring
// data sink
double sampleRate = af.getSampleRate();
int channels = af.getChannels();

// Debug out
if (DEBUG)
    System.out.println("AudioFormat: " + af);

// Create new format enforcing sample size, byte ordering, number
// or channels and signed samples. Samples leaving processor must be
// 16 bit, little endian and signed to fit with the processing
// architecture presented in this book.
```

```
        AudioFormat naf = new AudioFormat(AudioFormat.LINEAR,
                                    sampleRate,
                                    16,
                                    channels,
                                    AudioFormat.LITTLE_ENDIAN,
                                    AudioFormat.SIGNED);
        // Attempt to set this format on track
        tc.setFormat(naf);

        // Set output descriptor for processor
        processor.setOutputContentDescriptor(
            new ContentDescriptor(ContentDescriptor.RAW));

        // Now wait until processor transitions to realized state
        waitForState(processor, Processor.Realized);

        // Create a MediaLocator for our datasink
        MediaLocator destMediaLocator = new MediaLocator("intfc:");

        // Create a datasink from process data source and the media locator
        datasink =
            Manager.createDataSink(processor.getDataOutput(),
                                            destMediaLocator);

        if (DEBUG)
            System.out.println("DataSink: " + datasink);

        // We found our data sink. It is the real AbstractAudio device
        AbstractAudio ab = (Handler) datasink;

        // Link in the datasink device in place of the bogus device in
        // the AbstractAudio signal chain.
        ab.next = aa.next;
        aa.next.previous = ab;
        aa = ab;

        // Pass sample rate and channels for negotiation to the data
        // sink device.
        ((Handler) datasink).setSampleRate((int) af.getSampleRate());
        ((Handler) datasink).setChannels(af.getChannels());


        // Install callback so data sink can call back into this code
        ((Handler) datasink).setCallBack(this);
```

```
    // If we get here we are good to go
    if (DEBUG)
        System.out.println("Prepare was successful");

    return true;
}
catch(Exception e) {
    System.out.println("Prepare error: " + e.getMessage());
    return false;
}
}
```

The JMFFile Input Device

This device is used to read audio files and make the samples available for use in the *AbstractAudio* device signal chain. All of the file formats supported by JMF2.0 including AU, wave, aiff, gsm, and mp3 should work with this device or will eventually work with this device. The UI for the JMFFile input device is shown in Figure B.6 and the block diagram is shown in Figure B.4. This device is made up of the two code files, *JMFFileUI.java* and *JMFFileWithUI.java*.

Use with the AudioTest Program

When using the *AudioTest* program, the *JMFFile* input device is included in the signal path by specifying the command line switch "*–i jmffile.*" To play an audio file opened with the *JMFFile* input device, the following command line could be used:

```
java craigl.test.AudioTest -i jmffile -o winplayer
```

Using the JMFFile Input Device

This device works in an identical manner to the other devices of this type presented previously. The *Select File* button is clicked to bring up a file open dialog box for selection of the file to play. When the sink device is started, samples are served up until

Figure B.6   *The JMFFile Input Device Based on JMF2.0*

end of file is reached. Once a file is selected and playback has occurred, a new file cannot be selected.

The code from *JMFFileWithUI.java* that performs the interesting work within the device is shown here for reference.

```
// Given a media locator of the selected file, pipe the samples into
                        the AbstractAudio environment using our custom
// data sink.
public boolean jmfPrepare() {

    try {
        if (processor != null) {
            processor.close();
            processor = null;
        }

        // Create a data source from media locator
        dataSource = Manager.createDataSource(sourceMediaLocator);

        if (DEBUG)
            System.out.println("DataSource: " + dataSource);

        // Create a processor from the data source
        processor = Manager.createProcessor(dataSource);

        if (DEBUG)
            System.out.println("Processor: " + processor);

        if (processor == null) {
            System.out.println("createProcessor method returned null");
            return false;
        }

        // Advance processor to configure state
        processor.configure();

        // Wait until we get there
        waitForState(processor, Processor.Configured);

        // Get the track controls from the processor
        TrackControl [] controls = processor.getTrackControls();
```

```java
// Attempt to find an audio track control
TrackControl tc = null;
for (int t=0; t < controls.length; t++) {
    TrackControl tc1 = controls[t];

    // Get format of track
    Format f = tc1.getFormat();

    // Skip if not an audio format track
    if (f instanceof AudioFormat) {
        tc = tc1;
        break;
    }
}
if (tc == null) {
    System.out.println("Couldn't find an audio track in media");
    return false;
}

// We found an audio track to use
AudioFormat af = (AudioFormat) tc.getFormat();

// Extract parameters of audio source
double sampleRate = af.getSampleRate();
int channels = af.getChannels();

// Debug out
if (DEBUG)
    System.out.println("Orig AudioFormat: " + af);

// This should work but it doesn't yet
if (DOWNCONVERT) {
    if (sampleRate == 44100)
        sampleRate = 22050;
}

// Create new format enforcing sample size, byte ordering
// and signed samples. Samples leaving processor must be
// 16 bit, little endian and signed to fit with the processing
// architecture presented in this book.
```

```
AudioFormat naf = new AudioFormat(AudioFormat.LINEAR,
                                  sampleRate,
                                  16,
                                  channels,
                                  AudioFormat.LITTLE_ENDIAN,
                                  AudioFormat.SIGNED);
// Attempt to set this format on track
tc.setFormat(naf);

// Set output descriptor for processor
processor.setOutputContentDescriptor(
    new ContentDescriptor(ContentDescriptor.RAW));

// Now wait until processor transitions to realized state
waitForState(processor, Processor.Realized);

// Create a MediaLocator for our datasink
MediaLocator destMediaLocator = new MediaLocator("intfc:");

// Create a datasink from the media locator
DataSink datasink =
    Manager.createDataSink(processor.getDataOutput(),
                                      destMediaLocator);

if (DEBUG)
    System.out.println("DataSink: " + datasink);

// We found our data sink. It is the real AbstractAudio device
AbstractAudio ab = (Handler) datasink;

// Link in the new device in place of the bogus device
ab.next = aa.next;
aa.next.previous = ab;
aa = ab;

// Pass sample rate and channels for negotiation
((Handler) datasink).setSampleRate((int) af.getSampleRate());
((Handler) datasink).setChannels(af.getChannels());

// Install callback
((Handler) datasink).setCallBack(this);
```

```
        // If we get here we are good to go
        if (DEBUG)
            System.out.println("Prepare was successful");

        return true;
    }
    catch(Exception e) {
        System.out.println("Prepare error: " + e.getMessage());
        return false;
    }
}
```

The JMFFile Output Device

The *JMFFile* output device is used to write samples originating in the *AbstractAudio* environment to audio files of different formats. The audio file format written is driven by the file extension specified when the output file is selected. The UI for the *JMFFile* output device is shown in Figure B.7 and the block diagram is shown in Figure B.2. The code which makes up this device is contained for the most part in the files *JMFFileWriterUI.java* and *JMFFileWriterWithUI.java*.

Use with the AudioTest Program

When using the *AudioTest* program, the *JMFFile* output device is included in the signal path by specifying the command line switch "*–o jmffile*". To record an audio file using the *JMFFile* output device from the sound captured at the microphone input, the following command line would be used:

```
java craigl.test.AudioTest -i mic 11025 1 -o jmffile
```

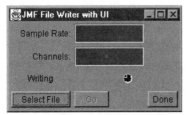

Figure B.7   The JMFFile Output Device Based on JMF2.0

Using the JMFFile Output Device

Once the UI for the *JMFFile* output device is visible, the *Select File* button should be clicked to bring up a save file dialog box for selecting the destination of the output file and giving it a name. The extension given to the file determines the format it will be written in. If "au" is specified as the extension, a Sun AU file will be written. If "mp3" is the file extension, an MP3 file will be written. This for the most part works but JMF2.0ea doesn't always write the type of file you would hope it would. I'm sure the FCS version of JMF2.0 will be better.

Once a file has been specified, the *Go* button is clicked to start the sample acquisition process. Once the samples are exhausted, the *JMFFile* output device resets and can then be used to write another output file. The *Done* button terminates the operation of the *AudioTest* program and closes all *AbstractAudio* devices in the signal chain.

The code within *JMFFileWriterWithUI* that does the bulk of the work is shown below:

```
// Write the output file from the audio samples provided by the
// AbstractAudio device.
public synchronized boolean writeOutputFile() {

    // If not output locator bail
    if (outputMediaLocator == null)
        return false;

    try {
        // If a processor is running close it down
        if (processor != null) {
            processor.close();
            processor = null;
        }

        // Create a media locator for our datasource
        MediaLocator sourceMediaLocator = new MediaLocator("intfc:");

        // Create a data source from media locator
        PullDataSource dataSource =
            (PullDataSource) Manager.createDataSource(sourceMediaLocator);

        // Set some parameters into the data source
        ((craigl.jmf20.media.protocol.intfc.DataSource)
                                        dataSource).setAA(this);
        ((craigl.jmf20.media.protocol.intfc.DataSource)
                            dataSource).setSampleRate(sampleRate);
```

```java
((craigl.jmf20.media.protocol.intfc.DataSource)
                        dataSource).setChannels(channels);

if (DEBUG)
    System.out.println("DataSource: " + dataSource);

// Create a processor from the data source
processor = Manager.createProcessor(dataSource);

if (DEBUG)
    System.out.println("Processor: " + processor);
if (processor == null) {
    System.out.println("createProcessor method returned null");
    return false;
}

// Advance processor to configure state
processor.configure();

// Wait until we get there
waitForState(processor, Processor.Configured);

// Get the track controls from the processor
TrackControl [] controls = processor.getTrackControls();

// Attempt to find an audio track control
TrackControl tc = null;
for (int t=0; t < controls.length; t++) {
    TrackControl tc1 = controls[t];

    // Get format of track
    Format f = tc1.getFormat();

    // Skip if not an audio format track
    if (f instanceof AudioFormat) {
        tc = tc1;
        break;
    }
}
if (tc == null) {
    System.out.println("Couldn't find an audio track in media");
    return false;
}
```

```
        // Create audio format for transcoding
        AudioFormat af = new AudioFormat(
                           encodingName,
                           sampleRate,
                           bitsPerSample,
                           channels,
                           Format.NOT_SPECIFIED,
                           Format.NOT_SPECIFIED);
        // Set the format on the track
        tc.setFormat(af);

        // Set processor output content descriptor
        processor.setOutputContentDescriptor(
                       new ContentDescriptor(ContentDescriptor.RAW));

        // Advance processor to configure state
        processor.realize();

        // Wait until we get there
        waitForState(processor, Processor.Realized);

        // Create a data sink for writing the file
        DataSink dataSink = Manager.createDataSink(processor.getDataOutput(),
                                            outputMediaLocator);
        if (DEBUG)
            System.out.println("DataSink: " + dataSink);

        // Write the file
        dataSink.open();
        dataSink.start();
        processor.start();

        // Indicate success
        return true;
    }
    catch(Exception e) {
        System.out.println("Error writing output file: " +
e.getMessage());
        return false;
    }
}
```

The JMFPlayer Device

The *JMFPlayer* device is a platform-independent player for samples produced in the *AbstractAudio* environment. It is designed to stream the PCM samples it receives to a JMF player for rendering. The UI for the *JMFPlayer* device is shown in Figure B.8 and the block diagram is shown in Figure B.1. The code which makes up this device is contained for the most part in the files *JMFPlayerUI.java* and *JMFPlayerWithUI.java*.

Use with the AudioTest Program

When using the *AudioTest* program, the *JMFPlayer* device is included in the signal path by specifying the command line switch "*–o jmfplayer*". To play audio samples captured from the microphone using the *JMFPlayer* device, the following command line would be used:

```
java craigl.test.AudioTest -i mic 11025 1 -o jmfplayer
```

Using the JMFPlayer Device

This device is used just like the *winplayer* and the *player* devices described elsewhere in this book.

The code within JMFPlayerWithUI that does the bulk of the work is shown below:

```
// Negotiate number of channels and sample rate with previous
// AbstractAudio devices.
public boolean doNegotiation() {

    if (initComplete)
        return true;
```

Figure B.8   The JMFPlayer Device Based on JMF2.0

```
// Propose using MINCHANNELS as the number of channels
MyInt channelsMin = new MyInt(MINCHANNELS);
MyInt channelsMax = new MyInt(MAXCHANNELS);
MyInt channelsPreferred = new MyInt(DEFAULTCHANNELS);

// Negotiate number of channels
minMaxChannels(channelsMin, channelsMax, channelsPreferred);
if (channelsMin.getValue() > channelsMax.getValue()) {
    System.out.println("Couldn't negotiate channels");
    return false;
}


// Propose using DEFAULTSAMPLERATE as the sample rate
MyInt rateMin = new MyInt(MINSAMPLERATE);
MyInt rateMax = new MyInt(MAXSAMPLERATE);
MyInt ratePreferred = new MyInt(DEFAULTSAMPLERATE);

// Negotiate sample rate
minMaxSamplingRate(rateMin, rateMax, ratePreferred);
if (rateMin.getValue() > rateMax.getValue()) {
    System.out.println("Couldn't negotiate rate");
    return false;
}
// All negotiation has been completed. Extract parameters.
sampleRate = ratePreferred.getValue();
channels = channelsPreferred.getValue();

// Inform all previous stages
setSamplingRateRecursive(sampleRate);
setChannelsRecursive(channels);

// Try to
try {

    // Create a media locator for our datasource
    MediaLocator sourceMediaLocator = new MediaLocator("intfc:");

    // Create a data source from media locator
    PullDataSource dataSource =
        (PullDataSource) Manager.createDataSource(sourceMediaLocator);

    // Set some parameters into the data source
    ((craigl.jmf20.media.protocol.intfc.DataSource)
                                        dataSource).setAA(this);
```

```
        ((craigl.jmf20.media.protocol.intfc.DataSource)
                            DataSource).setSampleRate(sampleRate);
        ((craigl.jmf20.media.protocol.intfc.DataSource)
                            dataSource).setChannels(channels);

        if (DEBUG)
            System.out.println("DataSource: " + dataSource);

        // Create a realized player
        player = Manager.createRealizedPlayer(dataSource);

        // Setup a controller listener for the player to listen for
        // end of media
        player.addControllerListener(new StateListener());

        if (DEBUG)
            System.out.println("player: " + player);

        // Signal initialization has been completed
        initComplete = true;
        return true;
    }
    catch(Exception e) {
        System.out.println("Error: " + e.getMessage());
        return false;
    }
}
```

SOURCE FILES . . . .

File Name	AudioTest Device	Package	Description
JMFFileWithUI.java	jmffile (input)	craigl.jmf20.devices	Support code for the jmffile input device.
JMFFileUI.java	jmffile (input)	craigl.jmf20.devices	User interface code for the jmffile input device. UI is shown in Figure B.6.
JMFFileCallBackIF.java	N/A	craigl.jmf20.devices	An interface definition for allowing callbacks from our datasink device to the JMFFile (input) and JMFMic devices.
JMFFileBase.java	N/A	craigl.jmf20.devices	A collection of static methods for interacting with the JMF registry. Used to register our datasource, datasink, and demultiplexer devices.
JMFFileWriterWithUI.java	jmffile (output)	craigl.jmf20.devices	Support code for the jmffile output device.
JMFFileWriterUI.java	jmffile (output)	craigl.jmf20.devices	User interface code for the jmffile output device. UI is shown in Figure B.7.
JMFMicUI.java	jmfmic	craigl.jmf20.devices	User interface code for the jmfmic input device. UI is shown in Figure B.5.
JMFMicWithUI.java	jmfmic	craigl.jmf20.devices	Support code for the jmfmic input device.
JMFPlayerWithUI.java	jmfplayer	craigl.jmf20.devices	Support code for the jmfplayer output device.
JMFPlayerUI.java	jmfplayer	craigl.jmf20.devices	User interface code for the jmfplayer output device. UI is shown in Figure B.8.

File Name	AudioTest Device	Package	Description
Handler.java	N/A	craigl.jmf20.media. datasink.intfc	This datasink device, associated with the "intfc" (interface) protocol, couples JMF2.0 input samples into the *AbstractAudio* architecture. Used in association with the jmffile (input) device and the jmfmic input device.
RawParser.java	N/A	craigl.jmf20.media. parser.audio	This demultiplexer plug-in is used with the datasource below to convert *AbstractAudio* samples to a format compatible with JMF2.0.
DataSource.java	N/A	craigl.jmf20.media. protocol.intfc	This datasource device, associated with the "intfc" protocol, couples the *AbstractAudio* signal processing chain into JMF2.0.

Appendix C– Bibliography

The following books, articles, and miscellaneous publications were of assistance in the preparation of this book. They contain lots of academic and practical information about audio, DSP, numerical algorithms, and programming that augments what is presented here.

BOOKS AND ARTICLES ·

Cronin, Dennis, "Examining Audio DSP Algorithms," *Dr. Dobb's Journal* on CD-ROM.

Kientzle, Tim, *A Programmer's Guide To Sound*, Addison-Wesley Developers Press, 1998, ISBN 0-201-41972-6.

Lyons, Richard G., *Understanding Digital Signal Processing*, Addison-Wesley Longman, Inc. 1997, ISBN 0-201-63467-8.

Moorer, J. A., "About this Reverberation Business," *Computer Music Journal*, vol. 3, no. 2, 1979.

Morrison, Michael, *Presenting Java Beans*, Sams.net Publishing, 1997, ISBN 1-57521-287-0.

Press, William H.; Flannery, Brian P.; Teukolsky, Saul A.; Vetterling, William T.; *Numerical Recipes in Pascal*, Cambridge University Press, 1989, ISBN 0-521-37516-9.

Rorabaugh, C. Britton, *Digital Filter Designer's Handbook*, McGraw-Hill, 1993, ISBN 0-07-053806-9.

Steiglitz, Ken, *A Digital Signal Processing Primer*, Addison-Wesley Publishing Company, 1996, ISBN 0-8053-1684-1.

Waugh, Ian, *Making Music With Digital Audio*, PC Publishing, 1997, ISBN 1-870775-51-1.

MISCELLANEOUS PUBLICATIONS . . . .

APR2—Digital Stereo 10-Band Graphic Equalizer Using the DSP56001, Motorola,
    Inc., 1988.

Java Media Framework API Guide, Version 0.7, dated May 21, 1999, (1998–99 Sun
    Microsystems, Inc.)

Lane, John; Hillman, Garth, *Implementing IIR/FIR Filters with Motorola's
    DSP56000/DSP5601 Digital Signal Processors*, Motorola Inc, 1993.

Appendix D—
CDROM Content

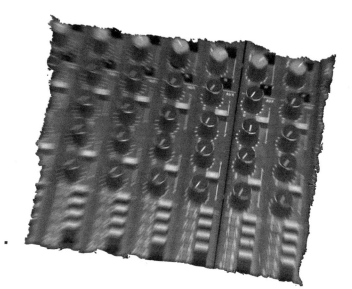

CDROM SOURCE FILES . . .

The files listed in Table D.1 are found on the accompanying CDROM. As you can see, there is a lot of code provided for your experimentation and use.

Table D.1   CDROM Source Files

Directory	File Name	Usage	Described in Chapter
\apps		Audio application program directory	15, 16
\craigl		Main code directory	All
\frontpanels		Simulated front panels code	7
\sounds		Audio files illustrating the various audio processing effects	13
\	beanjarmakefile	Makefile for producing Java beans from the UI components	1, 2, 3, 4, 5, 6
\	blinker.mk	Makefile for the blinker bean	1
\	buttons.mk	Makefile for the button beans	2
\	datagen.mk	Makefile for the data generator bean	1
\	javadocs.bat	Batch file for producing JavaDocs for the code in the book	Appendix A
\	javadocs.files	Package list from which to produce JavaDocs	Appendix A
\	leds.mk	Make file for the LED beans	4
\	makefile	Make file for building the complete source tree	Appendix A
\	makefile.rules	Rules used to build the source tree	
\	meters.mk	Makefile for the meter beans	5

Table D.1 (continued)

Directory	File Name	Usage	Described in Chapter
\	pots.mk	Makefile for the pot beans	3
\apps\guitartuner		Guitar tuner application program directory	16
\apps\phrasesampler		Phrase sampler application program directory	15
\apps	makefile	Makefile for building the guitar tuner and the phrase sampler application directories	
\apps\guitartuner		ComputeFrequencyWithFFT.java FFT support code for tuner	16
\apps\guitartuner	makefile	Make file for building the guitar tuner application	16
\apps\guitartuner	TunerUI.java	UI code for tuner	16
\apps\guitartuner	Tuner.java	Signal processing code for tuner	16
\apps\phrasesampler	makefile	Makefile for building the phrase sampler application	15
\apps\phrasesampler	RiffOMaticUI.java	UI code for phrase sampler	15
\apps\phrasesampler	RiffOMatic.java	Signal processing code for phrase sampler	15
\craigl\au		Code for reading and writing AU audio files	11, 14
\craigl\beans		Code for the Java bean UI components	Section 1
\craigl\compexp		Support code for the compressor/expander device of Chapter 13	13
\craigl\filereader		Code for reading audio files	11
\craigl\filewriter		Code for writing audio files	14
\craigl\filters		Code for IIR digital filters	13, 16
\craigl\JMF20		Code for JMF2.0 EA devices	Appendix B
\craigl\osc		Code for oscillator devices	11
\craigl\pcmplayer		Code for player devices built on JMF1.0	14
\craigl\processors		Code for all of the processing devices presented in this book	13
\craigl\reverb		Support code for reverb devices	13
\craigl\scope		Code for the sample scope monitor device	12
\craigl\spectrumanalyzer		Code for the spectrum analyzer monitor device	12
\craigl\test		Code for testing source, monitor, processor, and sink devices in an audio processing chain	9, Appendix A
\craigl\uiutils		UI support code used throughout the book	All
\craigl\utils		Base classes used as foundation of audio processing devices	All
\craigl\wave		Classes used to process wave files	11, 14

Table D.1 (continued)

Directory	File Name	Usage	Described in Chapter
\craigl\winplayer		Windows platform-specific code for playing audio samples	14
\craigl\winrecorder		Window's platform-specific code for recording audio samples	11
\craigl	makefile	Makefile for building all \craigl subdirectories	
\craigl\au	AURead.java	Code for parsing AU files	11
\craigl\au	AUWrite.java	Code for writing AU files	14
\craigl\au	AUWriteDevice.java	AbstractAudio device for writing AU files	14
\craigl\au	makefile	Makefile for building files in this directory	
\craigl\beans\blinker		Code for the blinker component/bean	1
\craigl\beans\buttons		Code for the button components/beans	2
\craigl\bean\datagen		Code for the data generator component/bean	1
\craigl\bean\displays		Code for the various display components/beans	6
\craigl\beans\leds		Code for the various LED components/beans	4
\craigl\beans\meters		Code for the various meter components/beans	5
\craigl\beans\pots		Code for the various pot (potentiometers) components/beans	3
\craigl\beans	makefile	Make file for building the \craigl\beans subdirectory	
\craigl\beans\blinker	Blinker.java	Code for the blinker	1
\craigl\beans\blinker	makefile	Makefile for building the blinker	
\craigl\beans\buttons	Button.java	Button base class code	2
\craigl\beans\buttons	ButtonTypeDisplay.java	Button demo program	2
\craigl\beans\buttons	makefile	Make file for building the button components	2
\craigl\beans\buttons	RoundButtonBeanInfo.java	Round button code	2
\craigl\beans\buttons	RoundButtonIcon16.gif	Icon file	2
\craigl\beans\buttons	RoundButtonIcon32.gif	Icon file	2
\craigl\beans\buttons	RoundButton.java	Round button code	2
\craigl\beans\buttons	SquareButtonBeanInfo.java	Square button code	2
\craigl\beans\buttons	SquareButtonIcon16.gif	Icon file	2
\craigl\beans\buttons	SquareButtonIcon32.gif	Icon file	2
\craigl\beans\buttons	ToggleSwitchButton.java	Toggle switch code	2
\craigl\beans\buttons	ToggleSwitchButtonIcon16.gif	Icon file	2
\craigl\beans\buttons	ToggleSwitchButtonBeanInfo.java	Toggle switch code	2
\craigl\beans\buttons	ToggleSwitchButtonIcon32.gif	Icon file	2

Table D.1   (continued)

Directory	File Name	Usage	Described in Chapter
\craigl\beans\datagen	DataGen.java	Code for the data generator component/bean	1
	makefile	Make file for building the data generator	
\craigl\beans\displays	DisplayDemo.java	Display demo program	6
\craigl\beans\displays	IntLEDDisplayBeanInfo.java	Integer7-segment display code	6
\craigl\beans\displays	IntLEDDisplay.java	Integer 7-segment display code	6
\craigl\beans\displays	LEDDisplayIcon32.gif	Icon file	6
\craigl\beans\displays	LEDDisplayBase.java	7-segment display base class code	6
\craigl\beans\displays	LEDDisplayIcon16.gif	Icon file	6
\craigl\beans\displays	makefile	Make file for building the display components	
\craigl\beans\displays	ReadoutLabel.java	Readout label component/bean	6
\craigl\beans\displays	SevenSegmentDisplay.java	7-segment display element code	6
\craigl\beans\leds	LabeledLED.java	Labeled LED component code	4
\craigl\beans\leds	LEDBase.java	LED device base class	4
\craigl\beans\leds	LEDTypeDemo.java	LED demo program	4
\craigl\beans\leds	makefile	Makefile for creating the LED components	4
\craigl\beans\leds	RoundLED.java	Round LED component code	4
\craigl\beans\leds	SquareLED.java	Square LED component code	4
\craigl\beans\meters	AnalogMeter.java	Analog meter component code	5
\craigl\beans\meters	LEDMeter.java	LED meter component code	5
\craigl\beans\meters	makefile	Makefile for building the meter components	5
\craigl\beans\meters	MeterDemo.java	Meter demo program	5
\craigl\beans\meters	Meter.java	Meter base class	5
\craigl\beans\meters	RoundLEDMeter.java	Round LED meter code	5
\craigl\beans\pots	BoostCutSlidePot.java	Boost/cut slide pot code	3, 13
\craigl\beans\pots	IntValuedPot.java	Int valued pot code	3
\craigl\beans\pots	IntValuedSlidePot.java	Int valued slide pot code	3
\craigl\beans\pots	makefile	Makefile for building the pot components	3
\craigl\beans\pots	PotBase.java	Pot base class	3
\craigl\beans\pots	PotBeanInfo.java	Pot code	3
\craigl\beans\pots	PotIcon16.gif	Icon file	3
\craigl\beans\pots	PotIcon32.gif	Icon file	3
\craigl\beans\pots	PotTypeDemo.java	Pot demo program	3
\craigl\beans\pots	Pot.java	Pot code	3
\craigl\beans\pots	RealValuedSlidePot.java	Real valued slide pot code	3

Table D.1 (continued)

Directory	File Name	Usage	Described in Chapter
\craigl\beans\pots	RealValuedPot.java	Real valued pot code	3
\craigl\beans\pots	SlidePot.java	Slide pot code	3
\craigl\beans\pots	SlidePotIcon16.gif	Icon file	3
\craigl\beans\pots	SlidePotBeanInfo.java	Slide pot code	3
\craigl\beans\pots	SlidePotIcon32.gif	Icon file	3
\craigl\compexp	GraphSurface.java	Graph surface used in compressor/expander device of Chapter 13	13
\craigl\compexp	LabeledGraphSurface.java	Labeled graph surface used in compressor/Expander device of Chapter 13	13
\craigl\compexp	makefile	Makefile for building this subdirectory	
\craigl\filereader	FileReaderWithUI.java	Device for reading audio files	11
\craigl\filereader	makefile	Make file for building this device	
\craigl\filewriter	FileWriterWithUI.java	Device for writing audio files	14
\craigl\filewriter	makefile	Makefile for building this device	
\craigl\filters	IIRBandpassFilter.java	Runtime bandpass filter class code	10
\craigl\filters	IIRBandpassFilterDesign.java	Design time bandpass filter class code	10
\craigl\filters	IIRFilterDesignBase.java	IIR filter design base class10	
\craigl\filters	IIRFilterBase.java	IIR filter runtime base class	10
\craigl\filters	IIRHighpassFilterDesign.java	Design time high pass filter class code	10
\craigl\filters	IIRHighpassFilter.java	Runtime highpass filter class code	10
\craigl\filters	IIRLowpassFilterDesign.java	Design time lowpass filter class code	10
\craigl\filters	IIRLowpassFilter.java	Runtime lowpass filter class code	10
\craigl\filters	makefile	Make file for building the classes in this directory	
\craigl\jmf20\devices		JMF2.0 devices directory	Appendix B
\craigl\jmf20\media		JMF2.0 media directory	Appendix B
\craigl\jmf20	makefile	Make file for building subdirectory	
\craigl\jmf20\devices	JMFFileWithUI.java	Processing code for JMF20 file reader	Appendix B
\craigl\jmf20\devices	JMFFileUI.java	UI code for JMF20 file reader	Appendix B
\craigl\jmf20\devices	JMFFileCallBackIF.java	JMF20 code	Appendix B
\craigl\jmf20\devices	JMFFileBase.java	JMF20 code	Appendix B
\craigl\jmf20\devices	JMFFileWriterWithUI.java	Processing code for JMF20 file writer	Appendix B
\craigl\jmf20\devices	JMFFileWriterUI.java	UI code for JMF20 file writer	Appendix B
\craigl\jmf20\devices	JMFMicUI.java	UI code for JMF20 sampler	Appendix B
\craigl\jmf20\devices	JMFMicWithUI.java	Processing code for JMF20 sampler	Appendix B

Table D.1 (continued)

Directory	File Name	Usage	Described in Chapter
\craigl\jmf20\devices	JMFPlayerWithUI.java	Processing code for the JMF20 player	Appendix B
\craigl\jmf20\devices	JMFPlayerUI.java	UI code for the JMF20 player	Appendix B
\craigl\jmf20\devices	makefile	Make file for building the JMF20 devices	Appendix B
\craigl\jmf20\media\datasink		Directory containing JMF20 datasink	Appendix B
\craigl\jmf20\media\parser		Directory containing JMF20 raw data parser	Appendix B
\craigl\jmf20\media\protocol		Directory containing JMF20 datasource	Appendix B
\craigl\jmf20\media	makefile	Make file for building subdirectories	
\craigl\jmf20\media\datasink\intfc		Directory containing JMF20 datasink	Appendix B
\craigl\jmf20\media\datasink	makefile	Make file for building subdirectories	
\craigl\jmf20\media\datasink\intfc	Handler.java	JMF20 datasink device code	Appendix B
\craigl\jmf20\media\datasink\intfc	makefile	Make file for building subdirectory	
\craigl\jmf20\media\parser\audio		Directory containing JMF20 raw data parser	Appendix B
\craigl\jmf20\media\parser\audio	makefile	Make file for building subdirectories	
\craigl\jmf20\media\parser\audio	makefile	Make file for building subdirectory	
\craigl\jmf20\media\parser\audio	RawParser.java	JMF20 raw data parser code	Appendix B
\craigl\jmf20\media\protocol\intfc		Directory containing JMF20 datasource	Appendix B
\craigl\jmf20\media\protocol	makefile	Make file for building subdirectories	
\craigl\jmf20\media\protocol\intfc	DataSource.java	JMF20 data source code	Appendix B
\craigl\jmf20\media\protocol\intfc	makefile	Make file for building subdirectory	
\craigl\osc	makefile	Make file for subdirectory	
\craigl\osc	Oscillator.java	Processing code for mono oscillator	11
\craigl\osc	OscillatorWithUI.java	UI code for mono oscillator	11
\craigl\osc	StereoOscillator.java	Processing code for stereo oscillator	11

Table D.1 (continued)

Directory	File Name	Usage	Described in Chapter
\craigl\osc	StereoOscillatorWithUI.java	UI code for stereo oscillator	11
\craigl\pcmplayer	ControllerAdapter.java	PCMPlayer device code	14
\craigl\pcmplayer	makefile	Make file for building the pcmplayer device	
\craigl\pcmplayer	PCMDataSource.java	PCMPlayer device code	14
\craigl\pcmplayer	PCMPlayer.java	PCMPlayer device code	14
\craigl\pcmplayer	PCMPlayerWithUI.java	PCMPlayer device code	14
\craigl\pcmplayer	PCMSourceStream.java	PCMPlayer device code	14
\craigl\pcmplayer	_PCMPlayer.java	PCMPlayer device code	14
\craigl\processors	AmplitudeAdjustWithUI.java	Processing code for the amplitude adjustment processor	13
\craigl\processors	AmplitudeAdjustUI.java	UI code for the amplitude adjustment processor	13
\craigl\processors	Cache.java	Processing code for the cache processor	13
\craigl\processors	ChorusUI.java	UI code for the chorus processor	13
\craigl\processors	ChorusWithUI.java	Processing code for the chorus processor	13
\craigl\processors	CompExpUI.java	UI code for the compressor/expander processor	13
\craigl\processors	CompExpWithUI.java	Processing code for the compressor/expander processor	13
\craigl\processors	DelayUI.java	UI code for the delay processor	13
\craigl\processors	DelayWithUI.java	Processing code for the delay processor	13
\craigl\processors	DistortionUI.java	UI code for the distortion processor	13
\craigl\processors	DistortionWithUI.java	Processing code for the distortion processor	13
\craigl\processors	GraphicEQUI.java	UI code for the graphic equalizer processor	13
\craigl\processors	GraphicEQWithUI.java	Processing code for the graphic equalizer processor	13
\craigl\processors	makefile	Make file for creating all processor devices	13
\craigl\processors	PannerUI.java	UI code for the panner processor	13
\craigl\processors	PannerWithUI.java	Processing code for the panner processor	13
\craigl\processors	ParametricEQWithUI.java	Processing code for the parametric equalizer processor	13
\craigl\processors	ParametricEQUI.java	UI code for the parametric equalizer processor	13
\craigl\processors	PhaserUI.java	UI code for the phaser processor	13
\craigl\processors	PhaserWithUI.java	Processing code for the phaser processor	13
\craigl\processors	PitchShifterUI.java	UI code for the pitch shifter processor	13
\craigl\processors	PitchShifterWithUI.java	Processing code for the pitch shifter processor	13
\craigl\processors	ReverbWithUI.java	Processing code for the reverb processor	13

Table D.1 (continued)

Directory	File Name	Usage	Described in Chapter
\craigl\processors	ReverbUI.java	UI code for the reverb processor	13
\craigl\reverb	AllpassNetwork.java	All pass network code	13
\craigl\reverb	CombFilter.java	Comb filter code	13
\craigl\reverb	makefile	Make file for building this subdirectory	13
\craigl\reverb	SchroederReverb.java	Schroeder reverb code	13
\craigl\scope	makefile	Make file for building scope monitor device	
\craigl\scope	ScopeUI.java	UI code for scope monitor device	12
\craigl\scope	Scope.java	Processing code for scope monitor device	12
\craigl\scope	StatusDisplay.java	More scope UI code	12
\craigl\scope	TriggerFlag.java	Triggering code for scope	12
\craigl \spectrumanalyzer	FFT.java	Fast Fourier code	12
\craigl \spectrumanalyzer	makefile	Make file for building spectrum analyzer monitor device	
\craigl \spectrumanalyzer	SpectrumAnalyzer.java	Processing code for the spectrum analyzer monitor device	12
\craigl \spectrumanalyzer	SpectrumAnalyzerUI.java	UI code for the spectrum analyzer monitor device	12
\craigl \spectrumanalyzer	StatusDisplay.java	More spectrum analyzer UI code	12
\craigl\test	AudioTest.java	Audio test application program	9, Appendix A
\craigl\test	makefile	Make file for building the audio test application program	
\craigl\uiutils	BaseUI.java	User interface helper utility classes	
\craigl\uiutils	Border.java*	User interface helper utility classes	
\craigl\uiutils	Box.java*	User interface helper utility classes	
\craigl\uiutils	CloseableFrame.java	User interface helper utility classes	
\craigl\uiutils	CloseableFrameIF.java	User interface helper utility classes	
\craigl\uiutils	DrawnRectangle.java*	User interface helper utility classes	
\craigl\uiutils	EtchedRectangle.java*	User interface helper utility classes	
\craigl\uiutils	EtchedBorder.java*	User interface helper utility classes	
\craigl\uiutils	Etching.java*	User interface helper utility classes	
\craigl\uiutils	makefile	Make file for building the helper utility classes	
\craigl\uiutils	MessageBox.java	Popup message box class	
\craigl\uiutils	Orientation.java*	User interface helper utility classes	
\craigl\utils	AbstractAudio.java	Base class from which all devices are derived	9

Table D.1 (continued)

Directory	File Name	Usage	Described in Chapter
\craigl\utils	AbstractDecoderIF.java	Audio file decoder interface	
\craigl\utils	Assert.java	Assert utility class	
\craigl\utils	AudioConstants.java	Collection of constants throughout	
\craigl\utils	AudioFileDecoder.java	Used in reading audio files	11
\craigl\utils	AudioUIIF.java	Used for controlling the position and size of simulated front panels used by audio processors	13
\craigl\utils	ConvertDataInputStream.java	Used in reading audio files	11
\craigl\utils	ConvertDataOutputStream.java	Used in writing audio files	14
\craigl\utils	DecodeG711MuLaw.java	Used in reading audio files	11
\craigl\utils	DecodePcm16BESigned.java	Used in reading audio files	11
\craigl\utils	DecodePcm16LESigned.java	Used in reading audio files	11
\craigl\utils	DecodePcm8Signed.java	Used in reading audio files	11
\craigl\utils	DecodePcm8UnSigned.java	Used in reading audio files	11
\craigl\utils	FileWriterIF.java	Used in writing audio files	14
\craigl\utils	LinkedListVector.java	Data structure that links AbstractAudio devices together into a audio processing chain	9
\craigl\utils	makefile	Make file used for building subdirectory throughout	
\craigl\utils	MyInt.java	Specialized integer object used in parameter negotiation	9
\craigl\utils	NegotiationCompleteIF.java	Used in oscillator devices to signal completion of negotiation	11
\craigl\utils	ReadCompleteIF.java	Used in reading audio files	11
\craigl\wave	makefile	Make file used for building subdirectory	
\craigl\wave	WaveRead.java	Used to parse wave files	11
\craigl\wave	WaveWrite.java	Used to write wave files	14
\craigl\wave	WaveWriteDevice.java	AbstractAudio device that can be used to read wave files and provide their samples for subsequence processing	11
\craigl\winplayer	craigl_winplayer_WinPlayer.h	Header file for native methods generated with javah -jni	14
\craigl\winplayer	makefile	Make file for building this subdirectory	
\craigl\winplayer	WinPlayer.java	Java interface to Windows native methods for playback	14
\craigl\winplayer	winplayerdll.dll	Windows DLL containing the native methods for sample playback.	14

Table D.1 (continued)

Directory	File Name	Usage	Described in Chapter
\craigl\winplayer	WinPlayerWithUI.java	Device for playing samples in the Windows environment	14
\craigl\winplayer	\winplayerdll craigl_ winplayer_WinPlayer.h	Header file for native methods generated with javah -jni	14
\craigl\winplayer \winplayerdll	winplayer.c	C code for Java native methods that interface into Windows sound API for playback of audio samples. Becomes winplayerdll.dll when built.	14
\craigl\winplayer \winplayerdll	winplayerdll.dsw	Microsoft VC++ version 5.0 project file to build winplayer DLL	
\craigl\winrecorder	craigl_winrecorder _WinRecorder.h	Header file for native methods generated with javah -jni	11
\craigl\winrecorder	makefile	Makefile for building this subdirectory	
\craigl\winrecorder	RecorderIF.java	Interface providing call back used during sample acquisition	11
\craigl\winrecorder	WinRecorder.java	Java interface to Windows native methods for acquisition	11
\craigl\winrecorder	winrecorderdll.dll	Window's DLL containing the native methods for sample acquisition	11
\craigl\winrecorder	WinRecorderWithUI.java	Device for acquiring samples in the Windows environment	11
\craigl\winrecorder \winrecorderdll	winrecorder.c	C code for Java native methods that interface into Windows sound API for acquisition of audio samples. Becomes winrecorderdll.dll when built.	11
\craigl\winrecorder \winrecorderdll	winrecorderdll.dsw	Microsoft VC++ version 5.0 project file to build winrecorder DLL	
\frontpanels	CompressorFrontPanel.java	Simulated equipment front panel	7
\frontpanels	DemoFrontPanel.java	Simulated equipment front panel	7
\frontpanels	EQFrontPanel.java	Simulated equipment front panel	7
\frontpanels	makefile		
\frontpanels	StereoVUMetersFrontPanel.java	Simulated equipment front panel	7
\sounds	See Table D.2	See Table D.2	

* code used by permission

CDROM SOUND FILES . . . .

The sound files listed in Table D.2 are provided to audibly illustrate the effect of the processing devices presented in Chapter 13. These files are located in the *sound* subdirectory of the CDROM. These guitar riffs are original so no copyrights are infringed. The original recordings, with no effects processing, are found in the files *craig1.wav* and *craig2.wav*. Both of these files were recorded at a sample rate of 44,100 samples/second and were recorded in mono. The descriptions in the table below will give you an idea of how each file was generated—that is, what parameter settings were used to achieve the effect.

These files were produced using the *AudioTest* program with a command line similar to the following:

```
java craig1.test.AudioTest -i file -p xxxx -o file
```

where the input file was specified to be *craig1.wav* or *craig2.wav*, the processing effect was specified in place of xxxx, and the *FileWriterWithUI* output device (-o file) was used to write the processed data out to the audio files.

Table D.2   CDROM Sound Files

Audio File Name	Description
craig1.wav	Original guitar riff played by me. Recorded in mono at 44,100 samples/sec.
craig1chorus.wav	Chorus/flange effect with Delay=2ms; LFO rate=1.0Hz; Depth=3.9ms; Dry=40%; Wet=30%; Feedback=10%
craig1choruswierd.wav	Chorus/flange effect with Delay=31ms; LFO rate=1.25Hz; Depth=23.4ms; Dry=40%; Wet=30%; Feedback=50%
craig1distortion.wav	Distortion effect up full
craig1eq1.wav	Graphic equalizer effect with 200Hz=+6dB; 400Hz=−9dB; 800Hz=−9dB; 3.2KHz=+9dB
craig1eq2.wav	Graphic equalizer effect with 200Hz=+6dB; 400Hz=+4dB; 800Hz=+6dB; 1.6KHz=+8dB; 3.2KHz=+8dB; 6.4KHz=+7dB; 12.8KHz=+8dB
craig1eq3.wav	Graphic equalizer effect with 400Hz=-4dB; 800Hz=−10dB; 1.6KHz=−10dB; 3.2KHz=−10dB
craig1panner.wav	Panner effect panning audio from hard left to hard right
craig1pshift12d.wav	Pitch shifter effect with halftone shift=−12; Dry=0%; Wet=100%; Feedback=0% (down an octave)
craig1pshift12u.wav	Pitch shifter effect with halftone shift=+12; Dry=0%; Wet=100%; Feedback=0% (up an octave)
craig1pshift3u.wav	Pitch shifter effect with halftone shift=+5; Dry=0%; Wet=100%; Feedback=0% (up a 3rd)
craig1pshift5u.wav	Pitch shifter effect with halftone shift=+5; Dry=0%; Wet=100%; Feedback=0% (up a 5th)

Table D.2   CDROM Sound Files

Audio File Name	Description
craig1pshiftharmony.wav	Pitch shifter effect with halftone shift=+5; Dry=50%; Wet=50%; Feedback=0% (weird harmony)
craig1pshiftwierd.wav	Pitch shifter effect with halftone shift=–12; Dry=50%; Wet=50%; Feedback=30% (weird harmony)
craig2.wav	Original guitar riff played by me. Recorded in mono at 44,100 samples/sec.
craig2delay1000ms.wav	Delay effect with Delay=1000ms; Dry=50%; Wet=20%; Feedback=0%
craig2delay100ms.wav	Delay effect with Delay=100ms; Dry=50%; Wet=50%; Feedback=10%
craig2delay10ms.wav	Delay effect with Delay=10ms; Dry=50%; Wet=50%; Feedback=10%
craig2delay50ms.wav	Delay effect with Delay=50ms; Dry=50%; Wet=50%; Feedback=10%
craig2misc1.wav	Combination of the phaser, pitch shifter, and delay effects, in that order
craig2phaser1.wav	Phaser effect with Sweep Rate=.96Hz; Sweep Range=4.96 octaves; Base Freq=100Hz; Dry=30%; Wet=30%; Feedback=10%
craig2phaser2.wav	Phaser effect with Sweep Rate=.2Hz; Sweep Range=7 octaves; Base Freq=140Hz; Dry=30%; Wet=40%; Feedback=10%
craig2phaser3.wav	Phaser effect with Sweep Rate=.96Hz; Sweep Range=7 octaves; Base Freq=140Hz; Dry=20%; Wet=50%; Feedback=80%
craig2reverb1.wav	Various reverb settings
craig2reverb2.wav	Various reverb settings
craig2reverb3.wav	Various reverb settings

Note: These files represent only a small fraction of the audio processing possibilities available with the devices in this book. Because numerous effects can be used in any order, with any number of different parameters dialed in, the total possibilities are too many to think about.

Index

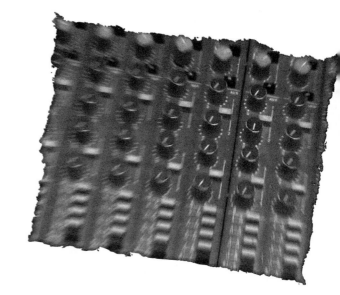

3D challenge, 10

A

AbstractAudio device, 96, 121, 122, 124, 126, 127, 131, 145, 161, 169, 172, 176, 178, 186, 193, 195, 210, 211, 221, 230, 235, 245, 250, 255, 257, 269, 276, 281, 289, 294, 297, 299, 304, 305, 314, 322, 329, 332, 342, 350
AbstractAudio utility methods, 125
Action(), 5
ActionEvent, 11, 16, 20, 61, 92
ActionEventListener, 61
ActionListener, 18, 59, 92
active filters, 133
addActionListener, 20, 92
addAdjustmentListener, 13, 35, 92
addDefaultComponent() method, 99
addPropertyChangeListener, 12
Adjustable interface, 30
Adjustment events, 67, 83
Adjustment interface, 33, 34
AdjustmentEvent, 11, 12, 33, 34, 35, 50
AdjustmentEvent data range, 11
AdjustmentEventListener, 50
AdjustmentListener, 13
AdjustmentListener interface, 67, 83
aliasing, 114, 232

all-pass filter, 250, 272
alpha, beta, gamma filter coefficients, 140, 143
Amplitude adjust processor, 196
amplitude control, 150
amplitude dynamics, 211
analog domain, 140, 252
Analog to Digital conversion, 113
analog waveforms, 109
AnalogMeter class/indicator, 13, 66, 93, 77, 78, 319, 321
apps.guitartuner package, 322
apps.phrasesampler package, 311
AT (Above Threshold) Ratio, 212
A-to-D converters, 113
attack count, 217
AU file format, 164, 278, 282
AU file header, 290
AU file varieties, 165
AU files, 159, 164
audio applications, 301
audio architecture, 103
audio file formats, 278
audio file reading devices, 159
audio monitor devices, 175
audio processing chain, 240, 277
audio sink devices, 277, 289, 297
audio source devices, 149
audio taper pot, 29, 30, 36, 157, 197
audio_raw, 335
AudioFileDecoder class, 160, 162

AudioTest program, 103, 127, 129, 130, 154,
157, 160, 162, 171, 183, 192, 201, 227,
230, 238, 244, 249, 257, 268, 275, 277,
279, 282, 289, 294, 295, 298, 325, 343,
346, 350, 354
AURead class/device, 162, 164, 289
AUWrite device, 279, 286

B

balance control, 239
band-pass filter, 134, 143, 231, 245
band-stop filter, 134, 137, 143
BaseUI class, 96
batch processing, 130
beanjarmakefile, 8
Beatles, 202, 258
Bell, Alexander Graham, 107
big endian integer format, 166, 172, 282, 284,
286
bilinear transformation, 140, 252
Blinker, 11, 12, 57, 59, 61, 75, 94, 128
Blinker class, 93
boost, 231
BoostCutSlidePot class, 33, 47, 93, 236, 237,
248
bottomCaption, 24
breathing effect, 212
brick wall filters, 134
BT (Below Threshold) Ratio, 212, 217
building the software, 324
Butterworth filters, 140
button caption, 24
Button class/controls, 11, 15, 18, 21
button modes, 15

C

Cache device/processor, 125, 199, 289
calculateFrequencyDifference() method, 319
CDROM content, 361
CDROM sound files, 371
cents, 318

Chorus processor, 202
chromatic tuner, 320
chunks, 166
circular buffer, 223
Classpath, 324
clipping, 110, 228
CloseableFrame class, 96
CloseableFrameIF interface, 97
code/platform requirements, 323
comb filter, 203, 224, 227, 271
common mode rejection, 270
component direct access method summary, 94
component even/listener summary, 93
compression, 212, 213
compression ratios, 218
compressor, 211, 213
Compressor/Expander device, 91
connecting components and algorithms together,
92, 96
connecting LEDs to ActionEvent Producers, 61
connecting pots to listener devices, 50
ControllerAdapter, 293
convolution, 140
craigl.au package, 172, 299
craigl.beans.blinker package, 93
craigl.beans.buttons package, 27, 93
craigl.beans.datagen package, 93
craigl.beans.displays package, 88, 93
craigl.beans.leds package, 64, 93
craigl.beans.meters package, 78, 93
craigl.beans.pots package, 52, 93
craigl.compexp package, 221
craigl.filereader package, 172
craigl.filewrite package, 299
craigl.filters package, 147
craigl.jmf20.devices package, 357
craigl.jmf20.media.datasink.intfc package, 358
craigl.jmf20.media.parser.audio package, 358
craigl.jmf20.media.protocol.inftc package, 358
craigl.osc package, 172
craigl.pcmplayer package, 299
craigl.processors package, 198, 201, 210, 221,
228, 230, 239, 245, 250, 257, 269, 276
craigl.reverb package, 276
craigl.scope package, 184

craigl.spectrumanalyzer package, 193
craigl.test package, 132
craigl.utils package, 132, 172, 299
craigl.wave package, 172, 299
craigl.winplayer package, 300
craigl.winrecorder package, 172
Cronin, Dennis, 259
cross fade coefficients, 260
cross fading, 260
crossover filter, 137
crosstalk, 158
cursor arrow keys, 31
cut, 231
cutoff frequency, 134
cycles per second, 106

D

damping factor, 135
data decoders, 163
data rate as function of sample rate, 115
Datagen class/device, 11, 12, 93
decibel scale pots, 30
decibels, 107, 191, 218
delay line, 260
Delay processor device, 222
demultiplexer, 335
derived button classes, 21
designing simulated front panels, 90
device, 119
device bypassing, 124
device order, 126
digital domain, 252
digital filter types, 138
digital filters, 133
Digital to Analog Conversion, 115
digitization, 113
distortion, 110
Distortion processor device, 111, 228
DLL (dynamic link library), 168
Doppler effect, 259
double buffering, 10, 17, 34, 69
drawDigit() method, 81
DRAWOFFSEGMENTS constant, 81

dry level, 204, 224, 253
DSP (Digital signal processing), 134
D-to-A converters, 113
duty cycle, 57
dynamic range, 107, 211

E

echoes, 222
electro-mechanical meter movements, 65
enhancements, 182
EOF indication, 124, 171, 201, 277, 281, 289, 296, 298
equalization, 133
even numbered samples, 122
Event, 5
Event model, 5
Expander process/device, 211, 214
expansion, 212, 214
expansion ratios, 219
extended scale pots, 30

F

Fast Fourier Transform, 109
feedback level, 205, 224, 253
feedback phase, 205
FFT, 109, 185, 187, 190, 314, 316, 320, 322
FileReader device, 90, 129
FileReaderWithUI class, 160, 162, 164
FileWriter device, 129
FileWriterWithUI device, 171, 279
filter coefficients, 140
filter design classes, 143
filter equations, 141
filter order, 135
filter rolloff, 135
filter runtime classes, 144
filter varieties, 134
filtering applications, 137
filters, 103
findClosestNoteIndex() method, 319
FIR filters, 138

fireActionEvent() method, 20
fireAdjustmentEvent, 35
Flanger processor, 202, 250
forward FFT transform, 188
Fourier transform, 185
Fourier, Jean-Baptiste, 109
frequency, 106
frequency control, 150
frequency domain, 185
frontpanel package, 102
fundamental frequency, 319
fuzz tone, 111, 228

G

gain management techniques, 246
generateSegments() method, 81
generateSwitchImage() method, 24
getAttenuation() method, 47, 197
getGain() method, 47
getPreferredSize() method, 16, 21, 24, 33, 45, 47, 60, 61, 83
getSamples() method, 124, 131, 145, 153, 158, 161, 166, 178, 187, 197, 199, 207, 215, 217, 224, 228, 235, 241, 254, 277, 284, 289, 291, 306, 308, 316, 340
getSamplesWithOffset() method, 306
getSamplingRate() method, 123
getState() method, 20
getValue() method, 35, 38
Graphic equalizer filter, 137
Graphic equalizer processor/device, 130, 146, 231, 245, 246, 316
GraphSurface, 219
GridBagLayout layout manager, 97, 179, 187, 208, 219, 226, 237, 248, 256, 267, 274
GridLayout layout manager, 97
Guitar tuner application, 126, 168, 180, 188, 190, 301, 313

H

half-speed playback, 305

Halftone, 258, 266
HandleEvent(), 5
headroom, 110
Hertz, Heinrich, 106
higher level semantic events, 20, 35
highlight property, 24
high-pass filter, 134, 143

I

IIR band-pass filter, 232, 236
IIR filter design, 140
IIR filters, 138
IIR high-pass filter, 245
initializeDecoder() method, 162, 166
input and output devices, 109
installation, 324
intfc (interface protocol), 329, 339
IntLEDDisplay class, 93
IntValuedPot class, 33, 48, 93, 248
IntValuedSlidePot class, 33, 50, 93

J

jar files, 325
Java AWT 1.0, 5
Java AWT 1.1 event model, 10, 92, 94
Java beans, 7, 30, 41, 47, 56, 64, 66, 85, 304, 314
javadoc utility, 325
javah utility program, 297
JavaSound, 168
JMF (Java Media Framework), 104, 130, 168, 288, 289, 295, 311, 329
JMF controller, 293, 299
JMF registration, 332
JMF states, 291
Jmffile device, 329, 341, 350
Jmfmic device, 329, 341
Jmfplayer device, 329, 354
JNI (Java Native Method Interface), 77, 168, 288, 296
JVM (Java Virtual Machine), 168

K

keyboard events, 31, 39
Kientzl, Tim, 119
knee, 212, 213

L

LabeledGraphSurface, 219
LabeledLED class/indicator, 63, 93, 318
Laplace transforms, 140, 252
latency, 77, 290, 295, 309
layout managers, 23, 45
LED features, 55
LED properties and methods, 59
LED state machine, 57, 75
LEDBase class, 56
LEDDisplayBase class, 81
LEDMeter class/indicator, 66, 74, 77, 78, 93
LEDs, 11
LFO (Low frequency oscillator), 202
limiter, 211, 214
linear interpolation, 204, 260
linear peak meter response, 76
LinkedListVector class, 121, 126, 128
Listener, 6
little endian integer format, 166, 172, 286
low-level keyboard events, 16, 18, 35
low-level mouse events, 16, 18, 35
low-pass filter, 134, 143, 245, 314, 316

M

Martin, George, 202, 258
mechanical integration, 76
Meter base class, 66, 78
meter modes, 68
meter range, 66
MeterColorZone class, 72
Meters, 11, 13
meters, analog and digital, 65
microphone, 109
MIDI note numbers, 314, 317

minMaxChannels() method, 240
momentary button mode, 15, 310
monitor device, 120, 128, 176
Moorer, J. A., 271
mouse events, 31, 39
MP3 files, 159

N

named scope instances, 181
negotiation, 121, 122, 145, 151, 152, 157, 179, 233, 240, 255, 279, 280, 286, 291, 297, 340
noise gate, 211, 214
noise generation, 152
number of channels, 121
Nyquist limit, 114, 247
Nyquist, Henry, 114

O

odd numbered samples, 122
optimum signal quality, 122
Oscillator device, 129, 149, 172, 190, 204
Oscilloscope device, 176

P

paint() method, 16, 18, 21, 33, 42, 47, 60, 69, 81, 180, 188
painting controls and indicators, 10
panner modes, 239
Panner processor device, 122, 239
Parametric equalizer processor device, 146, 245
pass band region, 135
passive electronic components, 133
Path, 324
PCM (pulse coded modulation), 113
PCMPlayer device, 129, 294
PCMPlayerWithUI, 294
period, 106
phase, 251, 257

phase shift, 189
phase shifter, 250
Phaser processor device, 250
Phrase sampler application, 168, 259, 301
ping-ponged delay, 260
pitch difference, 318
Pitch shifter processor device, 130, 258, 303,
     304, 307, 309
platform independence, 311
platform specific code, 168
polar coordinates, 38
polling pot values, 94
Poskanzer, Jef, 188, 316
Pot class, 32, 37, 93
pot presentation issues, 32
pot sections, 31
pot taper, 29
pot unit increment, 32
PotBase class, 32, 33
potentiometer class hierarchy, 32
pots, 11
PotType Demo Program, 51
power spectrum, 191
process bar display, 65
processKeyEvent() method, 18, 35
processMouseEvent() method, 18, 35
processMouseMotionEvent() method, 35
processor device, 120, 128
processStereoSamples() method, 207
properties and methods of BaseButton class, 17
properties and methods of the PotBase class, 33
properties and methods of the RoundLED class,
     60
properties and methods of the SquareLED class,
     61
PropertyChangeEvent, 11, 12, 57
PropertyChangeListener, 12, 59
pull architecture, 121, 124
PullDataSource, 293
pulling samples, 153
Push on/push off button mode, 15, 310

Q

Q (filter quality factor), 136
qualify factor (Q), 232
quantitative measurements, 175
quantization, 113

R

radians per sample, 252
ReadoutLabel class/indicator, 79, 86, 157, 208,
     209, 219, 220, 226, 256, 268
real time processing, 130
RealValuedPot class/control, 33, 50, 93, 248
RealValuedSlidePot class/control, 33, 50, 93
recording levels, 65
release, 212
release count, 217
removeActionListener, 20
removeAdjustmentListener, 13, 35
removePropertyChangeListener, 12
renderDigits() method, 82
reset, 201
reset propagation, 125
reset() method, 162, 166
Reverb processor device, 130, 222, 269
reverse FFT transform, 188
RIFF file format, 166, 286
round button controls, 15
round potentiometer, 30
RoundButton class, 16, 21, 93
RoundLED class/indicator, 56, 60, 61, 74, 93,
     94
RoundLEDMeter class/indicator, 66, 74, 78, 93,
     102

S

sample, 113
sample acquisition, 178, 186
sample code, 129
sample display, 178, 179, 187
sample players, 288

sample processing, 187
sample propagation, 178
sample rate, 114, 121, 122, 340
Sample scope device, 154, 176, 187
sample value range, 115
sample word size, 121
SAMPLEBUFFERSIZE, 296, 306, 308, 316
sampled sound, 112
SampleDoubler device, 306, 307, 309
Schroeder reverb, 271
Schroeder, M. R., 271
scroll bar positioning, 180
s-domain, 140
setButtonColor() method, 23
setCaptionAtButton method, 38
setChannelsRecursive() method, 240, 241
setColorRange() method, 72, 73
setGradUseTics() method, 38
setInterval() method, 12, 13
setKnobUseTic() method, 38
setLabelPercent() method, 73
setNumberOfSections() method, 74
setValue() method, 67, 87
seven segment display, 13, 79
SevenSegmentDisplay class, 79
sharpness (Q), 232, 245
shelving filters, 135
side pot, 30
signal path, signal chain, audio processing
    chain, 119
signal to noise ratio, 114
simulated equipment front panels, 89
sine wave generation, 151
sink or output device, 120, 128, 171
SlidePot class/control, 32, 46, 93
soft knee, 212
Sound, 105
sound production, 112
source device, 120, 128
speaker, 110
spectrum analyzer, 138, 156, 176, 184
Spectrum analyzer device, 90
square button controls, 15
square LEDs, 56
square wave generation, 152

SquareButton class, 16, 23, 93
SquareLED class, 61, 93
state machine, 217
Steiglitz, Ken, 271
stereo samples, 159, 207
StereoOscillator device, 90, 97
stomp box, 250
stop band region, 135
Straw Fields Forever, 258
sustain, 273
Swing UI toolkit, 7
synthesizers, 112

T

telephone system, 114
three dimensional properties, 60
threshold, 212
threshold detection, 212
time domain, 185
timing requirements, 217
ToggleSwitchButton class/control, 15, 16, 24, 93
tone controls, 138
transition band region, 135
triangle wave generation, 151
troubleshooting, 175
Tuner device, 127, 315
types of UI controls and indicators, 9

U

UI consistency issues, 100
User/potentiometer interaction, 31

V

VU meter, 76

W

WAV files, 159

wave file format, 278
wave form fidelity, 154
WaveRead device, 289
wavetable lookup, 151
WaveWrite device, 279, 288
WavRead class, 163, 166
wet level, 205, 224, 253
white (Gaussian) noise, 152
Win32, 169
windowClosing() method, 97
WinPlayer device, 129, 154, 158, 162, 168, 183,
      192, 295, 306, 308

WinPlayerWithUI device, 298
WinRecorder class, 169
WinRecorder device, 127, 129, 173, 304, 306,
      314, 322
WinRecorderWithUI class, 170, 171, 172

Z

z-domain, 140
zoom, 180

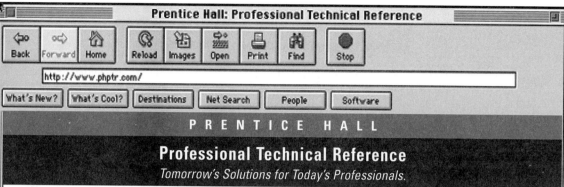

LICENSE AGREEMENT AND LIMITED WARRANTY

READ THE FOLLOWING TERMS AND CONDITIONS CAREFULLY BEFORE OPENING THIS DISK PACKAGE. THIS LEGAL DOCUMENT IS AN AGREEMENT BETWEEN YOU AND PRENTICE-HALL, INC. (THE "COMPANY"). BY OPENING THIS SEALED DISK PACKAGE, YOU ARE AGREEING TO BE BOUND BY THESE TERMS AND CONDITIONS. IF YOU DO NOT AGREE WITH THESE TERMS AND CONDITIONS, DO NOT OPEN THE DISK PACKAGE. PROMPTLY RETURN THE UNOPENED DISK PACKAGE AND ALL ACCOMPANYING ITEMS TO THE PLACE YOU OBTAINED THEM FOR A FULL REFUND OF ANY SUMS YOU HAVE PAID.

1.   **GRANT OF LICENSE:** In consideration of your payment of the license fee, which is part of the price you paid for this product, and your agreement to abide by the terms and conditions of this Agreement, the Company grants to you a nonexclusive right to use and display the copy of the enclosed software program (hereinafter the "SOFT-WARE") on a single computer (i.e., with a single CPU) at a single location so long as you comply with the terms of this Agreement. The Company reserves all rights not expressly granted to you under this Agreement.

2.   **OWNERSHIP OF SOFTWARE:** You own only the magnetic or physical media (the enclosed disks) on which the SOFTWARE is recorded or fixed, but the Company retains all the rights, title, and ownership to the SOFT-WARE recorded on the original disk copy(ies) and all subsequent copies of the SOFTWARE, regardless of the form or media on which the original or other copies may exist. This license is not a sale of the original SOFTWARE or any copy to you.

3.   **COPY RESTRICTIONS:** This SOFTWARE and the accompanying printed materials and user manual (the "Documentation") are the subject of copyright. You may not copy the Documentation or the SOFTWARE, except that you may make a single copy of the SOFTWARE for backup or archival purposes only. You may be held legally responsible for any copying or copyright infringement which is caused or encouraged by your failure to abide by the terms of this restriction.

4.   **USE RESTRICTIONS:** You may not network the SOFTWARE or otherwise use it on more than one computer or computer terminal at the same time. You may physically transfer the SOFTWARE from one computer to another provided that the SOFTWARE is used on only one computer at a time. You may not distribute copies of the SOFTWARE or Documentation to others. You may not reverse engineer, disassemble, decompile, modify, adapt, translate, or create derivative works based on the SOFTWARE or the Documentation without the prior written consent of the Company.

5.   **TRANSFER RESTRICTIONS:** The enclosed SOFTWARE is licensed only to you and may not be transferred to any one else without the prior written consent of the Company. Any unauthorized transfer of the SOFT-WARE shall result in the immediate termination of this Agreement.

6.   **TERMINATION:** This license is effective until terminated. This license will terminate automatically without notice from the Company and become null and void if you fail to comply with any provisions or limitations of this license. Upon termination, you shall destroy the Documentation and all copies of the SOFTWARE. All provisions of this Agreement as to warranties, limitation of liability, remedies or damages, and our ownership rights shall survive termination.

7.   **MISCELLANEOUS:** This Agreement shall be construed in accordance with the laws of the United States of America and the State of New York and shall benefit the Company, its affiliates, and assignees.

8.   **LIMITED WARRANTY AND DISCLAIMER OF WARRANTY:** The Company warrants that the SOFTWARE, when properly used in accordance with the Documentation, will operate in substantial conformity with the description of the SOFTWARE set forth in the Documentation. The Company does not warrant that the SOFT-

WARE will meet your requirements or that the operation of the SOFTWARE will be uninterrupted or error-free. The Company warrants that the media on which the SOFTWARE is delivered shall be free from defects in materials and workmanship under normal use for a period of thirty (30) days from the date of your purchase. Your only remedy and the Company's only obligation under these limited warranties is, at the Company's option, return of the warranted item for a refund of any amounts paid by you or replacement of the item. Any replacement of SOFTWARE or media under the warranties shall not extend the original warranty period. The limited warranty set forth above shall not apply to any SOFTWARE which the Company determines in good faith has been subject to misuse, neglect, improper installation, repair, alteration, or damage by you. EXCEPT FOR THE EXPRESSED WARRANTIES SET FORTH ABOVE, THE COMPANY DISCLAIMS ALL WARRANTIES, EXPRESS OR IMPLIED, INCLUDING WITHOUT LIMITATION, THE IMPLIED WARRANTIES OF MERCHANTABILITY AND FITNESS FOR A PARTICULAR PURPOSE. EXCEPT FOR THE EXPRESS WARRANTY SET FORTH ABOVE, THE COMPANY DOES NOT WARRANT, GUARANTEE, OR MAKE ANY REPRESENTATION REGARDING THE USE OR THE RESULTS OF THE USE OF THE SOFTWARE IN TERMS OF ITS CORRECTNESS, ACCURACY, RELIABILITY, CURRENTNESS, OR OTHERWISE.

IN NO EVENT, SHALL THE COMPANY OR ITS EMPLOYEES, AGENTS, SUPPLIERS, OR CONTRACTORS BE LIABLE FOR ANY INCIDENTAL, INDIRECT, SPECIAL, OR CONSEQUENTIAL DAMAGES ARISING OUT OF OR IN CONNECTION WITH THE LICENSE GRANTED UNDER THIS AGREEMENT, OR FOR LOSS OF USE, LOSS OF DATA, LOSS OF INCOME OR PROFIT, OR OTHER LOSSES, SUSTAINED AS A RESULT OF INJURY TO ANY PERSON, OR LOSS OF OR DAMAGE TO PROPERTY, OR CLAIMS OF THIRD PARTIES, EVEN IF THE COMPANY OR AN AUTHORIZED REPRESENTATIVE OF THE COMPANY HAS BEEN ADVISED OF THE POSSIBILITY OF SUCH DAMAGES. IN NO EVENT SHALL LIABILITY OF THE COMPANY FOR DAMAGES WITH RESPECT TO THE SOFTWARE EXCEED THE AMOUNTS ACTUALLY PAID BY YOU, IF ANY, FOR THE SOFTWARE.
SOME JURISDICTIONS DO NOT ALLOW THE LIMITATION OF IMPLIED WARRANTIES OR LIABILITY FOR INCIDENTAL, INDIRECT, SPECIAL, OR CONSEQUENTIAL DAMAGES, SO THE ABOVE LIMITATIONS MAY NOT ALWAYS APPLY. THE WARRANTIES IN THIS AGREEMENT GIVE YOU SPECIFIC LEGAL RIGHTS AND YOU MAY ALSO HAVE OTHER RIGHTS WHICH VARY IN ACCORDANCE WITH LOCAL LAW.

ACKNOWLEDGMENT

YOU ACKNOWLEDGE THAT YOU HAVE READ THIS AGREEMENT, UNDERSTAND IT, AND AGREE TO BE BOUND BY ITS TERMS AND CONDITIONS. YOU ALSO AGREE THAT THIS AGREEMENT IS THE COMPLETE AND EXCLUSIVE STATEMENT OF THE AGREEMENT BETWEEN YOU AND THE COMPANY AND SUPERSEDES ALL PROPOSALS OR PRIOR AGREEMENTS, ORAL, OR WRITTEN, AND ANY OTHER COMMUNICATIONS BETWEEN YOU AND THE COMPANY OR ANY REPRESENTATIVE OF THE COMPANY RELATING TO THE SUBJECT MATTER OF THIS AGREEMENT.

Should you have any questions concerning this Agreement or if you wish to contact the Company for any reason, please contact in writing at the address below.

Robin Short
Prentice Hall PTR
One Lake Street
Upper Saddle River, New Jersey 07458

About the CD-ROM

The CD-ROM included with Digital Audio with Java contains the following:

1. Java code for all audio devices and effects described in the text, plus some.
2. Code for connecting the audio processing architecture presented in the text with the Java Media Framework for platform independent audio input and output.
3. A Java bean library of custom controls and indicators suitable for audio and/or process control applications. Included are: various meters, bar graphs, simulated LEDs, 7-segment displays, buttons, switches, potentiometers and slide pots.
4. Two complete audio applications that illustrate various aspects of the technology presented. A phrase sampler for capturing musical phrases (riffs) and playing them back at a slower rate while maintaining correct pitch and a guitar/bass guitar tuner. These two applications alone are worth the price of this book.
5. Native code for the Win32 platform that interfaces the audio processing architecture presented with the Microsoft Windows WAV subsystem for sample acquisition and playback.
6. 26 example audio files that illustrate the affect of applying the effects presented in the book.
7. Makefiles for building all of the code described above

The CD-ROM can be used on Microsoft Windows® 95/98/NT®.

License Agreement

Use of the software accompanying Digital Audio with Java is subject to the terms of the License Agreement and Limited Warranty, found on the previous two pages.

Technical Support

Prentice Hall does not offer technical support for any of the programs on the CD-ROM. However, if the CD-ROM is damaged, you may obtain a replacement copy by sending an email that describes the problem to: disc_exchange@prenhall.com